CU00727063

Politics and Ideology in the Italian Workers' Movement

Politics and Ideology in the Italian Workers' Movement

Union Development and the Changing Role of the Catholic and Communist Subcultures in Postwar Italy

Gino Bedani

First published in 1995 by
Berg Publishers
Editorial offices:
150 Cowley Road, Oxford, OX4 1JJ, UK
221 Waterman Road, Providence, RI 02906, USA

Library of Congress Cataloging-in-Publication Data

A catalogue record for this book is available from the British Library

British Library Cataloguing in Publication Data

A catalogue record for this book is available from the
British Library.

ISBN 0 85496 827 X

Printed in the United Kingdom by WBC Bookbinders,
Bridgend, Mid Glamorgan.

To the loving memory of my sister
Carla

Contents

Contents

Contents

Acknowledgements

From among the numerous Italian union officials with whom I have come into contact, I must single out Johann Marzani, who, in addition to sharing his own experiences and reflections, obtained practical assistance and valuable documentary and bibliographical material for my use at the Camera del Lavoro Territoriale di Parma.

I have on numerous occasions had recourse to the specialist knowledge of Dr Tom Keenoy and Dr David Simpson in the field of industrial relations. Their valuable comments have served to sharpen my own observations, and on more than one occasion have helped me avoid potentially hazardous pitfalls. I am indebted to my colleagues Professor Lynn Mainwaring and Mr David Blackaby who adised me on matters relating to labour statistics used in the Appendix.

I am grateful for the constant encouragement and support of Dott.ssa Maria Giovanna Motta, who also read the entire manuscript and drew my attention to numerous problems of style, expression and meaning. I have learned much from my numerous and lengthy discussions with Dott.ssa Chiara Sfondrini, whose lively and critical intelligence I have shamelessly exploited on matters ranging from the broadest political issues to the detailed interpretation and exegesis of congress speeches.

Professor F. J. Jones is one of those rare colleagues and friends who knows how to combine the most trenchant criticism with constructive encouragement and support. No lapse in style, expression or reasoning escapes his attention. I can hardly begin to express my gratitude for the characteristically good-natured manner in which he has read one draft after another, filling their pages with comments, suggestions or corrections. Any shortcomings which remain are entirely my own responsibility.

The School of European Studies, University of Wales, College of Cardiff, kindly awarded me a research grant for the purpose of continuing my research in Italy throughout the summer of 1990.

Grateful thanks are due to the staff of the Biblioteca Archivio Nazionale Cgil in Rome, and in particular to Dott.ssa Teresa Corridori who has been of continual assistance on my numerous visits to the centre over recent years. Similarly, thanks are due to the staff of the Gramsci Institute and the Biblioteca Archivio Storico Cisl, in Rome. Also in Rome, I must thank Sig.ra Franca Sopalu of the Biblioteca Centrale Acli for her kind assistance in the summer of 1990, and at the Archivio Storico Uil, the Director, Paolo Ungaro, for allowing me access to unpublished material and to Segr. Paolo Saija for unravelling the material and making himself available to assist me when I needed to consult it.

In preparing the manuscript for the publisher my lack of expertise in the world of word-processing technology has fortunately been more than matched by the willingness of colleagues to come to my rescue. I am more than a little grateful to Glynis Storey for her work in converting from one system to another. On more technical matters, without the patience, guidance, generosity and skill of Dr David Basker, I could not have met my publisher's requests.

Finally, I must thank Gwen Rice who gave her time so generously to the painstaking tasks of copy-editing and proof-reading the work.

Gino Bedani
University College Swansea

Note on Translation

The Italian workers' movement has been shaped on ideological and political terrains which differ substantially from those of its counterparts in the Anglo-Saxon world. It has thus evolved a discourse and lexical corpus which at times have no equivalent in English. Consequently, even such basic terms as 'labour' movement, 'trade' unions, and many others cannot be used to describe social and institutional phenomena which reflect a quite different historical experience. Conversely, there are numerous Italian terms which express ideas and practices unfamiliar to the English reader. Sometimes, as in the case of the very term for union (*sindacato*), the only solution has been to retain the Italian. In all such cases, the reader is advised to refer to the glossary for clarification and assistance.

Most of the material quoted in this study is taken from Italian sources, nearly all of them unavailable in English. The translations from the Italian are my own.

Introduction

The initial idea for this book was conceived from within the discipline in which I have habitually worked, namely that of intellectual history. This is not surprising in the case of a country where 'ideology' has penetrated the fabric of postwar development in a particularly intense and explicit manner. In no aspect of recent Italian history is this more true than in the Italian *sindacato*, a workers' movement in which ideological issues have been debated with unparalleled energy and commitment.

The present study retains as its centre of gravity the ideological factors that have contributed to the development of the Italian *sindacato*. But such factors cannot themselves be properly analysed or understood in isolation from the broader context in which Italian unions have had to operate. Thus it will be necessary to touch on relevant aspects of the country's social, political and economic development. Inevitably, the major events and phases in the *sindacato*'s postwar history will form part of the discussion, as will areas of special interest, such as bargaining mechanisms, the content of negotiations and the internal organization of unions. Nevertheless, greater weight will be given to the distinctive features of Italy's own historical development than would be found in a more functionalist approach to the subject. In particular, a more important and positive role is attributed to 'ideological' factors in the evolution of the Italian *sindacato* than would be permitted within the more restrictive confines of such an approach. Nor is the difference of perspective adopted in the present study simply the outcome of my own professional preferences. Rather, it is determined by certain important features of postwar Italy itself.

Italy's experience of twenty years of fascist rule was of overwhelming importance in the subsequent development of the postwar republic. The unions were reconstituted towards the end of the war, when the struggle for liberation was still proceeding, and indeed as part and parcel of that very struggle. Shaped as it was within the political atmosphere of the anti-fascist alliance, a workers' movement capable of organizing and acting freely became part of the democratic fabric necessary for the country's future development. The idea was enshrined in the republic's Constitution. In this way the connection between workers' organizations and a free and democratic political system was established in the public mind, something Italy shared with other nations in continental Europe, most of which had either experienced or been occupied by fascist or Nazi regimes. It is no mere accident that in much of Western Europe which experienced in some form or other the trauma of fascist/Nazi oppression or occupation the political dimension of union activity is more readily acknowledged than in Britain, which did not share this experience.

But a study of the Italian *sindacato* is illuminating also for what is distinctive and different in its development from many other European labour movements. As we shall see, it has not only undergone more change than most, but in its postwar evolution has also engaged in an unusual degree of experimentation. English speakers in particular will be struck by the lexical apparatus used to discuss practices and institutions with which they are unfamiliar. Even the word *sindacato* has no equivalent in English. Italians use the word to describe individual unions, union confederations either singly or combined, and finally the whole corpus of union organizations considered either in their institutional form or as a collective social/political *movement*. The semantic range of this term reflects a perception of labour organizations and movements which differs in important respects from that which prevails in the Anglo-Saxon world.

As European integration proceeds it becomes more necessary than ever to understand not only the differences between union practices in the different nations, but also the diverse historical traditions which have produced them. Italian unions, for instance, did not originate, as they did in Britain, as *trade* unions, but were organized on the basis of industrial sectors, and with a strong centralising and confederate tradition. The term *tradeunionismo* has, in fact, passed into the Italian language as a manner of describing a particular approach to union practice, with distinctive ideological connotations. The confederations were never affiliated to a single party, with block votes determining that party's policies, but emerged instead with strong 'collateral' ties linking them with competing parties. This fact alone has drawn the Italian *sindacato* into the political arena in a highly distinctive manner, and forced it to confront a unique set of problems. In their quest for unity the confederations have had to loosen their party ties, establish their autonomy and, given the peculiar nature of Italian postwar governments, claim for the *sindacato* a specific role within the system as a political actor.

The ideological determinants of such developments are rooted in the two dominant subcultures in postwar Italy, the Catholic and the communist. Apart from a short period in the 1950s, when the Cisl's intellectuals showed an interest in the theory and practice of industrial relations in the United States, the Italian workers' movement has, on the whole, charted its own territory. For this reason the two major union confederations, the predominantly communist Cgil and the Catholic Cisl, provide the main focus of attention. This is not to say that the third, smaller, confederation, the Uil, has been ignored. It has, on the contrary, come to play an increasingly influential role in the latter part of the movement's development.

There have been times in the Italian *sindacato*'s postwar history when the ideological and political gulf which divided the movement's Catholic and communist components seemed unbridgeable. Two mutually exclusive conceptions of the nature of industrial relations seemed to be locked in deadly combat. This was so in the 1950s, for instance, when each component stood intransigently on its own side of the divide between the collaborationist views of the Catholics in the Cisl and the class ideology of the communists and socialists in the Cgil. There were, however, within each camp, sufficient reserves of ideological flexibility to transform the potential for a disastrous confrontation into the momentum for an interplay of contrasting views, which not only kept the movement from disintegrating, but which, at the same time, enabled it to develop and secure its place as an important interlocutor both with governments and employers.

Initially, politics and ideology were inextricably interwoven within both of the two major subcultures. In many ways the most engaging part of this study lies in tracing the tendency towards ideological convergence in a number of areas, a tendency which has, over the years, travelled laborious paths from points of origin in two deeply-rooted, divergent traditions. The process is by no means complete, nor is its outcome easily predictable, for alongside these developments political affiliations have not always changed in parallel. The gradual dislocation of ideology and politics in the Italian *sindacato* coincided with the growing importance of the third confederation, the Uil, within the movement, and its own increasing attachment, from the late 1970s, to the Psi. Thus, while ideological factors have by now become less of an obstacle to unity, divisions remain, although such divisions are now more pragmatically than ideologically based. One very significant indication of this changing pattern of relationships was given in October 1991, when the leader of the Pds (formerly Pci), Achille Occhetto, in a statement which drew little comment, announced the demise of the concept of a 'special relationship' between the *sindacato* and any political party. Coming from the leader of a former Communist Party, such a step may seem momentous to the outside observer. Yet the abandonment of the 'special relationship' theory is part of an organic and constructive process through which the Italian *sindacato*, originally so deeply-rooted in party identities, continues to reshape its identity. This is but one of the surprising developments which the reader will discover in the creative conflict which lies behind the evolution of a remarkable but little known workers' movement.

Part I

THE IMMEDIATE POSTWAR YEARS:
FROM UNITY TO SECESSION

1

A United Labour Confederation: An Accommodation of Minds and Wills

The Italian labour confederation (Cgil), which was formed in 1944, was a mirror-image of the anti-fascist coalitions which helped liberate Italy from 1943 onwards, and governed the country until 1947. The signatories to the Cgil's founding document, the *Patto di Roma*, Giuseppe Di Vittorio, Achille Grandi and Emilio Canevari, were leading figures within the Communist, Christian Democrat and Socialist Parties, which headed the government in these early years. The provisional settlement between the representatives of these major political forces was even given structural expression within the organization of the Cgil. Each of the signatories was designated General Secretary, thus institutionalising a tripartite division within the workers' movement. It is not surprising, therefore, that the break-up of the political coalition, initiated by the exclusion of the communists and socialists from the fourth De Gasperi government of May 1947, should have contributed to the eventual collapse of the *Cgil unitaria* itself.

There were also tensions within the Cgil which were independent of the political parties. Italian labour confederations did not emerge from within a 'trade union' tradition which restricted the legitimacy of union activity to 'terms and conditions of employment'. The debates and statutory formulations which accompanied the founding of the original Cgl in 1906, for example, stressed that industrial disputes and negotiations conducted by the unions could not be divorced from the broader social reforms which were also the proper and legitimate objectives of the movement.[1] This is not to say that the political dimension of union activity had always been proclaimed with unanimity, with a consistent degree of consciousness, or without ambiguity. And given the deeply-rooted subcultures of catholic, socialist and later communist origin which have both inspired and divided it, ideological and political

---

[1] See W. Tobagi, *Il sindacato riformista*, pp. 13-105.

factors have had an unusually critical role in shaping its development. This complexity of themes and objectives is immediately evident in the negotiations undertaken in 1943, as a prelude to the setting up of the Cgil in June of the following year.

The Question of Unity

The postwar Italian workers' movement was reborn in the spirit of the partisan struggle. Independently of the formation of the Committees of National Liberation (Cln), a series of remarkable industrial strikes had taken place in the north of Italy from late 1942 onwards. Communists had organized clandestine networks of factory groups, and used their influence to link the day-to-day demands of the discontented workforce to slogans which simultaneously gave these disputes an anti-fascist thrust:

> For bread and liberty!
> Down with the 12-hour day and this disastrous war!
> Away with Mussolini!
> Struggle for peace and independence!
> We demand immediate payment of a living wage!
> Action, strikes, struggle are the only arms we possess, our means of liberation.
> Strike, strike, strike![2]

Leaflets containing such slogans were secretly prepared and distributed by the thousand. They accompanied the wave of strikes in March 1943, as well as the dramatic general strike of 1944, an unprecedented demonstration, across the northern industrial belt, of mass opposition to the regime which was by that time bolstered by the Nazi occupation of northern Italy. As Paolo Spriano has observed, 'an exceptional event such as the general strike of March 1944 has the hallmarks of a partisan battle, an episode in a guerrilla war'.[3]

Although the communists were the main organizational force behind such events, anti-fascists of Catholic, liberal, republican and socialist origins were also involved. Taken together with the

---

[2] P. Spriano, *Storia del partito comunista italiano*, vol. iv, p. 170.

[3] Ibid., vol. v, p. 257.

politico-military struggles of these groups within the Cln, an overall atmosphere of unity deeply influenced much of the thinking about the future shape of a reconstructed Italy. The leaders appointed to negotiate the reconstruction of the workers' movement were heavily conditioned by this powerful wave of anti-fascist unity. The idea of a single labour confederation was, therefore, difficult to resist even for those who, in less exceptional times, might have preferred a different solution.

But unity did not have entirely the same meaning on all sides. For one thing, the communists were popularly perceived as the fiercest opponents of fascism. The extraordinary demands on its members by the party in exile had led to the return of wave after wave of would-be organizers to almost certain captivity in attempts to establish opposition cells within fascist Italy. Among the regime's captives who were eventually released, communists easily outnumbered the total of all its other opponents. The communist negotiators knew, therefore, that their party enjoyed a high level of prestige among wide sectors of the population.

Now while this newly acquired status of the communists proved a powerful bargaining counter for their negotiators, the communists could not overplay their hand if they were committed to the creation of a single, united confederation. Ideologically, the unity of the working class was a tenet of cardinal importance to communists, and especially so under the leadership of Togliatti, who had developed a new strategy for the Pci, in line with his view that postwar Italy was no longer a 'bourgeois democracy' of the old order. The popular masses had emerged, for the first time in Italian history, as active protagonists in the process of national reconstruction. This had implications for the classical communist conception of the bourgeois state. Within the new Italian state, Togliatti argued, popular strata, through new mass parties - Catholic, communist and socialist - would play a constructive role. This dramatic change of perspective, according to which the Italian state was no longer the instrument of class rule pure and simple, presented state institutions as part of a 'progressive democracy'. To be successful, however, the new strategy required not simply that popular forces be active in all areas of Italian life, but more significantly that they be united. And to maintain this unity the communists were prepared to make sacrifices.

When considering the Italian socialists it must be

remembered that the Psi, particularly within its strong maximalist tradition, had itself been profoundly influenced by Marxist thinking. The socialists were, however, a distinct political force, and while there were even those within its ranks who were attracted by the idea of a fusion of the two parties, most were opposed to a total merger. The prospect of a united labour confederation was nevertheless attractive to the fusionists for obvious reasons. Likewise it appealed to the majority, for by including the Catholics within it, the potential for communist hegemony over the whole movement would be minimised. In any case, neither side wished to see an organizationally divided working class.

The Catholics, however, brought to the negotiations a more complex set of motivating factors. The pre-fascist Catholic confederation of labour (Cil) had steadfastly rejected unity with what was at the time the socialist-dominated Cgl. Such a merger, in Catholic eyes, would have meant having policy determined by the more powerful and numerically superior rival organization. During the turbulent period of the occupation of the factories in 1920, the National Council of the Cgl had even debated and only narrowly defeated a motion calling for revolution! But in 1943 Catholic labour leaders recalled the fascist destruction of a divided movement, and many of them had drawn closer to socialists and communists in a common struggle against the regime. Achille Grandi, for example, a former Catholic labour leader and the General Secretary chosen in 1944 by the Dc, was committed to unity on both pragmatic and ideological grounds. But though Grandi himself was willing to embrace a class perspective, this did not mean that the Catholics were unambiguously free to do so in the negotiations. Many of Grandi's colleagues, together with the majority of the party leadership, were deeply worried about the consequences of a united movement, which would bring with it the influence of a powerful communist presence.

The party's choice of Grandi as the Catholic General Secretary was determined more by the respect he could command, as a militant anti-fascist, with his counterparts in the tripartite secretariat, than by his well-known progressive sympathies. Nevertheless, the importance attached by De Gasperi to the negotiations can be gauged by his remarks in a letter to Giulio Pastore, who was to become the Catholic labour leader after Grandi's death: 'I also am most concerned with this problem [i.e. a united labour confederation], which I regard as more important than the political one.'[4] Politically, however, the Dc had not yet found its centre of gravity. Although class solidarity was not high on De Gasperi's own list of priorities, there was a degree of anti-capitalist feeling in the ranks of the party, and it was by no means certain at that stage that it could rely on industrialists and employers in general for its base of support. Many newly enlisted Christian Democrats thought of the party as heading a mass popular movement. De Gasperi, as a prominent member of the pre-fascist Catholic 'Partito popolare' and its leader before its disbandment, could well remember the attitude of employers who had negotiated exclusively with the Cgl and totally ignored the relatively smaller and ineffectual Catholic Cil. He concluded, therefore, in his letter to Pastore, that to reject unity 'would be dangerous. We would certainly be excluded from any influence in industry; and even in agriculture we would only survive with difficulty if struggle were to break out'.[5]

If the Catholics were to enter a united labour movement, it was important, in De Gasperi's eyes, to maximise their potential for moderating the militant postures the confederation would be forced to assume under communist influence. To this end he proposed supporting the initiatives, already being encouraged in Vatican circles, to form parallel or flanking organizations of Catholic workers. From the start of the negotiations the Catholics had indeed raised the question of their right to form 'associazioni laterali' alongside the unions, with the object of promoting the study and application of Catholic social teaching. A preparatory meeting of such an association took place on 8 June 1944, only five days after the conclusion of the *Patto di Roma* itself, and four days after the liberation of the city. By August the *Associazioni cristiane di lavoratori italiani* (Acli) had come into existence, and as if to stress the purpose of the organization, Achille Grandi was appointed President and Giulio Pastore, Secretary.

The founding of the Acli has given rise to a number of interpretations. Some commentators, for instance, have seen in it a bid for ecclesiastical hegemony, and others a preliminary move towards an eventual Catholic secession. It must be remembered,

---

[4] M. R. De Gasperi (ed.), *De Gasperi scrive*, vol. i, p. 356

[5] Ibid.

however, that this was at a point when politically active Catholics did not constitute a homogeneous and well-defined ideological bloc. It is more likely that among its founder members there existed a variety of motives and aspirations. It is doubtful whether there was ever an overall master-plan lying behind its foundation. Moreover, the formation of the Acli was totally in keeping with the principles of the Catholic tradition of *collateralismo*. The existence of a separate forum for discussion was in all probability a necessity for Catholics entering a sphere of activity in which they felt themselves to be at a natural disadvantage in relation to the traditional labour leaders of the left. It certainly calmed the fears of the Vatican, at least temporarily. In March 1945, on the occasion of the Acli's first national convention, Pope Pius XII gave a positive, if cautious, appraisal of the principle of a united workers' movement.[6]

The Legal Framework

On the basis of the ideological traditions alone of Catholics and communists, one might expect conflict to have been immediately manifest on the question of the role of labour organizations *vis-à-vis* the state. Traditional Catholic social teaching in the nineteenth century, including the 'workers' charter' of Leo XIII (the encyclical *Rerum Novarum*), had strongly favoured the corporatist idea as a model for social organization. Conflict between labour and capital could be resolved through their structural integration into a single state organ. On the communist side, the 'transmission-belt' theory (*cinghia di trasmissione*) weighed heavily. According to this theory, labour organizations were regarded as the industrial arm of the party and were expected to put its policy into practice. It must be remembered, however, that such a theory was based on the conception of the bourgeois state as the instrument of class rule, whereas Togliatti had considerably modified this notion of the state as far as Italy was concerned.

On the Catholic side, the pre-fascist Cil had provided a valuable period of non-corporatist practice and also a body of

---

[6] This was a far cry from the Church's condemnation of the idea as a 'monstrous marriage' in 1925 when fascist union repression was producing the first indications among Catholics of a desire for unity. See S. Turone, *Storia del sindacato in Italia*, p. 84.

labour leaders such as Grandi committed to pluralistic models of organization. The fascist experience, moreover, had further strengthened the pluralist convictions of progressive Catholics, thus providing a core of seasoned opposition to the corporatist camp.[7] Nevertheless, traces of the corporatist tradition can be detected in the demands of the Dc for the workers' organizations to be included within the general corpus of state institutions.[8] The Catholic negotiators did not press their party's official line at the negotiations, however. They argued instead that the *sindacato* should be a free and autonomous body within a democratically organized state. Gronchi, who put the Catholic proposals, did, nevertheless, argue that both membership of unions and the payment of subscriptions should be made compulsory. The Catholic argument was that universal membership was more likely to ensure that union leaders took account of the interests of all members, and would provide a more democratic framework for drawing up demands. There was, however, a concealed motive behind the proposal, one which can be traced back to the pre-fascist Ppi and Cil demands for formal legal recognition for unions. Obligatory membership sanctioned by legislation would require a system of statutes and regulations guaranteeing legal parity to the Catholic component. Legislation would thereby secure for it a status in negotiations with employers which it might not otherwise achieve.

The socialist Buozzi supported demands for compulsory membership. Buozzi, General Secretary of the pre-war Cgl, was not on the most pro-communist wing of his own party and was apprehensive of the prospect of communist hegemony. He thus had considerable sympathy for the hidden agenda of the Catholics. But there were other arguments which could be used in open discussion. The fruits of labour struggles and organization were enjoyed by the

---

[7] For a brief discussion of the Catholic corporatist tradition in relation to the negotiations for the *Patto di Roma*, see S. Fontana, *I cattolici e l'unità sindacale 1943-1947*, pp. 35ff.

[8] This demand is stated in the Dc's *Programma sindacale*, produced in March 1944. See G. Merli, *De Gasperi ed il sindacato*, pp. 57-65. Earlier, however, De Gasperi had considered proposing a single union organization of workers and employers - an idea which belongs squarely within the Catholic corporatist tradition. See P. Scoppola, *La proposta politica di De Gasperi*, pp. 92ff.

whole workforce. It was not right that the burden should be borne entirely by a paying membership, who would be asked to subsidise the parasitically acquired benefits of the rest. This argument was in turn supported by the Catholics. Buozzi also appealed separately to the communists, arguing that failure to guarantee parity to the Catholic component could put the negotiations at risk, and cause unfavourable repercussions within the government coalition of which communists and socialists were both members.

The communists were opposed to attempts to resolve the internal problems of the movement within the framework of the law. Roveda was quick to remind Buozzi that in spite of the undoubted commitment of a few, the Catholic record in the labour struggles against fascism was, to say the least, ambiguous. The position they would gain through the arrangements which the communists were proposing was already disproportionate to their input, without recourse to additional legislative guarantees. They were thus unlikely to put unity at risk while it was to their advantage. However, there were other, more profound objections to compulsory union membership.

After the arrest of Roveda in December 1943, the communist objections were put forward by his successor at the talks, Giuseppe Di Vittorio. Di Vittorio was quick to see in such proposals an attempt to secure for union officialdom an assured and stable level of income and funding.[9] But far from forcing the Cgil to take account of its members' interests, added security would act as a buffer against the ire of disaffected members. Such a body of comfortably placed functionaries would be disinclined to challenge a political establishment which guaranteed its future. Worst of all, the compulsory payment of dues would be a continuation of the practice of the hated fascist unions. To workers who, after twenty years of fascism, wished to breathe the air of freedom, such compulsion would produce a feeling of remoteness and alienation. If it were truly to be part of the democratic fabric of Italian society, the workers' movement, if nothing else, would have to be the free expression of the aspirations of the working class. The Catholic

---

[9] In a report on the negotiations Di Vittorio talks of having to sit through an hour-long harangue by the socialist Buozzi on how obligatory subscriptions would provide financial security for the movement. See M. Pistillo's collection of Di Vittorio's speeches and reports, *Giuseppe Di Vittorio 1924-1944*, p. 249.

proposals would create an organization with a large membership, but much of it passive and resentful.[10]

In March 1944 partisan activities provoked Nazi reprisals, and led to the capture and execution of the chief socialist negotiator Buozzi. With his replacement by Oreste Lizzadri, the dominant party tendency to collaborate closely with the communists came to the fore. Having lost the support of Buozzi, the Catholics agreed to drop their proposals. Their desire for parity was met, nevertheless, by the creation of a tripartite secretariat structure.

The Political Dimension: Confederation, Federations and Parties

It is not surprising that 'integralist' tendencies should have been revived among Catholics during the fascist period. These tendencies gained impetus from the early thirties onwards, and began to modify aspects of the Catholic corporatist tradition in competition with the official fascist version. In some respects, however, Catholic corporatism was indistinguishable from its fascist counterpart, and was certainly no less hostile to political pluralism. It became influential among the younger generation of intellectuals and Catholic political leaders who had attended the Università cattolica in Milan in the thirties. It frequently gave rise to aspirations for the eventual replacement of fascism by a society organized on Catholic principles. But those heading the Catholic negotiations for union unity in 1943 were from an older generation. They had not received their formative political schooling in either the Catholic university or in the higher echelons of organized Catholic Action. They had either experienced labour struggles at first hand or had come into direct contact with anti-fascist activities. Despite the corporatist tones of their initial proposals for formal legal recognition and obligatory union membership, their perspective was imbued with a good deal of pluralism and with those liberal democratic values which had been accepted by the old Ppi.

A major concern of the Catholic negotiators was to avoid creating a movement which could challenge the liberal democratic structure of the state after the defeat of fascism. Many feared that

---

[10] See his reports of the discussions in ibid., pp. 219-24.

the communists, in arguing for a highly centralised movement which could be mobilised for anti-capitalist struggles, could spearhead precisely such an assault on the state. In his correspondence with labour leaders, De Gasperi had indeed warned of the dangers of a movement created around 'class' and political issues. The solution was to invest the movement's authority in national federations organized on an industrial basis, the *federazioni nazionali di categoria*.[11] If the command structure of the movement were built around categories of economic production, problems related to work, and not to political issues, would predominate.

Within such a scheme labour contracts would be agreed autonomously by the national industrial or 'category' federations, which would then exercise a controlling influence over federation organizations at provincial and local levels. The effect of making the federation the axis of union organization would be to minimise the need for policies of a political, economic or social nature, since the main thrust of policy would originate from within specialised industrial sectors.[12] As the Catholic commentator Sandro Fontana has noted, one of the main objectives of the proposals was 'to weaken the political capacity of the movement by stressing its technical dimension, in order to foster stability'.[13]

The communist rejoinder was strengthened by the fact that the quasi-'trade union' approach to labour organization which was being advocated by the Catholics did not have strong roots in Italian labour history. The Cgl formed in 1906 to unite the emerging industrial or category federations had had a much stronger policy-making role for the whole movement than was now being advocated. Moreover, there had been in Italy a vigorous tradition of union territorial or geographical organization based on chambers of labour (*camere di lavoro*), which had led many important struggles and had provided the movement with a strong focus of class solidarity. The communists did not, of course, accept the 'narrow' definition of the scope of union activity which was typical of *tradeunionismo*. There were large areas of social and economic

---

[11] See *federazione di categoria* in Glossary.

[12] The best summary of the Catholic proposals can be found in the *Programma sindacale* mentioned earlier.

[13] *I cattolici e l'unità sindacale*, p. 62.

policy which affected all working people equally, irrespective of job or trade. These wider interests were not protected by workplace negotiations alone, and were ignored by the Catholic proposals. On the basis of arguments such as these, the communists proposed that while the category federations should represent all the workers in a particular industry, they should do so within the framework of the policy guidelines of the confederation.

This was no ordinary item of negotiation for the communists. The very essence of the workers' movement was at stake. In spite of the main socialist negotiator Buozzi, there was widespread support for the communist view among the socialists, and when he was replaced by Lizzardi in the talks the case was won. This meant that the Cgil was to become the major policy-making body and would decide the social and economic strategies and objectives of the movement as a whole. This outcome was to have a lasting effect on the Italian workers' movement. It meant that the principle of worker solidarity was expressed in the very organizational fabric of the movement. Its command structure was such that workers could mobilise in common struggles without having to cope with the institutionalised divisions inherent in *tradeunionismo*. This sense of corporate identity would survive the forthcoming secession of the Catholics, and also their renewed attempt to promote the federations as the primary union organizations. Paradoxically, by later setting up a rival confederation, the Catholics would even intensify the sense of corporate belonging.

An associated problem which initially seemed to have been resolved with relative ease, was the question of the relationship between the movement and political parties. It is easily forgotten that as well as the socialist and communist parties, the Dc was also at this time widely regarded as a popular mass party. As a party of the Catholic masses it could, in principle at least, lay claim to the same kind of interest in, and organic connection with the movement as the others. But having accepted that there were strong historical and ideological links between the various currents in the movement and their respective parties, the communists in particular were anxious to secure a working relationship between all sectors of the movement which could survive an eventual break-up of the existing government coalition. A divided workers' movement would be a weakened one. The only practical option, therefore, was to declare the movement's independence from all political parties.

As a position of principle, the idea of independence from all political parties presented few problems for the Catholic negotiators. While there existed strong tendencies within the Dc itself to maintain control of Catholic union leaders, there were some committed 'autonomists' among the Catholics. Grandi, for instance, was known to have held such views from the days of the pre-fascist Cil.[14] Catholic declarations of independence did not, in any case, entail a rejection of all aspects of the 'collateralist' tradition, but of its inherent tendency to establish a system of command among flanking organizations. What the Catholic labour component wished to avoid was subservience to the party. It did, however, enjoy the advantage of having secured approval from the socialists and communists for establishing the Acli, the independent association of Catholic workers. The setting up of a separate body to promote the study and application of Catholic social teaching in the world of labour was a classic example of *collateralismo*. It was intended to protect the Catholic component from the danger of being absorbed into a movement hegemonised by a strong communist and socialist presence, and risking losing its identity.

For the communists this aspect of the negotiations was to be only the beginning of a prolonged and painful process of accommodation, compromise and self-examination, which would last for decades. Their equivalent of Catholic *collateralismo*, the *cinghia di trasmissione* (transmission-belt theory) was, of course, rooted in the Comintern tradition of the guiding role of the party. The problem facing the communists, who were being asked to establish their independence of the party, was qualitatively different from that of the Catholics. They were being asked to declare their autonomy in respect of a party which was profoundly pro-labour in essence, a party whose very existence was built around the history of labour struggles. There were, however, some important factors which eased their problems.

The communists were collaborating in the construction of a new workers' movement at a time when anti-fascist unity was at its most intense, when partisans from all parties were experiencing an unprecedented level of co-operation. The movement was also being projected within the framework of the Pci's new 'progressive

---

[14] See L. Bellotti, *Achille Grandi e il movimento sindacale cristiano*, pp. 209ff.

democracy', which postulated a new type of bourgeois state, capable of being transformed from within. This made it necessary to think in terms of new sets of co-ordinating principles. The guiding role of the party was not so crucial in a state environment which was less hostile to the working class. The communists were also witnessing an extraordinary influx of new recruits not formed within the party's traditions, and this helped to establish the non-sectarian stamp of the 'new party' Togliatti was trying to create. But perhaps of more immediate significance was the figure of the leading communist negotiator himself.

Giuseppe Di Vittorio could almost have been chosen by an act of providence. His schooling in labour struggles had earlier been conducted within the ranks of the revolutionary syndicalists, ardent defenders of the autonomy of the workers' movement and the fiercest opponents of the notion of party leadership. Di Vittorio describes his route to the Communist Party in 1924 as 'slow, hesitant because the syndicalist ideology on which I was reared from childhood made me feel the weight of its influence'. An additional difficulty for him had been that of 'bringing the masses, which I myself had taught for so many years to reject the very concept of party, to accept the Communist Party'.[15] Di Vittorio was to become a legendary figure in the communist movement, but he never became the archetypal party man. It was partly for this reason that he was appointed to head the negotiations for his own party only after the arrest of Roveda in December 1943.

But even when splits in the movement later occurred, and the rival confederations drew closer to their respective parties for support, independence had nevertheless been established in principle and would remain inscribed in their separate statutes.[16] At a later

---

[15] M. Pistillo, *Giuseppe Di Vittorio 1907-1924*, p. 177.

[16] An indication of the importance attached to the principle of independence from political parties can be seen in the document approved by a preparatory convention in September 1944 preceding the founding Congress of Naples of 28 January - 1 February 1945. Article 3 of the motion approved reads:

The declared independence of the workers' movement from all political parties and the state must be practised in the everyday activity of the *sindacato*. To this end it has been agreed that (a) no union will share its premises with a political party; (b) no union will display symbols,

stage the theme of autonomy would re-emerge, as the confederations took up once again the difficult search for unity.

The text of the final agreement guaranteed to all members of the nascent confederation full freedom of expression and respect for all religious and political views.[17] This was, of course, an essential declaration if unity were to be maintained, and also a guarantee that the formal independence of the confederation did not imply religious or political agnosticism on the part of its members. Indeed, after twenty years of fascism, the political commitment of members to the defence of democracy was universally proclaimed as essential to assure the survival of the movement if threatened.

Thus independence did not imply non-commitment to the defence of democracy. As we have seen, moreover, the Italian workers' movement from its very beginning had never totally surrendered the political and social dimensions of its activity to the political parties. It was thus agreed that the confederation would 'whenever it considered it appropriate, associate itself with the actions of the democratic parties which are the expression of the working masses, either for the protection or development of popular liberties, or for the defence of particular interests of working people or of the nation'.[18] The declaration would be expanded and reinforced in article 9 of the Cgil statutes, agreed at the founding congress a few months later. The idea of a political role for the workers' movement would remain an abiding theme in its postwar development, but not before article 9 had become a battleground prior to the Catholic secession of 1948.

Workers in Agriculture

All sides in the negotiations were agreed that Italy's agrarian sector

---

flags, portraits or other emblems which give it a particular political complexion; (c) no participation of political parties in the internal activities and organization of unions will be permitted.
'Convegno delle organizzazioni sindacali dell'Italia liberata. Roma, 15-16 settembre 1944', p. 50.

[17] For the text of the *Patto di Roma* see V. Foa (ed.), *Sindacati e lotte operaie 1943-1973*, pp. 50-2.

[18] Ibid., p. 51.

was in urgent need of reform. The agrarian South was the disadvantaged half of the country's intractable 'dual economy'. Forms of occupation and land-ownership were highly varied and problematic. There were *braccianti* (i.e. mostly seasonal workers and day-labourers), *mezzadri* (share-croppers), *fittavoli* (tenant farmers), *contadini proprietari* (peasant owners), *agricoltori* (farmers) and finally *latifondisti* (owners of large landed estates). Naturally, the base of support for Catholics and communists among such groups would differ. While the communists could expect support from the *braccianti, mezzadri,* and perhaps from the poorer *contadini,*[19] the Catholics could expect the support of the remainder.

From the time of Gramsci's leadership of the party in 1924, Di Vittorio, himself a southern *bracciante* by origin, had collaborated with Grieco and Gramsci in developing the party's agrarian policy. The complex stratification of the agrarian classes produced a disparity of social objectives and aspirations which made it difficult to unite them in a common purpose. In 1924, in open controversy with the socialists, Di Vittorio argued that their inability to understand the problems of the South was forcing the *contadini* to turn to other political parties, most notably to the Catholic Ppi. The socialist policy of placing the whole of agriculture under collective ownership was profoundly mistaken. It ignored important differences between simple workers of the land and small proprietors, and assumed that they could all be won over to support the socialisation of 'the large landed estates and properties along with the smallholdings of the peasants who cultivate them intensively, with their cows and their modest dwellings'.[20] Di Vittorio's argument was that the different social groupings of agricultural workers (some owned no land, others owned small plots, yet others rented the land they worked, while a

---

[19] See *contadino* in Glossary.

[20] Pistillo, *Giuseppe Di Vittorio 1907-1924*, p. 327. On later being attached to the Krestintern, the body responsible for agricultural labour organizations in the Comintern, Di Vittorio was surprised at the low level of analysis of problems of agrarian labour in other communist parties. For a discussion of the development of Di Vittorio's ideas in this area see G. L. C. Bedani, 'Giuseppe Di Vittorio e il movimento dei lavoratori. Un profilo ideologico', pp. 24-43.

further section shared a fixed proportion of the proceeds with the landlord) were crucial to how these created their own aspirations. Each group could be won over only to policies which were in its own interests, and would act effectively only in an organization sufficiently distinctive to serve those interests. The *bracciante*, who had little to lose and no possessions but his labouring capacity, might well join a movement seeking to socialise agriculture, for it would bring him stability and regular work. The peasant, or *contadino*, however, would see it as a threat to what little he already possessed. The communists were thus proposing to establish a separate organization for the *contadini*.

These were in substance the kinds of argument repeated at the negotiations by Di Vittorio. Essentially, he proposed that hired or wage-earning workers should be included in the Cgil. This would preserve the principle of unity with industrial and other workers on a class basis. Proprietors and tenant farmers employing small numbers should form an independent federation (detached from the large farmers' confederation) which would give it greater cohesion and enable it to focus on problems specific to them as an intermediate category, falling neither within the ranks of wage-earners nor in those of large landowners and employers. Thus taking their own programmes as a starting point, common ground could be found with agricultural wage-earners. A formal and permanent alliance could then be established to seek further co-operation and joint action between the agricultural workers' federation within the Cgil and the independent federation of *contadini* and related categories outside it. Di Vittorio concluded that in this way united action would be based on real points of convergence, and would stand a better chance of success than policies worked out on the basis of a confused and generic unity which ignored important differences.

Although the final outcome was in fact determined by Dc initiatives outside the negotiations, the arguments of the Catholic negotiators remain an important record of the ideological development of the Catholic world of labour. Whilst not unsympathetic to much of the communist argument, the Catholics started from different premisses. They were less tied to clearly defined class demarcations. Traditional Catholic social teaching had condemned the excesses of capitalism, not its essence. It mattered more to Catholics that many *contadini* were as impecunious as other agricultural workers. The little land they owned was often worthless or impossibly resistant to cultivation. For the Catholics there were strategic consequences which flowed from the conditions of real deprivation and the subordinate social status of Italy's mass of *contadini*. The Catholics argued strongly that peasants would be more effective in combating land monopolies by being included within the *sindacato*. It was essential, they argued, not to let the agricultural class based on wage-labour become isolated, drive the *contadini* into the arms of the large capitalist landowners, and eventually force them into their organizations.

These were compelling arguments, and they were not lost on the communists. But there was another dimension to the Catholic proposals: their fear of being swamped by a communist-dominated movement. The *contadini* were an historically important base of Catholic support, just as the *braccianti* were for the communists. Grandi estimated that Catholic strength in the nascent confederation could count for about one third of the membership. He wrote to a Catholic colleague: 'if the confederation could extend its sphere of influence over all categories of *contadini* and artisans, I am convinced that we could even reach 50%'.[21] The matter was not decided, however, in the negotiations for the *Patto* itself. The official outcome was decided at the constituent Congress of Naples in January - February 1945. But by this time the arguments and debates had been overtaken by events.

The Dc party leader, De Gasperi, was not altogether confident of either Grandi's ability or indeed determination to counter communist objections to Catholic proposals.[22] In the event the party had at some stage begun to prepare an alternative solution to the problem of representation in the agricultural sector. Unfortunately, there is no detailed and documented study of these contingency plans. However, in a letter dated 12 November 1944, De Gasperi informed Luigi Sturzo that the party had already taken steps 'to establish a federation of small proprietors and farmers which will gain support from union unity, but retain more autonomy [than

---

[21] Bellotti, *Achille Grandi*, p. 82.

[22] For a discussion of some of the differences between the two leaders, and of De Gasperi's preference for Gronchi as negotiator, see Fontana, *I cattolici e l'unità sindacale*, pp. 31ff.

other federations]'.[23] In fact the *Federazione nazionale coltivatori agricoli*, shortly afterwards to be known as Coldiretti, had already been established on 31 October under the leadership of the Catholic Paolo Bonomi.

This surreptitious initiative both anticipated and vitiated the debates at the founding Cgil Congress in January - February 1945, where Grandi successfully pressed to have the *contadini* and small farmers included in the confederation. The final resolution admitted all categories of small farmers who did not employ more than one permanent waged agricultural worker. For Grandi, anxious to secure a more substantial Catholic presence in the workers' movement, this would have been a considerable victory. Instead, the rival organization of *contadini* witnessed an immediate and spectacular growth in membership, and would go on to provide the Dc with a solid base of support.[24] This allowed the party in the succeeding years to establish itself more firmly than ever in the agricultural sector, but not without the use of the clientelistic practices for which it subsequently became notorious. For the communists, who had originally argued for a separate federation of small farmers, but one in which they would have had a voice, the creation of the Catholic Coldiretti was an even greater defeat than it had been for Grandi. The loss of the *contadini* would prove an insurmountable obstacle to communist influence in the agricultural sector.

In a letter to a fellow Catholic labour leader, Grandi, with bitter disappointment, described the Bonomi initiative as 'sectarian and damaging to the interests of the working class'.[25] In fact, once the political climate shifted to the disadvantage of the left, the Coldiretti operation began to eat into the ability of the *sindacato* to exert any influence over the *contadini*. Furthermore, with the impending loss of Grandi the workers' movement would lose its greatest Catholic advocate of unity. With Grandi gone, and replaced by a leadership more amenable to party influence, the externally contrived breach we have just discussed was to foreshadow a secession of even greater proportions.

---

[23] Scoppola, *La proposta politica di De Gasperi*, p. 290.

[24] The Coldiretti's number of associated families increased from about half a million in 1946 to a high point of almost two million by 1967.

[25] S. Magister, *La politica vaticana e l'Italia*, p. 46.

2

The *Cgil Unitaria*: A Highly Centralised Structure

Analyses of this early period of reconstruction have focused on what has been described as a certain *verticismo* in decision-making. The leaders of political parties took it upon themselves to make far-reaching decisions on matters of policy and organization without recourse to widespread consultation. It would be an error of historical judgement, however, to read such tendencies in an entirely negative light. Initiatives were taken in a situation of great urgency, while the country was in the throes of a struggle for liberation, and communications between North and South were intermittent and uncertain. The reconstruction taking place in the workers' movement was just as much a part of the turmoil as was the recreation of political parties. An important feature of this process, particularly strong among the communists but by no means absent on the Catholic side, was the aim to achieve a position of comparative organizational consolidation by the time of liberation. The determination on the part of a wide spectrum of Italian anti-fascists not to leave the future political destiny of the country in the hands of the liberating allies was very strong.[1] In order to secure indigenous control it was essential, by the end of Nazi occupation, to have functioning organizations in place.

The depth of conviction felt within the world of organized labour that it should become an essential component of the new democratic republic is reflected in the first article of the Italian Constitution: 'Italy is a democratic republic based on work.' But in the early days of reconstruction the world of labour was just as subject to the pressures of improvisation as were other aspects of the resurgent democracy. Leaders of the hastily regenerated *camere del lavoro* were being inundated with requests for membership. Luciano Lama, many years later to become General Secretary of the

---

[1] Togliatti was convinced, for example, that Churchill was determined to minimise as much as possible the partisan role in liberating the country.

Cgil, found himself in 1945 at the head of the *Camera del lavoro* of Forlì in precisely this predicament. His testimony is worth recounting at some length.

> We opened the headquarters of the *Camera del lavoro* [in Forlì] by breaking down the doors of the fascist unions, and from that point on we began to organize the people who came in. What were we organizing them for? In Forlì, most were unemployed, because the factories had been destroyed and it was a region ravaged by war. They were unemployed and wanted to work in the AMG shipyards, the shipyards of the allied forces which were the only source of work for many long months - apart, that is, from the countryside where thousands of acres of agricultural land had been planted with mines.
>
> What did we do? We gave them provisional membership cards ... and within six months we had organized 115,000 workers. Who had persuaded them to join? Was there *verticismo*? Was there democracy? Was there bureaucracy? They came to the *Camera del lavoro*, they did not join individual category federations, because they did not know to which category they belonged, they simply joined the *Camera del lavoro*.
>
> In these circumstances, those 115,000 people ... were propelled towards the *sindacato* by the general ethos behind the anti-fascist democratic forces, by what they had seen of these forces, and by what they had represented during the liberation of my land. And the *sindacato* was seen by them, by the workers, as an expression of those forces.[2]

Lama was typical of a generation of partisans who had had leadership thrust upon them. His testimony points to two features in the situation which it is essential to grasp. The workers' movement was faced first with an organizational task of unprecedented proportions both in urgency and scale. In the second place, the wave of anti-fascist feeling in the country included a great deal of hostility towards the large-scale capitalist enterprises which in the popular mind had benefited from the discredited fascist regime. The vast majority of labour leaders thus felt with great passion the legitimacy of the movement's anti-capitalist mission. Moreover, given the widespread conviction that the discredited capitalist forces would nevertheless receive strong

---

[2] L. Lama, 'L'impegno della Cgil per lo sviluppo e l'unità del sindacato in Italia', p. 354.

support from the allies once the war was over, it was essential to mobilise effectively in order to be able to oppose such forces. A highly centralised structure, with a centralised system of negotiations, responded to these requirements.

The founding Cgil Congress at Naples in 1945 established the priority of 'horizontal' over 'vertical' structures. There would be a single confederation, Cgil, at national level, incorporating all the individual category (industrial) federations. The horizontal or confederate body at the territorial (mostly provincial) level was to be the *camera del lavoro*, which, in turn, would incorporate the provincial federations. On the vertical level there was to be a single federation (*federazione di categoria*) for each major industry or area of productive activity, i.e. federations of metalworkers, textile workers, farmworkers, chemical workers, food manufacturing workers, etc. As already indicated, these were to be established both at national and provincial level.

The crucial factor in the centralisation of the movement lay in deciding which organizations would have the ultimate power to shape policy and negotiate with employers and the state. The bodies responsible for concluding agreements were set out in articles 53-58 of the new statutes of the Cgil.[3] Essentially, local agreements were to be the exception. National agreements for each industry would be negotiated by the industrial federations for the category or industry. But the autonomy of the federations was severely circumscribed, and their demands were first to be confirmed by the confederation which, since its function was to preserve global policy, reserved for itself the power to amend federal proposals. Likewise, the national leadership could intervene in negotiations at area level, and in any initiatives taken by the *camere del lavoro*.

Perhaps the most conspicuous feature of the new union negotiating machinery was the decision, contained in articles 100-101 of the statutes, to divest the internal commissions of the plant-level negotiating functions provisionally granted to them earlier by an ad hoc interconfederate agreement in 1943.[4] The

---

[3] For the text of these articles see 'Statuto approvato all'unanimità dal Congresso di Napoli 1945', pp. 264-5.

[4] Internal commissions (*commissioni interne*) had existed as plant-level organizations in pre-fascist Italy. See Glossary.

internal commissions, although not officially union bodies, were recognised as the appropriate organizations for protecting workers' interests at plant level. The communists valued these bodies as a means of involving the whole workforce in problems at plant level. But any initiatives taken by the internal commissions were to be strictly controlled by the unions. The recognition of the internal commissions was subject to their 'acting in conformity with union instructions' (article 100). There was also a pointed reminder that official negotiating activity was to be conducted by the union body 'which preserves the unity of all the workers in a particular industry or sector in any given locality ... and which alone is empowered to represent them' (article 101). What this meant was that no plant-level negotiating machinery as such was provided for. Employers would have to negotiate with representatives from larger federal and/or confederate organizations. From the beginning, particularly in its communist/socialist component, the Cgil was determined to avoid the dangers of *aziendalismo*.[5]

The communists were thus successful in establishing a framework which on the face of it safeguarded the unity of the working class. But this success was compromised by serious incongruities. Di Vittorio, in his speech at the founding congress, had included in his inventory of weaknesses of the movement up to that point the lack of development in the federations. Yet the congress had made no provision for curbing what could easily become a stifling confederate 'interference' in their affairs. In a speech to a Pci convention in August 1945, the Communist Party leader Togliatti had likewise stressed to labour leaders the importance of effective union organization at the lower levels.

> The trade federations, local union branches, the *camere del lavoro*, must study seriously the problems of production. They must concern themselves with the conditions of factory life, with the ways in which work is organized and can be developed. You will not succeed in improving the conditions of workers if you remain passive in this sphere. This is the new orientation which you must apply to union work, otherwise at some point you could be left behind.[6]

---

[5] See Glossary.

[6] P. Togliatti, *Opere*, vol. v, p. 171.

The desire of the leadership, at that juncture, to preserve unity at all costs, was clearly at the expense of an effective union presence at plant level. We shall later have occasion to note just how prophetic Togliatti's words of warning had been.

Class Unity: Stresses, Strains and the Appearance of Divergent Objectives

Although differences between Catholics and communists would emerge before very long, between 1945 and 1947 the centralised structure of the Cgil initially suited both sides, although for different reasons. The communists were anxious to preserve solidarity on the basis of guaranteed minimum conditions for all categories of workers. On the Catholic side, however, given the presence of communists and socialists alongside the Dc in the government coalition, the authoritarian structure of the Cgil was perceived as a way of keeping the movement's objectives in line with the government's programme of economic reconstruction. Catholic labour leaders were accordingly prepared to remain within the movement, even though communist influence over policy objectives was clearly establishing itself as predominant.

It did not take long for the moral authority and experience of Di Vittorio to establish him as the effective spokesman of the movement. This position was eventually formalised at the Cgil Congress of 1947 with his appointment as General Secretary with overall responsibility over the three General Secretaries heading the tripartite secretariat. But as a communist, Di Vittorio remained committed to the concept of the new type of 'progressive', popular democracy which was supposedly under construction. The workers' movement could no longer adopt a purely negative oppositional posture in this situation. The central core of Togliatti's theory of 'progressive democracy' was the idea that the new bourgeois state which had come into being offered the prospect of a constructive role in society for organizations of the working class. Thus, Di Vittorio stressed, the Cgil had emerged from the struggles to reconstruct Italian society and established its position as an essential component of the new republic. This structural relocation of the workers' movement had profound political consequences for Italian society. Why, he asked at the first Cgil Congress of 1945, should the programme of reconstruction be formulated in government ministries, in the banks and in the headquarters of joint stock companies? It must satisfy in the first place the needs of the people, which are the genuine needs of the country. It should be worked out with the participation of the people.[7]

In demanding a role in national reconstruction, the Cgil was not arguing for a programme of socialist measures. It accepted the role of small and medium-sized industries, and the Cgil programme at this stage was in the main supported also by the Catholics. The broad measures incorporated within the programme agreed at the 1945 Congress included: a minimum wage for the lowest paid workers; the introduction of a *scala mobile* (index-linked wage scale) for all workers; the derequisition of industrial establishments appropriated by the Anglo-American forces; the nationalisation of those key industries under monopoly control, and agrarian reform.

There is little doubt that the constructive attitude of the Cgil leaders immediately evident in the February 1945 negotiations with employers was heavily influenced by the parties in coalition. Di Vittorio had already stressed that the weak and unstable Italian economy could not sustain uncontrolled wage increases. For their part the employers were at this stage happy with a highly centralised union structure which could rigidly control wages, and which severely limited union power at plant level. The scene was thus set between union leaders and employers for a series of productive compromises. National contracts were signed in December 1945 for the North and in May 1946 for Central Italy and the South which prevented plant-level bodies from seeking to improve upon agreements made at a higher level. Further important precedents were set in this period. Wages were to be fixed industry by industry and province by province. The employers undertook to negotiate only with the official territorial organs, thereby guaranteeing confederate control on the union side. This in effect introduced the notorious *gabbie salariali*, or differentials between North and South, and between men and women, which it would take many years to eliminate. In return for wage control on the part of the unions the employers agreed to the introduction of the *scala*

---

[7] *La Cgil dal Patto di Roma al Congresso di Genova*, vol. i, 1949, p. 116.

mobile and a guarantee of no dismissals. These concessions were perceived even by the employers as stabilising factors in a period of urgent reconstruction. Subsequently, such agreements were renewed in 1946 and 1947, with further concessions on holidays and the granting of an additional 'thirteenth' month's wage.[8] On the negative side, the Cgil was forced to agree in January 1946 to unblock in part the veto on dismissals, and in October to accept a six-month wage freeze.

These early agreements have often been presented as a 'sell-out' by the union leadership. Among the many constraints within which the Cgil had to operate, and which are ignored in such an interpretation, were its internal tensions. The first critical division occurred at a meeting of the Cgil executive in July 1946, which met to discuss the deflationary policies put forward by the Treasury Minister, Corbino (Dc). Di Vittorio argued that while the Cgil was playing its full part in the programme of national reconstruction, it could not entirely abandon its proper function and ignore the urgent need for at least moderate wage increases. In his response Grandi recognised the justice of Di Vittorio's claim, but expressed the concern of the Catholic component at the inflationary pressures such increases would bring about. He warned that the Catholics would put forward a motion calling for support of the government. The motion was rejected by the communist/socialist majority. Many commentators have seen in this episode the first move on the part of the Catholics towards secession. Grandi himself, however, who was opposed to secessionist developments among Catholics, feared most of all for the unity of the movement, and stated poignantly that 'if the unity of Italian workers cannot be preserved my mission will be at an end'.[9]

In truth, the Cgil lacked a sufficiently coherent set of alternative proposals to bolster its position. And while it seemed to many of its members that the Catholics were simply supporting their own minister, the government programme was the only even

---

[8] The payment of an additional 'thirteenth' month's wage or salary, known as the 'tredicesima', subsequently became a widely accepted practice in many sectors.

[9] Turone, *Storia del sindacato in Italia*, p. 115. Grandi died two months later.

minimally co-ordinated course of action which had been proposed. It was clear that the schedule of proposals which had emerged from the 1945 Cgil Congress did not amount to a comprehensive programme of economic recovery. The vote of July 1946, clearly divided along Catholic and communist/socialist lines, was the first major split on policy, and established an ominous precedent. It certainly encouraged those elements in the Dc who favoured a Catholic secession. Opinion among historians of the workers' movement is still divided on the question of the number of Catholic labour leaders who favoured such a move. In all probability there were many Catholic union leaders who viewed such a prospect with misgivings. But as events unfolded such reservations were no match for the resolve of those who privately harboured such secessionist aspirations as, increasingly, they began to be voiced by powerful forces outside the movement.

In August 1947, Cgil leaders decided by a majority of votes to call an immediate national strike against rising prices and a general strike in Rome in December of that year against unemployment.[10] Without the restraining influence of Grandi to hold it in check, the Catholic current dissociated itself from these actions. Such a refusal to accept majority decisions brought calls for expulsion. It took all the mediating skills of Di Vittorio to keep the flickering flame of unity from being totally extinguished. But party allegiances were clearly making inroads into the heart of the organization as the Dc emerged as the dominant force in government.[11]

The events so far described highlight major problems in the position of the early experiences of the *Cgil unitaria*. Its highly centralised structure was devised to provide class unity and direction. But given the strong nature of diverse party allegiances within the movement, its direction was from the beginning always exposed to the unforeseen effects of divisions within the

---

[10] Given the predominance of the confederate structure in the Italian *sindacato*, the distinction between 'national' and 'general' strikes is important. See Glossary under both headings.

[11] In June 1946, national elections of a constituent assembly resulted in a coalition headed by De Gasperi. In May 1947, De Gasperi excluded the communists and socialists from government in an act which clearly alarmed the Cgil majority.

government coalition. Only a movement firmly held together by rank-and-file support could have overcome such difficulties. By investing its strength in the authoritarian style of a highly centralised organization, its leaders had gambled everything on their ability and willingness to preserve unity. Yet these leaders were the most vulnerable to party pressures. Decisions on policy and industrial action were based on executive voting but were not backed by popular mandate. Rank-and-file consultation could have invested such decisions with a legitimacy which would have made public disavowals by the Catholics more difficult to justify.

Yet Di Vittorio's speeches, at the 1945 Congress and subsequently, abound with references to the importance of popular participation in the life of the movement. To a large extent the Cgil's *verticismo* was a response to the urgent requirements of the situation. But this was not the whole story. A high proportion of the Cgil's leadership had emerged from the ranks of partisan formations and was accustomed to imposing a vigorous and decisive style of leadership. Indeed these were in many cases the qualities which had thrust them into positions of leadership in the new movement. Moreover, given their training in clandestine modes of operation, it is not surprising that many of the Cgil's new leaders were unpractised in the methods of peace-time, mass consultation.

For their part, the Catholics were in many respects even less equipped to meet the situation. The pre-fascist Cil had had its main base of support in the more conservative agricultural sector and had never experienced the same degree of pressure for rank-and-file consultation as had the more industrially based Cgl. Cil's leaders, moreover, had traditionally believed in delegating responsibility for reforms to government. Their model of democracy was unambiguously 'representational' rather than 'participatory'. In this respect, it is interesting to note Adolfo Pepe's criticism of Grandi, when comparing this most highly esteemed of the Catholic leaders to the communist Di Vittorio regarding their attitudes to worker participation in union affairs. Pepe refers to the debate on the agrarian question at the 1945 Naples Congress, 'where Grandi's report was totally lacking in the same democratic spirit [as Di Vittorio's] and limited itself to delegating the structural reforms in agriculture to the elected assemblies'.[12]

While Catholic weaknesses were rooted in conceptions of historical and social change in which there was little or no place for popular forces organized outside formal institutions, the communist defect was of a different order. Communists had always understood that elected 'representatives' are only as strong, in moments of conflict, as their rank-and-file support. Their first miscalculation was to rely too heavily on the communist/socialist presence in the government coalition. Their second weakness was largely attributable to the lingering combative instincts of leaders trained in the struggles of the preceding twenty years. They were too slow to realise that new methods for mobilising support were required, and remained all too ready to lead from the front.

It would take time for Catholics and communists to face up to their respective problems and to begin to question the traditions and ideologies in which such problems were rooted. But this would not occur until some hard lessons had been learned on both sides.

The 'Consigli di Gestione'

On 17 April 1945, a few days before the insurrection and liberation in the North, the Clnai, which represented the Bonomi government in the occupied territory, issued a decree creating the *consigli di gestione*, or management councils. These were to guarantee the participation of the workforce in the management of industry. While many employers had profited from fascism, collaborated with the occupying Nazi forces and abandoned the factories in the violent struggles, workers had engaged in acts of sabotage and conducted strikes against the enemy. The workers had prevented the transfer of valuable machinery to Germany and occupied factories during insurrectionary struggles. The *consigli di gestione* thus had a strong moral legitimacy in the North.

The *consigli di gestione* have been described as a compromise between 'an interclassist, Christian, profit-sharing notion and the revolutionary communist idea of worker control

---

[12] A. Pepe, *Classe operaia e sindacato*, p. 163.

-34-

following the expropriation of private companies'.[13] In reality, both the conception and the genesis of these councils are less clear. Irrespective of what some rank-and-file communists might have hoped, for Togliatti there was no question of their serving a revolutionary purpose or jeopardising the strategy of the *svolta di Salerno*. They were, however, a first step towards bringing the whole process of production under the control of the working class. At the first congress of the *consigli di gestione*, held in Milan in October 1946, the communists argued strongly that these organs of worker control should remain clearly distinct from the internal commissions and the unions.

Even before the congress, the socialists, led by Lelio Basso, put forward the idea that the councils should be seen as instruments for economic planning. The communist Emilio Sereni, however, argued that such functions were too wide-ranging and impractical for such bodies.[14] Against both communists and socialists, the Partito d' azione proclaimed in its typically radical fashion that it was impossible to manage production alongside the capitalist class and that the *consigli di gestione* should assume complete control of industry. The Christian Democrats, holding fast to principles of Catholic social teaching, supported worker-employer collaboration and profit-sharing.[15] The liberals, having emerged from their postwar internal contest between rival tendencies as strong supporters of the classical *laissez-faire* doctrine, were against the formation of *consigli di gestione*.

In January 1946, the Confindustria opposed the setting up of *consigli di gestione*, arguing that they would be an obstacle to change and would poison industrial relations. In spite of these arguments, a *consiglio di gestione* was established at the Fiat works in February 1946, but with a purely consultative role. This gave the movement a certain impetus, and the socialist Rodolfo Morandi set about drafting a bill for the Constituent Assembly. Estimates vary, but there seem to have been between 500 and 800 set up, mainly

---

[13] U. Morelli, *I Consigli di Gestione dalla Liberazione ai primi anni cinquanta*, p. 19. See *interclassismo* in Glossary.

[14] See ibid., p. 86.

[15] See ibid., pp. 49-55.

in the larger, northern factories, by 1949. Those with direct experience of the councils claim that industrial reconstruction would have been more difficult without them. Their modes of operation varied a great deal, as did the methods of selecting the membership of the *consigli*. Some included management among the members, others consisted of workers only. Their functions varied from simple consultation to the hiring of labour, and in some cases even the organization of production.

The Confindustria's hostility to the *consigli di gestione* grew in volubility and effectiveness as the employers regained confidence and self-respect. By late 1947 it was clear that the Dc, now strong in government, was back-tracking on its earlier support for the councils. In a reply to Di Vittorio, who, in a debate at the Constituent Assembly, was pressing the government to make up its mind about legislation, De Gasperi declared that he did not 'see the immediate need for *consigli di gestione*'.[16] With the defeat of the left at the national elections of April 1948 the Morandi Bill was forgotten and the *consigli* went into decline. It may afford some small consolation to those who feel that an opportunity for developing forms of industrial democracy was missed through the lack of clearsightedness on the part of the left, that in spite of the defeat of the *consigli di gestione* in the realm of *realpolitik*, and this was no small matter, discussions in the Constituent Assembly nevertheless ensured the permanent legitimacy of the principle of worker participation in the management of industry in the country's constitutional order, where it remains enshrined to this day.[17]

---

[16] *Atti della Assemblea Costituente*, vol. viii, pp. 1771-2.

[17] 'For the purposes of the economic and social advancement of labour, in harmony with the requirements of production, the Republic recognises the right of workers, according to the methods and within the framework established by the law, to participate in the management of companies'. *Costituzione Italiana*, Art. 46.

3

The Catholic Secession and the Formation of Rival Confederations

Looking back on political developments in Italy between 1946 and 1948, it is easy to see that there was a certain inevitability about the break-up of the *Cgil unitaria*. During this period, political and ideological divisions between Catholics and communists increased both in intensity and range. The critical division over policy in July 1946, the expulsion of communists and socialists from the government coalition in May 1947, and the Catholic disavowals of executive decisions later in the year were followed by an acrimonious electoral campaign for the parliamentary elections of April 1948. The spirit of anti-fascist unity which had inspired the activity of the Cln and informed the drafting of the republican Constitution dissolved into the bitter polemics of the cold war. The Christian Democrats, shortly before portrayed in communist speeches as leaders of a great mass popular party, became the priest-ridden puppets of an unqualified capitalist restoration. In a campaign which had all the hallmarks of a religious crusade, the communists, in their turn, from being the former backbone of the resistance, found themselves cast in the role of destructive enemies of God, the family and civilization.

Inside the Cgil, the resounding victory of the Dc in April 1948 delivered a coup de grace to any residual hopes which may have remained within the Catholic left for the preservation of labour unity. It strengthened the conservative wing and enabled the 'collateral' organization Acli to emerge as 'a controlling force over the Catholic union component'.[1]

Preparing the Ground for a Split

The prospect of Catholic-communist unity had always been viewed

---

[1] G. Baglioni, *Il sindacato dell'autonomia*, p. 221.

with varying degrees of disquiet within important sectors of Italian Catholicism and within the Vatican. As early as August 1945, Pope Pius XII expressed the traditional Catholic fear of Marxist contamination. And when, a few months later, the Catholic De Gasperi succeeded Parri as the country's leader, articles began to appear in the Jesuit periodical *Civiltà Cattolica* attacking the idea of unity within a movement in which a large part of the leadership was ideologically committed to the class struggle. After the Dc victory of April 1948 the hostility became even more pronounced. The Pope condemned the anti-Christian pursuit of worldly values which was allegedly penetrating the workers' movement and, in an address delivered in June of that year to a large Acli gathering of 60,000, warned that 'if the existing form of the *sindacato* should endanger the true purpose of the workers' movement, then the Acli would not fail to take the action which a sense of duty and the gravity of the situation demand'.[2] Pressure from official ecclesiastical quarters was simply one manifestation of the 'collateralist' network in operation. After its election victory, for instance, the Dc also began to press the Catholic component of the Cgil to 'clarify its position'. Statements from both ecclesiastical and party sources were in effect flanking fire in support of the action being taken at the real centre of operations in the Acli.

It is doubtful whether the Catholic secession from the Cgil was as unpremeditated as some Catholic commentators have maintained. We know from the minutes of meetings held in the offices of the presidency of the Acli in December 1947 that discussions at this stage were no longer about *whether* a Catholic confederation should be formed but about the *timing* of the split. The chief ecclesiastical assistant appointed to the Acli, Luigi Civardi, wanted the new confederation to be explicitly Catholic, whereas the leader of the Catholic component within the Cgil, Pastore, argued for an 'ideologically neutral' organization, since this would attract more members.[3] Some months later, Pastore, after refusing to speak at the Cgil May Day rally in Rome alongside other union leaders, on 6 May attended a highly confidential meeting of the National Council of the Acli. The meeting lasted

---

[2] C. Pillon, *I comunisti e il sindacato*, p. 444.

[3] See Magister, *La politica vaticana e l'Italia*, pp. 119ff, and also D. Rosati, *La questione politica delle Acli*, pp. 60ff.

three days, and also present were Dc government ministers, the President of Catholic Action, and the American labour leader James Carey. After lengthy talks a press release announced that the National Council of the Acli had come to the conclusion that the interests of working people required 'a truly free and democratic union organization, in which all workers could collaborate in the common task of national reconstruction'. This bland statement on its own might have meant almost anything. What was unknown to the public was the ending of the statement, not disclosed to the press but contained in the minutes of the meeting: '...and undertakes to realise this project'.[4] A memorandum dated 12 May from the president of the Acli, Ferdinando Storchi, to the Vatican official Montini (later Pope Paul VI) summarises the outcome of the meeting. The new confederation was to be established in such a manner as to take with it as many defectors as possible. The majority of some categories of membership seemed assured: teachers, bankers, white-collar workers, civil servants, etc.[5]

The presence of James Carey at the Acli meeting was a sign of the influence on Italian affairs of direct cold war strategies being worked out at higher levels of international politics. We now know from government documents that in March of that year the US Secretary of State had summoned the American union leaders Murray and Carey to discuss the importance of the forthcoming split within the Cgil. Murray and Carey were to assure the secessionists of financial and moral support.[6] After the defeat of the communists in the Italian elections in April 1948, the AFL sent a telegram of congratulations to Pastore (who was also a Dc deputy), asking to be informed of the effects within the Cgil of the Catholic victory. On 16 June, Pastore met Thomas Lane, the US expert on union affairs, at the US Embassy in Rome. Lane urged the Italians to break with the communist-led Cgil as soon as possible.

American intervention in Italian union affairs was, in effect, part of a broader series of cold war initiatives which led the

---

[4] Magister, *La politica vaticana e l'Italia*, p. 120.

[5] See G Pasini, *Le Acli delle origini*, pp. 199ff.

[6] See the documentation in R. Faenza and M. Fini, *Gli americani in Italia*, p. 306, n. 3.

American labour confederations AFL and CIO to overcome their traditional rivalry and, with the help of the British TUC, split the WFTU and go on to establish the ICFTU. The international division of union organizations into communist and non-communist camps was not simply a passive effect of cold war tensions at the political level, but the result of a planned strategy. Thus within the Cgil, differences which in other circumstances might have been resolved were deliberately exacerbated and kept alive by the would-be secessionists. It remained, however, for the Catholics to find a way of justifying the split which had already been decided.

The Controversial Article 9

At the founding Naples Cgil Congress in early 1945, the statutes of the newly-founded confederation had been approved unanimously. The Catholics were later reminded of this fact many times, for article 9 of the statutes affirmed the legitimacy of political strikes, a provision to which they subsequently objected, and around which there grew a bitter polemic. In the early days of 1945 the spirit of the resistance was still very much alive; political freedom had not yet been established and, as Di Vittorio repeatedly warned, even after victory it would be many years before the country could feel secure against the danger of a regression to authoritarian rule. Against this background it was not difficult to win congressional approval for an article committing the movement to the defence of democracy. Difficulties began to emerge, however, as the original threat from the common enemy receded into the background, and the notion of defending democracy began to take on new meanings.

To the majority of Cgil leaders the popular liberties which the confederation had undertaken to defend, if and when necessary, could be endangered not only by fascists but also by governments and other forces operating within a formal democratic framework. The polemic was first sparked off in December 1945, when it appeared to many within the Cgil that the Dc had had a decisive role in the fall of the Parri government, thus causing a political crisis and the fracturing of the anti-fascist coalition. Spontaneous work stoppages took place in many parts of the country, initiatives which the Cgil could hardly ignore. But anxious to avoid internal conflict with the Catholic current over the role of the Dc, the leadership of the confederation, in drawing up a resolution expressing 'grave concern' over existing developments, studiously avoided any mention of specific political parties. In spite of such efforts, Pastore, the most aggressive of the Catholic leaders, wrote an article in the Dc daily condemning the 'infusion of all forms of political expression in the activity of the *sindacato*'.[7] The Catholic attack on article 9 of the Cgil statutes had begun.

The debate on article 9 which took place at the next congress, held in Florence (1-7 June 1947), was bitter and intense. In what seems suspiciously like a carefully timed act of provocation, the day before the congress was due to start, De Gasperi announced the expulsion of communists and socialists from the new coalition government. De Gasperi, in constant touch with the new Catholic leader of the Cgil, Pastore, must have known of the attack the latter was to launch at congress on the article in question. It seems likely that the timing of the Dc leader's announcement was designed to provoke condemnation of his action by congress, thus facilitating, indeed justifying, a serious split in the movement. He could reasonably have hoped, moreover, that republicans and social democrats would support the Catholics and refuse to condemn his action since he had given both of their parties two ministerial positions where previously they had had none.[8]

A change in Catholic attitudes towards political strikes had taken place since the 1945 Naples Congress. The reason, of course, was that union *political* mobilisation was becoming increasingly directed against Dc-led governments as the Dc-Pci conflict intensified. It was clear in the 1947 congress debate that De Gasperi's decision to oust communists and socialists from the government coalition had angered many delegates, who accused him of deliberately destroying the anti-fascist coalition. Loyalty to their party in government led Catholic delegates to argue that the task of defending democracy belonged to the political parties and the government alone.[9] Given the failure of precisely these

---

[7] Pastore's outburst appeared in *Il Popolo*, 23 December 1945.

[8] The communists lost nine ministerial posts, the socialists eight.

[9] See, for example, the arguments of the Catholic leader Pastore, in *La Cgil dal Patto di Roma al Congresso di Genova. Atti e documenti*, vol. iii, pp. 130-4.

institutions to prevent fascism's coming to power in the first place, this was not the strongest of arguments. To most delegates it seemed that the Catholics were not arguing from a position of principle but adopting an opportunistic stance. Many Catholics, in other words, who had praised the political strikes of 1943 and 1944, now appeared to be trying to change the rules of the game.

In his 1947 congress speech, Pastore distinguished between the defence of democracy as such and actions aimed at undermining particular governments within a democratic state. His objection was that article 9 could be used as an instrument against particular parties in government. He was sure that if the need arose the workers' movement would respond without hesitation to any real threat to democracy. He asked the congress: 'Do you believe that after what happened in 1922 the Italian workers really need an article in the statutes in order to rise up unanimously the day such a threat should occur?'[10]

Given Italy's historical past, Pastore's argument was not difficult to counter. In the first place, it *was* essential to be able to act against the decisions or vacillations of elected governments. The fascist March on Rome, for instance, had itself taken place within a democratic framework and against a background of government confusion and indecision. It would be irresponsible to make no provision for the possibility of timely action should the need arise once again. Secondly, if Pastore were so confident of the Cgil's readiness to defend liberty, why, asked the socialist Santi, did he object to the formal declaration of so honourable a commitment?[11] Such a declaration would add to, not detract from the prestige of the movement. The result of the debate was a crushing defeat for the Catholics. Republicans, social democrats and *azionisti* joined the communists and socialists in defeating a Catholic resolution which sought to limit the *sindacato*'s activity in such a way as not to 'offend the convictions or limit the political or religious liberty of its members', a motion which, its opponents pointed out, made it possible to delegitimise almost any kind of activity.[12]

---

[10] Ibid., pp. 134-5.

[11] See ibid., p. 176.

[12] 'Mozione della corrente sindacale cristiana', pp. 19-20. The *azionisti* were members of the Partito d' Azione.

Throughout the proceedings Di Vittorio was at pains not to fuel unnecessarily either the initial fury or the subsequent exhilaration of the majority at the heavy Catholic defeat. Aware of the designs of De Gasperi and Pastore, he knew that humiliating the Catholics risked provoking their immediate departure. In reply to a Catholic attack on the alleged use of the Cgil for party purposes, he pointed out that for the sake of unity he had refrained from even mentioning what many regarded as the most provocative government action since anti-fascist unity had been established. He and other leaders then sought to modify article 9 in a manner that would allay Catholic fears. The original wording of the article was altered, and while the right to take action on social and political issues was retained, the introduction of a three-quarters majority voting requirement stressed the exceptional nature of such action.[13] Most communist and socialist delegates, though prepared to follow Di Vittorio's lead, thought his course of action too indulgent towards the Catholic minority.[14] But the fragility of the unity which the congress had managed to preserve was evident in the warning given by Pastore in the closing stages. If the exceptional nature of

---

[13] The amended article 9 which was approved with the abstention of the Catholic component read as follows:

> Union independence of political parties and of the state does not signify union noncommittal in the face of all problems of a political nature. The Cgil will be free to adopt a position on those political problems which concern not only particular parties, but working people in general, such as the defence of the Republic and the development of democracy and popular liberties; also on problems relating to social legislation and to the reconstruction and development of the nation's economy.
> Union action in relation to such problems, being of an exceptional character, can be pursued only if decided upon by the properly convened executive of the organization concerned and by a three-quarters majority of those present.

This amended version of article 9 is to be found alongside the original, among the documents of the 1947 Congress, in 'Modifiche proposte allo statuto confederale', pp. 363-4.

[14] See, for example, Luciano Lama's first-hand account of these discussions and debates in *La Cgil di Di Vittorio*, pp. 87ff.

the recourse to article 9 were to be violated, the Catholic minority would feel itself released from the obligation to observe union discipline.[15]

The Secession

The event which finally occasioned the major split was the assassination attempt on the Communist Party leader Togliatti on 14 July 1948. At about 11.30 am, as he left the Chamber of Deputies, a 25-year-old neo-fascist student fired four pistol shots into his chest. As the news spread, the public reacted with shock. All over the country spontaneous strikes were called; factories, shops and offices were closed and public services were brought to a standstill. Ex-partisans who still harboured hopes of insurrection brought out the arms they had kept in hiding.

The Pci leadership, while supporting the protest and condemning government cold war attitudes, was anxious that matters should not get out of hand.[16] Similarly, the leadership of the Cgil, particularly the communists and socialists, was aware of the opportunity that a violent reaction to the attempted assassination would provide for legal and repressive measures against the left. Indeed, many thought that the real purpose of the assassination attempt was to bring the climate of extreme tension to a point of civil crisis. On the other hand, it was intolerable in a democracy that the leader of an opposition party should have to exercise his function at the risk of his life. It was exactly this kind of threat which justified recourse to article 9 of the Cgil statutes.

In such an unstable and critical situation, the Cgil considered that it would be better placed to control its outcome by placing itself at the head of the protest. On the same evening, 14 July, the confederation thus issued an instruction extending the general strike

---

[15] See Pastore's declaration and Di Vittorio's rejoinder, *La Cgil dal Patto di Roma al Congresso di Genova. Atti e documenti*, vol. iii, pp. 342-3.

[16] The Minister of the Interior, Scelba, reported to parliament that the total number of casualties resulting from the disturbances of mid-July was 16 dead and 206 wounded.

to all categories of workers from midnight.[17] Catholic leaders, also shocked by the assassination attempt, were present at the meeting which took this decision.[18]

Within the Catholic leadership, however, there was a sudden change of mind. By about noon of the following day, 15 July, the eleven leaders of the Catholic component of the Cgil sent a letter to the rest of the Cgil executive stating that the decision taken the evening before was in conflict with article 9 of the statutes, and ending with a clear ultimatum: 'We are, therefore, obliged to inform you that we consider the announcement of the ending of the strike by today obligatory. Aware of its responsibility to the workers and to the nation, our component reserves the right to take whatever decision it sees fit, and we draw your attention to the gravity of such a situation.'[19] It was clear that the Catholic leadership was seizing the opportunity to make the break and at the same time shifting the responsibility for fracturing the unity of the working class on to the shoulders of the remainder of the executive, should it not accede to Catholic demands.

The remainder of the executive felt that, although a national protest had in any case already been made, it would still have been wrong to capitulate to what it saw as a clear act of blackmail. Thus, on the evening of 15 July, it called off the strike from noon the following day, failing to meet the deadline imposed by the Catholic minority group by 12 hours. The executive thus signalled its wish to compromise for the sake of unity, but at the same time indicated that decisions would continue to be taken by majorities. In all probability, the Catholics were hoping for a forthright rejection of their demands, and were not expecting so subtle a manoeuvre. The decision to call off the strike even by noon on the following day required prompt action, and would certainly have been interpreted publicly as an accommodating gesture. Thus to use the 12-hour

---

[17] For the full text of the instruction, see 'Cronache e documenti della scissione della corrente sindacale cristiana', pp. 321-2.

[18] For detailed and documented accounts of the events, see Turone, *Storia del sindacato in Italia*, pp. 144ff, and Pillon, *I comunisti e il sindacato*, pp. 444ff.

[19] 'Cronache e documenti della scissione', pp. 323-4.

delay to justify their departure would have made it abundantly clear that the Catholics were determined to abandon the confederation.

No reference was made to the delay. Instead, the Catholics announced on 16 July that the Acli was meeting to consider the question of the need for a truly autonomous workers' organization. It was clear that there was no longer any hope of reconciliation. On 5 August, after much shadow boxing about which side would assume responsibility for the formal declaration, the executive of the Cgil unanimously approved a resolution stating that the Catholic component had placed itself in such a position as to be no longer within the organization. A liberal journalist who had travelled to the Franciscan retreat where a meeting of the Dc national council was being held, met the Catholic labour leader Pastore by chance and gave him the news.[20] The scene of elation described by Gorresio contrasted sharply with the declared reluctance with which Pastore had placed his demands before the Cgil executive. It was, however, the natural expression of a long-awaited and hoped-for liberation.

It was not until May 1950, after a series of negotiations, that the definitive shape of the rival confederations was settled. In the meantime, the Acli Congress of September 1948 had announced the foundation of the new confederation, the Lcgil. The choice of name, with the simple addition of *Libera* in the new title, was meant to send a twofold message. First, that at the Acli Congress, those who had wanted a confessional, or avowedly Catholic organization had been defeated by the majority, who preferred a confederation open to members of all religious and political persuasions. In the second place, the new title was a thinly disguised cold war jibe aimed at the communist-dominated Cgil.

These developments increased the anxiety of the non-communists remaining in the Cgil, particularly the social democrats and republicans. It soon became clear that these components were not prepared to live with an enhanced communist majority strongly supported by the socialists. Thus a second secession, of social democrats and republicans, led to the formation of the Fil in June 1949. But even before this further split had taken place, the question had arisen about whether social democrats and republicans should join forces with the Lcgil. The argument, which continued after the foundation of the Fil, was between those whose

---

[20] See V. Gorresio, *I bracci secolari*, pp. 56ff.

priority was the creation of an effective and united anti-communist organization of labour, and others who were not prepared to replace communist domination with a Catholic one. The latter dismissed the idea that the Lcgil could be anything but a Catholic confederation which would inevitably support the Dc. There was considerable pressure from the American side, and a great deal of trans-Atlantic toing and froing of political and union leaders, aimed at bringing about a fusion of the two secessionist confederations.[21]

On 1 May 1950, after a period of negotiations, the Lcgil and the Fil merged to form a new confederation, the Cisl. However, a group of socialists, later to join the social democrats, led by Romita, had left the Cgil in 1949 to join the Fil, only to discover that secret negotiations were taking place to merge with the Lcgil. Totally opposed to such a union, this group had founded a further confederation, the Uil, in March 1950. The Uil later drew into its fold the republicans, who refused to join a confederation (Cisl) dominated by Catholics. Soon afterwards, social democrats began to desert the Cisl and to join the Uil, thus leaving the former with the original Catholic membership of the dissolved Lcgil. By mid-1950, therefore, the three confederations, the Cgil, the Cisl and the Uil, represented a fairly clear political division along communist/socialist, Catholic, and social democrat/republican lines.[22] According to statistics produced later in the year, the strength of the three confederations in terms of membership was: Cgil 4,782,090; Cisl 1,489,682; Uil 401,527.[23]

Conclusion

As the political parties' divergent visions of Italy's future were translated into day-to-day political activity, changes within the

---

[21] See 'Carteggio 1949-51 "degli intrighi e delle manovre" USA - Italia. Gli americani, la scissione sindacale italiana, le polemiche fra Cisl e Uil', pp. 519-46.

[22] Joseph La Palombara has asserted that US financial aid was vital for the survival of Cisl and Uil at their foundation. See his *The Italian Labor Movement*, pp. 57ff.

[23] A. Gradilone, *Storia del sindacalismo*, vol. iii, part 2, p. 315.

workers' movement and the political parties were almost bound to follow a series of parallel courses. For this reason, too negative a judgement on party influences in this period would be a mistake. As the Catholic Sandro Fontana has noted, political parties were 'in those crucial years, the sole instruments of social and political aggregation for large popular masses'.[24] A large measure of *verticismo* was as unavoidable in the process leading to secession as it had been in the original foundation of the *Cgil unitaria*.

One thing the Catholic secession in July 1948 did demonstrate was the scanty support which existed among all the non-Catholic components of the movement, social democrats and republicans included, for the idea of a politically and socially disengaged *sindacato*. The communists and socialists were not alone in condemning the attitude of the Catholics. The republican view was expressed thus:

> The *sindacato* must indeed act as *sindacato*, but not apolitically, in the sense that even it must live the political life of the citizens in its entirety and share the same patriotic concerns. It must also retain the right to act accordingly, with political strikes when in the general interests of the Republic, and protest strikes when, like the other day, it was a question of fundamental rights to political co-existence and social tolerance.[25]

There were undoubtedly Catholics in the Cgil who shared the opinions expressed in the passage just cited from *La Voce Repubblicana*. But Pastore's historic act of opportunism, with its recourse to deeply entrenched loyalties, swept aside the possibility of fine distinctions in its demand for an expression of Catholic solidarity which in reality left his co-religionists little choice.[26] Thus the founding of the Catholic *sindacato* took on the appearance

---

[24] *I cattolici e l'unità sindacale*, p. 125.

[25] G. A. Belloni, *La Voce Repubblicana*, 18 July 1948. Cited in Pillon, *I comunisti e il sindacato*, p. 450.

[26] It should be pointed out that the task was made easier for Pastore, in that the instruction issued by the Cgil on the evening of the assassination attempt contained a strong condemnation of the government. Pastore, a leading member of the Dc, would clearly use the argument that the Cgil was engaging in political acts against the *party* of government.

of an act of rebellion against the notion of a 'politicised' workers' movement. It would be many years before Catholic labour leaders were able to re-examine the question of the political dimension of union activity with equanimity, and without fear of appearing to suffer an ideological capitulation to the major rival confederation.

As a result of the split the Cisl was committed to creating for itself a new identity as an autonomous organization, independent of political parties. For many years this remained little more than a pious hope, as each of the confederations continued to reflect strong party loyalties.

Yet despite their inability to preserve unity, the forces which created the original *Cgil unitaria* had, in effect, performed a task of more lasting significance than might at first appear to be the case. The communists, for instance, inspired by the thinking behind the idea of a 'progressive democracy', became as much the creators of the new Italian Republic as were the other political groupings. Alongside socialists and Catholics, their input into the Constitution ensured that many of the aspirations of the workers' movement were given constitutional expression. Article 3, in particular, asserts the right to 'a real and effective participation of all workers in the political, economic and social organization of the country'.[27]

The much-debated article 9 of the Cgil statutes reflected the self-awareness of a movement which was not prepared to accept a role at the margins of Italian society. This perspective was momentarily lost, or at least stifled, within the Catholic world of labour led by the Cisl, in its anxiety to give support to the Dc. In the summer of 1949 the Dc Minister of Labour, Fanfani, proposed the banning of strikes which were 'political' in nature or had been called for reasons of 'solidarity'. Fanfani's proposals did not become law but, as Paul Ginsborg has noted, 'they were hardly a good advertisement for the Christian Democrats' attitude to trade unionism, especially with an industrial proletariat as class-conscious as the Italian'.[28] Such attitudes within its collateral party organization did not bode well for the Cisl. This was not such an ideological problem within the smaller but significant social democrat/republican current of the movement, newly organized in

---

[27] *Costituzione Italiana*, p. 3. See also articles 4, and 36-40.

[28] P. Ginsborg, *A History of Contemporary Italy*, p. 173.

the Uil. In article 3 section 4 of its statutes, the Uil asserted its right 'to intervene actively in all problems relating to economic and social policy and whenever, directly or indirectly, the future of the working class is at stake'.[29] Indeed, while rejecting 'collateralist' links with any political party, the Uil asserted, in the official report to its first National Congress in December 1953, that the *sindacato*

> is much more than a simple protector of wage levels or a body for drafting regulations. In the interests of the worker it co-ordinates all policies relating to the world of work, and these are inseparable from the worker's economic interests and social aspirations. The conception of a non-political *sindacato* is thus a dangerous piece of nonsense which risks inflicting serious and painful losses on the workers' movement.[30]

Yet despite its positive achievements, in 1950 the Italian workers' movement emerged to face the future with some notable disadvantages. A series of internal political battles had left it scarred and painfully divided. No attention had been given to the need for a union presence at workshop level, where it remained woefully unrepresented. Equally tragically, not only did the *Cgil unitaria* fail to create a new 'historic bloc' between peasants and the industrial working class, but it had thrust the *contadini* almost irredeemably into the hands of the larger landowners. With its complex ensemble of successes and failures, the Italian workers' movement prepared to face the bleak decade ahead.

---

[29] Uil, *Statuto approvato dal primo congresso nazionale*, p. 4.

[30] Uil, *Relazione presentata al primo congresso nazionale*, p. 24.

Part II

THE 1950s: YEARS OF DIVISION AND RIVAL IDEOLOGIES

4

A Weak and Divided Movement: Political and Economic Constraints

The Growth Pains of the 1950s

Once the steep inflationary tendencies of the late 1940s had been curbed, largely as a result of the harsh liberal economic policies of Luigi Einaudi, there followed, from the early 1950s onwards, a substantial increase in industrial production and profits. The decision to open the economy to international competition meant that it was essential to maintain low labour costs and freedom for employers to take on and lay off workers at will. From 1958 the developments under way entered their dramatic phase, and continued until 1963, a phenomenon which became known as the 'economic miracle'. Export markets were opened up to Italian goods in an unprecedented manner. Italy, a marginal economy at the time, was able to exploit a phase of international commercial development in which the increase in demand for goods could not be met by the internal supply of the major industrial economies.[1] This phase of enormous expansion and industrial development saw spectacular advances in a variety of sectors, and in terms of its global production, Italy was being transformed from a predominantly agrarian into an industrially-based society.

There were, however, some fundamental structural problems contained within this process of economic growth. The major one was that both the driving force and the beneficiaries behind this development were the manufacturing industries of the North. The age-old disparities between North and South were intensified by even greater distortions in the productive base of the economy and in structures of employment. For example, while there was an overall drop in unemployment, new jobs could be found only in the North. Thus a phase of internal migration began, with which the

---

[1] See R. Spesso, *L'economia italiana dal dopoguerra a oggi*, pp. 49ff.

northern urban centres were ill-equipped to deal. The social tensions created by the ensuing demographic upheavals would ultimately erupt with explosive force in the late 1960s. Northern cities then became the centres of an unbridled movement towards consumer-oriented investment, while no attention was paid to the additional demands made on essential services such as transport, health, education and housing.

A start on land reform which was intended to eliminate the North/South divide had been attempted earlier by the communist Minister of Agriculture, Fausto Gullo, in a series of decrees from July 1944. Gullo's legislation aimed to guarantee peasants at least half of their production, to hand over neglected land to production co-operatives, and abolish the hated intermediaries between the large landowners and peasants/workers. For three years, communists led land occupations and strikes, mostly in the South, where the Cgil also fought for greater work security and for a fair system of labour allocation. Share-croppers in central Italy were also supported by the communists in their attempts to modify their contracts with the landowners.[2] There were great difficulties with these attempts at reform. They were opposed by the Dc and the liberals, who were backed by a judiciary formed under fascism and not very sympathetic to left-wing reforms. Credit facilities which Gullo had made available to small and medium *contadini* were never extended, so that initial gains were frequently clawed back by the large landowners, with the help of their powerful friends. Furthermore, small peasant owners who had taken part in the struggles for land were not sympathetic to the Cgil's demands that labour should be secure and better paid. The communists had not given sufficient thought and attention to the potential divisions between peasants and *braccianti*.

In July 1946 De Gasperi replaced Gullo with the Christian Democrat Antonio Segni, himself a large landowner, who made promises about abolishing the large landed estates, but in effect presided over a major shift of strategy. The protests were ultimately defeated by the hostility of the landowners, the judges and a heavy dose of police brutality. The political situation after 1947 had

---

[2] For a more detailed account of Gullo's legislation and the peasant struggles, see Ginsborg, *A History of Contemporary Italy*, pp. 59-63 and 106-10.

changed decisively to the disadvantage of the left. In October 1950, parliament approved a measure of land reform which redistributed many of the latifundia 'in preparation for a general agrarian reform which would never follow'.[3] The passing of the law had been preceded by the struggles of 1949-50, in which violent clashes with the police had resulted in protesters being injured and even killed. From the beginning, these struggles had little chance of long-term success. Even if they had been able to overcome the bitterness of their recent split, the Cgil and the Cisl were aiming at quite different objectives. To the Catholics, the large landed estates were to be broken up into small properties. The communists, on the other hand, wanted only limited ownership, via collectives and co-operatives, and even that only after a larger-scale socialisation, involving the nationalisation of large industries and institutions of credit. In any case, the Cisl was by now, particularly in the South, unable to participate in any form of agrarian struggle because it would have meant acting in open defiance of the higher clergy who were solidly behind the large landowners. The 1950 reform, while modest in terms of immediate results, was effective in helping to destroy the parasitic system of latifundia which for millennia had allowed the large landed proprietors to amass their fortunes. What it failed to do was to improve the real conditions of the *contadini* and to lay the foundations of a more modern and effective system of agricultural production. As Renato Zangheri has argued:

> The land which was either sold or expropriated was generally the worst, and large sums of money passed from the countryside to the cities; the peasant purchasers or recipients of the land received neither the technical nor financial assistance which was indispensable; the land's excessive segmentation was not conducive to the modernisation of the country's agrarian structures. We must ask, however, why it is that progressive forces were not able to overcome these unfavourable circumstances.[4]

The reforms were carried out in a manner which was intended to reinforce individual/family rather than co-operative possession. Thus, in spite of the periods of strong mobilisation in

---

[3] R. Stefanelli, *Lotte agrarie e modello di sviluppo 1946-67*, p. 175.

[4] *Agricoltura e contadini nella storia d'Italia*, p. 37.

1944-7 and 1949-50, the collective spirit among the southern peasants and workers was broken by 1950. Crucial to this defeat was the role of the Coldiretti, established, as we saw in chapter 1, in 1944 under the leadership of Paolo Bonomi to undercut the influence of the nascent *Cgil unitaria*. Inspired, at least in its formation, by traditional Catholic populism, the organization aimed to promote small individual holdings. With the consolidation of Dc control of the government, it became an important power base in the hands of Bonomi, who enjoyed enormous influence in the Ministry of Agriculture, and controlled about fifty deputies in parliament. The organization was able to guarantee health protection to its members, and a variety of other benefits, including grants for equipment and cheap fertilisers. Through the influence of Bonomi in the Dc, the Coldiretti was also able to facilitate the award of old age and invalidity pensions. Also with the help of the Dc, special legislation establishing savings and credit institutions for small farmers was passed in parliament. In this way the peasant proprietor was lost to the left and won over increasingly into the political camp controlled by larger landed interests.

The objectives of the agrarian struggles of 1944-7 and 1949-50, led by the communists, had been set within an ideological framework which required a series of broader political measures for their success. But these measures were far from being on any conceivable government's political agenda. Even when Gullo was Minister of Agriculture from April 1944 to July 1946, his initiatives had been easy to undermine. Furthermore, although the communist leaders of the struggles enjoyed the steadfast support of the *braccianti*, their strategy failed to take account of the quite different aspirations of the *contadini*. There were the so-called 'capitalist peasants structurally tied to the dominant groups', but there were also poorer peasants who had to be detached from these and won over to the side of the *braccianti*. This was far from being a remote possibility since they 'remained at subsistence level along with those undergoing an increasing process of proletarianisation'.[5] Once again, we are faced with the failure of the left to forge a

---

[5] U. Romagnoli e T. Treu, *I sindacati in Italia: storia di una strategia*, pp. 151-2. For a more detailed discussion of these structural differentiations, see C. Daneo, *Agricoltura e sviluppo capitalistico in Italia*, Turin: Einaudi, 1972.

strategy which could have united these lower elements of the agrarian social strata.

The weaknesses of the Cgil and the Cisl to which we have referred are part of the reason for the failure of the forces to which Zangheri refers. A divided movement was not in a position to force the government to take seriously problems it preferred to ignore. But it must also be said that the greater part of the energies of the movement, albeit for reasons which differed between Catholics and communists, was directed towards developments in the North. For it must not be imagined that the expansion being witnessed in the northern industrial centres was without alarming consequences on the working conditions in the factories.

The period of expansion of the Italian economy was aided by the competitive nature of Italian prices, which was largely the result of low labour costs. One of the reasons that most western economies were unable to match the low prices of Italian goods was that their internal industrial relations systems did not permit practices which, by contrast, in Italy became the motor force of rapid, cheap expansion. While a number of advanced industrial economies chose a path of collaboration with the world of labour, Italian industrialists were able either to ignore or easily defeat the workforce's best efforts to negotiate the consequences of rapid change.

The large-scale introduction of Taylorist methods into a previously backward system made an enormous difference to productivity. The use of assembly lines reorganized working patterns into fragmented, self-contained, monotonous tasks. To this was added the stress of piecework production. In spite of the physically and psychologically oppressive nature of such work, the compensatory effects on the earning capacity of the workforce were astonishingly low. Between 1948 and 1955 production, productivity per worker and profits all rose by between 86 per cent and 95 per cent, while real wages increased by only 6 per cent.[6] In 1957 the Central Institute for Statistics (Istat) revealed that the average monthly family budget for essentials was L70,371, while the monthly earnings of the majority of industrial workers were

---

[6] See J. Barkan, *Visions of Emancipation*, p. 37.

between L50,000 and L60,000.[7] There had been no improvement in workers' pay since the beginning of the decade. It was clear that low wages were important for financing reconstruction.

It would, of course, be wrong to think that depressed pay, poor working conditions, or government complacency in the face of inadequate essential services did not meet with bitter union resistance. But to understand why such opposition was largely ineffectual, at least for many years, we must examine the way in which both government and employers were able to take advantage of the divisions within the workers' movement.

The Government

Given the cold war politics of the period, the effect of the organizational split in the *sindacato* was to polarise Catholics and communists even further. In the minds of the public the two confederations which mattered, the Cisl and the Cgil, became identified with support for the Dc government and the communist-led opposition respectively. Notwithstanding the confederations' statutes and numerous congress pronouncements to the contrary, the public's perception was broadly correct in practice.

This worked to the disadvantage of the communists. Catholic workers' organizations had the advantage of being a collateral force with the party of government. But this was not all. Catholic *collateralismo* embraced the Church, and in July 1949 Pope Pius XII issued a decree of excommunication on any Catholic who joined the Pci or any of its flank organizations such as the Cgil, or read or disseminated any communist newspaper or journal.[8] The legitimisation of anti-communism began to penetrate the day-to-day working of the government, the judiciary and the police in an alarming manner.

In such a climate, mere opposition to employers who sought to impose unilateral conditions at the workplace became seditious,

---

[7] See Spesso, *L'economia italiana dal dopoguerra a oggi*, pp. 51-74.

[8] The text of the decree can be found in Magister, *La politica vaticana e l'Italia*, pp. 132-3. Although the original text did not specifically name the Cgil, a more widely disseminated version did.

so that at the Venice Congress of the Dc in June 1949 Mariano Rumor was able to state: 'It is necessary to combat the political ferment which exists in the workplace and to resist, even with the force of law, those who carry out clearly subversive activity against the Italian economy. We must above all de-politicise the workplace.'[9] The forces of law and order responded to such promptings in a manner which made of the fifties a distinctly unedifying spectacle for commentators on postwar Italian labour history. Police commissioners were provided with forms to send to local employers for the collection of information on employees. They were to answer questions on the 'moral and political' conduct of workers who gave cause for concern, indicating also their party and union affiliations. Between 1948 and 1953, in Fiat alone, 164 workers were dismissed for engaging in union and political activity.[10] These, of course, were merely the recorded cases.

As one might expect in an atmosphere such as this, political hostilities became open and virulent. In 1953, the Dc was able to force through parliament an electoral reform which would have given the party or electoral bloc obtaining 50 per cent plus one of the votes 66 per cent of the seats. This tactic was so reminiscent of that used by Mussolini that it caused an uproar. In the 1953 elections which followed the passing of the new law, the Dc vote fell considerably, as did that of the centre parties, and the Dc-led bloc failed to reach its target. Communists and socialists increased their votes. Following this blunder, the law was swiftly repealed the following year. The Cgil, which saw the *legge truffa* ('swindle law'), as it came to be known, as almost a re-run of the fascist attempt, some thirty years earlier, to eliminate political opposition, had campaigned vigorously against this attack on democracy. There was a demonstrable increase in public support for the left because of its opposition to the law. Once more, it was felt, the necessity for retaining article 9 in the Cgil statutes had been demonstrated.

But this was not the only kind of political mobilisation organized by the Cgil. Strikes and protests were held against the setting up of NATO bases, the negotiations for the Common Market, the construction of atomic weapons and the American war

---

[9] *I congressi nazionali della Democrazia cristiana*, p. 234.

[10] See Turone, *Storia del sindacato in Italia*, pp. 179ff.

in Korea. Against this kind of open political activity, and assisted by the information passed to the police by employers, judicial reaction was severe. According to communist sources, between 1948 and the mid-1950s there were 92,169 cases of arrest and 19,306 recorded sentences in the courts, with varying degrees of severity.[11] Other sources confirm that during the same period some 75 Italians were killed by the police and well over 5,000 wounded.[12]

Among commentators and historians there is now universal recognition of the widespread discrimination practised at all levels against Cgil activists. Nevertheless, even the most sympathetic towards the communists and their socialist allies must concede that, given the grievances of their members in the workplace, global political and economic objectives were pursued, until the mid-1950s, with a serious neglect of problems at plant level. The ideological hostility of the communists to workplace bargaining was not, however, shared by the Cisl. But although the Catholic confederation came to make of such negotiations an official cornerstone of its union practice, it suffered from too little political independence from government and insufficient combativity in the face of high-handed employers to be effective. For this reason, both government and employers had a vested interest in promoting the hegemony of the Cisl over the world of labour. In 1951, for instance, Italian representation on the *Bureau international du travail* was due for renewal. Since this was a government nomination, De Gasperi selected Giulio Pastore, General Secretary of the Cisl, even though the Cgil was numerically far more representative of the workforce. While, therefore, it was true that the Cisl was more concerned with advancing claims along traditional trade union lines

> than those of a general political nature, it was also the case that these claims were strictly in conformity with the line of the 'Rinnovamento' (subsequently 'Forze Nuove') faction in the Dc. It has been observed that when this faction was in opposition [within the Dc] the claims

---

[11] A. Riosa, 'Le concezioni sociali e politiche della Cgil', p. 108.

[12] D. L. M. Blackmer, 'Continuity and Change in Postwar Italian Communism', p. 47.

were put forward with greater energy, while when it was in the majority the struggle was conducted with less vigour.[13]

Paradoxically, there were certain areas in which the Cisl's collateralist relationship with the Dc worked to the long-term advantage of the workers' movement as a whole. In the 1950s there were attempts by both government and employers to use article 40 of the Constitution to limit union activity. This article guaranteed the right to strike within the framework of the law. In 1951, for example, the government decided to attempt to limit strike action within the public sector, more specifically among the clerical employees of the state, where anti-communism was deemed to have a firm hold, and where such legislation was felt to have a good chance of success. The problem was, however, that for the same reason this was a stronghold of the Cisl, which was reluctant to reveal itself as incapable of defending its membership. Thus, with a combination of united union resistance and pressure from within its own faction of the party, the Cisl was able to weaken the Dc's resolve, and anti-strike legislation was dropped.

A second important example of *collateralismo* working to the long-term advantage of the *sindacato* as a whole was the Cisl's success in persuading the government to detach the state-controlled sector of industry from the employers' association, the Confindustria, in 1956. The ideological and strategic implications of this move will be discussed later, but it is sufficient to note at this point that the new association of state employers, Intersind, was to become a kind of pace-setter for new developments in industrial relations in Italy, often forcing the reluctant private employers' confederation to follow its lead.

For the most part, however, government activity in the 1950s worked to delegitimise what it saw as disruptive, Cgil-inspired activity in industry. With government encouragement, the courts pronounced some extraordinary judgements against the legitimacy of such practices as the work-to-rule, short-term stoppages, staggered strikes, and even the use of loudspeakers to call on

---

[13] G. P. Cella e T. Treu, *Relazioni industriali. Manuale per l'analisi della esperienza italiana*, p. 315.

workers to strike.[14] Wild-cat strikes, however, were acceptable. The reason for this was that this form of activity, discouraged by the confederations, was thought to undermine union organization, particularly in the case of the Cgil, where discipline was firm. Encouraged by the attitude of the judiciary, the Confindustria sent out circulars to employers declaring that certain forms of strike activity were illegal, and as a consequence many dismissals followed. It is not without relevance, of course, that in this period the higher courts were still largely dominated by judges trained under fascism, which had operated an extremely oppressive system of labour legislation and had even trained a special *magistratura del lavoro*. The attitudes and decisions of many of the high court judges were, not surprisingly, more in tune with the former system than with the judicial requirements of the new democratic Republic, towards whose institutions many of these judges retained a relationship of sullen hostility.

The Employers

Employer ascendancy in the 1950s was partly the result of the weakness of union representation in the workplace. We have already seen that at this level worker contact with the employer was maintained through the internal commissions, which were essentially non-union bodies. Thus the unwritten rules of plant bargaining and the mobilisation of whatever union action was possible at this level depended to a large extent on the capacity of these under-resourced, unofficial groups. Employers were able to dictate whether or not meetings could be held on the premises, whether they could take place in working hours, and whether notices could be displayed. In addition to the problem of their lack of official status, the internal commissions suffered from the same ideological rifts as the confederations and federations to which most of their members belonged. Naturally, employers were able to exploit such divisions and weaknesses to their own advantage.

In such a situation the internal commissions depended heavily on support and guidance from the local industrial or category

---

[14] See Romagnoli e Treu, *I sindacati in Italia*, pp. 52ff.

federations, which tended to function well only in the larger industrial centres. Consequently, the members of the internal commissions frequently had to rely entirely on their own resources and on establishing good relations with management. This in turn gave plenty of scope for employer discrimination against the more combative communist representatives.

The members of the internal commissions were elected by the whole workforce, irrespective of union membership, but the nominations and electoral lists were usually clearly aligned along Cgil-Cisl-Uil lines. The employers' tactic of favouring the Cisl and Uil representatives, whether in informal negotiations or in official agreements when the unions were called in, was aimed at weakening the movement as a whole, or at least at encouraging defections from the Cgil to the more docile or 'reasonable' rival labour organizations. Such a strategy was also supported in tangible form by the continuing availability of funds to the Cisl and the Uil from American union and State Department sources.[15]

Although the anti-communist strategy was central to employer behaviour in the 1950s, it would be futile to look for a master-plan or formula behind such a strategy. Employers varied in their favoured lines of approach, although Fiat tended to act as an important point of reference for many employers. In general, there was an attempt on the part of employers to undermine the centrality of national wage structures by promoting productivity bonuses and a series of other local or plant benefits which would lead the worker to question the advantages of union membership. No-strike bonuses, paid to workers who refused to participate in industrial action, were widely used in factories all over the country, and Fiat initiated the practice of transferring troublesome activists to 'isolation' or 'exile' sections, where they would all be separated from the remainder of the workforce.

In June 1954, the Confindustria signed the precedent-setting agreement over *conglobamento* with the Cisl and the Uil, excluding the Cgil. The labour confederations had approached the employers with separate proposals to rationalise a chaotic pay structure which included a fragmented system of supplementary payments which were not considered when calculating sickness benefits, entitlement

---

[15] See G. A. Bianchi, *Storia dei sindacati in Italia*, p. 133.

to pensions, etc. The Cgil had included in its proposals a demand for wage increases and parity of pay for men and women. From the beginning of these demands, first presented in 1951, the employers rejected the Cgil proposals but negotiated on the more 'reasonable' ones put forward by the Cisl and the Uil. The latter two, particularly the Cisl, were more than anxious to co-operate in isolating the Cgil. The communist/socialist confederation's attempts to moderate its demands were rejected in moves which made clear that the employers' intentions were motivated by more than simply contractual considerations. The Confindustria's tactics were eased considerably by the willingness of the other two labour confederations, particularly the Cisl, to collude in anti-communist discrimination. Many company and plant agreements subsequently followed this practice of negotiating separate agreements with the exclusion of the Cgil. Daniel Horowitz has estimated that between 1953 and 1957, out of 748 plant or company agreements, no more than 41 per cent included Cgil signatories.[16] Such separate agreements, moreover, which isolated the Cgil, were sought not only by employers. Both the Cisl and the Uil hoped to gain at the expense of the larger confederation by presenting themselves as willing and able to negotiate where the more militant organization could make no headway.

In the early 1950s, given the priority which global and national negotiations enjoyed, in the Cgil's thinking, over local demands, together with the Cgil's declared mistrust of workplace bargaining, and its preoccupation with social and political issues, it was clear that the confederation was heading for trouble. The Cisl, which by contrast was recasting its image as an organization which gave priority to workplace negotiations, was claiming a large share of the credit for the agreements which were being made with employers, even though the gains for the workforce were frequently more apparent than real. It was, after all, always a signatory where the Cgil was frequently absent. A large number of Cgil supporters began to wonder why they should be paying out of their wage packets for the confederation's 'ideological' positions, especially when the Cgil seemed to be consistently on the losing side.

The newly introduced Taylorist working methods in the large

---

[16] *The Italian Labor Movement*, p. 243.

industries were frequently oppressive. Minimal wage increases were accompanied by disproportionate gains to the employers who simply intensified the rhythm and altered the methods of production without consultation.[17] The introduction of the new industrial regime brought with it particularly harsh consequences for female workers. The president of the Confindustria, the arms manufacturer Angelo Costa, felt able to complain that women were paid too much at a time when, for example, in spite of the constitutional article on equal pay, in large metalwork establishments they received less than 25 per cent of the average wage of the lowest paid category of male worker.[18] Vigorous and courageous communist opposition, generally acknowledged by the workforce, was, however, seen as largely defensive and too often unproductive. Employer announcements of mass redundancies were followed by lock-outs when the Cgil refused to accept them. The occupations by the workers at Ansaldo of Genoa and at Ilva of Bolzaneto, for instance, which followed such lock-outs, were defeated. Membership of, or support for, communist organizations was a distinct disadvantage in a country where the practice of using letters of recommendation from the parish priest for securing employment had become a widespread practice.

From the early 1950s, therefore, there were many factors which began to eat away the support for the Cgil in the factories. The clearest indicators of this declining support were the elections to the internal commissions, which showed signs of diminishing communist majorities right up to 1955. From 1953, with the appointment of a virulent anti-communist Ambassador to Rome, Clare Booth Luce, US government support for the employers' strategy became public and explicit. US economic assistance would depend on the employers' ability to demonstrate their effectiveness in combating communist influence. Employers readily provided evidence of the measures taken, including sackings and investigatory methods of various kinds.

---

[17] For a well-documented case study of this style of management, see R. Giannotti, *Lotte e organizzazione di classe alla Fiat (1948-1970)*, Bari: De Donato, 1970.

[18] See M. Lorini, '30 anni di lotte e di conquiste delle lavoratrici italiane', p. 228.

In the lead-up to the 1955 Fiat elections, the employers undertook a campaign of intimidation of unprecedented proportions.

> Supervisors spoke to their workers one by one and warned them to consider their jobs and their families ... Company watchmen in civilian clothes were stationed in working-class neighborhoods and near FIOM [Cgil] headquarters ... Employees opening their pay-check envelopes found a cartoon drawing inside that showed a worker exiting from a doorway marked Cisl-Uil and happily entering Fiat's gates.[19]

Clare Booth Luce prevailed on the US Defense Department to add further pressure, and secured an announcement that no offshore contracts for the production of military equipment would be granted to industries wherever the Cgil obtained a majority in their internal commissions.

The unthinkable happened. In the very stronghold of communist labour organization, in the elections of 29 March 1955 to the Fiat internal commission in Turin, FIOM-Cgil lost its majority. It dropped from 63 per cent of the votes to 36 per cent. FIM-Cisl obtained 41 per cent and UILM-Uil 23 per cent.[20] Although the Cgil losses were not as great in other industrial centres, this was a humiliating defeat, which shook Italian communism. Most of the national press celebrated the event as the coming-of-age of the Italian workers' movement. The Catholics, ecstatic, spoke of the end of communist influence in the unions. The Italian Prime Minister Mario Scelba, in the United States at the time, was awakened in the middle of the night with the news. The following morning, at the State Department, he reported the good news to a delighted John Foster Dulles.

In the excitement of the moment, however, an important fact had been overlooked, particularly by the jubilant Catholics. The sensational 1955 election results at Fiat concealed an overall process of decline in support for the workers' movement as a whole, a process which only began to be reversed years later. In

---

[19] Barkan, *Visions of Emancipation*, p. 47. More detailed accounts of the 'dirty tricks' tactics employed can be found in A. Accornero, *Fiat Confino*, Rome: Edizioni Avanti, 1959, and also in G. Carocci, *Inchiesta alla Fiat*, Milan: Parenti, 1960.

[20] A. Accornero, 'Autonomia operaia e organizzazione sindacale', p. 201.

fact, very few of the communist losses accrued to the Catholics. Between 1954 and 1959 in Turin, while FIOM-Cgil lost a total of 37,744 members, the Catholic FIM-Cisl gained only 1,736. During the same period in Milan, FIOM lost 41,768 members, while FIM gained only 299. The process of de-unionisation is better seen, however, through another set of indicators. Between 1951 and 1959, the communist/socialist FIOM fell from a membership of 679 to an astonishingly low 76 per thousand employed in Turin, and from 621 to 158 in Milan. But the Catholic FIM also fell during the same period from 57 to 37 per thousand employed in Turin, and from 69 to 40 in Milan.[21] The industrial workforce was clearly punishing much more severely the failures of the organization on which it had placed greater reliance. But it was not turning to the Cisl. The fact that rank-and-file membership of the federations remained higher for the communists even after such a dramatic slump in popular support served only to highlight the weakness of the Cisl in the industrial world.

By the end of the 1950s, although the unions claimed a membership of six million workers nationally, this figure was undoubtedly inflated. But as the exhilarating effects following the Cgil defeats of 1955 faded into the distance, the Catholics gradually awakened to the negative side of the developments they had been extolling. In 1957 the Acli of Milan published statistics which showed colossal disparities between increased profits and productivity on the one hand, and unemployment and low wages on the other. The Acli, which for many years had used its influence to reinforce the Cisl's anti-communism, now pronounced a negative verdict on the practice of separate negotiations and called for unity. The Cgil leader Di Vittorio responded positively to this encouraging sign of self-criticism. The Cgil, moreover, was itself by this time in the middle of a process of self-criticism after the shock of 1955, and had taken the first steps towards recovering lost ground.

Within the Cisl, further changes were beginning to take place towards the end of the decade. At the confederation's third congress in March 1959, there were a number of attacks on the Dc government. Delegates from the Cisl's metalworkers' federation,

---

[21] A. Accornero, 'Per una nuova fase di studi sul movimento sindacale', p. 34.

FIM, called for more collaboration with the other confederations, although congress was not yet ready to respond warmly to such a call. Nevertheless, April and May 1959 saw the beginnings of united forms of action between the three metalworkers' federations. These were emerging as the vanguard of new developments, a position they would continue to occupy in the movement's subsequent progress. New problems, created by the massive transformations taking place in industry, were daily more in evidence. The *sindacato* as a whole was awakening to the fact that the terrain of struggle and negotiations required new methods, and above all a working relationship between the rival confederations.

Moreover, although the dark years of the fifties had been characterised by divisions and defeats, on the positive side there was the fact that in the latter part of the decade the confederations had begun a process of self-examination and reassessment, having learned important lessons for the future. At this point, a closer look at this reassessment within the two major confederations will help us understand more clearly the logic of subsequent events.

5

The Cisl in Search of a Distinctive Identity

In June 1951 the Cisl set up a special school, the *Centro studi* in Florence, to train its future leaders. It was the first of the confederations to found such an establishment, but it was also the organization most urgently in need of one. Unlike the communists, the Cisl did not have a body of cadres with experience in industrial struggles. And it had to overcome the traditional ambiguities and lacunae in Catholic thinking about the problems of labour.[1] It could not remain rooted in the paternalism of traditional Catholic social teaching, nor in the corporatist tendencies of this tradition. Finally, in the words of one of the theoreticians of the new Catholic confederation, Mario Romani, the Cisl had to leave behind it the nineteenth-century Catholic 'rejection of industrialisation as the key element in the country's future'.[2] It started by looking at the trade unions in industrially advanced countries, particularly North America, in the hope that they could provide a model for the creation of a modern, independent organization capable of rivalling or even replacing the Cgil as the major representative of Italian labour. Although its attention to foreign models proved more problematic than initially suspected, it was an important starting point.

Workplace Bargaining and 'Productivism'

The North American model was important as a support for some initial ideological reorientations within the Cisl. It is undoubtedly 'against the background of its profound ideological and political confrontation [with the Cgil] that the relevance of the North

---

[1] See S. Costantini, 'La formazione del gruppo dirigente della Cisl (1950-1968)', pp. 121ff.

[2] Cited in Baglioni, *Il sindacato dell'autonomia*, p. 16.

American experience must be understood'.[3] But the latter also provided a wealth of empirical data on workplace or plant bargaining to be analysed and adapted to the Italian scene.

After internal discussions which began in January 1951, the Cisl decision to promote the practice of plant negotiations as the central component of its union practice was taken at the General Council meetings which took place at Ladispoli between 24 and 26 February 1953. In theory at least, this is the birth of workplace bargaining (*contrattazione aziendale*) in Italy. The conceptual framework within which it was generated is all-important. In his introductory speech, the confederate Secretary, Dionigi Coppo, stated that 'the inspiring principle of the whole system [of plant bargaining]' is the recognition that 'the real possibilities of improvement in wages and conditions of work are strictly tied to the development of the efficiency and profitability of the system [of production]'.[4] The concluding resolution of the General Council endorsed Coppo's opening remarks. The Cisl went so far in this direction as to set up 'productivity committees' in numerous workplaces to monitor and encourage increased efficiency. Considerable advantages accrued to management from the Cisl's adoption of its new negotiating policy. The employers were helped by 'a model of industrial relations based on efficiency and productivity, and a less turbulent view of industrial conflict'.[5] Above all, however, the great novelty in Italian industrial relations was the fact that the introduction of new methods of production into the factories was being negotiated. Management undoubtedly called the tune in such negotiations, as it did also in the matter of the utilisation and massive redeployment of the labour force. Nevertheless, in spite of the force of communist complaints that the Cisl had allowed itself to become hegemonised by the employers, the Cgil leader Luciano Lama later observed 'the Cisl initiative did, at least, relate to a real process of change in the organization of work, and had an advantage over our position because we were

---

[3] S. Sciarra, 'L'influenza del sindacalismo "americano" sulla Cisl', pp. 291-2.

[4] Cited in Turone, *Storia del sindacato in Italia*, p. 194.

[5] Sciarra, 'L'influenza del sindacalismo "americano" sulla Cisl', p. 292.

refusing to engage in any discussions relating to such issues'.[6]

It was not the Cisl's intention to destroy either national wage bargaining, or other forms of centralised negotiation, as its opponents sometimes claimed, but to create the possibility of differentials. This was intended to enable wages to be related to productivity, and to a more flexible system of individual incentives. But the crucial element in the Cisl's new philosophy, which justified all the agreements on productivity bonuses and the introduction of more intensified work methods, was what Accornero has called its 'faith in industrial development'.[7] Its new thinking exhibited the unrestrained enthusiasm of a faith. Not only was industrialisation the only means of overcoming the country's economic backwardness, but central to the Cisl's belief was the idea that industrialisation 'leads inevitably to a better distribution of wealth, social opportunities and political power itself'.[8] In the early 1950s, therefore, the Cisl firmly rejected the hostility to industrialisation which had been central to traditional aspects of Catholic social teaching.

During this heady period of discovery, 'industrialisation' became synonymous with 'modernisation' in the language of the Cisl. In its anxiety to lead the movement into the 'modern' world, the organization identified with the 'productivist' ideology of the employers, and declared that in order to embrace the 'productivist' line it 'must in the first place abandon all recourse to ideology'.[9] There was also, however, a strong anti-communist critique implicit in this allegedly 'non-ideological' stance.

Numerous Catholic commentators have pointed out that the Cisl's assumptions during the 1950s concerning industrialisation as the 'inevitable bearer' of automatic benefits and social improvements for all were accompanied by a lack of social analysis. One looks in vain in Cisl documents for any reference to conflicting interests of social groups or forces. Social actors are absent from its discourse, so that power relations and the manner

---

[6] Lama, *La Cgil di Di Vittorio*, p. 209.

[7] Accornero, 'Per una nuova fase di studi', p. 79.

[8] Baglioni, *Il sindacato dell'autonomia*, p. 243.

[9] Ibid., p. 19.

in which these affect social and political development remain unexplored. For many years there was a conspicuous absence, in the Cisl's vocabulary, of terms like 'capitalism'. An important interpretative tendency within the movement even considered industrialisation to be 'the post-capitalist phase of economic development and therefore not subject to abuse in the interests of the privileged classes'.[10]

Given the Cisl's strongly collaborationist orientation in the 1950s, it is not surprising that plant agreements paid little attention to the human costs of rapid industrialisation and the introduction of new work methods. There were a variety of reasons for this. In the first place, negotiations were in the hands not of workplace union representatives, but of the provincial organs of the Cisl, which were more concerned with preventing than promoting conflict. Secondly, such agreements 'were for the most part the fruits of collaboration with the [negotiating] counterpart aiming at the erosion of Cgil support'.[11] Another inhibiting factor which prevented the Cisl from taking up confrontational positions lay in the hold which important aspects of Catholic social teaching still exercised over the faithful. More specifically, the Cisl was unable to accommodate any notion of conflict in its social theory. It was still dominated by the *interclassismo* of the tradition, and by the idea, propounded in all Papal social encyclicals from the late nineteenth century onwards, of the conciliation of labour and capital. Thus 'conflict' remained unambiguously tied to the *pathology* of human relations.

Once again, this differed from the American experience, where unions were often highly conflictual. There were elements in industrial relations theory within the American liberal tradition which utilised a variety of conflict models. Despite appearances, therefore, the Cisl maintained an ideological relationship with the capitalist world which differed from that of the AFL. This difference is fundamental, and requires some further elaboration.

The absence of the term 'capitalism' from the lexicon of Cisl intellectuals of the period was due to that notion's precarious position in the Catholic theoretical and historical tradition. This gap

---

[10] Ibid., p. 243.

[11] P. Kemeny e E. Rauci Ortigosa, 'La Cisl dei primi anni e l'ideologia del mondo cattolico', p. 68.

in its discourse was filled by 'industrialisation'. And it was this which became, temporarily at least, the basis of the Cisl's new article of faith. As such, 'industrialisation' was not necessarily any more a feature of capitalism than it was of socialism. But the Cisl's accommodation to capitalism was not an option. Given its hostility to socialism, the only other concrete historical form in which its enthusiasm for 'industrialisation' could find expression was within the capitalist reality of Italian economic development. But the Cisl's ideological development always stopped short of an outright and explicit acceptance of capitalism's underlying assumptions. The ambiguity in the Cisl's position on this point has deep roots in the Catholic transcendental tradition, a hallmark of which is a reluctance among some of its intellectuals to embrace fully, or 'surrender' themselves to the values and ideology associated with any particular secular, social or economic order. Moreover, Catholicism had for centuries extolled the virtues of the poor and the downtrodden, and its social teaching had repeatedly condemned the excessive polarities of poverty and wealth which it associated with capitalism. Indeed, the Cisl's collaborationism in the 1950s contained those ideological seeds of ambiguity *vis-à-vis* the capitalist order which, in powerful sections of the movement, would even erupt into outright opposition at a later stage of its development.

The Difficult Pursuit of Autonomy

From the moment of its foundation the Cisl began to lay stress on its autonomy. It had to project an image of independence from both employers and government in order to have any credibility as a viable alternative to the Cgil. This was also, in part, a reaction against the traditional *cinghia di trasmissione* theory of the communists, where unions and party formed part of the same 'movement'. The text of the course-book used at the Florence School, for example, when outlining the 'Fundamental Characteristics of the Cisl' begins with the statement: 'There is no doubt that the first and most important [fundamental characteristic] - in principle and historically - seems to us to be its autonomy and independence.'[12]

In general, however, such aims did not tally with the public perception of the Cisl's role, and for good reason. Most ordinary Dc party members could not conceive of the Cisl outside a collateralist framework. Both the party leadership and the Catholic hierarchy, the most powerful components within the collateralist framework, were more interested in the success of the anti-communist tactics of the Cisl than in anything else. For all its sincerity, the Cisl theme of 'autonomy' remained little more than an aspiration for future development. But from about 1953 onwards the educators at the Florence School began to give some serious thought to the negative effects of such close ties. There was a fundamental ambiguity to be faced, one which would plague the Cisl for many years to come. How was it possible to sustain a credible principle of autonomy within an organization tied to a *collateralismo* which few of its members were prepared to disown in practice? One of the Cisl's most prestigious leaders is witness to its difficulties: 'Whoever took part directly in such discussions will know how difficult it was to sustain the theses of union autonomy and freedom, both in the face of enduring ideological and sectarian attitudes and in opposition to initiatives from above to draw the *sindacato* into more institutionalised frameworks.'[13]

During the whole of the 1950s and beyond, the mass of the Cisl membership regarded the organization as a thoroughly 'Catholic' union confederation. Much has been said about the influence of Pope John XXIII in creating an atmosphere of co-operation between Catholics and communists in Italy. But the Johannine invitation to a dialogue with the Marxists did not come immediately after his elevation to the Papacy in 1958. In fact, in 1959, the decree of excommunication issued ten years earlier against Catholics who joined communist organizations was renewed with even greater vigour. Certainly at the level of official Vatican pronouncements, hostility towards the communists seemed stronger than ever: 'Approved by the Pope in person, signed by the Supreme

---

[12] Cited from *Il sindacato nella società democratica*, course notes for union training, School of Florence, Cisl, 1962-3, in Turone, *Storia del sindacato in Italia*, p. 192.

[13] D. Coppo, 'La Cisl e i partiti politici', p. 101.

Tribunal of the Church, annotated by official interpreters, applied by the Bishops, the decree of April 1959 goes well beyond the decree of July ten years before.[14] It is not difficult to understand, therefore, the widespread scepticism regarding the Cisl's claim to 'autonomy' while it remained tied to a *collateralismo* expressing such attitudes.

The Catholic organization was, in practice, caught in a web of complicated heterogeneous motivations. It enjoyed nothing approximating the ideological and political compactness of the communists and socialists, so that in the end collaboration with the employers and *collateralismo* with the Dc proved irresistible. But intentions, objectives and policy formulations relating to autonomy did mean something, particularly when, for all their ambiguity and lack of immediate application, they expressed the intellectual vigour and energy of the Cisl's most advanced sectors.

We have seen that the Cisl's thinking was in many respects still rooted in important aspects of traditional Catholic social thinking. A solid core of Catholic teaching had always rejected the purer forms of free market ideology, and had instead nurtured what amounted to a form of welfare or 'social' capitalism. If we look closely at the more important policy statements of the Cisl, particularly towards the end of the 1950s when it was beginning to reflect on its own *aziendalismo*, we can see that its notion of workplace bargaining becomes increasingly absorbed into the idea of a partially 'guided' capitalism.

From the very foundation of the Cisl, the concept of a 'directed' economy was always present. In the formal preamble to its new statutes, the organization set out the broad principles upon which these statutes were based. The preamble committed the Cisl to defending 'the right to introduce the forces of labour into the institutions which determine the direction of the nation's economic policy'. It asserted the same right in relation to the country's social policy, and placed the defence of the interests of working people within the context of 'the principle of the supremacy of labour over capital, since labour is the highest expression of human dignity'.[15] Thus the stress on plant negotiations, from the very beginning, must be viewed alongside early calls for a 'directed economy'.

---

[14] Magister, *La politica vaticana e l'Italia*, p. 246.

[15] 'Preambolo dello statuto della Cisl - 30 aprile 1950', p. 99.

The role of the public sector, which the Catholic social tradition had always attempted to promote as positive and constructive, also had to be woven into the fabric of a long-term strategic perspective. The first expression of a global Cisl position came from the support it gave to the first Dc economic plan, proposed by the minister Vanoni (the *schema Vanoni*) at the Dc Naples Congress in May 1954. The plan aimed to remedy the two major problems of the Italian economy: the uneven development of North and South, and the high level of unemployment. It aspired to achieve this by increasing public investment in agriculture, public works and services, and construction. It also sought to increase investment in small and medium industries.[16] Essentially, the Cisl inserted into the framework of this plan its thinking on plant bargaining, while at the same time broadening its perspective on negotiations to include bargaining at all levels. In his report to the Cisl's March 1959 Congress in Rome, Bruno Storti reaffirmed the confederation's strong support for the Vanoni plan. He attacked the laissez-faire economic doctrine as 'having given no positive results' and supported the government's use of public investment to initiate 'a phase of pre-industrialisation' in the South.[17] But this was no defence of what Storti called 'totalitarian planning'. Within this view of guided economic development, flexibility was provided by a system of bargaining at all levels, with agreements 'which offer the possibility of continual adaptation to the dynamics of the productive sector'.[18] In theory at least, the whole system of bargaining, starting from interconfederate agreements, down through agreements at category or industry level to the level of plant agreements, became a central feature of the Cisl's conception of the relationship between the state and other social agents in the management of the national economy.

Within this perspective planning seems to have been assimilated into the bargaining framework. Bargaining was the element which retained flexibility in the system and prevented

---

[16] For a more detailed account of the *schema Vanoni* see F. Cicchitto, *Pensiero cattolico ed economia italiana*, pp. 85ff.

[17] Cisl, *Terzo congresso nazionale*, p. 69.

[18] Ibid., p. 66. See also articles 10-15 of the congress resolution, pp. 383-6.

planning from becoming stultifying. In the thinking of the Cisl, this offered a strategy or form of social control which would preserve the capacity of industry to innovate and increase efficiency, and was also in direct ideological opposition to typically communist centralist tendencies. On the other hand, a planning element was inspired by the traditional Catholic hostility towards the free market anarchy and social irresponsibility it associated with the purer forms of liberal economics.[19] It is for this reason that in the period immediately following the 1959 Congress, Cisl spokesmen began to speak more openly of 'democratic planning'.

In effect, the peculiar Italian invention of a state holding sector which combined public control with private-style management, even though historically a creation of the fascist period, was nevertheless a typical syncretist product of political Catholicism. In 1956 the government acceded to the request of Pastore, the Cisl leader, to detach the public sector industries from the Confindustria by act of parliament.[20] The subsequent creation in 1958 of Intersind as the employers' association for the state holding sector fitted in with the Cisl view of public industry as the means through which the development of a capitalist economy could be combined with social equilibrium. The Cisl believed that the Dc's influence over state-controlled industry could be used to ensure a measure of co-operation from Intersind in the creation of a new model of industrial relations. By the end of the 1950s, the Cisl's experience with the private sector, as we shall see, left it with serious doubts about the possibility of co-operation from that quarter. The confederation's aim was to create an industrial relations system which was democratic, sufficiently impervious to communist pressures, and at the same time genuinely open to

---

[19] Two years after the Cisl congress, we find Pope John XXIII's encyclical stating that 'the civil power must also have a hand in the economy.' The document also asserts that 'there can be no such thing as a well-ordered and prosperous society unless the individual citizen and the state co-operate in the economy', because where 'the good offices of the state are lacking or deficient, incurable disorder ensues; in particular, the unscrupulous exploitation of the weak by the strong'. *Mater et Magistra*, translated as *New Light on Social Problems*, London: Catholic Truth Society, 1963, Part II, Section I, paragraphs 52, 56 and 58.

[20] This request was first made by the *Cgil unitaria* in 1947.

reform. The fact that most of the top posts in the state holding sector were controlled by political allies of the Cisl gave the organization's leaders some reason for optimism.

The End of the 1950s: First Signs of a Change of Direction

Despite the ambiguities we have described, the ideological ferment of the new thinking gave a certain vigour to the direction of the Cisl. Nevertheless, the latter part of the decade saw the emergence of some serious misgivings in Catholic quarters. At a Cisl conference on economic development in February 1958, Pastore called on the government to shoulder its responsibility for establishing a political framework within which such growth could proceed in a balanced manner. The attacks on the Segni government the following year, at the 1959 Congress of the Cisl, concentrated on its failure to accept this responsibility. There was a marked nervousness about the operation of an unfettered market mechanism, and the congress resolution demanded more public investment, vigorous stimulation of the southern economy and selective credit controls.[21] Congress discussion, moreover, reflected a perceptible change of attitude on the part of many delegates towards the employers. What had brought about such a change?

In March 1958, on the very terrain of its own victory over the FIOM-Cgil in Turin three years earlier, the Catholic FIM-Cisl itself suffered an even more embarrassing defeat in the internal commission elections at Fiat, one which was illustrative of the position of subordination to the employers which many in the Cisl had begun to regard as humiliating. The FIM-Cisl's list of candidates for the Fiat elections was actually prepared by Valletta himself, the Fiat manager. The company, moreover, declared that the list was not subject to modification. This was the last straw for the Catholic metalworkers' federation, which asked the national confederation to intervene. Pastore, after coming to Turin and presiding over a series of stormy meetings, announced that the Cisl would not present its candidates unless the management guaranteed free elections. Valletta refused, and the Cisl subsequently expelled

---

[21] See Cisl, *Terzo congresso nazionale*, pp. 387-9.

its leader at Fiat, Edoardo Arrighi, who refused to stand down. Arrighi, with the help of the company, set up within a few days a new automobile workers' union, Sida, a *sindacato giallo* or 'employers' union, which never gained a single member outside Fiat and was not destined to last, and at the elections roundly defeated his former associates, taking between 100 and 105 of the former 114 Cisl members of the internal commissions with him into the new union. Although different in kind, this was as salutary a lesson for the Cisl as that learned by the Cgil three years earlier.

The first to be vindicated by these experiences were elements on the left of the Cisl which had been marginalised in the early 1950s, but which had survived in such places as the *unione sindacale* of Modena.[22] In its training manual for local union leaders, produced in 1954, the local confederate organization insisted on the need to transform bourgeois society in the interests of the working class, and thus attacked the notion of apolitical unions.[23] In addition, new Cisl leaders were emerging from the Florence School in the late 1950s with a less favourable attitude towards the capitalist economy. Although we should remember that the vast majority of Cisl cadres were *not* shaped by the perspectives of the Florence School, its importance lay in influencing the intellectual leaders of the movement. The themes which began to emerge from this quarter were: that industrialisation in Italy was too dependent on cheap labour; that the economic policies of Dc governments ignored the structural and geographical imbalances of the national economy; and that the workers' movement had little effect on what happened in the workplace, counting for little or nothing in the minds of the political actors on the national scene.

These themes were reinforced from yet another direction, by a growing demand for social commitment from within the ranks of Catholic Action. This was influenced by theological developments in France and the worker-priest experiments which were an offshoot of such developments. Although the Vatican moved to suppress such initiatives, this did not prevent independently minded young leaders of Catholic Action such as Mario Rossi from protesting, as early as 1953, that the Gospel

---

[22] For *unione sindacale* see Glossary.

[23] See particularly pp. 23ff. and pp. 50ff. of this manual, *Il sindacalismo libero*.

does not teach us to support systems of patronage, nor to protect the devotions and riches of the wealthy. Justice and works of mercy come before all privileges, and having a chapel in the employer's villa will not be enough to bring us salvation on the day of judgement.[24]

An increasing number of Catholics were looking back over the plant bargaining experience with a new scepticism. In 1958 the General Council of the Cisl expressed disappointment at the small number of agreements signed, the categories of workers covered, and the meagre results in terms of pay and improved conditions. Even anti-Cgil discrimination was beginning to give rise both to objections among some members and to the tarnishing of the Cisl's image as the confederation began to be thought of as a kind of *particeps criminis*. Although the Cisl had undoubtedly broken new ground in Italian industrial relations, the results were not unambiguous, nor did they seem very encouraging as matters stood. When, at the historic meeting of the General Council at Ladispoli in 1953, the Cisl had originally unveiled its plant bargaining strategy, its note of optimism betrayed a pristine innocence which subsequent events would soon dispel. The key report of the General Council had pinned its hopes on 'the possibility of collaboration in good faith between employers and workers for the maximum utilisation of company resources in the spirit of an equal distribution of the benefits which this can bring'.[25] Placed alongside events such as those at Fiat, these early aspirations now seemed embarrassingly naive. Their original strategy of plant bargaining had been collaborationist and had misled the workers in one important respect. Their account of the benefits of local bargaining contained no reference to the uncomfortable fact that workers might have to fight for their demands. What they presented to them instead, in the shape of their *aziendalismo*, was a *produttivismo disarmato*. This was clearly the beginning, but only the beginning, of a change of direction. The Cisl seemed to be moving into terrain familiar to the Cgil.

---

[24] M. Rossi, *I giorni dell'onnipotenza*, p. 181. For Rossi's account of his encounter with Vatican officials and the existence of a 'hit list' of Catholic union leaders, see ibid., pp. 85ff.

[25] Cisl, *Una economia forte per un sindacato forte*, p. 34.

6

The Cgil: The Return to Class Politics, Defeat and Self-Criticism

The 'Piano del Lavoro' and the Global Perspective

In the political climate of the cold war, in which virulent anti-communism held sway, the Cgil's problems were markedly different from those of the Cisl, which was associated with the forces on the offensive. But in order to offset its image as a supporter of the Dc government and as a union which was on good terms with the employers, it was imperative for the Cisl to stress its autonomy as a confederation. The rank-and-file membership of the Cgil, on the other hand, felt the need for even greater solidarity with the parties of the working class, first and foremost with the Pci, which was, after all, a pro-union party. There existed, also, the 'unity of action' pact between the Pci and the Psi which meant that there was a strong basis for political agreement between the majority communist component and the socialists within the Cgil. Thus the question of union autonomy from political parties raised completely different problems within the Cgil.

After the Cgil's liberation from the need to accommodate a Catholic component within its organization, it returned, from 1948 onwards, to a more vigorous class position. We have already remarked on some of the negative effects of the Cgil's intensification of global class politics at the expense of the more immediate problems experienced by workers at shop-floor level. The defeat at Fiat in 1955 expressed only the negative side of the Cgil's post-1948 development. It must be remembered that the results, bad as they were, could have been worse, and that the confederation might have been obliterated. Indeed, this was the objective of its opponents. But although the Cgil had little choice regarding the tactics of its opponents, it could, nevertheless, examine its own mistakes.

The literature covering the Cgil in the 1950s has tended to present it as having been, during this period, wholly subservient to the Pci. Communist commentators themselves, anxious to distance the confederation from past mistakes, have frequently endorsed such conclusions. But a brief reconstruction of the ideological debates of the period will demonstrate that the situation was not so simple. For whereas it would be accurate to talk of Cgil-Pci solidarity, this does not in itself entail union subservience to the party.

At the October 1949 Cgil Congress in Genoa Di Vittorio launched his *piano del lavoro* (labour plan) for economic reconstruction. The plan called for the nationalisation of electricity and a programme of electrification, which would greatly increase productive capacity, particularly in the South; a project of land reclamation and irrigation to go along with much-needed reforms in the country's agrarian structure; the setting up of a national body which would oversee the building of schools, hospitals and houses; a programme of essential public works, i.e. roads, aqueducts, drainage systems, lighting, telecommunications, etc. Essentially, the plan was proposing the expansion of internal demand and public spending as the basis of economic development and reconstruction. In this respect the plan was in conflict with the international, externally oriented free-market model of development adopted by the government in 1947. But it is not so much the details of the plan which concern us, as its significance for assessing the development of the Cgil itself. It was not put forward as a complete economic plan, far less was it conceived of as an exercise in socialist economic planning. A number of important Pci members themselves had reservations about it, and given the parties in government, it was unlikely to receive a serious hearing. Its weaknesses have subsequently been indicated by communist and non-communist economists alike. Nevertheless, in spite of all this, the plan was of enormous significance for the Cgil's developing sense of identity. It is this aspect of the plan which has suffered neglect and even distortion.

Romagnoli and Treu, for instance, have seen in the *piano del lavoro* 'the high point in the working of the *cinghia di trasmissione*'.[1] This view belittles the historical significance of the plan. It was indeed, as the above historians have correctly observed, based on important theoretical assumptions which were shared by

---

[1] *I sindacati in Italia*, p. 204.

Pci intellectuals. But this does not make it an instance of the *cinghia di trasmissione* in operation. The Cgil was advocating a policy for directing productive investment into given sectors and geographical regions of the Italian economy, to produce, among other improvements, structural reforms in agriculture. Though it has been said that in doing this the Cgil was 'going beyond the limits of a movement trapped within traditional union canons',[2] even this is something of an understatement. The 'transmission-belt' arrangement was based on the clear understanding that it was the party which developed economic and social policy and the union which applied it within its own sphere of action. But the *piano* was not put forward by the party; it was produced and elaborated by the Cgil itself. This was an historic moment for the Italian worker's movement. It was adopting a policy-making role which was unprecedented and certainly not in conformity with existing theories about the nature of union activity. The new role of the *sindacato* was, however, very much in line with Di Vittorio's statements at the founding congress of the *Cgil unitaria* in 1945, where he had argued that there was no good reason why the programme for economic recovery should be worked out in the board rooms of joint stock companies, to the exclusion of the organizations of the working class. It is no accident that it should have been Di Vittorio himself, as we shall see, who later led a more explicit attack on the concept and practice of the *cinghia di trasmissione*.

This is not to say that the *cinghia di trasmissione*, and particularly the attitudes which historically had grown up around it, had already ceased to exist. The consequences of Di Vittorio's initiatives were not promptly or self-consciously explored in relation to the 'transmission-belt' theory. Between 1949 and 1952, the plan did indeed receive support from workers and *braccianti* who collaborated with local unions to produce plans for land reclamation, for the opening up of neglected plants, etc., in various parts of the country. The long-term effects, however, were disappointing. The *piano* was not sufficiently linked to the day-to-day struggles of northern workers and in many respects not

---

[2] A. Piccioni, *La Cgil nei suoi congressi*, p. 57.

even in tune with the struggles for land taking place in the South.[3] But for all its limitations the *piano* survived in the repository of the Cgil's experience as the *sindacato*'s first 'programmatic' attempt to express a broader social and political sphere of representation, one to which it would later lay claim in a more explicit manner.

The negative side of the Cgil's perspective was its total opposition, in the early 1950s, to plant bargaining. The Cgil's great fear was that such practices would encourage different rates of industrial and productive development in an already unbalanced, 'dual' economy. It also argued that wage and bonus differentials would further divide the working class. In the very congress in which Di Vittorio presented the *piano del lavoro*, Luciano Lama declared: 'the existence of the union in the place of work inevitably leads to plant agreements, and we are opposed to such agreements'.[4] As Lama later reflected, 'in this way we ended up by offering the workers, in the name of a more profound class consciousness, an abstract and isolationist strategy'.[5] The 1955 defeats at Fiat and elsewhere, to which we have already referred, along with a massive loss of membership, were enough to force the Cgil to re-examine its opposition to a model of industrial relations which the workforce clearly favoured.

Some Early Criticisms Ignored

The Cgil defeats in the 1955 elections were the turning point in the confederation's attitude to plant bargaining and to union organization in the factory. These defeats were followed by an immediate self-criticism and the launching of the *ritorno alla fabbrica* (return to the factory) slogan. Two things must, however,

---

[3] For more detailed discussion of the *piano*, see the contributions to the conference organized in 1975 at the University of Modena, in *Il piano del lavoro della Cgil, 1949-50*.

[4] *I congressi della Cgil*, vol. iii, p. 339. Lama also stresses the extensive nature of small industry and crafts in Italy, where plant agreements would either be impossible to reach or difficult to implement, thus creating greater disunity and discontent in the movement. See pp. 340ff.

[5] L. Lama, *Intervista sul sindacato*, p. 34.

be said about this dramatic change of direction. First, the change of course, when it came, was painful and initially patchy in its implementation. Secondly, the Cgil was able to change direction quite swiftly because there was in fact a background of criticism which, although ignored at the time, events conspired to vindicate in a quite impressive manner. Even though the electoral defeats had been devastating, they were nevertheless a confirmation rather than a sudden revelation of the major defects of the Cgil. Before the defeat at Fiat the socialist Cgil leader Santi had written: 'We are paying for the mistakes of poor union democracy, in which leaders take decisions without consulting the mass of the membership. For two years I have been speaking and writing about union democracy with few, very few results.'[6] Santi wrote these comments in his diary in February 1955. But the Cgil had already recommended, at a national convention on the confederation's organization in December 1954, the setting up of workplace branches against the background of the type of self-criticism voiced by Santi.[7] In fact, we must go back even further than 1954 to find the earliest criticism of the methods being employed by the Cgil. A brief survey of these early warnings will also provide additional insights into the relationship between the Cgil and the Pci.

We recall from chapter 2 Togliatti's warning, dating from as far back as 1945, that if the movement ignored issues relating to the organization of work in the factory it would be defeated. This was before the confederation split in 1948. Subsequently, the Cgil drew closer to the Pci, but the views expressed by the two organizations were not always in harmony. There was, of course, a strong socialist component within the Cgil, of which the communist majority had to take account. But it is a mistake to assume that even communists within the Cgil, despite their common difficulties, were always in accord with their comrades within the Pci.

Some surprisingly sharp differences surfaced at the Pci Congress in Rome in April 1951. On opposite sides in the debate were Di Vittorio for the Cgil and Pietro Secchia and Luigi Longo,

---

[6] Riosa, 'Le concezioni sociali e politiche della Cgil', p. 138.

[7] See Bianchi, *Storia dei sindacati in Italia*, p. 124, and also Romagnoli e Treu, *I sindacati in Italia*, p. 158, where the importance of the convention held in December 1954 is recognised.

the two deputy party Secretaries of the Pci. The status of the disputants was in itself an indication of the seriousness of the differences which had emerged. Both party leaders were clearly out of sympathy with the Cgil's reluctance to create official union branches in the workplace. The Cgil had reached the situation, argued Secchia,

> where certain leaders sometimes prepare strikes or other actions in their own offices, without knowing sufficiently well what the workers think or feel about the matter; without first calling together the leaders and activists in the factory, and without arranging meetings of the organized or even non-organized workers of the industry concerned in order to work out the best form of action or struggle to undertake in any particular case.[8]

Secchia further complained about the party's direct involvement in organizing activities which were clearly the responsibility of the Cgil. Longo took up this point and related the experiences of many party members in industry who had pointed out that while the FIOM-Cgil was losing members, the Pci itself was successfully recruiting them. This was 'a consequence of the fact that in the factory everything is done by "communists", by "experts", and very little is seen of union activists and organizations'. He continued: 'This acts as a constraint on the development and prestige of the FIOM and renders union organization in the factory ineffective. The party increases its membership but the mass organizations decline.'[9]

Secchia and Longo were objecting to party energies and resources being used to make up for the Cgil's refusal to establish proper union representation in the factory. This refusal also led, they argued, to a *verticismo* in the *sindacato*, which was losing it support. But there were further distortions of workplace democracy which Longo attributed to the confederation's reluctance to organize in the factories. As a leading member of the Cln and of the Constituent Assembly immediately after the war, Longo had learned the value of co-operation with other political forces. He also knew

---

[8] Secchia's congress speech, published separately as P. Secchia, *Organizzare il popolo per conquistare la pace*, p. 16.

[9] Longo's speech, in A. Cecchi (ed.), *Storia del Pci attraverso i congressi*, p. 113.

that more could be gained through non-sectarian alliances than from attempts to take over or control organizations through the skilful, even if formally legitimate, use of victories in elections to committees. Such tactics, always very tempting, were nevertheless self-defeating in the long term. Longo felt that the Cgil, given its numerical superiority over the Cisl and the Uil, and its ability to win elections, was using the internal commissions as a substitute for union organization in the factories. After reminding the delegates that 'the internal commission is and must remain the unitary organization par excellence in the factory, and that under no circumstances must this characteristic be forgotten or compromised', he goes on to complain that some comrades behaved as if the internal commission were an organ of the unions, or worse still, of a majority within its composition.[10] The majority component to which Longo was referring was, of course, almost invariably communist. Problems relating to the internal commissions, he argues, 'must not be resolved by majority coups, but through discussions involving everybody and by an attempt to find a field of action which would unite all the workers and all the categories [of workers] in the factory'.[11] This is why the *sindacato* must create its own organization in the workplace. 'It cannot compensate for its own deficiencies by commandeering and debilitating other structures in the factory. By doing this it does not overcome its weaknesses, but makes them worse.'[12]

This was a perceptive critique. Di Vittorio accepted that the level of worker participation in union life was low, but repudiated the idea that a failure to set up union branches at plant level was responsible for the confederation's problems. He admitted that 'among comrades in the union leadership there is not unanimity of opinion on this question. For my part, believe me, I do not understand what is meant by a factory union branch. I do know that factory unions can constitute a very great danger.'[13] It would take

---

[10] Ibid., p. 111.

[11] Ibid., p. 112.

[12] Ibid., p. 111.

[13] Pillon, *I comunisti e il sindacato*, p. 457.

the devastating defeats of 1955 to make Di Vittorio think again.

On the question of internal commissions Di Vittorio, in his turn, accused the party of contributing to their malfunction. He accepted that these organizations had to remain representative of the whole workforce, and on this basis he argued: 'I wish to ask the comrades who lead the party to remember these prerequisites and not to give, especially to members of the internal commissions, party responsibilities which often prevent them from carrying out their duties on behalf of the whole workforce.'[14] Di Vittorio was really raising two points here. In the first place, he was arguing that if the party was complaining that it was itself being involved directly in strictly union affairs, this was because it was hijacking the energies of those members who ought to have been left free to attend to their factory responsibilities. This in a sense was a circular argument because the party was asserting that it was precisely these members who lacked an instrument (i.e. a union branch) through which to act as true Cgil representatives. But more positively, Di Vittorio was also indirectly raising for the first time in the Cgil the problem of *incompatibilità*, i.e. the inappropriateness of holding positions of responsibility simultaneously in a union and in a political party. This would later become a crucial problem in seeking greater unity between the confederations.

There is one further point which needs to be made in connection with the problem of factory union branches. It has sometimes been argued that the Cgil dragged its feet on the issue simply because the communists already had effective 'cells' of Pci members in all the large factories. The better-organized even had factory committees, such as the *comitato sindacale dello stabilimento Mirafiori* at the Fiat works. On the other hand, as we have already seen, the communist movement was not a monolith, and there were frequently points of friction and disagreement between party and union. The Pci cells were indeed under strong *party* influence. But communist Cgil officials who negotiated with the employer came from outside the factory, and had to contend not simply with the hostility and competition coming from the Cisl and the Uil, but also had to shape their own positions alongside their socialist colleagues within the Cgil. The idea, therefore, of setting

---

[14] Ibid.

up union branches within the factories which would have internal communist negotiators presented some problems. It could not be taken for granted, for instance, that such militants, under strong Pci influence, would automatically fall into line with the tactical and strategic objectives of Cgil officials from outside with a more 'global' and long-term set of priorities. While the Cgil was certainly anxious to increase communist influence in the factory, it was communist *union* influence which it wished to extend, rather than that from party sources. This was one further reason why Di Vittorio was attentive to the need for independence from the party.

The 'Ritorno alla Fabbrica'

After the defeats of the Cgil in the internal commission ballots of March 1955, it was no longer feasible to resist the arguments of the Pci members which we have just noted. At this point self-criticism became determined and intense. At a meeting of the Executive Committee on 26 April, Di Vittorio gave a report which contained all the elements of this self-criticism, and of the change of direction which then came to be known as the 'ritorno alla fabbrica' ('return to the factory'). The substance of Di Vittorio's report was subsequently put to the Cgil's Rome Congress in February-March 1956 and accepted as policy.

In his report, Di Vittorio rejected the criticism of those who argued that the Cgil had undertaken too many 'political' strikes or had wasted its energies in such activities. This was not true, he argued, nor was it the cause of its recent defeats. The workers respected and understood the Cgil's defence of democracy. Others argued that in the run-up to the March elections of the internal commissions there had been unprecedented intimidation and interference by the employers, the government, the police, and even the US government. The press had warned of a possible flight of capital, a withdrawal of investment and economic ruin. Di Vittorio accepted that these things had happened, but he warned that if the Cgil placed the blame for its defeat on the actions of others, it would not understand its own failures. The major cause of the defeat lay with the leadership's

    not having studied seriously the new production processes and conditions of work which have been introduced into the workplace. Nor have we studied the new forms of pay incentive, the complex forms of super-exploitation, very different from one company to another, from one workshop to another, which are imposed on workers and which are constantly being modified. We have also neglected to acquire a concrete grasp of the new methods and managerial strategies and pressures applied to workers in the workplace, ranging from the most brutal threats, to enticement to corruption.

From such deficiencies, continued Di Vittorio,

stems our serious error in pursuing over-schematic and over-generalised wage claims, instead of working out with the workers themselves, in the factories and workshops, demands which corresponded to their needs as felt by them.[15]

Essentially these were the same arguments Di Vittorio took to the 1956 Congress of the Cgil a few months later. Both he and the socialist Santi assured the delegates that the new thinking was not a capitulation to the Cisl's *aziendalismo*, which accepted uncritically the changes which were taking place and which lacked a strategic approach to workplace bargaining. On the contrary, the 'return to the factory' was necessary in order to dominate and direct the course of change rather than suffer it passively. The *ritorno alla fabbrica* was necessary precisely to avoid having the effects of *aziendalismo* thrust upon the movement unwillingly. The objective remained that of guaranteeing 'a primary role for the workers' movement in making choices in relation to production, in controlling and influencing the decisions of management, in the struggle against monopoly power and the internal logic of capitalist profit'.[16] But the movement also had to concern itself more with factory conditions as such. 'The new machinery', argued Santi,

operates even faster than the old. The work-rhythms they [machines] impose on the worker, beyond a certain limit, are absolutely intolerable. The physical and psychological well-being of the worker are placed under strain ... Our workers rightly tell us that today the working hour

---

[15] *I congressi della Cgil*, vols iv & v, p. 377 (these volumes constitute a single tome).

[16] Riosa, 'Le concezioni sociali e politiche della Cgil', p. 140.

consists of ninety, not sixty, minutes. And you can't breathe. The factory has become an inferno.[17]

The perspective which emerged from the 1956 Rome Congress was one in which demands and negotiations at plant level were to be linked to the broader social and economic objectives of the movement. Thus agreements made at plant level were to improve upon 'the minimum established by the national category [i.e. federal] agreements which remain the fundamental and obligatory points of reference for the union's bargaining activity'.[18]

But as we have also seen with the Cisl, it is one thing to set objectives, but quite another matter to act consistently according to them. There were years of ingrained centralised practice to overcome. The new approach to bargaining required analytical flexibility from negotiators whose background had taught them to assume that whatever the employers suggested could not be in the interests of workers. It also entailed relating new and more complex bargaining postures to a predetermined social and political strategy. The Cgil could not abandon its class perspective. To give just one example, when it accepted the principle of articulated bargaining it had to come to terms with the problem of wage differentials on a regional basis. The employers argued that such differentials were justified because of the different costs of living in different parts of the country. Thus the wage bargaining strategy of the Cgil, in the different areas, had to be linked to a further set of proposals and objectives aimed at eliminating the disequilibria between these areas. It could not, as the Cisl had done, simply ignore this problem. Such then were the commitments expected of a movement which aimed to defend not simply the particular interests of disparate groups of workers, but also the interests of all of them as a class.

The 'Cinghia di Trasmissione'

Although normally associated with communists, the 'transmission-

---

[17] *I congressi della Cgil*, vols. iv & v, p. 359.

[18] E. Bartocci, *Alle origini della contrattazione articolata*, p. 84.

belt' theory in fact originated before the existence of communist parties as such, in the form of a resolution at the Stuttgart Congress of the Second International in 1907. The relationship of effective subordination of union to party was created in a period when in some countries the very legitimacy of union activity was still in question. The leaders of unions were normally drawn from socialist or social democratic parties, which were in effect the union's protectors in hostile bourgeois states.

Luciano Lama has rightly pointed out that the Cgil, given the sturdy independence of Di Vittorio, 'never reached the point of total subordination [to the party] of which we were accused'. But he went on to add that 'this was not the case in all the federations'.[19] In the thinking of many rank-and-file members, and even in that of some federation leaders, the attitude of subordination to party instructions was far from dead. But the issue that highlighted the problematic nature of the *cinghia di trasmissione* was the need to unite a workers' movement whose members had a variety of party affiliations. In a speech to union leaders as far back as 1944, Di Vittorio had stressed one of the fundamental principles underlying the foundation of the *Cgil unitaria*, namely that it had to be

> the organization which unites the workers of all political views, all religious convictions and also those who belong to no party and with no religious faith. If it is to achieve this unity in the very essence of the organization and effectively protect the interests of all workers, the *sindacato* must be independent of all political parties as it must be of the state.[20]

In an article prepared well before the Cgil's defeats in March 1955 but published that very month, Di Vittorio analysed the relationship between party and union. He argued, among other things, that 'the natural foundation of the unity of all workers in their own union is based on the identity and common nature of their most vital professional interests [as workers]...'. But to this homogeneity of interests as workers corresponds a 'heterogeneity

[19] Lama, *Intervista sul sindacato*, p. 38.

[20] Lama, *La Cgil di Di Vittorio*, p. 38.

in their political and religious opinions'.[21] The former is the sphere par excellence of the *sindacato*'s activity, the latter that of political parties and religious bodies. 'From this it follows that the *sindacato* must be "non-party"', but also that 'the party must be "a-professional".'[22] The party, argues Di Vittorio, 'is based on a particular ideology and on a corresponding political programme'[23] and operates in the sphere of parliament and the state. The unity of a party is based on the identity of political perspectives, which may differ between members of the *sindacato*. The conclusion of Di Vittorio's argument is contained in his statement:

> From this profound difference in nature between the *sindacato* and the party, it follows that any confusion of roles between the two, and any relationship of interdependence between them, is completely inconceivable, since it would be damaging to both ... In the final analysis, any mutual interference and interdependence between party and *sindacato* would bring about a situation in which we have both a bad *sindacato* and a bad party, would certainly damage both, and particularly the workers.[24]

Di Vittorio was in effect preparing the ground for his attack on the *cinghia di trasmissione*, which was to come at the Pci's Rome Congress in December 1956. In the meantime, he made public statements about the Cgil's willingness to co-operate with the Cisl and the Uil in creating 'a great united organization, strong, democratic, autonomous and independent of the state and of all parties'.[25] At the party congress, Di Vittorio repeated his ideas in the strongest terms: 'It is necessary to destroy completely the famous "transmission-belt" theory... . Unions, if they are to be united, cannot be the "transmission belts" of any party. I propose that this principle be clearly affirmed in the resolution concluding

---

[21] A. Tatò (ed.), *Di Vittorio, l'uomo, il dirigente. Antologia delle opere*, vol. iii, p. 345.

[22] Ibid., pp. 345-6.

[23] Ibid., p. 345.

[24] Ibid., p. 346.

[25] Turone, *Storia del sindacato in Italia*, p. 223.

the work of the congress, and that all Italian communists should commit themselves to observing it scrupulously.'[26]

This was an appeal to the party to play its part in respecting the autonomy of the Cgil. Once again, however, there is a strong parallel with the Cisl in the sense that it takes more than congress resolutions to alter the direction of deeply-rooted traditions and practices. However, in both cases also, the process had officially begun even though the historical realisation of their respective ideals would be long, arduous, and accompanied by frequent lapses.

It is worth recounting one final episode from the 1950s which is of some significance in the Cgil's struggle to break loose from the political habits and instinctive reactions associated with the *cinghia di trasmissione*. The worker uprising in Hungary, which was crushed by the invasion of Russian tanks, began on 24 October 1956. On 27 October, three leading socialists went to Di Vittorio's office with the draft of a statement declaring that the events in Hungary represented a 'definitive historical condemnation of anti-democratic methods of political and economic government and leadership'. Di Vittorio approved it immediately, and it was issued on the same day.[27] The Pci did not condemn the Russian intervention. Di Vittorio's agreement to sign the statement was in effect a concrete expression of internal unity within the union confederation. In the circumstances it also entailed a corresponding expression of autonomy from the Pci on the part of its communist component. To differ from its party comrades at such a time constituted an important act of solidarity with the socialists within the *sindacato*, and would not be forgotten in the difficult times ahead.

---

[26] *Ottavo congresso del Partito comunista italiano. Atti e risoluzioni*, p. 437. For the relevant section of the final resolution, see p. 982.

[27] Turone, *Storia del sindacato in Italia*, p. 220.

7

Conclusion: Ending the Fifties with Lessons Learned

The Lesson of Events: First Experiences of United Action

For most of the 1950s, the two major confederations followed separate, even mutually antagonistic paths of development. Towards the end of the decade circumstances began to favour a tentative rapprochement.

The Cisl criticisms of the Dc government in March 1959 came after nearly a decade of disappointed hopes that the confederation's readiness to collaborate with employers would bring tangible improvements in wages, matched by government commitment to better services. In May of the same year, the new General Secretary of the Cisl, Bruno Storti, deplored the repressive anti-union climate which shortly before had led to police brutality against not only Cgil strikers, but this time also against their Cisl comrades who had joined in the action.

The Catholic metalworkers' union (FIM), moreover, was forcing the pace of change within the Cisl. After the humiliating experience at Fiat in March 1958, further protests occurred at the Om factories in Brescia in the autumn of that year. Along with the usual communist objections (this time widely supported by the rank-and-file) to employer interference in the internal commission elections, there were also those of the FIM representatives. The latter refused to recognise the results of the ballots.[1] A battle ensued within the provincial FIM which resulted, at the Brescia Congress of the federation in November, in the election of a new secretary, Franco Castrezzati, who supported the stand of the Om Brescia representatives. Although the new line of the provincial FIM was at this point not followed by the Brescia Cisl, nor was it shared at

---

[1] See G. P. Cella, B. Manghi and P. Piva, *Un sindacato italiano negli anni sessanta; la Fim-Cisl dall'associazione alla classe*, pp. 113ff.

national level by either the Cisl or the FIM, the provincial (Brescia) FIM developed its line further. Castrezzati objected to the practice of excluding the FIOM-Cgil from negotiations and undertook a re-evaluation of the expediency of strike action. Together, the FIM and FIOM organized a stoppage at the Om Brescia factories, in protest against the payment of six-monthly, anti-strike bonuses to workers with a clean no-strike record.

In 1959, at the expiry of the existing national agreements with the metalworkers, the employers decided to use delaying tactics to avoid opening the new round of negotiations. Given the announcements about increased profits, this attitude angered workers. Pickets and strikes were organized, this time with national approval and including the UILM, in April and May. For the first time since the split of 1948, slogans such as 'united we can win' began to make their appearance. On 4 June, a metalworkers' strike in Milan saw representatives from all three provincial confederations, the Cgil, the Cisl and the Uil, speaking on the same platform. This was followed later in the month by a national strike, once again called by the three metalworkers' federations, to bring pressure on the employers to conclude negotiations.

In the Italian workers' movement, united action has always raised the problem of the relationship of its leaders to their respective parties. How could union leaders be expected to commit themselves to strategies worked out in common when their parties pulled them in opposing directions? The question of the incompatibility of holding simultaneous positions of responsibility in union and party was raised at a conference of socialist *sindacalisti* in October 1959. Most high-ranking union leaders, on all sides, also held parliamentary seats and frequently important posts in the hierarchies of their respective parties. At the Acli National Congress in December 1959, a combative minority advocated the principle of *incompatibilità* between union leadership and parliamentary representation.[2] Although such problems would take years to resolve, these first tentative debates on the theme of *incompatibilità* were a sign that the united forms of industrial action which made their first appearance in the late 1950s were developing into something more than temporary expedients.

---

[2] Coppo, 'La Cisl e i partiti politici', pp. 109ff.

The Preconditions for Dialogue Established

The erosion of hostilities taking place by the late 1950s had not yet evolved to the point where a constructive dialogue was under way. At this stage the rapprochement was largely piecemeal, mainly in the metalworkers' federations, and consisted of united action on specific occasions rather than unified strategies. A strong partisan spirit continued to have a firm hold on the rank-and-file within the confederations as a whole. The metalworkers, particularly when they tried to speed up the process of co-operation, found themselves isolated within their respective confederations.

Nevertheless, the ideological changes which were taking place within the divided confederations were the results of a mutually reactive process which would take the movement forward. The Cisl's *aziendalismo*, which, left to itself would have produced a 'freezing of the social dynamic, by fragmenting and isolating conflict at the level of the workplace'[3], was nevertheless productive in 'shattering the cultural isolation of the Italian workers' movement which had marginalised the Cgil in a pseudo-Marxist cultural ghetto'.[4] Once shifted from its hitherto stubborn position of exclusively centralised bargaining, the Cgil initiated a new phase, in which workers' problems at the point of production would be given much more attention. But this differed profoundly from the *aziendalismo* of the Cisl. As the events of 1958 at Fiat and Om Brescia had shown, the Catholic confederation's 'approach to productivity was uncritical, and in some respects had the flavour of "propaganda" about it. What was lacking was the force of the dialectical and conflictual element with which to participate in production'.[5] Without it, workers were at the mercy of the employers' wishes. The difference between the Cisl, and indeed the Uil, on the one hand and the Cgil on the other, was that, by contrast with the communist-led confederation after its *ritorno alla fabbrica*, the former pair 'did not develop a position for defending

---

[3] P. Craveri, *Sindacato e istituzioni nel dopoguerra*, p. 312.

[4] Bartocci, *Alle origini della contrattazione articolata*, pp. 115-16.

[5] Accornero, 'Per una nuova fase di studi sul movimento sindacale', p. 84.

the rights of working people in relation to productivity'.[6] Evidently, the confederations had a great deal to learn from one another.

One of the effects of the communist insistence on global solidarity, and of the Cgil's lasting suspicion of *aziendalismo* was the virtual absence in Italian industry of 'worker aristocracies', i.e. groups of highly paid workers in particular trades who jealously protected the differentials which gave them their privileged positions. With regard to what in the mid-1970s became known as the 'pay jungle' or wages free-for-all, Luciano Lama has observed:

> In Italy, however, by contrast with what has taken place in other countries, we have not created out of the 'pay jungle' a system of worker aristocracies. Why is this? In my view it is because of our suspicion, excessive if you wish, at least during a particular period [i.e. that of *aziendalismo*], which has reinforced in the Italian workers' movement, and especially among the working masses, the awareness of a danger [i.e. *aziendalismo*] which in other countries has not been seen as a danger. On the contrary it has been considered a victory, but it has gone on to shape the very nature of the *sindacato* in other capitalist countries, and this differs from the Italian experience.[7]

The absence in Italy of well-entrenched differentials among groups of workers, is related to another feature of the Italian *sindacato*, namely the absence of official union branches at workplace level. Thus the pressure from below on category federations to go their own way, and to establish levels of pay according to their differing positions of industrial strength in negotiations was lacking. Although by 1960 all the confederations had taken decisions to set up workplace branches to work alongside the internal commissions, such organizations never took root in Italian industry. On the other hand, given the divided state of the *sindacato* in Italy at the time, it is difficult to see how workplace branches could have functioned effectively. Thus the Italian workers' movement went into the 1960s having learned some important lessons but also with a number of problems still to be resolved.

---

[6] Ibid., p. 83.

[7] Lama, 'L'impegno della Cgil per lo sviluppo e l'unità del sindacato in Italia', p. 359.

Part III

1960-7: THE REDISCOVERY OF COMMON GROUND

8

A Changing Political and Industrial Scene

The Political and Economic Setting

The first three years of the 1960s saw a struggle within the world of political Catholicism to achieve the formal entry into government of the Psi. The 'opening to the left' (*apertura a sinistra*) was opposed by powerful sections of the Dc, within Italian industry, and in the Vatican. It was a development brought to fruition with the entry of Psi ministers into the Moro-led coalition in December 1963. The tensions and divisions to which the operation gave rise were in reality part of a much wider process of transformation taking place in Italian society at a multiplicity of levels.

The 'opening to the left' really became irreversible in July 1960. In March of that year, Fernando Tambroni formed a government which relied on the external support of the neo-fascist Msi to survive. In other words, Tambroni, without conceding ministerial posts to the Msi, was able to secure a guarantee of that party's vote in parliament. Emboldened by this social legitimation, the Msi decided to give maximum publicity to its forthcoming congress. It decided to hold the congress in Genoa, the Italian city with the country's proudest anti-fascist record stemming from the time of the resistance. This ominous decision was followed by the announcement that the honorary president of the congress would be Carlo Emanuele Basile, the prefect who had ordered reprisals against the activities of Genoese partisans in 1944. This final act of provocation by the *missini* sparked off protests in Genoa and in other Italian cities. Demonstrations were organized by the Cgil. Support from the Cisl and the Uil was patchy. Union protest united with that of anti-fascist groups, and forced the authorities, on 1 July, to postpone the Msi Congress. Anti-fascist demonstrations continued, however, in different parts of the country, and met with brutal police repression. Over the period of protest, participants had been fired upon in Genoa itself, along with Palermo, Licata, San Ferdinando (Puglia), Catania and Reggio Emilia. A number of demonstrators were killed, and many more wounded.

Within the Dc, the original unease and opposition to government reliance on Msi support turned to revulsion when Tambroni defended the behaviour of the police. He was forced to resign, and a government of a new complexion was formed under the leadership of Amintore Fanfani. Under the new leadership, Aldo Moro set about persuading his own *dorotei* faction of the party, and other potential opponents, that the situation was now right for the *apertura a sinistra*. The protests had demonstrated the depth of feeling which remained in the country against the right of the political spectrum, inevitably associated in the postwar Italian historical memory with the country's fascist experience. It also revealed that the Cgil had retained a powerful capacity to mobilise in moments of tension. Naturally, the Dc was anxious to counter any revived support for the communists, and engaging the socialists in coalition was intended to achieve this. But more than two years of internal manoeuvres and shifting alliances, which also involved the Vatican, were to pass before the centre-left government (*centro sinistra*) could be formally established in December 1963.

This shift to the left was seen by the Cisl as a victory for its own current within the party. But the Cisl still nurtured certain reservations regarding the socialists. After the Kruschev revelations of Stalinist atrocities in 1956, and the Russian invasion of Hungary in the same year, the Psi had begun to distance itself from the Pci, and it showed interest in the growing pressure within the Dc for the 'opening to the left'. But the socialists within the Cgil, who were drawn mainly from the left of the party, remained much closer to their communist partners. Thus the Cisl's hope for a government coalition with a strong reforming tendency which would find a partner in a corresponding coalition in the *sindacato* lacked foundation.

The Catholic confederation had helped to strengthen the reformist wing of the Dc. In December 1960, the Prime Minister, Fanfani, announced the commencement of tripartite talks involving the government, the employers and the unions, to discuss a plan for the social and economic revival of Sardinia. Although this initiative was disappointing in terms of concrete achievements, it was nevertheless important as a sign that a tendency was emerging within the party favourable to the idea of economic planning. The *apertura a sinistra* was part of this movement of the Dc towards a new planning and reformist culture. Fanfani began to stress the important role of the state holding sector in economic development, thus alienating the Confindustria, from which the sector had been detached in 1956.

In May 1962, the government presented to parliament a document on economic planning which was highly critical of the 'economic market spontaneism' of the fifties, and which spoke of the need for a planned approach to the problems of the South. In August the government set up the Cnpe, a national committee for economic planning. This committee included the presidents of the employers' organizations and union confederations, an expert nominated by each of the latter, and a further panel of independent experts. In a demonstration of its seriousness about economic planning, the government secured, in December, the passage of a bill through parliament for the nationalisation of the electrical industry. In arguing its case, the government was helped by the reluctance of the industry's private sector owners to install networks in the South, where they were badly needed but costly to develop and less profitable than in the industrially advanced North.

The 'opening to the left' was, however, motivated by more than a simple desire to introduce an element of planning into the economy. The Dc thought that by involving the Psi in government it could, without conceding too much to a party with modest electoral support, satisfy the political demands of the working class. It also hoped to detach the Psi from Pci influence and marginalise the communists in the process. The socialists, for their part, were looking increasingly on the Pci as a competitor, and were anxious to use their status as a party of government to strengthen their support in the country at the expense of both the Pci and the Dc. The Cisl, which supported the 'opening to the left', also hoped that its development would weaken the bond of unity between socialists and communists in the Cgil. The 'opening to the left' thus included an attempt to give a particular direction to the workers' movement through a combination of conditioning factors. Developments at the political level could help shift the internal relations between the *sindacato*'s components in favour of stronger Catholic-socialist links at the expense of the communists.

But the creation of the *centro sinistra* did not weaken the communists. The inclusion of the Psi in government created a new set of problems. In the first place, it led in January 1964 to the creation of a new socialist party, the Psiup, by dissident elements from the left of the Psi, many of whom were leaders in the Cgil. Along with the communists in the Cgil, and many of the remaining Psi members, they did not believe that structural reforms in the Italian economy could be brought about in coalition with the Dc. Nevertheless, as a condition of entering the government coalition, the Psi leader, Nenni, insisted on placing a range of social reforms on the political agenda. But by broadening the government's objectives in this direction, the Dc intensified its own internal factional behaviour, so that increasing internal opposition blocked the implementation of policies. The government also found it more difficult than it had expected to control a Psi which came increasingly under pressure from its base of support, frustrated by its lack of achievement. In the words of Sidney Tarrow, 'the reforms of the Centre-Left were significant, not for what it accomplished, but for demonstrating what it could *not* accomplish and for revealing the extent of the cleavages in the elite'.[1]

As for the Pci, far from being weakened or marginalised by the *apertura a sinistra*, it saw its support begin to increase from the elctions of 1963. Visceral anti-communism was being eroded by changing social and cultural values, which diminished the appeal of the Catholic 'crusading' spirit. Besides, although the inclusion of the Psi in the government aroused widespread social aspirations among popular strata, the communists were thus assured of increased support among those sectors of the population capable of being mobilised against the government when reforms were not forthcoming.

The changing political and social climate was also of benefit to the Cgil, even though the employers were vigorously opposed to the 'opening to the left'. For the Cgil, the early sixties brought to an end a period of severe repression in the legal sphere and the automatic support of employers' decisions which had been a feature of previous governments. In fact the government, with Cisl support, was pressing the *sindacato* to act as a third partner, along with public sector employers, in promoting planned development. It was the socialist Santi, whose own party was being introduced into

---

[1] S. Tarrow, *Democracy and Disorder. Protest and Politics in Italy 1965-1975*, p. 56.

government, who made the Cgil position clear in 1962. Eager to safeguard the autonomy of the *sindacato* and to avoid a move towards a neo-corporatism which would tie its hands, he asserted: 'The best way for us to contribute to this positive experiment and to its progressive development is not to stifle our own demands for fear of inconveniencing those at the helm [of government], nor to make a blind act of faith that things will come from above, that others will somehow resolve our problems for us.'[2] Santi's message was clear. Socialists within the Cgil should not allow themselves to be used, through the presence of their party in government, to compromise the autonomy of the Cgil or to bring about divisions within its ranks. The five-year plan eventually presented to parliament by the socialist minister Giovanni Pieraccini in March 1965 did, however, create division within the confederation over the plan's proposal that future wage rises should be linked to productivity. At the Cgil Congress in Bologna at the end of March, the Cgil communists were joined by Psiup members in condemning the proposed incomes policy. Oddly enough, both the Cisl and the Uil rejected the idea of an incomes policy, thus showing greater independence in relation to their respective parties than the Psi union leaders within the Cgil. The Cgil congress did, however, show greater unity over resolutions which stressed that successful planning could be achieved only by decentralising the forms of participation to regional levels, where planning could more easily take account of territorial and social demands.[3]

For the communists, such ideas had first been raised in a conference which the Pci had organized, in 1962, on the tendencies within modern capitalism. This initiative inaugurated a new, and less 'doctrinal' approach to economic problems. This was no mere chance undertaking. By 1962, the 'economic miracle' had almost run its course. In 1963-4 a recession occurred which, although short-lived, introduced some new and ambiguous features into the

---

[2] F. Santi, 'Il movimento sindacale di fronte alla nuova situazione politica', p. 2590.

[3] See Novella's report to the VI Congress in March 1965, *I congressi della Cgil*, vol. vii, 22-9. For a discussion of the debates in both the Cgil and the Cisl, see also M. Bordini, 'I sindacati e il dibattito sulla programmazione (1960-67)', *Quaderni di rassegna sindacale*, n. 77, 1979, pp. 3-16.

Italian economy. Inflation rose from 1-2 per cent in the previous period to 4-5 per cent; employment, having almost reached full capacity for the first time in modern Italian history, ceased to expand after the winter of 1963-4; there was also a fall in profits, and the balance of payments ran into difficulties. After an initial decline in industrial production, accompanied by an immediate fall in employment, production began to increase once more during the latter part of 1964, and continued to do so until 1969, with an average rate of increase for the period 1963-9 of 6.2 per cent. Although employment began to rise again from mid-1966, it took until 1969 to regain its 1963 level and was not commensurate with the rapid increase in production. Moreover, the period of increased productivity was accompanied by an overall fall in capital investment in plant and machinery, even though new technology was introduced in some key areas of the Italian economy, such as at the Fiat plants, in the latter part of the cycle.[4]

There are various reasons for these anomalies. Between 1958 and 1964 wages had increased, albeit from a very low starting point, faster than anywhere else in Europe. Thus 1964-5 witnessed an outflow of capital and of deposits to foreign banks. These were clearly a response to the appearance of a new militancy among the working class. But the flight of capital was not, on the whole, of direct capital investment, but consisted rather of what Michele Salvati has called 'purely financial stratagems'.[5] How then was increased productivity achieved? As Salvati has observed, it was brought about by increased pressure at the point of production. The effect of this on the workforce, however, was a sustained build-up of tensions which eventually exploded in the 'Hot Autumn' of 1969. The employers continued during the 1960s to speed up work rhythms, to impose extra shifts on the workforce and to replace skilled labour by the unskilled labour of largely non-unionised, southern migrants. The major grievances of the period, therefore, revolved around an intensification of the psycho-physical strains on the workforce, which were necessary for employers to increase their profits. But industrial workers were not compensated for this by

---

[4] For a more detailed analysis, with statistics for sectors of industry, see *Annali dell'economia italiana*, vol. xiii, part 2, pp. 15-136.

[5] M. Salvati, *Economia e politica in Italia dal dopoguerra a oggi*, p. 93.

improved public services.[6] Thus, mounting social tensions brought increased protests in the areas of housing, health, education and transport.

Women from families in the lower social groups looked increasingly for work, but less as an expression of changing social attitudes than out of economic necessity. In 1960 an interconfederate agreement between the employers' and the unions' confederations finally implemented the constitutional requirement of equal pay for equal work between men and women. This did not, however, eliminate discrimination, because women were not promoted, remained largely unqualified, and were seriously disadvantaged in their career structures. Certain forms of sexual discrimination in the labour market actually grew worse. For instance, an economic boom in the textile industry between 1960 and 1962 brought with it a huge increase in outwork or work-in-the-home (*lavoro a domicilio*). With the dramatic technological advances in the electromechanical field from the mid-sixties onwards, this practice was extended into the production of consumer goods such as transistor radios. The advantages to the employer were many. Labour was cheap, and companies avoided having to pay their normal contributions towards state benefits. Women engaged in such work, trapped by the contradictions of their economic plight, could not seek the protection of the unions without fear of losing what was to them an important source of income for the family.

Neither an increase in industrial productivity nor in the earning capacity of the workforce was able to reverse the trend in the national economy towards an ever greater disparity between North and South. If we compare earnings per capita in the various regions in 1967, for example, we find the national average to be L617,209. But the average in the province of Milan in the North was L1,043,000, while in the southern province of Avellino it was as low as L290,000, i.e. considerably less than one third of that of the northern province. While these two sectors of the population reflect the extremes, we find nevertheless that, with the exception of Rome, the thirty-two provinces where earnings were above the

---

[6] For an empirical study of these problems based on interviews and meetings with workers, see G. Flamini, *Operai nell'Italia industriale*, Naples: Edizioni Dehoniane, 1969.

national average were all in the North, whereas the remaining provinces were in the Centre-South, with the ten lowest in the deep South and the Islands.

Changes in Industrial Relations

It is customary to view the 'Hot Autumn' of 1969, and the period immediately following it, as the beginning of a new system of industrial relations in Italy. Important as this period was, it cannot be understood in isolation from the *sindacato*'s development in the earlier part of the decade. These were developments which produced that combination of increasing demands, frustrated expectations and indignation, which triggered the explosion. The writing was on the wall, however, even before the 1960s. Of all the advanced economies of Western Europe, the postwar industrial settlement was the least stable in Italy. The 'economic miracle', it must be remembered, was fuelled by low labour costs. Between 1953 and 1960, 'while industrial production rose from a base of 100 to 189, and workers' productivity from 100 to 162, real wages in industry fell very slightly from 100 to 99.4'.[7] EEC statistics on its early member countries indicate that during the 1950s the 'strike coefficient' (i.e. the ratio of hours lost in strike action to total hours of work) was highest in Italy.[8] And this was in the period of anti-communist repression in the factories, before the intensification of industrial action which took effect from 1960 onwards. Between the years 1955 and 1962, the total of hours lost per year in industry rose from 45 to 181 million.[9] Moreover, as the country moved towards almost full employment by 1963, there was less risk involved in taking strike action. Labour unrest thus continued throughout the decade, but more important than the amount of

---

[7] Ginsborg, *A History of Contemporary Italy*, p. 214.

[8] 1.4 in France, 0.2 in West Germany, 1.9 in Belgium, 0.05 in Luxembourg, 2.1 in Italy. Spesso, *L'economia italiana dal dopoguerra a oggi*, p. 69.

[9] Istat, *Sommario di statistiche storiche dell'Italia 1861-1975*, table 114, p. 152.

disruption was the change in temper and the appearance of new social actors which gave grievances a dimension and an intensity which could not be contained within existing forms of protest.

In 1960, a dispute broke out at the Cotonifici Valle Susa in Piedmont over piece-work and increased rates of production. The dispute quickly spread to the group's other plants. The Cgil and its textile workers' federation which led the industrial action departed from past practice, however, in some important ways. Instead of coming in from outside and immediately conducting the dispute according to nationally established criteria, the union organized factory assemblies of all the workers, and not just of its own members, to decide how they wanted the dispute to be dealt with. New forms of industrial action were deployed, such as the *sciopero a scacchiera* (chessboard strike), where stoppages were concentrated in succession in strategically chosen sections of the plant. Some plants were occupied by the workers. After 140 days an agreement was reached, which the union submitted to the factory assemblies for approval. Such forms of rank-and-file consultation, together with the new forms of industrial action, were subsequently taken up by other federations and became important precedents for what have often been regarded as inventions of the1968-70 period.

The industrial struggles which began in the 1960s broke new ground in establishing various levels of 'articulated' bargaining. Important in this context was the dispute in 1960 in the electromechanical sector.[10] On 4-5 June 1960, the FIOM-Cgil organized a conference to prepare a platform of demands which would be a basis for discussion with the FIM-Cisl and the UILM-Uil. A set of demands was soon agreed between the labour federations. The dispute began when the FIOM, on 11 July, and the FIM and UILM a few days later, sent a request to the Confindustria and the Intersind to negotiate. Both employers' associations replied that such sector-based negotiations were not possible because there were already category-based agreements in force, and that such a precedent would lead to contractual anarchy.[11]

The existing national agreement at category level did in fact

---

[10] See Bartocci's account of this important dispute in his *Alle origini della contrattazione articolata (1960-64)*, pp. 197-242.

[11] For the relationship between 'sector' and 'category' see Glossary.

contain provisions for unions to present demands at sector level. But the employers chose to ignore this provision. The demands related to productivity bonuses, the reduction of the working week, equal pay for women, piece-work rates, and agreements on skills and grading. The employers wished to continue with the old practice of discussing these matters with the internal commissions, thus resolving problems on their own terms. The prospect of sector-level bargaining threatened to raise problems of production in terms which were far more specific than those which could be raised at the more generalised level of category negotiations. At the latter level bargaining was remote from the point of production and left the employers free to negotiate with the easily manageable internal commissions at local level.

This time the hard-line response of the employers to the new union initiatives provoked an angry reaction. From May to early September 1960, the sector saw the dispute spread in the industrial centres of Genoa, Turin and Milan, at this stage involving about a third of the total workforce, and inevitably bringing the FIOM, FIM and UILM closer together. Numerous plant agreements were made, but this did not stem the rising tide of discontent, for workers were now also beginning to react against aggressive styles of management. The unions organized referenda in the workplace in support of union demands, and meetings were organized outside the factory to gain public support. On 19 September, the FIM, FIOM and UILM called a one-day national strike, ordered an overtime ban from the following day, and this was followed by a general escalation of industrial action thereafter. In many places the action went well beyond what was proposed by the unions at national level. A popular form of industrial action became the use of the 'staggered' strike, for example a half-day stoppage on alternate days. This form of action would contain wage losses within tolerable levels but cause maximum disruption of production.

In Milan, which contained 60 per cent of the total electromechanical workforce, students began to support strikers and appeared on picket lines with slogans calling for greater democracy on the shopfloor. On 1 December, a rally was held in the crowded Piazza del Duomo in Milan. On 10 December, the public sector employers' association Intersind broke ranks with the Confindustria and signed an agreement with the federations FIM, FIOM and UILM. The Minister of Labour, Fiorentino Sullo, criticised the attitude of the private employers and declared that weak unions and aggressive employers were bad for the country's balanced development because they made any prospect of planning implausible.

The effect of the Intersind's agreement, and to a minor extent also the remarks of Sullo, was to increase hostility towards the Confindustria, which still refused to bargain. The dispute thus continued to intensify in the private sector. On Christmas Day, 20,000 electromechanical workers, with their families, met in Milan's Piazza del Duomo. At the rally, messages of solidarity from politicians, intellectuals and foreign workers were read to the public. Collections were held to support the families of the strikers. Although the Confindustria remained adamant, it could not control its members. One by one, its private company associates came to individual agreements with the unions on more or less the same terms as the Intersind. Falck attempted, as of old, to reach a separate agreement with the FIM and the UILM, and at least exclude the communists. This was rejected by the workers, and FIOM had to be included in the reopened negotiations. In the final analysis the Confindustria could manage only a formal and rather ragged opposition to the new demands. An irreversible change in the climate of industrial relations had taken place.

The electromechanical sector dispute of 1960 was important for a number of reasons. It employed for the first time many of the forms of pressure which were later developed during the 1968-70 cycle of worker protest. It also saw the beginning of student-worker co-operation which was one of the hallmarks of the later period. But in terms of industrial relations it was a turning-point, in that the Intersind began the practice of negotiating separately from the Confindustria. This had undoubtedly come about under pressure from elements within the Dc. The dispute of 1960 had taken off at the tail-end of the anti-fascist protests in Genoa and elsewhere, when the Tambroni government, which relied on neo-fascist support, had been brought down, and when the new Fanfani government was engineering its 'opening to the left'. Fanfani was anxious not to put this new strategy at risk, and it was felt that the Intersind could play an important role in developing a new climate in industrial relations. It was also the period in which the FIM-Cisl was led by the first group of leaders to emerge from the Florence School. These were less inclined than previous Cisl leaders to collaborate at all costs with the employers. They were more determined to pursue a line independently of the government and to collaborate with the mainly communist-led FIOM. These elements within the FIM were close to the Dc left, indeed they formed part of it, and were, therefore, anxious to support the inauguration of a new era in industrial relations in which the Intersind would be a major partner.

The private employers, on the other hand, could foresee an expansion in the electromechanical sector and were more determined than ever not to lose their position of dominance in industrial relations with the unions, which they feared were becoming bolder. This further divided them from the Intersind, whose higher echelons were dominated by Dc appointees and were thus subject to government pressures.

The 1960 agreement between the unions and the Intersind was important as a recognition of the right of the former to negotiate both company *and* sector-level agreements, and highlighted the need to establish clear norms regarding the relationship of both to national category agreements. It broke the employer front and gave greater legitimacy to those who argued for the desirability of articulated bargaining, i.e. with a series of agreements at different levels. It is important to bear in mind, however, that the dispute, although it did in the end greatly increase the legitimacy of this demand, was concentrated on the electromechanical sector and had involved only the most advanced elements of the Cgil, the Cisl and the Uil. There were still numerous problems which divided the confederations, and co-operation, although becoming increasingly frequent, was at a lower level in most other federations. The employers were aware of this, and continued to use the divisions to their advantage and resist any move towards a normative consolidation of the Intersind precedent at interconfederate level.

A fair amount of attention has been given to the electromechanical dispute, at the expense of a discussion of other disputes later in the decade, owing to its importance in breaking the mould of previous practices. But even this episode was only the first stage in a massive reorientation of Italian industrial relations. It took the prolonged struggle of the metalworkers, which lasted from June 1962 until February 1963, to take the process a stage further and bring about a substantial consolidation of new bargaining procedures, which would continue well into the following decade. The dispute was unusual in its complexity and in the range of issues it eventually touched upon. It caused further splits among the employers, and drew an increasingly wide range of workers into industrial action.

In March 1962, the UILM made a unilateral request to the Confindustria to reopen negotiations on existing national agreements in the metalworking sector. The Confindustria agreed to negotiate. The FIM and the FIOM, however, did not agree to do so until May, by which time they had worked out a broader platform of negotiations. The Catholic and communist federations were determined to discuss issues which went further than pay and conditions of work and right to the heart of industrial relations procedures. Faced with this threat to their hegemony, the employers adopted delaying tactics, and the federations called a national metalworkers' strike for 13 June. The strike was supported by 90-95 per cent of workers all over the country, except at Fiat in Turin, where the workers were the best paid, and where the employers had successfully marginalised not only the Cgil but also the 'troublemakers' within the Cisl. After further strikes the public sector employers' associations, the Intersind and the smaller Asap, concluded an agreement on 5 July which established three negotiating levels: the national category agreement, which covered broad matters relating to all levels; national sector negotiations which agreed hours of work, job classifications and wage levels for each sector; and plant agreements on piece-work rates and on the classification of unskilled workers. The formal recognition of these levels was an important step forward. Further agreements on 2 October and 20 December with the Intersind extended the scope of plant negotiations. At this stage, however, important as these advances were, plant and sector-level bargaining remained *applicative* and not *integrative*.[12]

The private sector employers were more resistant. Nevertheless, a strike on 23 June this time brought out 60,000 Fiat workers in Turin. Immediately following the agreement with Intersind on 5 July, strikes were called in the private sector for 7,

---

[12] This meant that such agreements were limited to applying or interpreting national category agreements. Nationally-agreed norms could not be used as a minimum on which to make improvements at lower levels.

8 and 9 July. Fiat immediately signed a hasty 'separate' agreement with the local Uil and Sida (yellow union) representatives. Ninety-two per cent of Fiat's workforce ignored the agreement and supported the strikes. Angry workers, in spite of Cgil and Cisl appeals for restraint, attacked the Uil's headquarters in a 24-hour siege of Piazza Statuto. There were clashes with the police. The effect of these disturbances was to bring to a definite end the era of 'separate' negotiations (i.e. on the union side). Worried about the effect of repeated stoppages on production, Fiat, along with Olivetti, broke ranks with the Confindustria and signed an agreement with the unions on 3 October. It took further industrial action, and a general strike of workers in all industries on 8 February 1963, to bring the Confindustria to the negotiating table. On 17 February, the Confindustria signed an agreement with the unions which made even greater concessions than that of the Intersind some months earlier. More important than the improved wages and conditions, plant agreements were accepted as *integrativi*, i.e. they could improve locally on nationally agreed norms.

The disputes of 1960 and 1962-3 established a totally new agenda in Italian industrial relations. Numerous disputes followed on which space does not permit us to dwell. Their significance lay in broadening this agenda and in sharpening the workers' awareness of the problems which remained to be resolved. A further cycle of vigorous disputes in 1966-7 involved construction workers, food workers, metalworkers, shipyard workers, farmworkers and others. The chemical and construction workers, in particular, followed the earlier example of the metalworkers and showed a high degree of unity among the federations. From the mid-sixties, in the metalworkers' disputes the Catholic FIM frequently showed itself to be more combative than either the FIOM or the UILM. New demands began to appear, e.g. for a *classificazione unica* between manual workers and clerical staff, for major improvements in health and safety standards, and for more regular consultation with the workforce. There were important ideological changes, together with a process of secularisation, in Italian society which stimulated this new phase of combativeness. Large sections of the population were slowly being liberated from the traditional Catholic ideological opposition to conflictual patterns of social behaviour. But before moving on to discuss these ideological changes, we must return briefly to one of the movement's major internal problems.

The Unresolved Problem of Factory Representation

The explosive nature of the 'Hot Autumn' of 1969 was due in part to the advances made in the earlier part of the decade in expanding negotiating levels, which greatly increased the areas of potential strife. But with the intensification of conflict there was a corresponding need for the *sindacato* to adapt its structures and organization if it hoped effectively to harness and constructively direct its demands. But the reshaping of organizational structures deeply entrenched in ideological and political divisions was of necessity a slow and painful process. The problem was that its own members became part of an impatient and accelerating movement in the whole social fabric of Italian society, which later in the decade showed all the signs of being out of control. All the agencies of social control, and not simply the unions, would be caught by surprise in the intensified cycle of protest which began in 1968.

The launching of decentralised bargaining in the early 1960s called for adequate structures at the lower levels, and during the pre-1968 period the *sindacato* was able to respond only partially to this need. It was the federations, such as the FIOM, FIM and UILM, which 'established a more solid organizational structure and brought a greater degree of regularity and systematicity to the workings of the apparatus'.[13] This was inevitable, for it was the success of the federations' negotiations which brought them 'the formal recognition, on the part of the employer, of the unions' right to recruit and to provide for their own financing' from subscriptions automatically deducted at source.[14]

Given the cohesive role of the confederate structures of the Italian *sindacato*, the consolidation of the federations also strengthened the provincial structures or chambers of labour. But in spite of decisions in the late 1950s to set up factory union branches, attempts to consolidate these bodies met with little success. And notwithstanding efforts to define their relationship with the internal commissions, a major stumbling block to their formation remained

---

[13] G. Della Rocca, 'L'evoluzione delle strutture di categoria', p. 67.

[14] Ibid.

the very different conception which the two major confederations held regarding the nature and function of union branches. The Cgil by instinct and tradition saw their potentially strategic role, i.e. of creating greater unity in the workforce as a whole, as equal in importance to the 'representative' function they would have. But the continued existence of 'separate' union organizations militated against this. Within the Cisl, with the exception of the metalworkers' federation, the 'separatist' conception of union organization still persisted.[15] It was this aspect of the Catholic labour tradition which 'continued to make the [Cisl] confederation, in contrast with the Cgil, think of the factory union branch [Sas] as not so much an instrument of dialogue with the mass of the workers as a projection into the workplace of a *sindacato* from outside'.[16] But in any case, given the increasing perception on the part of the workforce of the need for greater unity, it is by no means certain that the introduction of union branches, which would have been divided along confederate lines, alongside the already existing internal commissions, would have been a positive move. In fact, following the fierce disputes of 1960, internal commissions were set up in many factories where they had previously not existed. A similar pattern emerged between 1967 and the 'Hot Autumn' of 1969. Thus a further factor which inhibited the move towards factory union branches was the increased perception of the internal commissions as vehicles of mobilisation. From the mid-sixties a debate took place within the Cgil about the possibility of revamping the internal commissions as organs of greater rank-and-file unity, but such a development was not encouraged by the Cisl.[17]

A more promising parallel development was the emergence of the *ad hoc* assemblies referred to earlier, for example in relation

---

[15] See, for example, the report to the fifth congress of the Cisl in 1965, where an increase in industrial membership is actually perceived as presenting problems in retaining control of union representation in the factory. Cisl, *Le politiche e l'attività della confederazione nel triennio 1962-65. Relazione della segreteria confederale al V Congresso nazionale*, pp. 107-113.

[16] G. Romagnoli, 'La Cisl e il sindacato in fabbrica', p. 652.

[17] See, for example, A. Accornero, *Dalla rissa al dialogo*, Rome: Editrice Sindacale Italiana, 1967, where the case for such a development is argued exhaustively.

to the 1960 dispute in the textile industry. In the period between 1960 and 1963 there were, in fact, numerous categories of workers in both industry and agriculture who resorted to the use of assemblies for consultation during disputes.[18] In 1963 the Cgil pressed for worker-delegates to be present at negotiations taking place between the chemical workers' unions and the employers. This practice was later formally accepted in an agreement with the Intersind in 1966. Prior to the contract renewals of 1966-7, there was an increased use of factory assemblies to support national category negotiations.

It was clear that worker consultation which crossed the boundaries of union divisions was investing negotiators with a base of support which made it difficult for employers to exploit the traditional weaknesses of Italian labour organizations. Workers, both unionised and non-unionised, were acquiring a new sense of their strength when united. But these innovations were still largely improvised, and it was equally clear that the existing organizational structures of the movement were incapable of harnessing this ground swell of popular involvement. There were serious doubts, moreover, about the ability of the confederations to overcome their divisions sufficiently to attend to the problem themselves. These doubts were shared by many union activists and cadres within the *sindacato*. But, as we shall see, profound ideological and cultural shifts taking place within Italian society, inextricably combined with the aspirations of the workers' movement, generated a pressure for change with an irresistible momentum.

---

[18] An important discussion of these developments is contained in R. Chiaberge, 'Le strutture di base negli anni sessanta', pp. 124ff.

9

Values and Perspectives in Transition

The Changing Religious Climate

The transformation of Italian society into a predominantly industrialised economy by the early 1960s was accompanied by a profound secularisation of attitudes and practices, a process encouraged by the theological upheavals promoted by the Second Vatican Council, which took place between 1962 and 1965. Although Vatican II was a Council of the Universal Church, the traditional involvement of the Holy See in Italian affairs gave its proceedings an immediacy and relevance which were peculiar to the peninsula. Pope John XXIII was not altogether representative of the Italian hierarchy, among whom he soon became widely regarded as a devout and well-meaning, but dangerous Pontiff. Before the opening of the Council, in 1961, he issued an encyclical, *Mater et Magistra*, which contained a reassessment of Catholic social teaching. Its discussion of social issues displayed an awareness of economic and labour problems which departed quite markedly in tone from the spirit of lofty detachment characteristic of previous Papal pronouncements. One of the areas on which it touched was that of greater worker participation in industry and the commanding heights of the economy.[1] This was combined with a more detailed attack than in the past on unregulated forms of market behaviour. Although the encyclical was thus generally seen in Italy as reflecting greater sympathy towards the left, it nevertheless contained a reminder that earlier teachings had 'emphasised the fundamental opposition between communism and Christianity'.[2]

The condemnation of communism was, however, restrained by comparison with previous ecclesiastical documents. In another

---

[1] See *New Light on Social Problems*, encyclical letter of Pope John XXIII *Mater et Magistra (1961)*, paragraphs 51-121.

[2] Ibid., par. 34. The frequently repeated assertion that the encyclical omits any such condemnation is mistaken.

important encyclical, *Pacem in Terris*, promulgated two years later, in April 1963, Pope John omitted the accustomed ritualistic censure altogether. The encyclical, moreover, took an important step in distinguishing between materialism as the philosophical origin of communism, and its political and social programmes, since there could be 'good and commendable elements in these programmes, elements which do indeed conform to the dictates of right reason, and are an expression of man's lawful aspirations'.[3] The communist leader Togliatti had some weeks earlier devoted a speech to the theme of Catholics and communists in Italian politics, in which he elaborated upon the Pci's December 1962 Congress resolution on the positive role of religious belief as a stimulus to progress.[4] A productive dialogue ensued between Catholic and communist intellectuals in the pages of such journals as the Florentine Catholic monthly *Testimonianze* and the communist weekly *Rinascita*.[5]

Agreement on the desirability of such a dialogue was, however, far from universal. On the communist side, it was approved, indeed encouraged, by the party leadership. On the Catholic side, it had the support of the Pope himself and of the movement which became known as the 'Catholic dissent' (*dissenso cattolico*). But the Dc was noncommittal and wary, while there was widespread opposition among the Italian hierarchy. In fact, Pope John's call for a relaxation of hostilities was widely blamed for the Pci's advances in the elections in April 1963. After the Pope's untimely death in June of that year, the Italian bishops began to revise the Johannine teachings and initiate a change of course. In a 'Message to the Italian People' released in October, they renewed the traditional condemnation of 'atheistic' communism, and this was followed by pastoral letters in which numerous bishops called for a halt to Catholic-communist dialogue.[6] The new Pope, Paul VI, in an audience granted to Acli leaders in December, added his own authority to this reversal of his predecessor's initiative. He warned

---

[3] *Peace on Earth*, encyclical letter of Pope John XXIII, *Pacem in Terris* (1963), par. 159.

[4] See P. Togliatti, 'Il destino dell'uomo', in Opere, vol. vi, pp. 697-707.

[5] For a more detailed discussion see M. C. Giuntella, '*Testimonianze* e l'ambiente cattolico fiorentino', pp. 289-93.

[6] See A. Prandi, *Chiesa e politica*, pp. 140ff.

Italian workers not to fall victim to the influence of 'atheistic, subversive Marxism'.[7] Some nine months later, in August 1964, Paul VI devoted an entire chapter of his encyclical *Ecclesiam Suam* to the question of relations between the Church and 'atheistic communism'. In this authoritative statement to the faithful, he undermined John XXIII's call for dialogue by arguing that the time for such an encounter was premature, and restated traditional doctrinal condemnations. Yet neither a return to such denunciatory postures on the part of the Pope himself, nor the efforts of the Italian hierarchy, could fully stifle the dialectical process which had been set in motion by John XXIII's original call for greater mutual understanding. But part of the reason for this is also to be found in changes which were taking place within the Church itself.

Essentially, the authority of the Church was being questioned from two directions. In the first place, it was being challenged by the general atmosphere of protest which characterised the sixties. But also, the Vatican Council was decentralising the Church's internal power structures under pressure from new ideas such as the 'priesthood of the laity' and a general demand for greater decisional powers to be devolved to national Churches and their bishops.[8] Such pressures came mainly from non-Italian delegates, while the stubborn resistance of the Italian hierarchy to the new spirit of the times served simply to generate further protest in Italy itself.

The unreflecting conservatism of Italian prelates was, in the long term, self-defeating. For the first time in its history, the country saw the emergence of public dissent among a small but significant number of the lower clergy. Priests who championed the cause of the socially deprived and attempted to place the resources of their parishes at the disposal of the homeless and unemployed were accused of neglecting the traditional devotional practices of the bulk of the faithful. Others showed an interest in the newly developing 'theology of liberation' and attempted to give a social and political dimension to their ministry, which was deeply anti-establishment in flavour, thereby once again encouraging

---

[7] The full text of Paul VI's speech is in A. Boschini, *Chiesa e Acli*, pp. 119-25.

[8] See the Vatican Council's Dogmatic Constitution *De Ecclesia*, published in English as *Dogmatic Constitution on The Church*, London: Catholic Truth Society, 1965, particularly chapters 2 and 3.

protest. Numerous condemnations followed, with disciplinary actions which in some cases alarmed even the Vatican.[9] These internal problems diminished the capacity of the Church to maintain its hegemony, and the process of secularisation already in progress began to erode many hitherto unquestioned assumptions. 1966-7 witnessed the first debates on the introduction of divorce and the need to modify the long-standing Concordat between Church and state which guaranteed a range of privileges to the former. The mere fact that such debates were possible was an important indication of the degree to which religious attitudes had changed.

Ideological Change within the Catholic Workers' Movement

One idea which seemed to achieve a large measure of consensus within the Catholic workers' movement was that of the *risparmio contrattuale*, a centrally administered form of savings from the wages of workers, negotiated with the unions. The idea, first launched in 1956, was by the early 1960s being incorporated into the new 'planning' perspective of the Cisl. The objective became one of directing workers' savings to 'exert a positive influence over the financing of balanced development' and combine 'the accumulation of savings with a wider distribution of wealth in favour of the workers'.[10] The Cisl suggested, moreover, that the *sindacato* should manage the funds. The proposal was by this time part of the Cisl's broad support for the government's movement in the early 1960s towards economic planning. But it did not want economic planning to be too rigid or too centralised. In its advice to the government, it stressed the importance of ensuring that economic programmes remained open to market forces in such a way as to increase efficiency and productivity. To this end, negotiations between employers and unions should cover such areas as the selective targeting of investment, the training of a more skilled workforce, and the use of more efficient methods of production. It is within this context that the Cisl felt that by instituting and managing a savings scheme based on the earnings

---

[9] For a more detailed account of these developments, see M. Cuminetti, *Il dissenso cattolico in Italia*, pp. 102-86.

[10] Cisl, *Il risparmio contrattuale*, pp. 21 and 23.

of the workforce, the *sindacato* would obtain a certain amount of leverage in negotiations.

The *partecipazioni statali* [11] were to have a guiding role in such an experiment. Indeed, the Cisl conceived of the state-holding sector as a potential partner for the *sindacato* in creating a new system of industrial relations. The general intention was that within this sector the advantages of public control, alongside union influence through the Cisl's links with the Dc, would be combined with those of private management, and the resulting achievements would serve as an example to the private sector. Such a strategy was indicative of a distinctive feature of the Cisl's industrial culture, one to which it would cling tenaciously in the years ahead. In spite of the Catholic confederation's abandonment of its original, uncritical *aziendalismo*, it continued to project a more positive appraisal of market mechanisms, and was less inhibited in extolling the virtues of efficiency and productivity than its communist counterpart, which at the time had to filter the development of its own 'productivist' culture through the fabric of an ideological and political tradition historically hostile to the market.

Paradoxically, the permanence in office of the Dc helped to produce an historical corrective to these original positions. Through this party's increasing penetration of the institutions of the state and of the state-holding sector, the communists were encouraged to take up critical positions *vis-à-vis* all aspects of Italian society under the influence of the state. Their increasingly critical stance in this regard helped them liberate their thinking from many of the pro-statist postures traditionally associated with the left. This enabled them to attack the Dc for corruption and inefficiency, and produced positive calls from communists for greater efficiency, and eventually led to an open attitude to the importance of the market, a source of astonishment to foreign observers.

At the same time, the Dc's state hegemony created within the Cisl some ambiguities from which the confederation has found it extraordinarily difficult to extricate itself. Despite its declared intention to remain autonomous of the Dc, the Cisl was drawn by the Dc's penetration of state institutions into the sphere of public administration for example, and created one of the power bases of the Cisl, where it has been traditionally stronger than the Cgil. At

---

[11] See Glossary.

its National Congress in Rome, in May 1962, the Cisl asserted the *sindacato*'s right to deal directly with state and public bodies without intermediaries. The Cisl's congress statement was in essence a message to the Dc, within which there was a widespread assumption that, as the party of Catholics which also controlled the sector of public administration, the Cisl could leave it to the Dc to protect its interests.[12] Clearly the Cisl felt compromised by this form of tutelage. Its position of dominance within this sector, given that it was in any case heavily staffed by Dc personnel, many of whom were also members of the Cisl, put the confederation in a difficult position. As the Catholic scholar Baglioni has noted, this was the period during which the relationship

> between the *sindacato* and the state underwent a decisive change, in the sense that it introduced a greater presence of employees' representatives into the structures of public administration. The *sindacato* went from being on the margins to participating in the elaboration of economic and social policy, and both institutionally and in practice became a party to either the maintenance or the undermining of governments.[13]

The dominance of the Cisl in this sphere of Italian political life has thus turned out to be a source of compromise and weakness. Far from being able to apply pressure to bring about much-needed reforms in public administration, the *sindacato* itself became one of the major obstacles to change.

These neo-corporatist leanings within the Cisl were supported by the majority element in the confederation, which consisted of the federations in the public services sector, agriculture, the underdeveloped regions of the South and the traditionally 'white' or Catholic areas of the North-East.[14] The least enthusiastic were the industrial federations most committed to autonomy and in more direct contact with the advanced areas of capitalist production. These were the Catholic labour components least taken by surprise

---

[12] See *Relazione della segreteria confederale al quarto congresso nazionale*, pp. 149-51.

[13] G. Baglioni, *La politica sindacale nel capitalismo che cambia*, p. 100.

[14] The tendencies being discussed here should not be confused with the neo-corporatist sympathies which developed from the late 1970s onwards, which emerged from different quarters within the Catholic confederation.

by the emergence of industrial disputes in the early sixties. The official documents of the Cisl, however, continued to express the neo-corporatist concepts of advancement which banished conflict to the realms of industrial pathology. Much of the Catholic workers' movement remained alien to the demands and new forms of participation which the conflicts of the sixties were proposing. The minority components, on the other hand, such as the federations of metalworkers and chemical workers, were deeply involved in the rough and tumble of most disputes, and were consequently more sensitive to the changing situation.

At the National Congress of the FIM in 1962, the existing leadership, all proponents of a neo-corporatist constraint on the federation's conflictual tendencies, found itself roundly defeated in the elections for a new leadership. The new leaders, products of the Florence School, thereafter rejected the concept of the 'non-political' union. With this went a rejection of the excessive reliance on the idea that all problems in industrial relations could be resolved within a 'contractual' framework, to the exclusion of conflict and struggle. In thus abandoning the Catholic-inspired doctrine of 'harmonious relations', the FIM was giving greater expression to the aspirations of young militant Catholic workers who, influenced by the changing religious climate we have already discussed, were increasingly making common cause with their communist colleagues. In the face of social and industrial pressures, religious differences began to seem increasingly irrelevant to these workers.

For the new leaders of the FIM, the social and industrial discontent of the 1960s demonstrated the invalidity of the correlation posited by the early Cisl between economic development and automatic social advancement for the mass of the population. Catholic intellectuals close to the FIM began to employ Marxist concepts to analyse structural problems within capitalist economic development. On to such analyses, the new *cislini* grafted the traditional moral perspective of the Catholic tradition which frequently injected into the tone of their critiques a sharpness and vigour which sounded fresh by comparison with the more orthodox arguments of the communists.

Yet contradictions and ambiguities remained. One of the most intractable perspectives of the Catholic labour tradition was its *associazionismo*. The Cisl was reluctant to abandon the principle that agreements reached with employers should cover members only. Throughout the sixties, communists and socialists argued that in spite of giving a superficial appearance of justice, such a view was fundamentally at variance with a class-based orientation. In the first place, the communists objected, a class union defends the interests of the whole class, not simply those who have sufficient commitment to join a union. Furthermore, it was argued, it is not the wealth created by its members alone which the workers' movement is attempting to distribute more equitably, but the surplus value created by the whole workforce. Moreover, if it were to be coherent, the Cisl should refrain from seeking the support of non-members in industrial action. There was an additional, practical reason for insisting that the benefits of negotiations should be extended to all. By arguing that only union members should obtain wage increases, the Cisl was in effect encouraging the creation of pools of cheap labour, for it was difficult to see why any employer should not recruit from non-unionised labour.

Yet despite the increasing class orientation of the more militant *cislini*, the attachment to forms of *associazionismo* persisted, even within the FIM, at least until 1968. In an agreement, for example, between the federations FIM-FIOM-UILM and the ironwork group of employers within IRI, where IRI undertook to provide back-pay for Sunday working, the FIM insisted that union members should be the first to be compensated.

The most dramatic ideological shifts within the world of Catholic labour during the 1960s, however, took place within the Acli. At its National Congress in Bari in December 1961, the delegates elected the left-wing Livio Labor as president. This was the outcome of the first of two important contests between the proponents of autonomy and those who wished to tie the movement more closely to the Dc and to the Church as a 'workerist' form of Catholic Action, under ecclesiastical tutelage.[15] But the increased tension in the workplace, together with the very obvious secularisation taking place in Italian society, served to strengthen the determination of the new Acli leadership to break its collateralist links with those sections of the Catholic world which were least sensitive to the needs of a changing society.

The depth of this resolve became very clear during the next stage of the confrontation which emerged at the Acli National

---

[15] See Prandi, *Chiesa e politica*, pp. 86-93.

Congress in Rome in November 1966. In his address to the congress, Labor declared that it was time to face the fact that although the Dc represented the political tendencies of many Italian Catholics, it did not enjoy the support of all of them. Labor led the attack on the Dc and argued that it must decide whether it wished to head a conservative force in Italian society or become a genuine party of reform. In an unusual show of anti-Dc emotion, the delegates shouted down Rumor, the party's guest-speaker, when he appealed for the Acli to rally to the support of the Catholic party. To make matters worse, the fraternal message sent to the congress by the socialist Cgil leader, Santi, was greeted with loud applause. The ecclesiastical representative of Catholic Action left the congress to demonstrate his disapproval of the proceedings. The Pope himself, in an audience granted to Acli leaders some days later, while more circumspect, gave a clear indication of the Church's concern over developments at the congress.[16]

This leftward shift of the Acli, which some years later would lead to Labor's open espousal of socialism, continued to lend vital support to the left within the Cisl in the latter part of the sixties. The growing support for the left within the Catholic *sindacato* was clearly indicated by the unprecedented difficulty experienced by the conservative Cisl General Secretary, Bruno Storti, in being elected to the Acli's new National Council at the 1966 Congress. Instead of the usual automatic high quota of votes for the leader of the collateralist worker organization, Storti was lucky to obtain, by a very narrow margin, one of the last places on the Acli National Council.

The Communists

In the early 1960s the communists had to respond to the new thinking on economic planning developing within the government and among its socialist partners of the centre-left. The obstacle they had to overcome was the traditional Marxist view that economic planning could be meaningful only within the context of a socialist

---

[16] See Magister, *La politica vaticana e l'Italia*, p. 342.

economy.[17] In 1962 the Pci organized a conference on the new developments within Italian capitalism. The conference took as its premiss the idea that doctrinal verities, namely articles of Marxist faith, could hold no privileged position in a genuinely open-ended debate. It turned out to be a watershed in communist economic thinking. The speakers for the most part abandoned the usual condemnatory postures and dropped traditional teleological assumptions regarding the inevitable collapse of capitalism, thereby putting the Pci many years ahead of other western communists. The importance of the conference went well beyond its particular message. It inaugurated a phase of analysis in which communists began to think with a more open and flexible attitude than hitherto about the capitalist economic system.[18] Almost immediately, and before its December 1962 Congress, the party made clear that it was dropping its opposition to the EEC. A more constructive approach began to emerge in the arguments of the communists towards what became known as the 'productive' strata of small and medium industrialists, artisans, the middle classes and others. For the Pci this entailed the development of strategies involving new social and political alliances. In the case of the Cgil, the new thinking encouraged it to chart new territories within its own domain and to respond in a more flexible manner to the behaviour of the government and the employers in the economic field.

Thus the same process of secularisation which had affected the Catholics began to undermine the strictly 'doctrinal' aspect of the Italian communist tradition. This would eventually lead to an explicit renunciation in official documents of any binding or *a priori* commitment to Marxist philosophical positions as articles of faith. This form of liberation from 'ideology as creed' enabled Italian communists to adapt their thinking and policies to the realities of social and economic developments in a way which eluded the more doctrinally orthodox communist parties operating

---

[17] The Pci had already broken with this traditional view at its first postwar December 1945-January 1946 Congress. See Togliatti's speech to the congress in P. Togliatti, *Rinnovare L'Italia. Rapporto al V Congresso nazionale del Pci*, particularly pp. 66ff.

[18] The papers presented at this important conference can be found in Istituto Gramsci, *Tendenze del capitalismo italiano. Atti del convegno di Roma*, 2 volumes, Rome: Editori Riuniti, 1962.

in other advanced capitalist economies. It also explained their frequent isolation within the international communist movement.

In its reply to the government, contained in the Cgil report to the Cnel in 1964, the confederation made a number of statements which are a useful guide to its new thinking on the question of economic planning. In accepting the idea that forms of planning can be contemplated within the framework of a capitalist economy, the communists went further and argued for a form of economic planning which included devolution at regional level. From this point, Italian communists became openly sceptical of the highly centralised forms of planning to which their tradition had been wedded, and they began to argue for legislative and administrative powers for regional programmes. This put pressure on the centre-left to set up the regional administrations which were required by the Constitution, a measure then being urged on the government by its minority socialist component.[19]

The need for regional planning and development was also stressed by the Uil. This confederation was ahead of both Catholics and communists in linking such a demand to the country's membership of the EEC. After the decision of the Uil's Central Committee in 1962 to stress the importance of European development, the confederation was the first to bring the question of European economic integration to bear on its thinking about domestic planning.[20] This was to some extent the result of the Uil's feeling of political isolation in a country dominated by deeply-rooted Catholic and communist sub-cultures, alongside a weak social democratic tradition. By binding its future more closely to Europe, it was argued, the country would benefit from contact with strong socialist and social democratic parties with experience of government. In reality, there were also some important changes taking place within the country itself. The 1960s was the period in which the Italian communists, although still critical of the EEC, dropped their ritual condemnation of the European Community as the economic arm of NATO. Instead, as indicated by Togliatti in his report to the Pci Congress of 1962, they began to focus on its development as part of 'an irreversible process of international

---

[19] See the Cgil report to the Cnel in *Cgil e programmazione economica*, vol. ii, pp. 5ff.

[20] See F. Simoncini, *Dall'interno della Uil*, pp. 115-32.

integration of the structures of production', not in itself undesirable but needing to be democratised and wrested out of monopoly control.[21]

By the time the Cgil came to hold its 1965 Congress in Bologna, the centre-left government had finally produced an economic plan, at least on paper. A short time before the congress, the Cgil presented a report to the Cnel, and decided to abstain in the vote which the Cnel took in support of the government's plan.[22] Within the confederation, the socialists were more sympathetic in the tone of their observations than the communists. Both, however, agreed on the fundamental points of criticism. At the congress itself, a more carefully meditated response was given. The congress resolutions welcomed those parts of the plan which were meant both to create employment and stimulate development in the South. The criticisms, however, focused on the failure to provide the necessary support for implementation: sufficient public investment, adequate credit selectivity, targeting of monetary resource allocations, and finally, incentives for private capital to invest in areas requiring development. At the parliamentary vote, the Pci voted against the government proposals, while communist Cgil parliamentarians abstained.[23]

A sense of plurality of allegiances was clearly beginning to undermine the traditional communist sense of belonging to a monolith. As we shall see shortly, this was also due to a greater sense of urgency about the need to achieve unity within the workers' movement itself. But it was much easier to deplore the lack of unity in the *sindacato* than to understand the nature of the obstacles to its realization.

---

[21] *Decimo Congresso del partito comunista italiano*, p. 48.

[22] See *Cgil e programmazione economica*, vol. ii, pp. 195ff for the text of the Cgil's declaration.

[23] In the parliamentary votes Cisl and Uil deputies voted in favour of the bill.

10

Unity: The Emergence of a Difficult Agenda

Changing Conceptions of Unity

The workers' struggles in the early 1960s forced the confederations to face the problem of unity. The first confederate encounters took place via interconfederate negotiations with the employers. Between 1962 and 1968 six such meetings resulted in agreements across a range of matters: equal pay for comparable categories of clerical workers; 'just cause' as a basis for dismissals; guidelines on reduction of staff; the assessment of the functions of internal commissions; and the fixing of minimum wage levels. But the success of the confederations in gaining concessions on these matters was due less to a unified strategy of demands than to the employers' anxiety to placate an increasingly militant labour force.

The period of economic crisis between 1964 and 1965 marked the dividing line between a phase in which united action was occasional and spontaneous and a further stage in which common strategic aims became urgent. In 1965 demonstrations were jointly organized to protest about the housing situation. Following discussions on economic planning, all reports to the Cnel from 1966 were jointly agreed by the national confederations. Things were on the move, but these indications of a growing desire for unity were part of a complex set of motivations which gave the concept of unity, at least in its initial stages, a variety of meanings.

The communist majority within the Cgil was the only component within the workers' movement which, from the beginning, conceived of the final objective of unity, or 'organic unity' as it was called, as a complete merger of the three confederations. In the early 1960s, however, this was not a feasible proposition. At a press conference in January 1960, for example, the Cisl General Secretary, Bruno Storti, declared his confederation's support for the creation of a *sindacato democratico* which would exclude the communist component of the Cgil.[1]

---

[1] Bianchi, *Storia dei sindacati in Italia*, p. 145.

The Catholic proposal had as its aim the creation of a *sindacato* reflecting the political centre-left coalition then in the process of gestation. Although this remained the official position of the Cisl until the mid 1960s, it was consistently rejected by the socialists in the Cgil who could see few benefits, but numerous disadvantages in such a move. In 1966 a different option surfaced from another direction in anticipation of the merger between the Socialist and Social Democratic parties. On this occasion the initiative came from the General Secretary of the Uil, Italo Viglianesi, for the creation of a *sindacato socialista*, once again with the objective of marginalising the communists, but this time as a movement parallel to a newly created 'third force' in Italian politics which would result from the Psi-Psdi merger.

The Uil proposal depended on the willingness of the socialists within the Cgil to break with the communists and form a new confederation in competition with the Cgil and the Cisl, since 'the majority of the leaderships within the Cisl and the communist component of the Cgil had taken up positions of complete indifference to the problems facing the development of our society'.[2] The initiative was doomed to failure for a number of reasons. The Uil enjoyed no mass support within either the industrial or agricultural working class, where it was still deeply mistrusted. Nor was this totally undeserved. In many of the workers' struggles up to that point the Uil had dragged its feet. To most workers the accusations it levelled at the other two confederations were simply empty rhetoric. For the majority of socialists within the Cgil, therefore, the Uil initiative was no more than an invitation to disaster. But the proposal received its final *coup de grâce* from a series of statements by the socialist secretaries and the socialist members of the General Council of the Cgil. Not only did they reject the idea of a *sindacato socialista* but they insisted that the only way in which lasting unity could be achieved was by accepting the idea of a plurality of organizations as a starting-point, and proceeding from there to encourage greater autonomy within the existing confederations from their respective

---

[2] *Documento della sezione sindacale del Psi*, p. 9. For a detailed assessment of debates around the question of unity at this time, see the collection of documents from the three confederations in Acli, *Idee e documenti per l'unità sindacale*, Rome: Industria grafica moderna, 1969.

parties.[3] The proposals for a *sindacato democratico* and a *sindacato socialista* placed excessive reliance on bureaucratic manoeuvres; both were made with no consultation with the membership in the proposing confederations. Additionally, both initiatives were tied to the interests of party coalitions and/or party mergers in a way which would have diminished rather than increased the space for the autonomous development of the movement.

In January 1966 there was public disagreement between the Cisl and the Uil over the latter's proposal for a *sindacato socialista*. Agostino Novella, General Secretary of the Cgil, intervened in the debate and proposed a series of meetings between the three confederations to discuss the possibility of a skeleton agreement (*accordo quadro*) on the objectives of the movement and on the manner of conducting negotiations with the government and the employers. The proposal was deliberately uncontroversial, and was difficult for the Cisl and the Uil to reject. After some initial delays, the first meetings took place in 1966.

These events quickly overshadowed discussions about the original Uil proposal. The encounters continued into 1967, but their importance lay more in the fact that the leaders of the confederations were meeting than in the contents of the talks themselves. Before April 1966, in the words of a prominent Cgil leader, relations between the confederations had been such that 'for ten years union leaders had known one another simply because they read one another's names in the newspapers, but they were not acquainted personally'.[4] This statement gives some indication of the depth of the divisions. The meetings had great symbolic importance and began to break down the immediate psychological barriers to fruitful discussion. The reaction of the membership was immediate.[5]

From the early sixties the gap between the increasing demand for unity among the workers and the confederations' capacity to

---

[3] The most important of these statements were made in the Psi daily *Avanti!*, on 11 September and 26 October 1966.

[4] Interview with Luciano Lama, cited in Turone, *Storia del sindacato in Italia*, p. 328.

[5] See the results of a rank-and-file survey carried out between October 1966 and and May 1967, in *Inchiesta sull'unità sindacale. Mille risposte alla rivista Rinascita,* Rome: Editori Riuniti, 1967.

achieve it began to grow. This was due not to a lack of movement on the part of the confederations, but to the more rapid momentum of developments among the rank-and-file. In the federations, however, the picture was not so uniformly gloomy, for by 1964 both the FIM and the FIOM had moved beyond the perspective of 'unity of action' and were slowly edging towards the prospect of 'organic unity' or merger. In this connection each federation had received congress approval for resolutions calling for the application of the principle of *incompatibilità* as a first step towards unity. But the metalworkers' organizations faced different tasks within their respective confederations. Within the Cgil, the position of the FIOM was well in advance of that of the confederation as a whole, not so much on the question of 'organic unity' as such, which was accepted as desirable within the organization, but on its preconditions and the time needed to bring it about. The Catholic FIM had a more difficult task to perform. At the Cisl Congress in April 1965, which reaffirmed its commitment to the notion of a *sindacato democratico*, the leader of the FIM, Luigi Macario, opposed the exclusion of the communists from any scheme of unification. Although defeated, Macario gained the support of about 15 per cent of the delegates, and this support increased substantially following his proposal for the introduction of the principle of *incompatibilità*.

Catholic scholars have observed that it was the experience of the FIM leaders in representing the more militant sectors of Italian workers which led them to the *scoperta della classe* (discovery of the class perspective), thus drawing them closer to the FIOM. Abandoning the earlier 'productivist' ideology of the Cisl, they argued that the very rationale of the system of production operated in the interests of the employers. Wages and profits were locked into permanent conflict. The 'class' nature of the FIM argument was initially somewhat muted and interlaced with the ethical overtones of Catholic social teaching. But as the FIM and the FIOM drew ideologically closer, the question of unity became more urgent and the problem of *incompatibilità* increasingly important.

The Principle of Incompatibility

The principle of *incompatibilità* became the test of the

confederations' seriousness in achieving autonomy from their respective parties. As we have seen, this was in many repects an uneven demand. While there was a natural link between the objectives of the pro-union Pci and the Cgil, the Cisl-Dc connection was causing the Catholic confederation increasing problems regarding its very credibility as a union. It will come as no surprise, therefore, that a greater sense of urgency on the matter of *incompatibilità* was felt within the more militant sectors of the Cisl.

Early in 1964 the leader of the Catholic FIM, Pierre Carniti, urged the FIOM and the UILM to take the matter up in their forthcoming congresses. This appeal was in response to a document released by the General Council of the Cisl in December 1963 expressing alarm at the haste with which the FIM was engaging in unified forms of industrial action, particularly with the communists. The other two metalworkers' confederations, admittedly to a lesser degree, were in the same position of being ahead of their own confederate organizations. They thus had similar problems. So, far from heeding the warnings of his confederate leaders, Carniti was attempting to force the pace of unity from below by seeking to extract explicit declarations of intent from the FIOM and the UILM.

The readier, and more important response came from the FIOM at its Rimini Congress in March 1964. A FIM delegation attended and was invited to speak. The UILM was not represented. In the debate on the question of *incompatibilità*, a division emerged between the communists and the socialists. While the former wished to see the principle applied to the simultaneous holding of union and party positions, the latter wished to extend it to include seats in parliament and local government. The communists opposed such an extension of 'incompatibility', arguing that this would depoliticise the union and deprive it of its influence on legislation. The extension argued by the socialists was deferred to the next Cgil congress, but the delegates accepted the principle of *incompatibilità* between executive positions in the union and political parties.

The importance of this internal debate went well beyond the confines of the FIOM. It raised the question of the manner in which labour was to be represented in parliament. Were union leaders in parliament representatives of the parties on whose lists they stood for election, or did they represent the interests and views of their confederations? This was a particularly burning question for the Cisl as the divisions between it and the Dc became more pronounced, and as an increasing proportion of the membership of the Catholic labour confederation questioned the Dc's ability to represent its interests. Hence for the Catholics *incompatibilità* was related to the increasing division between the two wings of the collateral alliance and to the growing incapacity of one component to function as the political expression of the other. It is not by chance, therefore, that the development, at a later stage, of the idea of the *sindacato* as a *soggetto politico*, or political actor, should find its strongest supporters within the Catholic labour movement.

By contrast, the increasing differentiation between party and union among the communists, although a real enough process, was not motivated by the same diminishing confidence in the Pci's capacity to represent the interests of labour. On the whole, *incompatibilità* was experienced by the communists as the price they had to pay for the unity of the workers' movement. Fewer rank-and-file members of communist organizations felt the need for autonomy than their Catholic counterparts since communists had a more enduring trust in their party. Class solidarity, however, which they did feel more keenly than the Catholics, required unity. Thus, albeit for different reasons, *incompatibilità* was seen as essential by the more advanced elements on both sides. The matter was debated at the congresses of the two confederations in 1965. At the Cgil Congress in Bologna at the end of March, the delegates accepted a resolution introducing the principle of incompatibility between leading positions in local organs of the Cgil on the one hand, and membership of parliament, and positions of leadership in local government and political parties on the other. But it was not extended to national executive posts in either the Cgil or the category federations. The holders of such posts could continue to act as parliamentarians and hold leading positions in political parties.[6] The congress did, however, highlight one of the persistent problems within the Cgil, namely that of the Cgil's *componenti* or 'components'. In the lead-up to the congress the confederation declared that over 100,000 members had participated in pre-congress discussions. But the choice of delegates attending the congress was negotiated between the three parties of the 'components', the Pci, the Psi and the Psiup, which resulted in a 56

---

[6] For the text of the Cgil resolution, see *I congressi della Cgil*, vol. vii, pp. 631-2.

per cent, 28 per cent and 16 per cent representation of the respective party 'components'. The communists were happy to acquiesce in this method of selection, for although a ballot would have given them a larger share of delegates, it was important to keep the socialists within the confederation. Increasingly, positions within the confederation's structure would be dominated by this kind of 'arrangement' whereby socialists would gain a higher proportion of posts in return for staying within the organization, a practice which clearly, in the eyes of many members, had perverse effects on internal democracy.

At the Cisl Congress some weeks later, the unitarians in the confederation were able to extract only a much weaker commitment to the principle of incompatibility out of the congress, which in its final resolution stated that 'the liberty of its members to participate in the life of political parties constitutes a fundamental individual right which does not affect the union sphere in any way'. As for elective political institutions, the confederation reserved the right 'to judge, case by case, the advisability and manner in which Cisl representatives are to be present in such bodies'.[7]

The congress debates which led to the resolutions nevertheless produced a greater degree of self-consciousness in the behaviour of confederate parliamentarians. It was against this background that the communist Cgil parliamentarians broke ranks with the Pci in the parliamentary vote on the government's economic plan in early 1967. Henceforth confederate parliamentarians would feel increasingly uneasy about their ambiguous roles and come under greater pressure to demonstrate a degree of autonomy from the party while at the same time expressing their loyalty to the cause of unity. Yet it could hardly be said that the confederations were rushing headlong towards unification. Within the Uil it was the republican, and not the social democratic or socialist components which supported the principle of *incompatibilità*. Socialists and social democrats were worried about weakening the political force of their parliamentary components. The republicans, however, although beset by similar problems, came from that current which represented, in Italian society, a strong tradition of constitutional and institutional correctness. Within both the Cisl and the Cgil, the more determined

---

[7] Cisl, *Atti del V Congresso Nazionale, Roma 22-25 aprile 1965*, p. 484.

minority of *incompatibilisti* continued to press for the full implementation of the principle, while the Catholics did so with a degree of ferocity which alarmed their own confederate leaders.

In July and October 1967, the Cisl and the Cgil both held national conferences. At both, the leaderships managed to contain the mounting pressure to remove confederate leaders from parliament. Nevertheless, the pressure continued to intensify. Within the Catholic camp, for example, the voice of the Federchimici (chemical workers' federation) leaders and others were added to those of the FIM. At the Cgil Conference some FIOM leaders wanted the confederation to implement the principle unilaterally, against the arguments of the Cgil General Secretary, Novella, who favoured a multilateral policy alongside the Cisl and the Uil. Although Novella won the vote, the FIOM leader, Bruno Trentin, announced his withdrawal from the Pci list in the forthcoming parliamentary elections, the first high-ranking federal leader to do so.[8] Nervous about facing the elections without their traditional collateral support, both the Dc and the Pci urged caution upon their union colleagues. But the momentum was gathering speed, and in some quite unexpected ways.

The problem of representation had reached a climax in the Cisl. The emergence of the idea of the *sindacato* as a *soggetto politico* was closely related to this problem. The development of the *sindacato*'s role as a political actor is frequently regarded as having followed the turbulent 1968-70 cycle of events which dramatically changed the industrial relations scene in Italy. But to attribute it entirely to the events of this period is to underplay the roles of the Catholic and communist subcultures and their readiness to introduce modifications into liberal democratic forms of representation. More immediately, the idea of the *sindacato* acting as a *soggetto politico* had arisen on numerous occasions before the outbreak of protest surrounding the 'Hot Autumn'.

Once more, we have to look outside the guarded pages of official Cisl documents to see how things were changing. In a newspaper interview in December 1967 for instance, the General Secretary of the confederation, Bruno Storti, declared

---

[8] Shortly afterwards, a joint declaration of the FIM-FIOM-UILM federations of the province of Milan stated that the leaders of the metalworkers' federations would not be standing in the 1968 national elections.

I would give up my seat in parliament at any point at which I thought it was damaging rather than helping the *sindacato*. Leaving this aside, it seems to me that an essential precondition for this is the establishment of new areas of representation for the *sindacato* which guarantee substantial levels of input. This would prevent the *sindacato* from being excluded from the decision-making process on economic and social matters, which are its legitimate concern.[9]

Storti had, in fact, proposed the abolition of the Senate and the transformation of the Cnel (which contained union representatives) into a second parliamentary chamber.[10] The importance of his comments did not lie in the *form* of his proposal, which did not gain widespread support. Given his moderate position within the Cisl, and his personal closeness to the Dc, the proposal was an important indication of the depth of unease felt within the confederation, and of the growing sense of autonomy within its ranks. The world of Catholic labour was finally beginning the search for a new political space. Finally, it illustrated an important factor within the ideological fabric of Italian thinking about industrial relations, one which differentiates it substantially from the Anglo-Saxon tradition, namely, the ready acceptance within Italian society of the legitimacy of a social and political representational function for the *sindacato*. It is essential to grasp this point in order to understand why the cycle of events soon to follow were to have such a consolidating effect on the *sindacato*'s social and political role in the post-'68 period. These events helped to further the movement's claim to be accepted as a *soggetto politico*. They did not, however, as some readings of the 'autunno caldo' seem to suggest, create it.

---

[9] 'I tre interrogativi', interview given to Lama (Cgil), Viglianesi (Uil) and Storti (Cisl) in *Il Giorno*, 27 December 1967, p. 13. The interview also reveals the favourable attitude of Lama and unfavourable position of Viglianesi in relation to the whole question of *incompatibilità*.

[10] A proposal for a similar form of representation had been supported by many elements within the pre-fascist Catholic labour confederation, Cil and the Catholic party, the Ppi. Some early Dc political figures were also favourable to such a body.

Part IV

THE SOCIAL CONSOLIDATION OF THE
WORKERS' MOVEMENT

11

The Unforgettable Autumn of '69

Mounting Social Tensions

The protest movements of the late 1960s affected most of the industrialised countries of the West, focusing on a wide variety of global issues ranging from the war in Vietnam to the repressive nature of traditional sexual values. There were undoubtedly some common underlying factors contributing to this widespread phenomenon, particularly the fact that the protagonists were, on the whole, the first postwar generation of young people coming to maturity in a highly consumer-oriented Western world and attempting to shake off many traditional beliefs. It was a period during which young people were extremely receptive to new ideas. But the feeling of being part of a vast international wave of protest frequently concealed important differences specific to national situations.

In Italy, the period of protest involved wider sections of society than almost anywhere else, rooted as it was in the social fabric of a society caught up in an unusually intense and rapid transformation. The 'economic miracle' had profoundly changed the material basis of Italian society, but had left its framework of social supports untouched and in need of urgent reform. It is important, therefore, when we examine the industrial disputes at the centre of the 'autunno caldo', not to perceive them in isolation. While there was undoubtedly a continuity in strictly contractual terms between the demands of the period and earlier industrial struggles, the explosive quality of the 'Hot Autumn' was fuelled by the broader social tensions which had been mounting from the beginning of the decade. The increasing demands on the nation's social and productive resources were being made with an assertiveness that could no longer be controlled by traditional methods of containing protest, which had lost their effectiveness and credibility. Old-style labour repression was no longer possible. Not only had it lost both its social and ideological legitimacy in the country at large, but it could not count on the support of the centre-left government. The political realignment brought about by the *centro sinistra* also prevented the government from using the traditional mechanisms of deflationary economic policies to bring the unions into line. The Church had lost a great deal of its hegemonic power over an increasingly secularised flock. Although this was on the one hand the effect of protest, it was equally on the other a direct cause of it, since it was the result of a dynamic process of ideological liberation that proved difficult to control.

Religious dissent had been growing throughout the decade, not simply *around* the Church but also *within* it. The protests took a variety of forms. In September 1968, for example, Catholic students in Parma occupied the Cathedral. They were protesting both against the authoritarian attitude of the Church and the low level of lay participation in its daily life. The new teachings of Vatican II regarding the 'priesthood of the laity' were simply ignored by the Italian hierarchy, which was determined to cling to every fragment of power. Messages of support for the protesters came from Catholic groups all over the country, particularly from the large urban centres. The most controversial of these was sent by the priests of the Isolotto in Florence, led by the parish priest Enzo Mazzi, and signed by 150 parishioners. Mazzi, who had made his parish premises available to the unemployed and the deprived, was already at the centre of a stormy debate about the Church and its mission to the poor. Prompted by the Vatican, Cardinal Ermenegildo Florit threatened to suspend Mazzi if he did not withdraw his message of support for the occupation in Parma.[1] Mazzi's refusal to recant was supported by local factory workers, who went on strike in protest against the threat.[2]

This kind of activity highlights one of the most striking features of the two-year cycle of revolt in Italy, which began in 1968: the exceptionally high level of sympathy which existed between the protagonists of the different protest movements. It was the cross-fertilisation of grievances which gave the period its extraordinary vigour and emotional charge. Underlying these

---

[1] See C. Falconi, *La contestazione nella chiesa*, pp. 355ff.

[2] The events surrounding the whole Isolotto incident are documented in *L'Isolotto. Documenti. La crisi della chiesa locale di Firenze*, edited and published by the periodical *Il Regno*, Bologna, 1969.

manifestations of solidarity were ideological developments which were not always evident on the surface of events. Partly owing to the non-sectarian cultural habits of the Pci under Togliatti's leadership, but also to the leftward cultural shift of large sections of Italian society in the wake of fascism, the easing of cold-war tensions saw the gradual appropriation of Marxist currents of thought and analysis by Catholics and important sectors of the lay or secular intelligentsia (the *area laica*).

It was significant that one of the major centres of student protest in the late sixties was the Catholic University of Milan.[3] Yet the appropriation of a protest culture had origins earlier than the late sixties. As Sidney Tarrow has amply demonstrated, contrary to what is frequently asserted, student protest had begun earlier and was considerably more mature in Italy by the late sixties than it was, for example, in France.[4] The original stimulus for student radicalisation was provided by the Gui bill of 1962 which aimed at restricting access to universities. After initial protests at the bill, the groups which had emerged in the universities turned their attention to broader political issues, particularly to forging links with the organizations of the working class. Ultra-left groups such as *Potere Operaio* (worker power) and *Lotta Continua* (perpetual struggle) did not originate in working-class organizations, but were transported there in 'entryist' fashion from the universities. The contribution of Catholic student leaders in the three leading centres of the student movement, the Faculty of Sociology of the University of Trento, the Catholic University of Milan, and the Sapienza of Pisa, was substantial. By the time of the occupation of university institutions all over the country in 1967, opposition to renewed attempts by Gui to restrict university entry was only one of the campaigning issues, the movement having become increasingly drawn into solidarity with labour struggles. Action programmes and policy statements were exchanged between the main centres of student activity, culminating, in one important centre, in the definition of students as 'a labour force in the process of training'.[5]

---

[3] See G. E. Rusconi e C. Saraceno, *Ideologia religiosa e conflitto sociale*, pp. 58ff.

[4] See Tarrow, *Democracy and Disorder*, pp. 155ff.

[5] Ibid, p. 251.

From the summer of 1968, these groups, together with others such as the pro-Maoist *Avanguardia Operaia* and the more orthodox Stalinist *Movimento Studentesco*, with its main centre this time at the State University of Milan, began to push the movement in a 'workerist' (*operaista*) ideological direction, and became critical of the reformist policies of the Pci and the official unions. This has led some critics to overstate the importance of ultra-left groups in the formation of rank-and-file workers' committees in the factories, ignoring the process of ideological change that was also taking place within the Pci, the Cgil, the Cisl and the Uil. Radical groups developed among the intellectuals of the labour organizations, particularly the FIM and the FIOM, and played a major part in shaping the new social and economic demands which the workers' committees would soon be making.

Perhaps the most striking feature of the period, one which once again distinguishes Italy from neighbouring France, was the high level of collaboration between students and workers. With some minor exceptions, neither students nor workers tended to coalesce exclusively around the radical or reformist camps mentioned earlier. A strong sense of solidarity led each group to organize meetings in support of the other. But the high level of collaboration between protesting groups was not due solely to ideological factors, but also to the interpenetration of the social and material problems expressed by these groups.

By 1965 access to university had in effect been widened by the abolition of selective entry, which meant that student numbers began to increase rapidly, thus drawing an increasing proportion of students from the lower social groups. These were well attuned to the grievances which were bringing their brothers, sisters and fathers onto the streets in labour demonstrations. This awareness was reinforced by the absence of a system of grants, which forced students to live at home and study at their local universities. Trapped in their local communities, they were only too familiar with the inadequacy of the educational, social and material provision on offer to them and their families. Overcrowded lectures, absent professors, lack of staff-student contact, and the indifference of university authorities further fuelled their grievances. Far from being an opening to new and exciting experiences, as it was for many university entrants in other western countries, enrolment at Italian universities, for many students, simply added to their personal and family problems.

Similar observations can be made in relation to another important factor in Italian social life: the family. In a country where traditional family bonds were strong, grandparents and other elderly relatives were readily accommodated in the family home. It takes little imagination to perceive the strains such a practice placed on millions of working-class families, particularly in overcrowded urban centres, where, as late as 1969, southern immigrant families found 'many flats without lavatories, some without running water, and landlords willing to let for only six months at a time'.[6] The lack of public provision in matters of health, transport and many other services was both a strain on family income and a continual source of anxiety. In some ways the extended Italian family was a microcosmic nucleus of protest movements. It is clear that there were determining factors woven into the very fabric of Italian society which bound the wider social issues to those of employment in a clear and unmistakable manner. The social and political demands which the post-1969 *sindacato* added to its agenda were not simply the products of an ideological understanding of the connections between work and society. They were embedded within the daily experiences of working people.

The most urgent problem requiring attention was the need for an adequate system of pensions. After numerous meetings with the labour confederations, the question was debated in parliament in 1967, but with no immediate results. In December, the confederations threatened to call a general strike, but withdrew after an appeal by the Prime Minister, Aldo Moro, for further meetings. After the *sindacato* had come to an initial agreement with the government in February 1968, the Cgil unilaterally withdrew its support from the government scheme because of the immediate protest of its members.[7] The confederation called a general strike, which was boycotted by the Cisl and the Uil, but the support for the Cgil's action throughout the country was such as to force the

---

[6] Ginsborg, *A History of Contemporary Italy*, p. 310.

[7] The agreed proposal fixed the pension at 65 per cent of the average of the workers' last three years' earnings provided they had paid 40 years' contributions. The objections were to the government's proposal to raise the retirement age of women from 55 to 60, and to the low level of compensation for existing pensioners.

other confederations also to withdraw their support from the government's pension plan. On 14 November the three confederations jointly called a national general strike, which forced the government to come to a more satisfactory agreement following talks in February 1969.[8]

Although overshadowed by the more dramatic events of the autumn to come, the February agreement represented an important turning-point in the history of the *sindacato*. It was reached after the first national general strike to be called by the three confederations since 1948. Not only was this action an important demonstration of unity, but it also engaged the non-communists, and in particular the Catholics, in a significant show of independence from the Dc government. Equally important, the talks established the *sindacato* as a major interlocutor with the government, at the same time enhancing the legitimacy of its claim to act in a political capacity. Thus the movement's first concrete act as a *soggetto politico* was to negotiate over pensions. This was also the birth of the *sindacato*'s 'reform strategy'.

The Build-up of Tension in the Factories

The mounting social tensions we have discussed were aggravated by the stresses of an industrial system which imposed conditions of work so appalling as to raise public alarm about the high incidence of mental strain in the factories. The statistics were alarming.[9] Ten, twelve, even fifteen-hour days were common practice. In many factories, operatives of forty years of age and over, unable to cope with the fury and pace of machine operations, were being laid off with inadequate pension provision and replaced by younger workers. Alongside the increasing combination of frustration, anxiety and anger generated by conditions at plant level, we have to place the problem of a still-divided *sindacato*, which was far from having solved the problem of union representation at factory

---

[8] The basic pension for 40 years of contributions was raised from 65 per cent of wages prior to retirement, to 74 per cent.

[9] In February 1968 the Milan daily newspaper *Il Giorno* carried a series of investigations into the phenomenon, the results of which surprised the nation.

level. Thus many workers, particularly those belonging to that generation which had not lived through the movement's difficult and traumatic years, cared and understood little about union divisions, and even felt abandoned by the *sindacato*. Much of this resentment found expression in the rank-and-file committees of workers which emerged with a high degree of spontaneity in the factories from early 1968 onwards, and manifested itself in such slogans as '*we* are the *sindacato*' ('il sindacato siamo noi'), which typified the period. But these sentiments, while expressing a deep sense of frustration with official structures, were not a wholesale rejection of the movement. The situation was, in reality, more complex.

Commentators have sometimes given the impression that the rank-and-file committees which emerged in the industrial centres did so in automatic opposition to the official unions. The history of the bewildering variety of popular collectives, action groups, assemblies and works committees which played a part in this cycle of events remains to be written. But it is slowly becoming evident that the *sindacato*, or at least its local members and leaders, will be seen to have served a more positive function than was thought at the time. It has been shown, for instance, that the first inter-union factory committees were organized by official union members in the course of disputes over the renewal of national agreements in 1966.[10] Enrico Galantini further observes that these committees gave rise to assemblies of workers, which received added stimulus from the subsequent involvement of the student movement. A major break with the past occurred at this point. Workers were led by their intolerable working conditions to assert their right to determine the very structure of the working environment. This explains the vigour and ferment underlying the growth of these popular organizations. It also demonstrates that the profoundly anti-capitalist nature of these developments grew out of the experiences of the workers themselves and was not grafted on to the situation from outside by radical groups, although these may have added to the fury and momentum of such developments.

Therefore, the view that has sometimes been expressed that the first rank-and-file committees (*comitati unitari di base*, or Cub)

---

[10] See E. Galantini (ed.), 'Delegati e consigli nei documenti sindacali', p. 108.

to emerge did so in the spring of 1968 is not entirely correct.[11] But this is not to underrate the importance of the Cub. Where the student movement was strongest and most influential within these workers' committees, such as in Milan, Pavia, Trento, Bologna, Pisa, Florence, Rome and Latina, militant elements within them questioned the right of the official unions to represent the workers. In some cases, such as at the Pirelli works in Milan between 1968 and 1969, where workers and members of *Avanguardia Operaia* joined together to create a Cub, rank-and-file committees managed to obtain improvements on agreements already signed by the unions. Whereas this challenge to the official unions was ultimately doomed to failure, since it never gained mass support among the workers, it nevertheless helped bring about an irreversible change in attitudes to workers' rights to self-determination. New demands, which would have come very slowly if at all, from the official unions 'outside the factory', erupted within the heart of the rank-and-file movement: the abolition of piece-work, overtime and methods of production causing undue physical or mental strain; equal pay increases for all and parity between blue- and white-collar workers.

The assertiveness of these new bodies took the official unions by surprise, but here again much of the mythology which has surrounded the period has had a distorting effect. Asked in an interview about these developments shortly after the calming of the storm, the new General Secretary of the Cgil, Luciano Lama, declared that the confederate leadership did not view the 1968 period as one of opposition to the official movement, but 'on the contrary we thought it was a very important development, which certainly contained great dangers, but which would be a strong force for evolution and progress if we could channel it into a strategy of demands for the class'.[12] This was undoubtedly the intention of the Cgil and of the more advanced sections of the other two confederations from the beginning. The major weakness of the Cub was that they were not equipped for such a strategic task. Not

---

[11] See, for example, G. Bianchi, F. Frigo, P. Merli-Brandini, A. Merolla, *I Cub: comitati unitari di base*, pp. 11ff.

[12] 'Dieci anni di processo unitario. Conversazione con Luciano Lama', p. 18.

surprisingly, it was the metalworkers' federations which were most sympathetic to the new groups. The communists in particular understood that in order to have a long-term effect once their initial *élan* had subsided, their demands would have to be promoted by the official unions, but to do so they, in turn, would have to act quickly and adapt their organizations to accommodate new forms of rank-and-file participation.

The waves of conflict which began in 1968 were continuous until the 'Hot Autumn' of 1969 and beyond. The disputes gathered momentum, drew new conflictual actors into the arena, and from early 1968 gradually spread to industries and localities which had previously been strike-free. The wide diffusion of conflict eventually involved skilled workers, young non-unionised southern immigrants, women, white-collar workers and public sector employees, and saw the creation of new, inventive forms of industrial action. Contrary to much of what has been said about the period, in many of the important strikes, such as the 'wildcat shop strikes in the summer of 1968 at Pirelli, and in the spring of 1969 at Fiat the first shops to stop spontaneously were those composed largely of skilled workers from northern regions'.[13] These workers, moreover, were attempting to maintain their privileges *vis-à-vis* other groups of workers. More typical, perhaps, of the period was the strike at the Montecatini and Edison works in July 1968, where the demands of the workers went well beyond the proposals of the official chemical workers' federations representing them. The workers rejected the link between wage increases and productivity, and demanded equal pay increases for all grades of workers. Students joined in the protest, the strike gained widespread support, and eventually the whole of the chemical sector was forced to renegotiate agreements made earlier. By the end of the year workers all over the country were demanding equal pay rises and equal status with white-collar workers. This dispute, and many which followed its example, saw the official unions either pushed to the margins or forced to present to management demands decided upon directly at workers' assemblies over which they had little control.

The intensity and force of the protest was evident by the close of 1968. Although this was a year in which no major category

---

[13] I. Regalia, M. Regini and E. Reyneri, 'Labour Conflicts and Industrial Relations in Italy', p. 109.

agreements were due for renewal, there had been 3,870 plant agreements involving 1,568,293 workers and 33.5 million hours of strike action.[14] But its significance, as it moved close to its climax in the 'Hot Autumn' of 1969, lay in the developments which had taken place below the surface of the turbulent events. For the first time in the postwar history of the movement, the workers were speaking for themselves in a manner which could not be ignored. By 1968 it was clear to the confederations that speedy and massive restructuring would have to be undertaken to regain a position of influence at plant level. The nature of working-class demands had undergone a qualitative shift and presented a challenge to the very system of production well beyond anything the official unions had been prepared to mount. Numerous commentators have talked about the large number of Catholic labour leaders who were radicalised by the experiences of 1968-9. An important precondition for this change was the fact that the masses of Catholic workers, influenced by the process of secularisation already in progress, now abandoned all vestiges of traditional Catholic reserve towards ideas of conflict. The long-standing confederate and federal rivalries had become meaningless to these workers. It mattered little in the popular committees and assemblies whether workers were Catholic or communist. This would put increasing pressure on the unions to strive for unity. Yet in spite of union shortcomings, and of the ultra-leftist critiques which exposed them mercilessly, the new rank-and-file organizations emerged to compensate for existing weaknesses rather than destroy what was already in place:

> The new production line and piece-work delegates, the unitary strike committees, superseded the old structures and replaced them without direct confrontation, sometimes even without discussion. It was a juncture, created in 1968, in which *spontaneity created organization*, because now worker autonomy was an active force and created what was lacking without wanting to destroy what was shaky. In fact, in many situations these new organizations appeared in order to fill a void.[15]

---

[14] See Bianchi, *Storia dei sindacati in Italia*, p. 166.

[15] Accornero, 'Per una nuova fase di studi sul movimento sindacale', p. 56.

The 'autunno caldo' of 1969

Notwithstanding the radicalising force underlying worker protest from 1968 to the middle of 1969, the 'Hot Autumn' was the point at which the unions regained the initiative and began to take control of rank-and-file organizations in what became thereafter an irreversibly transformed industrial relations system. A further intensification of protest was inevitable, given that in the autumn of 1969 agreements were due for renewal in all the major industrial, agricultural and service sectors. The 'autunno caldo' was thus principally a period of heightened *contractual* conflict in which the official unions were necessarily involved. This was an important vantage point, which provided them with the opportunity to regain their somewhat weakened hegemony over the movement and deal with the protestations of the ultra-left and radical groups. Success in regaining a position of leadership was far from being a foregone conclusion, however, and would depend on the *sindacato*'s ability to succeed in reflecting the new mood of the working class.

In an almost symbolic manner, the autumn season of disputes opened, after the traditional national holiday period, with a strike at two Fiat workshops in Turin on 1 September 1969. The strike was not initiated by the official unions. In May, June and July, the city had already witnessed a series of strikes organized by joint committees of workers and students alongside official union activity. On 3 July an official one-day general strike was accompanied by a parallel demonstration organized by the ultra-left, which ended in a running battle with the police, and became known as the battle of Corso Traiano. Such events convinced the official unions still further that they had to take control of events. The autumn strike of 1 September was the eighty-fourth dispute at Fiat since the beginning of the year and the first after the summer recess. It was occasioned by the company's refusal to honour an agreement made in June concerning the reclassification of a large number of workers. Within days the stoppage brought other sections of the plant to a standstill, and the management suspended those unable to work. In itself, the strike was not a huge success in terms of volume of support, though it was extremely disruptive. The official unions intervened, and the employers, clearly worried by now about low production levels, dropped the suspensions, and work resumed normally on 6 September. The management thought it had obtained at least a partial victory in not capitulating to the original demands. In reality, the management decision had allowed the metalworkers' federations to gain control of the workers' demands by putting themselves at the head of the industrial action.[16] The suspension of the strike was only the prelude to a more strategic initiative for which the federations had been preparing for some time.

On 25 September, encouraged by the apparent success of Fiat, Pirelli decided to respond to a strike in its own works by introducing a lockout. On that very day, tens of thousands of metalworkers converged on Turin from all over the country, marching through the city. The period of the large open assemblies in the country's major cities had begun. By entering the fray, Pirelli simply inflamed the situation, for the chemical workers' national agreements were themselves due for renewal. Workers in other industries began to prepare for battle in a growing mood of intransigence on all sides. In October, tens of thousands of construction workers demonstrated and held rallies in Rome, adding urban and housing demands to their negotiations. By now, all the major categories of industrial workers were in dispute, and conflict began to spread to the public sector, to hospital workers, the services sector and agriculture. Strike action became increasingly frequent and varied in form: wildcat strikes, staggered or selective strikes, sit-down strikes, strikes in shifts or chequered strikes, demonstrations and marches *within* the factory to draw in stragglers, and other forms of disruptive activity. For the first time since the days of liberation, meetings and rallies were held inside the factory gates at Fiat and other large establishments. Contrary to precedent, industrial action continued *during* negotiations, something not even the official unions could have prevented. The activities of the 'Hot Autumn' involved a total of 5.5 million workers all over the country. It was the most profound manifestation of worker discontent in the country's history.

In spite of a widespread feeling that the situation was out of control, a different picture begins to emerge if we focus our analysis on the activities of the official unions. In July 1969, that

---

[16] During the dispute, radical elements from outside were allowed access to workshops and sections of the factory. Union leaders at the time saw this uncharacteristic relaxation of vigilance as a deliberate attempt to undermine and disrupt official union organization.

is before the events we have just described, the three metalworkers' federations, FIM, FIOM and UILM, after the most extensive rank-and-file consultations ever witnessed, took the unprecedented step of organizing a conference at which they jointly prepared the platform of demands they would present to the Confindustria for the whole industry.[17] The new types of demand were the most important, and would prove to be the most contentious. The first of these, about which the communists were uneasy, for fear of alienating skilled operatives, was the claim for equal pay increases for all categories of workers. The working week was to be reduced to 40 hours, with 5 working days. Blue- and white-collar workers were to have equal status. Finally, the federations were demanding the formal recognition of union representation within the factory. Plant union representatives, moreover, were to be recognised not simply for the purposes of consultation, but as negotiators. Further pressure was put on the employers by the new Dc Minister of Labour, Donat Cattin, who supported the federations' wage demands, declaring that they were modest by comparison with increased profits and the amount of capital being invested abroad.[18]

Following their earlier success over pensions in February 1969, the confederations were once again on the move. During the time of the troubles at Fiat in September, the Cgil proposed further social objectives for the movement. These were discussed and agreed by the three confederations Cgil, Cisl and Uil in early October. The confederations thus initiated a fresh 'dispute' with the government, demanding an immediate and concrete commitment to reforms in housing, rent control, health provision and taxes. The strategic sense and leadership of the Cgil was crucial in the new reform strategy. Its objective was to take advantage of the mood of the times and mobilise sectors of the population not directly involved in industrial disputes, such as the unemployed, pensioners and families on low incomes and in poor housing conditions. Despite the reservations of some Cisl *contrattualisti*, who complained that a new set of *social* demands would create confusion during a period of *industrial* conflict, such demands in

---

[17] Barkan, in *Visions of Emancipation*, pp. 74ff, estimates that 2,300 assemblies were held around the country, involving 300,000 workers.

[18] The statements were made in an interview given to the weekly *Panorama*, 15 September 1969.

fact displayed an enormous mobilising capacity. The new goals also considerably enriched, and gave a clearer sense of direction to the emerging *political* identity of the *sindacato*. The confederations called a national general strike for 19 November to press for their demands. It was the most widely supported general strike ever seen in Italy. Empty cities with closed shops saw only columns of marchers crossing their streets. Sectors of the population with no previous record of involvement in protest joined forces with workers in a common expression of discontent.[19] The success of the occasion confirmed the movement's capacity to mobilise support for its new reform strategy and gave greater legitimacy to the *sindacato*'s declared intention to promote the interests of working people and their families in wider areas of social policy.

The events of 19 November had repercussions on the other major dispute in progress, namely that between the employers and the metalworkers' federations, for which the latter had prepared. Early in the discussions the employers had insisted that national agreements should be a guarantee against plant-level disputes. In the wake of the high point of activity of the rank-and-file committees in 1968, and in the light of their own conversion to plant-level negotiations, the federations would have destroyed the very credibility they were attempting to regain had they agreed to bind the workers in such a manner. In any case, they could not have done so even if they had wished. The employers thus withdrew from the talks in September and rejected calls for further discussion. After the success of the general strike of 19 November, the FIM, FIOM and UILM called a national metalworkers' strike for 29 November. The widespread support it received led the state-holding sector employers' association, the Intersind, to negotiate. There was undoubtedly government pressure behind the Intersind's willingness to do so. The metalworkers intensified their action against the intransigence of the Confindustria. In an atmosphere of national anxiety about the possible consequences of mounting tension, the Minister of Labour made a series of appeals

---

[19] A policeman was killed in clashes with radical groups in Milan. This incident was used by the political right to call for the use of emergency powers by the government. Fiat, with no evidence of involvement, immediately suspended 260 activists, but was persuaded to withdraw this hasty measure after a meeting with union leaders and the Minister of Labour.

to the Confindustria to negotiate. Shortly after the last of the meetings at which these appeals were made, on the morning of 12 December, bombs exploded in banks in Milan and Rome and at the national war monument in the capital, the *Altare della Patria.* The incident, for the timing of the explosions was clearly co-ordinated, shocked the nation. Sixteen people were killed at Piazza Fontana in Milan. The slaughter was initially blamed on radical left-wing groups and suspects were immediately arrested. The whole episode, which included the alleged suicide of an anarchist detainee in suspicious circumstances, was later found to be the work of the extreme right. The intention was to destabilise the political situation in a moment of great tension, to generate a state of emergency and provide the conditions for the creation of a government prepared to impose its authority. This was the the beginning of the extreme right's 'strategy of tension'.

In this tense political climate there was talk of 'coups' from the right. Nevertheless, in time-honoured fashion, the security forces arrested thousands of union activists. The movement continued its protest. The government, clearly worried by the continued unrest, held a series of meetings with the employers at the Ministry of Labour. What transpired is unknown to this day, but on 21 December the Confindustria agreed to most of the unions' demands: the 40-hour week; equal pay rises of a substantial nature for all categories of workers; the right of assembly in the workplace and the recognition of the workers' committees or councils.

The workers' movement emerged from the 'Hot Autumn' into a new phase of its history with unprecedented strength. A new, deeply-rooted rank-and-file democracy gave strength and legitimacy to the factory-level organizations which had been created. Membership of the official unions increased and reinforced the *sindacato's* recently developed multiple role as a force for social, as well as economic advancement. It was now necessary to consolidate the achievements of the rank-and-file organizations in the factory.

12

The Consolidation of Representation in the Workplace

The Formation of the Factory Councils

The structure and organization of the early factory councils (*consigli di fabbrica*) varied considerably from one establishment to another, so that the relationship between these new bodies and the official unions did not conform to a single pattern. By late 1969 the latter had regained the initiative in the factories, but in a completely changed environment. According to one study carried out at the time, 90 per cent of the delegates of the new workers' committees were members of official unions. Well over half of them were close to parliamentary parties of the left, a sizeable number had links with the Dc left, and about 12 per cent were sympathetic to extra-parliamentary groups.[1] At first glance such figures seem to indicate a close assimilation to traditional forms of leadership, but such a conclusion would be highly misleading.

After regaining the initiative in the disputes of the 'autunno caldo', the *sindacato* had to decide how to relate to the new rank-and-file bodies which had emerged in the factories. The debates within the movement suggested a range of options. Should the official unions create their own parallel organizations alongside the new committees, or should they accept the new committees in some agreed form as the factory negotiating bodies? If the latter option were chosen, how would the new organs relate to the official unions outside the factory? The final settlement, in which the factory councils were accepted by the *sindacato* as its official voice, was in fact strongly conditioned by the events of the 'Hot Autumn'. During this period, in spite of the problems to which such a settlement gave rise, its advantages had become clear to all concerned. About sixty national contracts had come up for renewal.

---

[1] See R. Aglieta, G. Bianchi and P. Merli-Brandini, *I delegati operai*, pp. 86ff.

In the course of the ensuing disputes and negotiations the unions successfully rallied the workers around coherent unitary platforms and consolidated their own leadership into the bargain. In the process, the limitations of the factory councils also became evident. Only a broader organizational framework could generalise demands which emerged from particular plants and incorporate them into national programmes. There was also the advantage that the confederations could co-ordinate the campaigning activities of various categories of workers. Radical, non-union activists, despite their revolutionary rhetoric, were unable to match these advantages in strategic terms, and began to decline in number and influence.

The *consigli di fabbrica* were unique in the history of the labour movement. A brief analysis of how their eventual structure was established will make this clear. The *sindacato* faced a difficult problem when it began to discuss the future pattern of worker representation at plant level, for no clear organizational model emerged from the period of intense protest. Rank-and-file mobilisation had developed in the heat of the struggles, without any agreement over the shape and functions of any future organization. The *sindacato* had to reflect on the structural patterns of the new movements which had emerged, in order to find a model which could channel their energies and aspirations.

One of the most striking of these developments, and perhaps the most difficult for the unions to control, was the 'assembly' of all the workers, unionised and non-unionised. Following the earlier student assemblies, and partly through contact with them, there had been an impressive development of *gruppi di studio, comitati unitari di base* (Cub) and *comitati di agitazione*, particularly in factories in the North. Some of these groups, such as those at the Philips (Milan) and Dalmine (Bergamo) factories, which were created to study the problems of white-collar workers, were direct union initiatives.[2] Such committees or groups soon developed the practice of calling assemblies of all the workers in order to achieve wider consultation. The assemblies, because of their broad-based representative nature, acquired prestige and quickly became centres for decision-making. In many of the plant agreements reached in 1968, the employers recognised the 'right of assembly' in the

---

[2] See G. Couffignal, *I sindacati in Italia*, p. 226.

workplace for the first time. The print workers' national agreement in February 1968, for example, sanctioned this right for all firms with more than forty employees. The disputes led by the official unions during the 'autunno caldo' in the following year were reinforced by the widespread support from the workers' assemblies.

The debates within the unions focused on the problems posed by assemblies which included non-members. Should there be separate assemblies for union members? If the different assemblies expressed divergent views, should the *sindacato* put forward the demands of only the unionised workers? It was clear that the vigour and strength of the new rank-and-file movement lay precisely in its unitary force. To introduce an element of division would weaken the movement, deprive the unions of much of the new support they were gaining, and be swimming against the tide of events. The 'Hot Autumn' thus delivered a heavy blow to the *associazionismo*, which had such deep roots within the Catholic labour tradition.

Almost as problematic for the unions was the figure of the *delegato*, destined to become the negotiator at plant level. The earliest reference to the term appears in plant agreements in the electrodomestic sector in the mid-sixties.[3] Frequently referred to as *delegati di cottimo* (piece-work delegates), and initially nominated by the unions rather than elected by the workforce, in the disputes of 1968 and 1969 *delegati* began to emerge in a baffling variety of ways: as a result of plant agreements; as union nominees; as delegates elected by plant sections or workshops during disputes; and as workers chosen by assemblies to chair discussions, to organize industrial action or maintain contact with official unions.[4]

Understandably, the *sindacato* was anxious to bring some uniformity into the system of electing delegates. By the time of the 'Hot Autumn', the *delegati* had become the automatic negotiators for the assemblies, which were by now an established feature of plant-level activity and were increasingly determined to appoint their own nominees. The vast majority of the *delegati* were union members, but this did not mean that they had previously been active in union affairs, a fact which caused the *sindacato* some concern. There were, however, compelling reasons for accepting a system of representation which had emerged so powerfully from the

[3] See Cella e Treu, *Relazioni industriali*, p. 113.

[4] See E. Guidi, 'Analisi e valutazione degli accordi sui delegati', pp. 54-72.

rank-and-file, who were asserting their determination to achieve not only improved wages and conditions, but also greater control over the whole process of production. This made a deep impression on the leadership of the confederations, particularly in the Cgil. Moreover, the workers were now less inclined to entrust the representation of their demands to delegates appointed from outside. Given the criticism which the official unions had received prior to the 'autunno caldo', this new development could not be ignored. That such criticism was often mixed with loyalty to the movement was not clear to all within the *sindacato* at the time. The desire to retain control over the delegates was forcefully expressed in a policy document produced by Fiat workers in May 1969. It is worth quoting parts of this document to provide a flavour of the atmosphere within which the *sindacato* had to operate.

> The strength and power which we have won recently must become permanent ...
> In all workshops, in all sections of the plant, we must *create assemblies and choose delegates* and use the force of industrial action and unity to bring about a complete change in our working conditions *through worker control.*
> It is essential to unite the workers' delegates in a powerful and united *workers' delegate movement* for the purpose of exercising permanent workers' control over conditions of work ...
> The assembly is the instrument through which workers, united in work-groups, plant sections and workshops, discuss and decide on objectives and assert their power and control over work.
> The assembly appoints delegates and can recall them at any stage ...
> The workers' delegate ... is neither nominated nor chosen by any organization outside the factory ... and *is therefore responsible solely to the workers and to nobody else.*[5]

It is clear with hindsight that the sense of suspicion towards the official unions, which was in some ways the product of Fiat's own industrial relations history, and which is the sub-text of the policy document, was not so strong in other establishments. Numerous empirical studies have confirmed this view.[6] But in the turbulent atmosphere of 1969 the confederations could not be sure of it.

---

[5] Foa, *Sindacati e lotte operaie*, Documenti della storia 10, pp. 174-5.

[6] See, for example, *Delegati e consigli di fabbrica in Italia.*

There was, however, for the official unions, something particularly worrying about the notion, expressed in the Fiat delegates' document, of a 'workers' delegate movement'. The Cgil in particular was concerned that plant-level representation, if too delegate-centred, would weaken the movement's broader strategic objectives and introduce divisions between workers from different plants and industries. The official unions had recently had some notable successes in uniting workers across industries and the country's traditional North/South divide. For example, the successful campaign which was led by the metalworkers' federations against the regional wage traps (*gabbie salariali*), and which had the full support of workers in the North where wages were higher, was typical of the new spirit of solidarity, which was winning new members among southern workers.[7] It was therefore essential to inject a coherent strategic direction into the sense of self-determination which was being expressed by the delegates' movement.

The debates on the role of the factory councils were lively and wide-ranging.[8] Among the more radical groups, positions varied considerably, from an outright rejection by *Lotta Continua*, which saw the councils as organs whereby the unions and employers would attempt to stifle the increase in spontaneous struggles,[9] to an enthusiastic welcome by *Il Manifesto*.[10] Comparisons were made with the factory councils of Gramsci's early years in Turin. But many Cgil communists denied that there could be any meaningful comparison between the factory councils of the late 1960s and those of Gramsci's day. While there was indeed in the rank-and-file factory organizations of the late sixties a desire to question fundamental aspects of capitalist production, Gramsci's factory

---

[7] See the document produced by the FIM-FIOM-UILM of Turin on the occasion of the national strike against the *gabbie salariali* in February 1969, in Foa, *Sindacati e lotte operaie*, pp. 171-3.

[8] See Couffignal, *I sindacati in Italia*, pp. 236-55, and M. Bergamaschi, *Statuti dei consigli di fabbrica*, pp. 49-67.

[9] *Lotta Continua* subsequently modified its position. See L. Bobbio, *Lotta Continua: Storia di una organizzazione rivoluzionaria*, pp. 60ff.

[10] See L. Castellina, 'Il movimento dei delegati', in *Il Manifesto*, n. 1, gennaio 1970, pp. 26-7.

councils were part of a wholesale revolutionary strategy challenging the very existence of the bourgeois order. Luciano Lama, General Secretary of the Cgil from 1970, later explained his confederation's position on this aspect of the radical left's argument:

> First of all, we have always firmly rejected the notion that there could emerge in the factories a movement alien to the *sindacato*, a kind of Soviet, councils of delegates aiming to overturn the country's political system ... as potential alternatives to parliament, the government and political parties, in other words in opposition to the institutions of the Republic.[11]

Many of the reservations which were felt towards the councils of delegates by confederate leaders came from the latter's failure to understand how limited the influence of the radical groups and charismatic figures really was among the rank-and-file. The genuine desire among the masses of workers to exercise more control over the system of production was not identical to the revolutionary objectives of the more radical groups, despite the latter's claims that they were. The leaders of the metalworkers' federations, particularly the FIM and the FIOM, who had been at the forefront of workers' struggles throughout the sixties, were able to distinguish more readily between mass movements and the smaller circles of ultra-left activists. For this reason, the FIM and the FIOM were pressing heavily from late 1969 for the confederations to declare their support for the factory councils.

The most constructive ideas about the councils came from the left of both the Cgil and the Cisl, particularly from within the FIOM and the FIM. Initially, many Catholics were, if anything, more adventurous than the communists in their total acceptance of the new bodies as the representatives of the official unions at plant level, even though the Catholic federations as a whole were more cautious than the communists. There were good reasons for the initial hesitation of the communists. They possessed, after all, over the whole spectrum of industrial federations, the highest number of disciplined and trained cadres whom they were anxious should not be excluded. In the end, however, the positions of the FIM and FIOM which eventually won the day, converged on essentials. The

---

[11] Lama, *Intervista sul sindacato*, p. 53.

factory delegates, it was agreed, elected by the workshop assemblies, and organized in councils, were the most direct expression of rank-and-file democracy. The *sindacato* should thus accept them, including non-unionised delegates, as their own structure, within the factory, with full negotiating powers. Since the councils had clearly swept aside all traditional confederate and federal divisions, they were to serve as the starting-point for the construction of an organically united workers' movement.

By early 1970 workers at many plants were drawing up statutes for factory councils.[12] In 1970 the factory councils became the official choice of the FIOM, the FIM and the UILM.[13] Together, the FIM-FIOM-UILM then prepared a model statute for factory councils.[14] A few months later, the executive of the Cgil also accepted them as the plant negotiating bodies.[15] The Cisl and the Uil took longer to be won over, but by July 1972 they too had officially recognised the factory councils as the unitary representatives of all the unions at plant level.[16]

The essential feature of the factory council was that its delegates were elected by workshop assemblies of all the workers, whether unionised or not. With the normalisation of relations between unions and employers it soon became apparent that only committed union members were prepared to take on the heavy burden of a delegate's responsibilities. In large establishments the council both elected an executive and created sub-committees with special responsibilities and expertise in particular areas. Where the legitimacy of its decisions or of its policy direction was in question,

---

[12] Numerous examples of statutes can be found in M. Bergamaschi, *Statuti dei consigli di fabbrica.*

[13] For the important role of the FIOM in subsequent developments see L. Albanese, F. Liuzzi and A. Perella, *I consigli di fabbrica,* pp. 34ff.

[14] This is reproduced in T. Treu, *Sindacato e rappresentanze aziendali,* pp. 289-91.

[15] See the document of approval reprinted in *Quaderni di rassegna sindacale,* n. 100, gennaio-febbraio 1983, pp. 54-5.

[16] The recognition formed part of the *Patto federativo* of the Cgil-Cisl-Uil. The full text of the *Patto* can be found in G. Giugni, *Diritto sindacale,* Appendix I, pp. 269-72.

an appeal was made to the plant assembly.[17]

An extension of the factory councils at the territorial level was promoted initially by the FIOM, and supported by the other metalworkers' federations, and subsequently by the textile unions. The *consigli di zona*, as the name implies, were intended to co-ordinate the activities and demands of various categories of workers at local area level. Although these bodies were not successful in taking root, they did add to the stimulus towards unity which was already inherent in the factory councils. It was clearly anomalous to operate in a unitary manner at the level of the factory or plant and yet retain the traditional divisions at all federal and confederate levels. However, before examining the renewed call for organic unity, we must turn our attention briefly to the question of how the profound changes in the social standing of the movement were reflected in the legal framework of Italian society.

The *statuto dei lavoratori*

The demand for a statute or charter to protect the rights of workers was first made by Di Vittorio at the Third Cgil Congress in 1952, during the period of febrile anti-communism in the factories. Despite article 39 of the Constitution which guaranteed freedom of union activity, Di Vittorio's initiative was not supported by the Cisl or the Uil. Article 3 of the Constitution, which affirms the right of 'all *workers* to participate in the political, economic and social organization of the nation', also protects all citizens against discrimination on the basis of sex, religion, race or political beliefs.[18] Debate on the need for legislation received greater impetus after the famous case of the dismissal from Fiat, in January 1952, of the company's Director of Welfare Services, Giovanni Battista Santhià, for belonging to the Pci. Still the Cgil remained isolated in its call for legislation throughout the 1950s. The Cisl argued in favour of a 'contractual' approach to protecting workers' rights in the factory, which in practice, given the habit of excluding the

---

[17] For further details, see I. Regalia, *Eletti e abbandonati. Modelli e stili di rappresentanza in fabbrica,* pp. 145ff.

[18] *Costituzione italiana*, p. 3. My italics

communist unions from negotiations and the strong employer ascendancy, amounted to no protection at all. But a more fundamental objection to the Cisl position was the argument that the constitutional right to belong to a union or party without fear of reprisal ought to be enshrined in legislation and did not need to be negotiated with employers.

With the labour struggles of the early 1960s, the attitude of Catholics began to change. The question of the need for protective legislation was kept alive by the Cgil, particularly in the pages of its labour law journal, *Rivista giuridica del lavoro*. The first centre-left government, led by Aldo Moro from December 1963, committed itself to examining the issue, included it in its development plan for 1965-70, and asked the employers and the unions for their views. The Cisl was by now also in favour of legislation.[19] Between 1966 and 1968, the Psi came to favour legislation. This meant that the centre of gravity within the government coalition began to shift in favour of acting upon the proposal for a *statuto*.

From early 1969, when protest started to switch from the social to the industrial scene, the government began to pay more attention to the drafting of a *statuto*. This created the suspicion within parts of the *sindacato*, and even more on the extra-parliamentary left, that one of its main purposes was to stifle protest and the development of rank-and-file mobilisation in the factories. There is no doubt that the relatively speedy enactment of the *statuto* was the outcome of the events of 1969. But this fact does not in itself either reveal the motives of its drafters or determine the final thrust of the document. In the first place, the conspiratorial suspicions of the ultra-left were belied by the opposition of the employers to a *statuto*. Secondly, the overriding concern of the government was to restore a measure of stability, which the lack of protective legislation had clearly undermined, in a situation in which the terrorist acts of December 1969 seemed to be creating a crisis of law and order, with unpredictable consequences. Accordingly, the government looked increasingly to legislation in order to resolve a long-standing malaise in the

---

[19] For an account of the debates about what such legislation should cover, see M. Ricciardi, 'La Cgil e lo statuto dei lavoratori', pp. 157-70, and M. Grandi, *L'attività sindacale nell'impresa*, pp. 3ff. Grandi argues that, in spite of their debates, it was not the unions who made the running on legislation.

country's system of industrial relations, one which all by now recognised as having left 'the power of employers virtually unchallenged'.[20] Draft proposals were amended in response to the unions, and the suspicions of many on the left of the *sindacato* began to diminish.

The extra-parliamentary left, however, remained implacably hostile and referred disparagingly to the new charter as a *statuto dei diritti del sindacato*, that is, guaranteeing the rights of the unions, as opposed to those of the workers. In reality, the *sindacato* was reluctant to have its own rights defined too closely, since this could restrict its manoeuvrability. The protection afforded to workers, however, was very specific. In fact, 'even before the passage of the *statuto*, there was a gradual but almost constant increase in the use of the courts to resolve industrial disputes, particularly on the part of workers, who quickly perceived that the courts were deciding more and more often in their favour'.[21] Legislation thus put the seal on a process already in motion. The conscience of the nation had been pricked. Even a casual reading of the *statuto* shows clearly that it is the *workers'* rights which are its central concern. The rights and duties of unions are firmly conditional on the those of the workers.[22] Luciano Lama has appraised the position accurately:

> The *statuto* has its point of departure in the defence of the rights of individual workers. This is its major feature. The right to organize unions derives from the sum of the rights of individual workers, as does any power which the *sindacato* may have. For example, the *statuto* states that workers have the right to meet in assemblies, whether or not unions exist in the factory. In turn, an assembly can establish itself as a *sindacato* and it is at this point that the rights of union organizations come into play.[23]

The *statuto dei lavoratori* was approved by parliament in its

---

[20] Romagnoli e Treu, *I sindacati in Italia*, pp. 84-5.

[21] Tarrow, *Democracy and Disorder*, p. 313. See also the statistical graph on which Tarrow's assertion is based.

[22] See Giugni, *Diritto sindacale*, pp. 56ff.

[23] Lama, *Intervista sul sindacato*, p. 58. The relevant parts of the *statuto* are Section II, articles 14-15, and Section III, articles 19-27.

final form in May 1970.[24] It was the first significant piece of labour legislation to follow the promulgation of the Constitution in January 1948. It is possible to perceive from its articles the history of labour repression in Italy. The *statuto* guarantees workers the right to express, in their place of work, their religious, political and union views without fear of reprisals, and pointedly denies employers the right to conduct investigations into the opinions of their employees (arts 1 and 8). The surveillance of workers through the aid of audio-visual equipment and specially-employed guards is either prohibited or subject to certain requirements (arts 2, 3, 4 and 6). Important principles are laid down on such matters as health and safety (arts 5 and 9), disciplinary procedures (art. 7) and the right of employees to insist on compliance with job descriptions (art. 13). Penalties are prescribed for employers found guilty of dismissal without 'just cause' (art. 18).

Regarding union activity itself, workers are free to establish unions in the workplace, and are protected against discrimination for belonging, or not belonging to unions and for engaging in union activity (arts 14, 15 and 28). Employers are forbidden to finance or create unions of their own (art. 17). Freedom of assembly is guaranteed in the workplace (art. 20), and workers are free to establish unions affiliated to confederations or otherwise (art. 19). Wherever a union is established, it enjoys the right to display information, levy dues and have premises provided to conduct its affairs (arts 25, 26 and 27). Workers elected to union or political positions, at national or local level, have rights either of exemption from work or of job retention while in office (arts 31 and 32).

The passing of the *statuto* in May 1970 was important for consolidating the new legitimacy which the workers' movement had achieved in the public mind over the previous decade.[25] It not only granted protection against a return to the levels of anti-union repression witnessed during the 1950s, but also placed Italian labour law at the forefront of European systems in protecting both the individual and collective rights of working people.

---

[24] Legge 20 maggio 1970, n. 300.

[25] For the full text of the *statuto*, see L. Pestalozza, *La costituzione e lo stato*, pp. 335-49.

13

Broadening the Sphere of Action: From Workplace to Society

New Conflictual Agents

The cycle of protest which led to the 'Hot Autumn' of 1969 engendered a transformation in the Italian industrial relations system in which the *sindacato* achieved a new social and ideological legitimacy. Its fluctuating positions of relative strength and weakness *vis-à-vis* employers and government would henceforth operate within new boundaries. Immediately after the 'autunno caldo', the movement extended the scope of its demands in both the industrial and political spheres. It was able to do this because its conflictual capacity had, in a short space of time, acquired a force well beyond anything which could have been predicted. Not only had the popular committees and assemblies of the late sixties developed a staggering variety of forms of industrial action, but they had given vast, formerly non-militant sections of the population their first experiences of conflict and resistance.

The period of heightened protest lasted from 1968 to 1972. Among workers in industry the most significant change was the increase in the militancy of unskilled and semi-skilled workers (*operai comuni*). Strictly in terms of pay and the working environment the conditions of these groups of workers had been even more intolerable than those of their skilled colleagues, on whom the more militant Cgil had traditionally relied for support. There was thus an even larger pool of labour now ready to mobilise in its own interests. The demands of these *operai comuni* for equal pay increases, for regrading, for the rejection of Taylorist working methods and for the reduction of noise and other health hazards drew on new areas of support, particularly from the socialist left and the Catholic left, namely from those elements of the labour movement traditionally less dependent on a skilled workforce for the recruitment of cadres.[1] The centre of gravity of industrial protest had thus shifted decisively to the centre of the mass of workers. The unskilled Catholic worker of southern extraction was now just as prone to industrial action as the politicised skilled operative close to the Pci. The added strength this gave to the bargaining power of the *sindacato* was incalculable in this period.

The enlargement of the conflictual base of Italian society was not, however, restricted to the industrial working class. In addition to the dramatic and sustained increase in union membership set in motion by the events of 1969 among industrial workers, there was an equally consistent growth of membership in the public sector which, for example, raised the teacher membership of the Cgil from about 4,000 in 1968 to 90,000 by 1975. Sidney Tarrow's detailed study of the period of protest shows how the strike, 'the quintessential weapon of the industrial working class ... became a conventional expression of dissent or a bargaining tool among such groups as civil servants, bank clerks, doctors and lawyers, who had previously tried to differentiate themselves from the proletariat.'[2] Many of the strikes in the public sector which followed the 'autunno caldo', were aimed at keeping pace with the gains of workers in industry. Moreover, employees in the public sector were important, 'for their strikes could damage consumers, commuters, pensioners, and welfare clients. Tram drivers, customs officials, Finance Ministry clerks, toll collectors and licensing officials may not be central to the productive apparatus of a capitalist society, but they can disrupt its daily life more easily than most workers'.[3]

From about 1973, the movement of the 'organized unemployed' (*disoccupati organizzati*) took hold in Naples and tried to break the corrupt and clientelistic system of job allocation in the city. Although not hugely successful in the long term, it gained the grudging recognition of the official unions, helped raise the combative spirit of the local unemployed, and for a few years gave hope and purpose to its thousands of active members.

---

[1] See E. Reyneri, 'Il ruolo della Cisl nel ciclo di lotte 1968-1972', pp. 737ff.

[2] Tarrow, *Democracy and Disorder*, p. 71.

[3] Ibid., p. 93.

Both in the industrial and tertiary sectors the increased participation of women in strike action and protest movements also strengthened the hand of the unions, although it cannot be said that problems relating to sexual discrimination in employment were high on the *sindacato*'s own agenda at the time.[4] The general increase in activity of that section of society which had traditionally been most reluctant to take part in protest was indicative of a profound change in the *senso comune* of Italian society. It was yet another sign that the psychological and ideological barriers to conflictual activity, deeply-rooted in the Catholic tradition, had broken down.

Further evidence of this was the decisive shift of important sections of the Cisl towards the acceptance of a conflictual model of industrial relations. Although the Catholic labour movement as a whole had adapted to the inevitability of conflict as a component of industrial relations in a modern society, significant portions of the Cisl, particularly the industrial federations, consolidated the explicit class positions which had been emerging within their organizations from the mid-sixties.[5] Even the Acli had adopted such positions, to the dismay of the Catholic hierarchy. On 6 March 1970 the Acli President, Emilio Gabaglio, was summoned before the Cei to receive an official letter of protest over the political direction the movement had taken. The bishops were concerned that the Acli had adopted the subversive postures of the Church's traditional enemies, which did not befit a social movement of Catholic workers.[6]

Unions and Employers: New Relations of Power in the Workplace

In the early 1970s, the Italian workers' movement enjoyed a degree of social and ideological hegemony unparalleled in its history.

---

[4] See B. Beccalli, 'Le politiche del lavoro femminile in Italia', pp. 253ff.

[5] See Baglioni, *Il sindacato dell'autonomia*, pp. 183ff. Baglioni's writings are themselves part of the corpus of these ideological developments.

[6] For the text of the episcopal letter, see Boschini, *Chiesa e Acli*, pp. 128-40.

Equally, its bargaining position was at its strongest. It was thus well placed to increase both the substance and range of its demands in negotiations with the employers. But important changes had also taken place within the *sindacato* itself. The *operaio comune*, or unskilled worker, and his egalitarian demands had acquired a central position on questions relating to pay.

Egalitarian demands had been proposed as early as 1966 by ultra-left groups to win the support of the mass of unskilled workers. These were strongly supported by the Catholic labour left, particularly the FIM, which saw in the tendency towards *ugualitarismo* an opportunity to rival the Cgil. At the Cgil Congress in 1969, Luciano Lama had in effect proposed the rejection of the emerging egalitarian tendency, arguing that 'levels of pay must correspond to levels of skill', and that to ignore this 'would introduce irreconcilable conflict into the ranks of the workers rather than unite them'.[7] Even the FIOM of Turin produced a document in June 1970 making the same case.[8] The communist argument was not simply a defence of the privileges of skilled workers amongst whom the Cgil had its traditional base of support. It did recognise positive features in the new *ugualitarismo* and it conceded that the existing system of differentials was chaotic. The communists insisted, however, that the new strategy which the movement as a whole was developing was trying to increase worker control over production by persuading the employers to acknowledge both the value of workers' skills and also their ability to make constructive proposals about the use of new skills and processes. There was, therefore, a contradiction between arguing for recognition of these skills on the one hand and promoting egalitarian demands which minimised their importance on the other.

In the longer term the communists were to be proved right. But in the short term, *ugualitarismo* was too strong to resist, and by late 1970 the three metalworkers' federations were united in heading a series of fierce disputes with the employers, in which the question of job classification was paramount. The most important of these disputes, the outcome of which was to serve as a model

---

[7] *I congressi della Cgil*, vol. viii, part 1, p. 146.

[8] See the document, 'Mansioni, qualifiche, professionalità e salario nella analisi della FIOM di Torino', pp. 46-8.

not only in industry but also in the public and tertiary sectors, was the one settled between the metalworkers' federations and Italsider in December 1970. In an imaginative compromise between the Catholic egalitarian FIM and the communist-led FIOM, the demand for an *inquadramento unico impiegati-operai* (single scheme of job classification for white- and blue-collar workers) produced a range of categories based on a new and more meaningful classification of skills. After hard negotiations with the employers, the existing system of job classification, with its distinction between 24 grades of blue-collar workers and 16 of white-collar workers, was replaced by a single scale of 8 grades including both.[9] After the Italsider agreement, the *inquadramento unico* was increasingly sought in all industries, reaching a high level of consolidation in contract renewals between 1972 and 1974.[10]

The *inquadramento unico*, however, was for the *sindacato* only one element within a broader set of objectives aimed at achieving control over the working environment. The Marxist and anti-capitalist orientation of the *gruppuscoli* of the late 1960s undoubtedly helped keep the question of worker control of production at the top of the movement's agenda. While rejecting the revolutionary aims of these ultra-leftist groups, the communists nevertheless saw in the new developments a genuine desire among the workers to claim greater control over all aspects of factory life. Although less ideologically compact than the Cgil, the Cisl was equally committed to the idea of greater worker control over the production process. Minority sections of the Catholic confederation, however, more open to the *gruppuscoli* than the communists, were often more radical and less cautious, as was evident from their unrestrained *ugualitarismo*. Within the Cisl as a whole, moreover, there was a new emphasis on the theme of 'alienation' as the product of the Taylorist organization of production. The concept of

---

[9] See A. Lettieri, 'L'inquadramento unico all'Italsider', pp. 48-50.

[10] See, for example, the important agreement on the *inquadramento unico* reached in 1971 at the Breda of Milan. A detailed description of the eight categories agreed upon, along with corresponding pay differentials can be found in R. C. D. Nacamulli (ed.), *Sindacati e organizzazione d'impresa in Italia*, Testo e casi, pp. 274-7. For subsequent agreements in other industries see pp. 336-41 and pp. 602-10.

'alienation' was one which could be shared by most sections of the Catholic movement, uniting those who now argued that capitalist production was inherently oppressive and those who saw the recent wave of protest as a reaction to the employers' sustained attack on the 'dignity of labour', an idea central to Catholic social teaching.

The early seventies witnessed a series of agreements in which control committees were set up to monitor working conditions, health and safety regulations and work rhythms in the factory. By 1973, in many factories, piece-work had been abolished, danger money was rendered superfluous by the installation of safer procedures at the employers' expense, and the reliance on overtime was reduced by a significant increase in pay for normal hours.[11] In addition to such gains, many workers in industry obtained increased holidays and the right to 150 hours' annual paid leave for the pursuit of non-work-related education.[12]

Equally indicative of the *sindacato*'s new assertiveness was its demand to exercise a measure of control over investment, and the use of credit and industrial development, particularly in the South. The 'southern question' was crucial to this aspect of the movement's strategy. From the time of the successful struggles over the *gabbie salariali*, eventually abolished in March 1969, there had been a rapid unionisation of southern workers, particularly in those areas with the highest concentrations of industry, such as Naples. After a series of demonstrations and strikes, an agreement was reached between the unions and Fiat in July 1970, which included a commitment on the part of the employers to set up 20,000 new jobs in the South. This was the first of many company-level contracts containing provisions for investment in the South.[13]

The period between 1968 and 1972 produced a degree of

---

[11] Many national agreements succeeded in reducing the working week from 48 to 40 hours with no loss of pay.

[12] On all these matters, see the collection of contracts contained in L. Bellardi, A. Groppi, F. Liso and E. Pisani (eds), *Sindacati e contrattazione collettiva in Italia nel 1972-74*, pp. 180-235.

[13] Contracts sometimes limited overtime in northern factories in order to encourage the transfer of work to southern plants. For agreements containing provisions for investments in the South, see ibid., pp. 191-2 (Fiat), pp. 223-5 (Italsider), p. 235 (Motta-Alemagna-Star).

North-South labour solidarity unparalleled in the nation's history. The most powerful expression of this solidarity was the popular demonstration, on 22 October 1972, in the southern town of Reggio Calabria, which followed a series of disputes, lockouts and occupations of northern factories. Neo-fascist attempts to sabotage trains carrying tens of thousands of workers from the North failed to stop the event from taking place, but were an indication of the wider dimensions of the problem, with which the unions were ill-equipped to deal. The *sindacato*'s demands for the right to inspect investment plans and the use of credit, and for fair procedures in taking on labour, were a threat to the clientelistic systems which were woven into the very fabric of social and economic life in the Mezzogiorno.

The demands of the unions for investment in the South were not a total failure. If we take two five-year periods, we find that between 1966 and 1970 the state-holding sector directed an average of just over 43 per cent of total investments to the South whereas between 1971 and 1975 the average rose to almost 50 per cent. In the same two periods financial aid from government sources rose from 0.98 per cent of gross national income to 1.77 per cent.[14] The results, from the *sindacato*'s point of view, were disappointing, however, for too much was invested in large and wasteful petrochemical and steel plants, which proved economic disasters. The unions had wanted a greater variety of investment which was more labour- and less capital-intensive. One of the major problems was that in negotiations concerning investments in the South, the *sindacato* could not be sure of facing a genuine bargaining partner able to honour agreements. In the Mezzogiorno the byzantine complexity of the systems of patronage limited the room for manoeuvre of its economic actors in unfathomable ways. Thus if the country as a whole could be described as a 'partyocracy' (*partitocrazia*) in which the political parties, and the Dc in particular, had colonised large sectors of Italy's administrative, civil and economic institutions, in the South this distortion of democracy was interwoven with more straightforward, criminal forms of

---

[14] See tables in T. Fanfani, *Scelte politiche e fatti economici in Italia*, pp. 154-5.

corruption.[15]

Thus in spite of its contractual successes, the *sindacato*'s long-term achievements in shifting valid economic resources to the South were disappointing. Nevertheless, the period was important in establishing the solution to the southern problem as one of the abiding strategic aims of the movement. Henceforth pressure to resolve the great economic disparities between North and South would penetrate all aspects of the *sindacato*'s thinking on the national economy, and become an area in which the movement would construct a lasting internal consensus between its traditionally divided components.

The Reform Strategy and the Arguments about the Movement's Political Role

The *sindacato*'s reform strategy looked beyond its members' working conditions to wider concerns in the country's economic, social and political life. Although many of the consequences of the *strategia delle riforme* affected the employers, who were frequently brought into such discussions, the unions' negotiating partners were principally the government and the country's public institutions. The reform strategy began with the movement's long dispute with the government between 1967 and 1969 over pensions. Its victory in February 1969 on a social question of such importance to the country at large was crucial in helping it sustain its demands for reform following the meagre results which lay immediately ahead.

After the success of the campaign on pensions, and during the industrial disputes of the 'autunno caldo', the three confederations announced that the new priorities of the movement were reforms in the areas of housing, tax and health provision. Housing reform, with a demand for a three-year ban on all rent increases and the launching of a construction programme for council houses (*case popolari*), was immediately given a high profile, and a series of staggered general strikes was held in the country's major cities in the autumn and winter of 1969. A law was

---

[15] See M. Carrieri e C. Donolo, *Il mestiere politico del sindacato*, pp. 177-209.

eventually passed in October 1971 handing control of the system of public housing over to local authorities, enabling them to expropriate land. For a number of reasons, including the manipulation of state bureaucracy by the scheme's opponents, the new law was not successful in spite of the funds made available. Although campaigning on social issues was frequently a failure in terms of direct results, it was successful in generating a sense of legitimacy for the movement's reform strategy as a whole. From late 1969 the confederations began to produce jointly-drafted documents and reports on the major areas of social provision, ranging from transport to education. All these issues were taken up, and throughout 1970 and 1971 further discussions with the government helped establish the movement as one of its main social and political bargaining partners. This role became increasingly central to confederate activity, for as the industrial federations and factory councils became more effective in negotiating with the employers, the confederations felt freer, and to some extent impelled, to concentrate on developing the broader social and political objectives which would give a coherent direction to the movement's struggles on all fronts.

With the *strategia delle riforme* the Italian *sindacato* began to put into practice its mission as a *soggetto politico*. Although unions world wide have traditionally maintained close ties with political parties, few, if any, have developed as explicit a claim to social and political representation as the Italian *sindacato*. A variety of explanations for this apparent anomaly have been advanced.

In discussing the role of the unions after the period of increased industrial conflict, Tarrow has made the point that 'the greater access to the polity that this accorded them was one of the major acquisitions of the cycle of protest'.[16] Although industrial conflict and urban protest were closely linked for the whole period studied by Tarrow (1965-75), this is not in itself sufficient to explain the emergence of the Italian *sindacato* as an actor on the political stage. In other advanced industrial nations unions have frequently supported protest movements, but without transforming the social and political demands of these movements into primary objectives of their own.

---

[16] Tarrow, *Democracy and Disorder*, p. 314.

The element which seems common to many explanations of the *sindacato*'s emergence as a *soggetto politico* in Italy is the notion that it was a result of weaknesses in the country's social, economic or political structures. Some commentators have seen it as a consequence of an accelerated and uncontrolled process of capitalist development 'to which the Italian ruling classes were unable to respond with any regulatory or rationalising capacity',[17] thus producing enormous social and economic strains which the traditional agencies were unable to keep in check. The immaturity of Italian capitalism, linked to the backwardness and oppressive tendencies of Italian employers, the relatively late development of an 'autonomous bourgeois class' in Italy, and the weakness of the country's civic structures, have all been advanced as factors which have radicalised the *sindacato* and caused it to develop a strong 'ideological' and political orientation of its own.[18]

Further reasons have been sought in the inability of governments to meet the country's political needs. The *strategia delle riforme* has been advanced as evidence of this: 'At a stage in which it was clear that the *centro sinistra* had exhausted all its political vitality, and had outlived its time, the confederations thought it was necessary to take an initiative which went beyond the contractual sphere and into new areas.'[19] Thus 'the *sindacato* entered the political system as an autonomous and united agent, acting in a surrogate capacity for parties considered incapable of representing or satisfying the new social demands.'[20] The inability of the parties to fulfil their representational function was seen as the result of the failure of the Italian system to produce alternating governments, and also of the tendency of the main governing party to serve interests other than those of the electorate. Accordingly, it has been argued, the *sindacato* began to function as a partial remedy for the absence in Italian political life of a functional

---

[17] Regini, *I dilemmi del sindacato*, p. 111. This is only one of the causes put forward by Regini.

[18] A summary of these views can be found in G. Pirzio Ammassari, *Teorie del sindacalismo e delle relazioni industriali*, pp. 119ff.

[19] S. Turone, *Il sindacato nell'Italia del benessere*, p. 39.

[20] Reyneri, 'Il ruolo della Cisl nel ciclo di lotte 1968-1972', p. 736.

adversarial system.

The analyses mentioned so far have all, in some way or other, highlighted the surrogate role of the *sindacato* as a political agent. What such explanations have in common is their tendency to attribute the movement's development to external causative factors. These undoubtedly played a part, but only insofar as the decision to compensate for weaknesses in the system, or to broaden the scope of the movement's demands, corresponded to objectives and tendencies already existing within the *sindacato*. This is crucial, and highlights a problematic feature of the surrogate arguments, namely the underlying assumption that unions have a given role in society, broadly equivalent to that of representing work-related interests and nothing more. To argue that most industrial relations systems work according to these assumptions is one thing, but to grant them axiomatic status is another.

This point is particularly pertinent to the Italian experience. As we have already seen, important sections of the Italian *sindacato* have always laid claim to a broader social and economic representative function in Italian society. The development of the *strategia delle riforme* was not seen by the *sindacato* itself simply as the surrogate function described by many analysts. The reforms were confederate-inspired initiatives to consolidate the factory-based advances being made simultaneously by the federations and workers' councils. The confederations were thus consciously promoting a strategically co-ordinating role for themselves, which entailed entering the political arena. To many, such a development was not without a Constitutional basis. Lelio Basso, socialist leader and jurist who had taken a prominent part in the drafting of the Constitution in 1947, echoed a widely-felt sentiment when he commented apropos the general strike of 19 November 1969:

> When Italian workers held a national general strike in support of legislative reform aimed at securing for all a decent home at reasonable cost, I was able to argue that through their strength and their struggles they were writing once more, but this time in the real world, those articles of the constitution which we, immediately after the war, had simply written on perishable paper.[21]

---

[21] 'L'utilizzazione della legalità nella fase di transizione al socialismo', pp. 852-3.

The tendency to justify the political activity of unions was given further support by an important ruling of the Constitutional Court in December 1974 establishing the legitimacy of 'political' strikes.[22] The significance of this decision put the whole question of the *sindacato*'s claim to a political role in a new light.

The debates on the issue, however, did not reflect straightforward left and right divisions. Certainly, elements of the ultra-left actually projected the workers' movement as a fully autonomous political force, with the new factory councils as the seeds of an alternative form of state power. The *Manifesto* group even conceived of a '[factory] council road to socialism'. But such tendencies gained no support within the orthodox left, the Pci and Psi. Although these parties did not oppose the *sindacato*'s reform strategy, many of their leading figures warned of the dangers of a *pansindacalismo*, which might seek to supplant the parties or some of their functions. Even some well-known figures on the left of the Cgil itself echoed such warnings.[23] Most of the reservations tended to highlight the chaos that could ensue from confusing the roles of unions and parties, or from undermining, however unintentionally, the role of parliament in producing social legislation. Within the political parties, those most sympathetic to the new developments saw them either as confirmation of the reform policies for which they had been pressing in government in the case of the Psi, or as an antidote to the risk of the *sindacato*'s focusing too narrowly on workplace issues in the case of the Pci.

The *Soggetto Politico* and the Confederations

The need to enter the political arena was discussed at the General Council of the Milan Cisl in September 1968. Those elements within the Catholic movement which had adopted a class position began to argue that contractual gains could never be secure without improvements in the social fabric of working people's lives. As the

---

[22] See Giugni, *Diritto sindacale*, Appendice VI, pp. 371-5. The ruling rejected as unconstitutional part of article 503 of the Criminal Code which made political strikes indictable offences.

[23] See V. Foa, *La cultura della Cgil*, pp. 232ff.

cycle of protest intensified, so did such arguments from Catholic quarters. What weighed heavily with the Cisl left was its mounting loss of faith in the willingness or capacity of the Dc to sustain a commitment to social reforms. It appeared to many within the confederation that it had become a movement without a party. Thus as the traditional collateral Cisl-Dc links weakened the Cisl began to strengthen its own political perspectives.

The Catholic labour left developed its arguments vigorously. The employers, it was stated, particularly the large multinationals, had at their disposal powerful means of influencing the decisions of government and of intervening in the functioning of the country's democratic institutions. The parties of the working class alone were unable to counteract this influence. The areas in which it was legitimate for the *sindacato* to act ranged from the need to control industrial development and investment to the distribution and use of publicly created wealth in a wide range of services to the community.[24] In this way work-related demands were linked to social demands and were to be promoted in an organically connected manner by the *sindacato*.

Following the early critiques of a potential *pansindacalismo*, some of the movement's Catholic intellectuals responded by asserting that the 'legitimacy of the *sindacato*'s political activity is not inferior to that of the parties. On the contrary it is based on the everyday experiences and struggles of its members rather than on electoral allegiances or traditional ideological preferences.'[25] The arguments of the Cisl left stressed the particular features of the Italian situation. The largest pro-labour party was in permanent opposition, and the static nature of the political system was unable to give direction to the social dynamic of Italian society. But although, as we have already seen, the Catholic labour left was distancing itself from its traditional collateralist partner, it was not prepared to tie itself to a communist political culture which had different historical roots from its own. There were, moreover, some positive features to be found within the Italian situation, namely that 'the *sindacato* in our country finds itself in a situation which

---

[24] This position is clearly formulated by Guido Baglioni, one of the major exponents of these ideas, in *Il sindacato dell'autonomia*, pp. 80ff.

[25] Ibid., p. 179.

has no parallel in any other capitalist nation, both because it is no longer shackled by legislative impediments and also because it is in a position to pressurise, to "bargain" with the government, of which it has become an important bargaining partner'.[26] It should be remembered, moreover, that it was the very existence of a large Catholic component within the workers' movement, with its own distinct current within the Dc, that had facilitated the creation of a constructive relationship with the government.

On the Cgil side, at its Livorno Congress in June 1969, the General Secretary, Novella, expressed concern at the possible development of *pansindacalismo*. Congress documents did stress, however, that gains within the factory could easily be dissipated in a society with inadequate social provisions. Thus the *sindacato* did indeed have to address itself to broader policy matters, otherwise workers would find that their remunerative gains from bargaining would be lost through the excessive costs of such provision, for which they would be made to pay.[27] Such arguments were not new within the Cgil. We have seen that from the beginning, with its *piano del lavoro* of 1949, the Cgil had itself staked a claim to a broader role within the polity than that of a narrow *tradeunionismo* of Anglo-Saxon derivation. Nevertheless, how such a role could be managed within the institutional structure of the system had never been worked out in any detail.

There were, however, powerful forces propelling the Cgil towards embracing the role of a *soggetto politico*, irrespective of opinions within the Pci. First, both communists and socialists within the Cgil began to argue that such a role was complementary to the efforts of the Psi and the Pci to push for reforms. Secondly, there was general agreement that the public image of the movement had improved as a result of the *sindacato*'s being perceived as looking

---

[26] Ibid., pp. 167-8.

[27] Novella's argument that the *sindacato* should not assume the role of a political party was not, however, an argument in favour of 'circumscribing the limits of union activity to purely economic and contractual matters at a point when its activity is rightly spreading beyond such limits ... This would be to expect the workers' movement to function in only one dimension while the dominant forces retain many forms and instruments for exercising their power'. *I congressi della Cgil*, vol. viii, part 1, p. 55.

beyond the short-term interests of its members and working for broader social improvements. Finally, the new role of the *sindacato* assumed critical proportions in relation to the question of organic unity. And when, as we shall see shortly, this objective was not realised, as planned, by 1973, the movement's new social and political role was seen by many disappointed leaders as the strategic focus around which it could sustain its unitary momentum. Thus the Cisl in its June Congress of 1973, and the Cgil in its July Congress some two weeks later, gave the idea of the *sindacato* as a *soggetto politico* the status of a formally approved and articulated objective. The Cisl broke with its traditional reserve to declare that it no longer placed any limits on its spheres of activity, now explicitly defined as 'una politica di classe'.[28] Speakers at the Cgil July Congress stressed the importance of the confederation's new tasks in consolidating what were called the 'social wages' of workers, making it necessary for the *sindacato* to become 'a protagonist of Italian society's economic, social and cultural development'.[29]

With what promised to be the emergence of the *sindacato* as a major protagonist of public policy, Italy's system of collective bargaining, already in the process of profound transformation, seemed open to yet further developments. National contracts agreed between the industrial federations and employers became the norm, and established *minimum* conditions upon which company and/or plant-level agreements could improve. The broader strategic task of co-ordinating the demands of the category federations and of relating them to broader social and economic objectives became the task of the confederations. As we shall see, the hoped-for entry of the *sindacato* into the realms of national economic and social policy signalled the beginning of a new phase in the movement's history but was also the source of a new set of problems.

---

[28] Article 3 of Motion 1. See Cisl, *Atti del VII Congresso Confederale, Roma, 18-21 giugno 1973*, p. 590. Congress support for this class line expressed, in my view, the ascendancy of the left at this time rather than the more enduring convictions of the wider network of federal and local leaders within the Cisl as a whole. For a good illustration of the 'twin souls' of the confederation, see the congress speeches of Paolo Sartori (ibid., pp. 155-63) and Pierre Carniti (pp. 225-34).

[29] Speech of Aldo Bonaccini, *I congressi della Cgil*, vol. ix, p. 150.

14

The Question of Unity: Political Parties and Hidden Agendas

Preparations for Unity

The industrial struggles which culminated in the 'Hot Autumn' of 1969 brought with them a widespread demand for organic unity at all levels of the *sindacato*. From the start, rank-and-file mobilisation had bypassed traditional divisions, and this had clearly been a source of strength. The three confederations thus found the question of unity forced on to their congress agendas in 1969, before the disputes of the 'autunno caldo' had been concluded.

For the first time since the split in the late forties, delegates from other confederations were present at each congress. In his opening report to the first of these, in June, the General Secretary of the Cgil, Novella, while supporting unity, struck a note of caution. His major reserve lay in meeting all the demands of *incompatibilità*. Although in agreement with the principle in relation to election to parliament, he argued against its extension to positions of leadership in the party.[1] The majority of speakers, however, both socialist and communist, wished to go further, arguing that autonomy from political parties was essential if the Cisl and the Uil were to be convinced that Cgil leaders would be free of divided loyalties. It was finally agreed that 'incompatibility' with parliamentary positions and political committees of parties would be put into immediate effect and that within a matter of months it would apply also to the executive committees of parties.[2] In February 1970 a meeting of the General Council of the Cgil decided that this requirement should be enforced from March, and Novella, who had already given up his parliamentary seat, resigned

---

[1] See *I congressi della Cgil*, vol. viii, part 1, pp. 57-60 for Novella's arguments on 'incompatibility'.

[2] For the text of the resolution, see ibid., pp. 512-13.

his leadership of the confederation in order to remain on the party executive. Luciano Lama, who by this time had withdrawn from parliament and from a position of leadership in the Pci, was elected General Secretary of the Cgil in March 1970. Having made these commitments, there were no further obstacles from the communist point of view, and the Cgil remained essentially compact and unanimous in its desire for unity.

On the Catholic side the Acli, at its June 1969 Congress, voted to support organic unity and for an end to the collateral bond with the Dc. At the Cisl's July Congress in Rome, however, there was a fiercely fought battle in which the old guard of Bruno Storti was attacked by an increasingly unitarian minority, led by FIM leaders such as Macario and Carniti, for its complacency and reluctance to change.[3] There was a clear impression that the leadership was in difficulty when arguing against unity, but owing to the numerical strength of its support among delegates from the agricultural and public sectors and the teachers' federations, together with the backing of most southern delegates, it won the votes, although the principle of *incompatibilità* was agreed for parliamentary and local government posts and extended to positions of leadership in political parties.[4] The question of organic unity was hedged around, with the statement that such unity would be possible once 'each of the three *sindacati* had achieved autonomous control and ... the freedom to choose its leaders, and the elimination of internal political currents'.[5] Despite these reservations, the success of the 'Hot Autumn' some months later strengthened the hand of the unitarians, and led in March 1970 to the General Council of the Cisl declaring more firmly in favour of unity. In many ways, the Storti victory at the Cisl Congress of July 1969 had been the swansong of the old leadership which could not conceive of Catholic union activity outside the confines of a strong

---

[3] For a sample of speeches illustrating the deep divisions at the congress, see those of Storti, Scalia, Romei and Carniti, in Cisl, *Atti del VI Congresso confederale, Roma, 17-20 luglio 1969*, pp. 17ff, 166ff, 183ff and 189ff respectively.

[4] See ibid., pp. 424-5.

[5] Ibid., p. 426.

collateralist relationship with the Dc. By early 1970, although some backsliding would occur later, a clear majority within the Cisl had come to favour organic unity.

Following the split in July 1969 of the Partito socialista unificato, formed in 1966 by the merger of the Psi and the Psdi, the two original parties were reconstituted. A higher proportion of the Uil leadership than in the years prior to 1966 followed the socialists rather than the social democrats, thus changing the political configuration of the confederation. At the Uil Congress in Chianciano in October 1969, in his congress report, Italo Viglianesi asserted that unity was essential 'to create a stable and valid democratic worker-oriented alternative to the authoritarian rule of the employers'. Although social democrats such as Lino Ravecca and Bruno Corti warned of the dangers of rushing into unity, socialist voices such as those of Gino Manfron, Giulio Polotti and Giorgio Benvenuto were strongly in favour, insisting that organic unity was 'the unavoidable consequence of our new strategy, of the political role which the *sindacato* must take on in the nation'. The congress voted in favour of the principle of *incompatibilità* for both parliamentary seats and positions of leadership in political parties. The enhanced socialist presence in the confederation secured approval for organic unity, although this would have to proceed in the light of the messages which would come to the confederation 'from the workplace, from the schools, and from society'.[6] The social democratic element, still largely anti-communist, however, remained opposed to unity and the republicans, lukewarm. These factors would weigh heavily on subsequent developments.

The first formal meeting of the confederations to consider the question of organic unity, subsequently known as 'Firenze 1', took place in Florence 25-28 October 1970. 'Firenze 1' took the form of a meeting of all three General Councils, 178 from the Cgil and 128 and 97 representing respectively the Cisl and the Uil. Although a clear majority of those present favoured unity, this first convention had no decision-making powers. The debate did, nevertheless,

---

[6] The citations are from the unpublished speeches of Viglianesi and Benvenuto at the 1969 October Congress. I am indebted to Paolo Saija of the Archivio Storico Uil in Rome for his help in gaining access to the as yet unpublished speeches and debates of the 1969 Congress, together with the concluding resolution.

reveal certain significant factors. The relatively advanced position of some federations (e.g. metalworkers, textile workers, construction workers and food workers, who wanted to bind the confederations to a firm commitment to organic unity from the start) contrasted with the more cautious approach of confederate leaders. At the end of the proceedings, a resolution was voted upon requesting the various components of the *sindacato* to hold meetings at all levels to discuss the question of unity. Significantly, the social democratic component of the Uil abstained from voting.[7]

Although 1971 opened with great hopes for unity, signs soon began to appear that all was not well. The Uil, shortly after 'Firenze 1', embarked on an internal polemic in which the unitarians were placed in a minority.[8] The Cisl leader, Storti, under pressure from the right of the confederation, stated at a press conference at the end of January: 'We do not consider the Cisl decision in favour of unity to be irreversible.'[9] It was therefore something of a surprise when, a few days later, it was announced that 'Firenze 2', which had met on 1 and 2 February, had approved an outline programme for unity. All three confederations had given guarantees on the principle of *incompatibilità*. Following a further meeting of the three General Councils, which, it had been decided, would be held later in the year, the confederations would hold their respective congresses of dissolution, to be followed by a constituent congress of the new united confederation.

Two intervening meetings of smaller groups were held in June and October 1971 to resolve remaining difficulties. The Cisl's request to allow the *contadini*, small peasant landowners, to join the new confederation was accepted. Difficulties in interpreting *incompatibilità* were overcome when the Cgil agreed to apply the principle to all levels of union and party organization, and not

---

[7] For the contributions to the debate at 'Firenze 1', see *Esperienze, problemi e sviluppo della prospettiva sindacale unitaria*, Rome: Edizioni Stasind, 1971.

[8] In a stormy meeting of the Central Committee in December 1970, the republican leader Raffaele Vanni sided with the social democrats and proposed a resolution declaring that the conditions for unity were still unfulfilled. The resolution was carried by 37 votes to 35.

[9] A. Forbice, *La federazione Cgil-Cisl-Uil fra storia e cronaca*, p. 97.

simply nationally. A further problem was the fact that while the Cisl and the Uil belonged internationally to the ICFTU, the Cgil was affiliated to the WFTU. Given the increasing feeling in all the confederations about the irrelevance of cold war postures, the agreed solution was that all three confederations would disaffiliate from their respective world bodies.[10]

Hopes for unity reached a climax at the meeting of the three General Councils of the Cgil-Cisl-Uil, held in Florence between 22 and 24 November 1971 ('Firenze 3'). Immediately before 'Firenze 3', between 18 and 21 November, the three confederations met separately to consider the 'Documento programmatico Cgil, Cisl e Uil', which contained outline proposals for unity to be put to the meeting of the General Councils. The text of the document, together with the three confederations' resolutions accepting the proposals, were presented in the opening address of 'Firenze 3' by Vito Scalia of the Cisl.[11] In his opening report, Scalia spoke of unity as certain.[12] Those against unity were few and unrepresentative of the mood of the delegates.[13] There was a strong feeling that obstacles had been overcome, and that the forthcoming unity would 'bind together in a single association the whole of the Italian working class, the North and the South, the worker and peasant, the clerical worker and technician, the labourer and the intellectual.'[14] Gino Manfron of the Uil referred to unity as consolidating the three major innovations in the Italian workers' movement: 'the basic elimination of the party/union transmission belt; the new political role of the *sindacato* which finds expression in our reform strategy;

---

[10] This decision was never implemented. Shortly afterwards, however, the Cgil decided to leave the WFTU. Many years later, at its October 1991 Congress, the delegates passed a resolution agreeing to seek membership of the ICFTU, to which the other confederations still belonged.

[11] The text of the 'Documento programmatico' is contained in *Atti della riunione unitaria dei consigli generali Cgil-Cisl-Uil. Firenze 22-24 novembre 1971*, pp. 11-18.

[12] Ibid., p. 8.

[13] See the speeches by Lino Ravecca and Gildo Muci of the Uil (ibid., pp. 75-9 and 189-92 respectively) and Paolo Sartori of the Cisl (ibid., pp. 146-53).

[14] Speech by Scalia, ibid., p. 19.

and the new union structures in the workplace.'[15] The final resolution fixed on 21 September 1972 for the winding-up congresses of all three confederations and committed the General Councils 'to the common task of calling, within the following five months, the constituent congress of the new unitary organization of Italian workers'.[16] By March 1973 the new confederation would be in place.

The Surfacing of Latent Opposition: a Compromise Solution

Determined to lead the way to unity, the metalworkers' federations had decided at a meeting of their own General Councils shortly after 'Firenze 1', in December 1970, to accelerate the pace of unity for their own category. Thus in September 1972 the single metalworkers' federation FLM was founded, but without disbanding the separate federations in order to keep within the terms of the agreement made at 'Firenze 3'. The metalworkers' decision drew sharp criticism from quarters within the Cisl and the Uil which argued that such an initiative was premature, since unity had to proceed according to the principle of 'all or none'.[17] In effect, such criticisms became incorporated into the obstructionist tactics of the anti-unitarians within the Cisl and the Uil who, alongside forces outside the movement, had been working behind the scenes to ensure that unity did not occur.

Opposition to the creation of a united movement came from numerous quarters. Shortly after the decision of 'Firenze 3' to proceed towards unity, Santo Quadri, Bishop of Pinerolo with special responsibilities to the Cei for labour organizations, delivered a short report to the Conference of Italian Bishops strongly suggesting that since the unity of the *sindacato* would effectively amount to communist hegemony over the whole movement, steps

---

[15] Ibid., pp. 167-8.

[16] Ibid., p. 333.

[17] In July 1971 the Central Committee of the Uil voted by a majority of 39 to 32 to expel the UILM from the confederation, a decision which was later revoked.

should be taken to prevent it.[18] Attacks on unity were not, however, always so direct. Usually they were more measured, presenting quite destructive arguments in the form of minor reservations.[19]

Among the political parties, initial communist fears centred on the unpredictable effects of loosening relations with a confederation in which the Pci enjoyed a substantial hegemony. The majority within the party, however, were confident of being able to exercise a strong influence on a new united workers' movement. In any case, the traditional ideological commitment to the unity of the working class was strong enough to outweigh any lingering doubts about the overall desirability of the project. Although officially, like the communists, the Psi supported unity, as an habitual government coalition partner it was nervous about the probability of a rapprochement between a more independent movement and the Pci opposition. Thus although the Psi did not actively undermine unity, a preoccupation with its possible electoral consequences blunted its enthusiasm.

It seemed to the major, non-communist parties, therefore, that the Pci would be the most likely beneficiary of unity. Most Dc members were convinced that a more united workers' movement would also be more conflictual, which would render the practice of its own *interclassismo* far more problematic and damage the party electorally. But opposition to unity came also from the left of the party. The left, which wanted to effect a shift within the Dc, was afraid of losing the collateral ties with the Cisl, which traditionally

---

[18] The text of Quadri's report is contained in G. Gherardi, *Amici e compagni. Le Acli, la gerarchia e il socialismo*, pp. 226-36. Quadri's name appears in a judicial report some years later as having been connected with anti-communist and anti-union organizations, and as having passed money to a certain Luigi Cavallo in connection with a range of anti-union activities. See A. Papuzzi, *Il provocatore. Il caso Cavallo e la Fiat*, which includes the text of the judicial report (pp. 95-162).

[19] See, for example, the comments of Giuseppe De Rosa, published in the Jesuit review *Civiltà cattolica*, shortly after 'Firenze 3', where he claims not to be attacking the unity of the *sindacato*, for insofar as it 'wishes to be a class-based *sindacato*, so far so good. The only problem is that *class* is understood in a Marxist sense. Certainly, this is not stated explicitly, but one can read it between the lines'. G. De Rosa, 'Sindacato unico per il 1973', p. 599.

strengthened its own position inside the party. Consequently a growing Dc opposition to unity, which included important figures from left to right, from Donat Cattin to Forlani, found its parallel within the Cisl in an opposition which went from Scalia to Sartori.[20]

Both the Pri and the Psdi were traditionally strong within the smaller confederation, the Uil. Although subject to the same fears as those of the Dc and the Psi, these smaller parties were under additional pressure. As minority parties, substantially smaller than even the Psi, a labour confederation of their own was a prize possession, of which the organic unity of the *sindacato* threatened to deprive them.

Although, as we can see, most political parties had strong reasons for wishing to see the unitarian project fail, these were not reasons which they could publicly declare. Behind the scenes, however, a great deal of pressure was being applied on union leaders, particularly within the Cisl and the Uil. Clear indications of this were the abrupt changes in the attitudes of leaders within the two confederations which began to occur soon after the decision to unite.

One month after the close of 'Firenze 3', Giovanni Leone was elected President of the Republic by parliament after twenty-three ballots, the longest and most bitterly fought presidential contest in the Republic's history. The election of Leone was a clear sign that the Dc was attempting to shift the country's politics to the right. The most significant feature of his candidature was that it was clinched by the decision of the republicans and social democrats to go for him rather than for the socialist, Nenni.[21] It is in the very nature of such behind-the-scenes negotiations that we cannot be sure what deals were made. Nevertheless, the burning

---

[20] Scalia, who had delivered the opening address at 'Firenze 3' in November 1971, led the anti-unitarian current to a victory at a meeting of the Cisl's General Council on 25-27 May 1972, overturning the decision to go ahead with the winding-up congress by a vote of 58 to 57. See Simoncini, *Dall'interno della Uil*, p. 187. The figure is given as 68 votes to 57 in C. Brezzi, I. Camerini, T. Lombardo (eds), *La Cisl 1950/1980. Cronologia*, p. 219.

[21] For an analysis of the twenty-three ballots, and a discussion of Pri and Psdi support for Leone's candidature, see N. Valentino, *Il presidente. Elezioni e poteri del capo dello stato*, pp. 161-85, particularly pp. 180ff.

issue of the day, namely the proposed unity of the labour confederations, must have figured in private discussions. Shortly after the election of Leone as President of the Republic, the republican leader of the Uil, Raffaele Vanni, whose position as General Secretary had in fact been secured by the support of the socialists in exchange for republican votes for unity, declared in the weekly *Europeo* in February 1972 that unity within the time prescribed was not possible.

Although Vanni was careful to avoid any suggestion that unity as such was being called into question, his comments were clearly intended to create an opening for others to do so. Critics of unity gained courage and began to issue warnings that a united confederation would be communist-dominated. Given such developments, many were puzzled by the Cgil General Secretary Luciano Lama's statement in his speech at the Pci Congress in March 1972 that 'unity is an act of faith in ourselves, in our capacity to exercise hegemony over wider masses than those normally led by us', comments which the anti-unitarians seized upon as proof of their contentions.[22]

The turning point came immediately after the general election held on 7 May. It was well known that the Dc wished to form a centre-right government. In February 1972, Giulio Andreotti had formed a totally Christian Democratic government. After the election of 7 May, and following lengthy negotiations which lasted until June, he invited the social democrats to join the government, but excluded the socialists. Since the Psi was now in opposition, this produced immediate tensions between social democrats and socialists within the Uil. What price had the social democrats paid in order to join the government? During the negotiations, fewer than ten days after the election results, the republicans and social democrats defeated the socialists in the Central Committee of the Uil and voted to support a motion in line with Vanni's reservations on unity expressed earlier. Vanni's proposal to put off the

---

[22] *Tredicesimo congresso del Partito comunista italiano. Atti e risoluzioni*, p. 207. Lama's comments were intended to allay the fears of those within the party who feared that the principle of *incompatibilità* would lose the Pci valuable leaders in the organization and in parliament. The congress reaffirmed its unconditional support for unity. See ibid., p. 495.

winding-up congress till the following year was accepted.[23] The anti-unitarians were clearly playing for time.

Although the Cisl joined the Cgil in officially criticising these developments, changes were rapidly taking place also within the Catholic confederation. Scalia, who had earlier championed unity at 'Firenze 3' eventually emerged as the leader of an anti-unitarian rebellion within the Cisl. At its meeting of 25-27 May, the General Council of the Cisl decided, with regard to its own disbanding congress, on 'the immediate cessation of all congress preparations in progress at all levels of the organization'.[24] As Turone and others have hinted, the whole episode smacked of a process of political trafficking and corrupt dealing, set in motion at the time of the negotiations for Leone's presidency, a suspicion strengthened later when the President of the Republic was forced to resign over a series of scandals.

In order to harness the considerable feeling for unity which remained within the Cisl and the Uil and retain a unitary impetus, the Cgil renewed a proposal it had first advanced in 1970, that is, the creation of a federation of the three confederations, a body which would not deprive the confederations of their autonomy but which would nevertheless acquire a structure of its own to formulate united policies and strategies.[25] Although the right wing of the Cisl initially opposed even this, once it was clear that the links between parties and their factions within the confederations were no longer threatened opposition to the new proposal was easily defeated. On 24 July 1972, the *federazione unitaria* Cgil-Cisl-Uil came into existence. Although this fell a long way short of organic unity, it represented a considerable advance on the three hitherto totally unconnected confederate structures. To the Cgil, moreover, and also to many within the other confederations, it was a transitional arrangement towards total unity, whose time, in spite of 'Firenze 3', had perhaps not yet come.

---

[23] See Simoncini, *Dall'interno della Uil*, pp. 187ff.

[24] Brezzi, Camerini, Lombardo (eds), *La Cisl 1950/1980*, p. 219.

[25] The proposal was passed as a resolution of the Cgil executive on 31 May 1972 and approved unanimously. See 'La risoluzione del Direttivo approvata all'unanimità il 31 maggio 1972', *Rassegna sindacale*, pp. 12-13.

The unitary federation Cgil-Cisl-Uil consisted of a fifteen-member secretariat, five from each confederation, and an executive of ninety, with thirty members from each of the three bodies. Bargaining platforms and social and economic policy would be formed on the basis of discussion within the federation, while each confederation continued to create its own policies through congresses as before. The autonomy of the confederations was safeguarded first by the parity structure of the unitary federation, and secondly by the adoption of the 4/5 majority rule for voting, which in practice gave the power of veto to each confederation. This structure was to be reproduced at all levels of the *sindacato*, so that the industrial or category federations were themselves to reproduce unitary federations at national, regional and provincial level. Area horizontal structures would be similarly organized, while the only fully integrated union structure without divisions remained the factory council at plant level, which continued as the unitary conscience of the movement.

Having created the *federazione unitaria* Cgil-Cisl-Uil, all three confederations, at the 1973 Congresses, declared that the *patto federativo* upon which the new structure was based was a preparation for organic unity. The unitarians in both the Cisl and the Uil regained the upper hand, but the immediate prospect of organic unity was lost. The Cgil took the decision to disaffiliate from the WFTU and to join the ETUC.[26] With this decisions the Cgil intended to remove any possibility for anti-unitarians to advance objections of a technical nature to renewed attempts at unity. In his report to the Cgil Congress in July 1973, the leader Lama declared:

> We were and remain ready for organic unity at any time, even now; if it had depended upon us this congress would have taken place some months ago and would have been the Cgil's winding-up congress. We still hold to this position, and repeat here today not only that we are willing to create organic unity as soon as possible, but that we will take all sections of the Cgil with us.[27]

---

[26] For a discussion of the mounting tensions between the Cgil and the WFTU and the growing importance at the time of the former's European orientation, see Lama, *Intervista sul sindacato*, pp. 76ff.

[27] *I congressi della Cgil*, vol. ix, p. 49.

Nobody doubted that the Cgil could deliver. With Lama's statement, however, the communists were placing the responsibility for the continued divisions of the workers' movement elsewhere.

Conclusion: Beneath the Surface of Events

It is, in my view, a mistake to regard the failure to achieve organic unity simply as a lost opportunity. The political obstructionism of the opponents of unity was the result of widely divergent conceptions still existing within the movement of the very nature of the *sindacato*. These differences meant that essentially the unitarian project was pulling the *sindacato* in opposing directions. The hidden agendas of the opponents of unity were to some extent the unarticulated expression of these unresolved differences.

The Cisl was internally divided into at least three camps. The middle-ground of the Catholic confederation tended to favour the principle of *incompatibilità* but nevertheless reacted with mixed feelings, ranging from mild satisfaction to anxiety, over the tendency of the confederation as a whole to loosen its collateralist ties with the Dc. Most *cislini* remained members of the party, but a growing number uncomfortably so. The anti-unitarians, successful in wrecking the programme for organic unity, although roundly defeated shortly afterwards at the Cisl Congress in June 1973, nevertheless became a powerful minority close to the party and one determined to maintain those links. The left, however, having adopted a clear class position saw the principle of *incompatibilità* as a form of liberation from the Dc. But having emerged from within the Catholic social tradition, the Cisl left had deep-rooted reservations about the Pci and did not wish to end up in a position of ideological and/or political subservience to that party. The Cisl's leaders thus had little sympathy with what seemed to them the less than enthusiastic attitude of the communists towards 'incompatibility'.

Although the Uil had by 1972 shifted considerably towards a class position, with a greater proportion of its leadership coming from the Psi, it still depended substantially on its republican and social democratic components. These were wedded to a strong 'institutional' conception of the *sindacato*, and some were even vaguely suspicious of its political and social ambitions. In their view, the loosening of formal ties between the confederations and political parties created a situation of open competition in which the Pci, with its strong links with the labour movement, could spread its influence beyond the Cgil. Indeed Lama's comments at the Pci Congress in March 1972, stating that unity was an expression of communists' confidence in their own capacity to achieve hegemony, reinforced this fear.

Given such diversity of views within the *sindacato*, it is easy to see that the conditions for organic unity were anything but ripe. In such circumstances, the *federazione unitaria*, with its capacity for a structured, united approach to the problems the movement had to face, and its simultaneous guarantee of autonomy for the confederations, can be argued to have been a better option than organic unity built on still unresolved differences of perspective within the *sindacato*.

The *federazione unitaria* could, in any case, look forward to operating on an industrial relations terrain which had been profoundly transformed in its favour. By 1972, the pay, working conditions and rights of workers had been raised to the standards of the most advanced industrial economies. Total union membership had risen from 4.5 million in 1968 to 6 million by 1973 and would continue to rise. The *sindacato* had spread to small and medium industries and to geographical areas where it had traditionally been weak. Collective bargaining was secure and effective at all levels, and the accepted representational role of the movement had been extended into areas of public policy traditionally closed to trade unions in most other countries. Finally, in spite of enduring collateral links with political parties, these ties had been weakened. A more autonomous, effective and united workers' movement seemed ready to embark upon a new phase of its development.

Part V

THE YEARS OF CENTRE-STAGE PERFORMANCE

15

Changes in Economic Patterns and Employer Behaviour in the 1970s

Economic Trends

The unions emerged from the early 1970s less divided than at any time in their movement's postwar history, well-established in the institutional fabric of Italian society, and with a strong sense of strategic purpose. These changes had been accompanied by the profound transformation of Italy into an advanced industrial nation. For the whole of the 1960s the country had sustained an impressive growth rate in GDP of 5.7 per cent, higher than West Germany and the United States.[1] A rapid growth of consumption continued throughout the sixties until 1970,[2] by which time, in manufacturing industry, real wages per unit of production were the highest among all the advanced western economies.[3] Until 1969 wage increases had been matched by productivity, but subsequently this state of affairs was not maintained. Throughout the 1970s hourly wages, and from 1973 the rate of inflation, rose on average twice as much as in other western economies. Such domestic difficulties occurred, moreover, at a fundamental turning point in the world economy. The ensuing economic problems require some comment if we are to understand their effect on the movement's strategic and ideological development.

By 1970 the sharp increases in wages had completely eliminated one of the major advantages enjoyed by much of Italian

---

[1] See United Nations, *1981 Statistical Yearbook*, Table 30, pp. 140-3.

[2] See statistics per capita and per family, Tables 4 and 15, 'Appendice statistica', Fanfani, *Scelte politiche e fatti economici*, pp. 245-70. In the 1960s private consumption more than doubled by comparison with the previous decade, i.e. it increased from 10.6 to 25.1 billion lire. See Istat, *Sommario di statistiche storiche dell'Italia 1861-1975*, table 116, p. 154.

[3] See statistical table in P. Frigerio e G. Zanetti, *Efficienza e accumulazione nell'industria italiana*, p. 73.

industry, namely, cheap labour. In 1970 alone, the first full year after the contracts of the 'Hot Autumn' had been signed, the national wages bill increased by 16.9 per cent,[4] and it was over 18 per cent in industry. The new strength of the *sindacato* likewise ensured that wage increases could not be easily halted. The Italian economy, weak in natural resources, was hit in 1971 by an increase in the price of raw materials on the international market. Other shocks were to follow. The resurgence of Arab nationalism and the block on oil supplies which followed the Yom Kippur War in October 1973 led, in the winter of 1973-4, to the quadrupling of oil prices. The deflationary policies which followed produced the deepest recession in the postwar period. Italy took expansionary measures immediately, and growth resumed between 1976 and 1979, but with serious distortions and inflationary tendencies. For the period between 1970 and 1979, the annual growth rate of GDP slowed to 2.9 per cent.[5]

In addition to the inflationary tendencies deriving from the world economy, Italy had to cope with further domestic pressures, many of which were directly related to major shifts in the balance of power in the industrial relations system. It was clearly undesirable that the substantial wage increases between 1969 and 1973 should permanently weaken industrial profitability. The result was an increase in prices, further aggravated by the cost of the oil crisis.[6] There followed, between 1973 and 1975, a devaluation of the lira and an inflationary spiral. The *sindacato*, moreover, was sufficiently strong to bring about, and the government too weak to prevent, further wage increases to compensate for the erosion of the real value of the original gains. Furthermore, with the important agreement in 1975 on wage indexation (*scala mobile*), the *sindacato* managed to link wages to price increases, with a negative effect on

---

[4] See Istat, *Annuario di contabilità nazionale. Serie 1960-85*, vol. xv, table 5.19, p. 340. As in many other cases which follow, the figures in the text are my own calculations based on statistics to be found in the works quoted.

[5] United Nations, *1981 Statistical Yearbook*, Table 30, pp. 140-3.

[6] In the three years between 1974 and 1977 prices increased at a yearly average of around 20 per cent. See table 207, Istat, *Compendio statistico italiano*, p. 273.

profits.

A high level of inflation could have been prevented if either or both of two sets of circumstances had prevailed. First, if a high degree of increased productivity of labour had absorbed rising wage costs. Secondly, if both wages and prices in other sectors (agriculture, commerce, professional and civil service groups) had increased at a substantially lower rate than in industry, workers in these sectors would admittedly have lost their advantages over the industrial workforce, but inflation could have been contained. Neither of these conditions prevailed. Labour productivity increased too modestly to absorb inflation. Moreover, not only was the 'lateral spread' of increased wages and prices into other sectors not contained, but it actually intensified in the years following 1975. Thus, although production increased at a higher rate than in most other European countries from 1973 onwards, the cost of labour per unit of production remained too high to counter the inflationary tendencies.[7] Consequently, from 1973 onwards, Italian inflation rates were on average twice those of most western economies.[8]

The other great problem of economic policy in the 1970s was that of public spending. This increased steadily in Italy from 38 per cent of GDP in 1970, at which point it was lower than that of the major developed countries, to become by 1982 more than 55 per cent of GDP. In the same period government income rose from only 33 per cent of GDP in 1970 to 43.3 per cent by 1982, thereby increasing the public deficit from 5 per cent to around 12 per cent of GDP, by far the highest among the developed countries. Thus while the reform strategy of the *sindacato* was indeed helping to secure improvements in such areas as social security, health and pensions, given the country's traditionally wasteful use of resources and grossly inequitable taxation system, traditional wage-earners found themselves bearing an increased proportion of the costs of an

---

[7] See Tables 7 and 8, 'Appendice statistica', Fanfani, *Scelte politiche e fatti economici*, p. 254. Between 1973 and 1978, productivity per hour increased at a rate of 4.1 per cent, although for the whole decade the figure is nearer 5 per cent. See tables 10 and 14, *Annali dell'economia italiana*, vol. xiv, part 1, pp. 239 and 244.

[8] See Eurostat, *Basic Statistics of the Community, 1981*, Table 114, p. 142. Also United Nations, *1981 Statistical Yearbook*, Table 37, pp. 169-76.

expanding welfare system which was generally accepted as being far less cost-effective and also inferior in quality to those of Northern Europe.[9] Additionally, in 1971 the government created Gepi (Gestione esercizio partecipazioni industriali), a body with the task of taking over an increasing number of private companies in difficulty. This was a socially useful, but highly expensive initiative.

From 1973 the government shifted the burden of the public levy and transformed the system from one traditionally reliant on indirect taxation to one based more on direct taxes. Direct taxes increased from 6.8 per cent of GDP in 1973 to over 14 per cent by the end of the decade. Indirect taxation declined from 10.9 per cent to 10.2 per cent of GDP while employers' contributions increased slightly from 12.6 per cent to just over 13 per cent. The Italian system was also notorious for its toleration of tax evasion, and also left enormous scope for tax avoidance. As the unions were quick to point out, the burden fell disproportionately on those groups on whom the fiscal levy was deducted at source and the nature of whose employment did not offer the opportunities for tax avoidance enjoyed by other sectors of society.[10]

As in the case of inflation, the burden of public spending was worsened by the government's unwillingness to take measures which would have been electorally unpopular. In addition to the more prosperous sectors of Italian society, its electorate included employees at all levels of a public sector whose institutions the Dc had been 'colonising' since the fifties. Thus from the early seventies to the early eighties the public sector supplied 75 per cent of the country's increased employment, at a time when industry was unable to make headway. An additional burden on state spending was the government's willingness to help employers in difficulty and to cushion the effects of reductions in employment by paying most of the bill for the *cassa integrazione.*

---

[9] For a breakdown of state expenditure in Italy in the 1970s, see tables 9 and 10, *Annali dell'economia italiana*, vol. xiv, part 1, pp 371-2.

[10] The major culprits in the Italian system are the self-employed. See table 15, ibid., p. 384, which provides a comparison of declared incomes by profession. The fully self-employed stockbroker is registered at the same level of earnings as the lowest-paid manual worker.

After an early period of relative stagnation, there followed, between 1972 and 1974, a renewal of quite vigorous economic activity which, paradoxically, coincided with the oil crisis. This was referred to by commentators as a *ripresa drogata*, an artificially induced recovery, which in effect made skilful use of the devaluation of the Italian currency and of inflation, allowing companies to recoup part of the income lost in the preceding three years of union ascendancy. Although this would eventually lead to the massive recession of 1975, one of the features of this recovery was a shift in the pattern of economic activity, namely, a decentralisation of industrial production, with important long-term effects, which will be discussed later.

It may seem puzzling that the year of Italy's greatest postwar recession, 1975, should also be the year in which the Confindustria and the *sindacato* reached their important agreement on the *scala mobile*, 'by far the most favourable indexation scheme towards workers established in Europe during the decade'.[11] One reason is that the Italian *sindacato* was perhaps the strongest in Europe at this period. Another was that the Italian government, which shared a general international optimism about the short-term nature of the crisis, was over-confident about its ability to stimulate the economy.

Despite Italy's economic difficulties in the late seventies, the situation could have been worse. Two of the major problems during this period were the low value of the lira among the international currencies and the high cost of labour. The devaluation of the currency, however, led, from 1976, to a recovery of competitiveness in Italian goods on the international market.[12] And as the lira continued to slide, the value of Italian exported goods more than compensated for the increasing prices at home, producing towards the end of the decade an export-led recovery.[13]

The second problem, that of the high cost of labour, could

---

[11] Salvati, *Economia e politica in Italia*, p. 144.

[12] The balance of payments was again in credit in 1977, for the first time since 1971. See table 15, *Annali dell'economia italiana*, vol. xiv, part 1, p. 285.

[13] Inflation was, in fact, reduced by 1979, from a peak of over 19 per cent to 13.5 per cent, but this was still very high. See ibid., table 12, p. 242.

have been even worse if the unions had continued to make elevated wage claims over and beyond the *scala mobile*. This problem was kept in check after 1975 by the new-found strength of the *sindacato*, particularly by its centralised control of the movement, and also by virtue of the government's skilful handling of the changes in the political situation. The years from 1976 to 1979 were the period of 'national solidarity', during which the communist proposal of the 'historic compromise' produced an explicit form of *consociazione*, or co-operation between the opposition and the government. The communists were anxious to ease their way into government, and the Dc, although as determined as ever that this should not occur, nevertheless made use of the former's aspirations to create a more consensual framework for its own policies. 'National solidarity' at the political level had its impact upon the *sindacato*, whose components were favourably disposed to co-operate in a period of economic crisis. Despite difficulties and ambiguities, which will be touched upon later, union co-operation was able to contain the high costs of wage indexation. This was achieved partly through agreements to eliminate some of the remaining costly anomalies in the scheme, and also through an important interconfederate agreement in 1977 between the unions and the Confindustria on containing labour costs. Additionally, for the whole period between 1976 and 1979, the *sindacato*, both in national and local agreements, co-operated in restraining the demands of workers. This was a practice, as we shall see, for which it would pay dearly.

The Employers

We have seen that by 1970 Italian wages had reached the levels of other advanced countries and had wiped out all trace of the traditional advantages of Italian industry. This convinced many of the country's employers that the domestic economic crisis which followed was due in large measure to the increased power of the unions. In 1972 the employers within the metalworking industry, in response to the leading part played by the metalworkers' unions in the *sindacato*'s advances, yet still within the framework of the Confindustria, formed their own association, the Federmeccanica, with the express purpose of meeting head-on the FIM-FIOM-UILM challenge to employer authority. More aggressive in its approach to the unions than the Confindustria, its formation signalled the end of the defensive era for the employers. Although it enjoyed neither the prestige nor the negotiating authority of the larger organization, and numerous employers did not favour its hawkish approach to industrial relations, it did stiffen resolve on the employer front as a whole to win back its command of industry. From 1972 employers began to demand a return to the use of overtime, a greater use of shift-work and holiday work.

In early 1973 the Confindustria proposed to the unitary federation Cgil-Cisl-Uil a series of meetings in which the employers would undertake to support the unions' strategy of reforms in exchange for wage moderation and the dropping of union demands for greater participation in matters of production and investment. The unions firmly rejected this offer, seeing in it simply a desire to return to traditional authoritarian practices. But by 1974-5 it became clear that the economic difficulties of the country were not simply employers' inventions, and that objective economic forces were playing a part in producing threats of unemployment and closures.

Although many employers wished to take advantage of the worsening economic situation to weaken the power of the unions, most, particularly in large-scale industry, were doubtful about the wisdom of a head-on clash with the unions, given the level of public support these now enjoyed in the country. Thus despite its costs, the majority within the Confindustria felt that the agreement over the *scala mobile* mentioned earlier could provide a much-needed measure of industrial relations stability.

The President of the Confindustria in 1975 was Fiat's Giovanni Agnelli. Agnelli was anxious at this stage to promote communist co-operation with a government of 'national solidarity', both because this would provide political stability, and also because the communists were the only party which could moderate union militancy. The agreement on wage indexation was the price he was prepared to pay for this. The unions for their part were anxious to establish a mechanism which would protect wages without continual recourse to industrial action. After some not unexpected skirmishes with the unions, an agreement was reached on 25 January 1975. For the *sindacato* this was a major turning point in wages policy and the most important interconfederate agreement of the decade. Although the *scala mobile* had existed in industry since 1945, its ability to protect wages was limited and its application had lacked uniformity. The 1975 agreement both increased the level of protection and standardised the mechanism throughout industry. An important part of the negotiations comprised an agreement to extend the scope of another protective mechanism, the *cassa integrazione guadagni*,[14] which had formally existed since 1941. This mechanism, sanctioned by legislation in May 1975, guaranteed workers who were laid off up to 80 per cent of their wages for a maximum period of twelve months, with the possibility of an eventual return to work. The cost of 72 per cent of wages was borne by the government and 8 per cent by the employers.

These agreements, although effective in reducing industrial conflict, were extremely costly. The Italian government, which was trying to persuade the IMF to extend its credits, put pressure on the unions to modify the costly *scala mobile*. The Communist Party, which was seeking to promote its image as a potential party of government, was urging the unions to present themselves as 'responsible' agents of development, mindful of the country's problems. Together with further pressures on employment, these factors persuaded the *sindacato*, at the end of January 1977, to reach another interconfederate agreement containing the cost of labour. On this occasion the major concessions were made by the unions. In return for the further elimination of anomalies in the *scala mobile* and a greater willingness to co-operate in the reintroduction of shift-work and working holidays, the basic indexation scheme was maintained and the employers made a number of commitments, in retrospect more generic and ritualistic than specific, on improving working conditions and increased investment in the South.

In spite of the hardening of attitudes by the employers towards the unions, the more hawkish among the former were kept sufficiently under control to achieve the two major interconfederate agreements. Nevertheless the pattern was clear. Although the *sindacato*'s position of legitimacy in the country was consolidated as the 1970s progressed, the balance of power in industrial relations within this new framework was shifting back to the employers. One of the most powerful signs that such a change was taking place

---

[14] See Glossary.

could be perceived in an important transformation of the country's economic activity, namely, the decentralisation of production and the increased activities of smaller firms. Numerous commentators have interpreted this phenomenon almost entirely as a reaction to the position of strength gained by the unions by 1972.[15] For a time, workers in Italy were better protected than almost anywhere in the capitalist world. In 1974, for example, Fiat froze the hiring of labour but signed an agreement guaranteeing no redundancies, and even imposed limits on overtime to protect jobs. But industry was not willing to tie its hands indefinitely in this way, and decentralised production offered numerous advantages. Chief among these was the simple fact that unions were weaker and less organized in smaller units of production. In fact, when Fiat, after much criticism for not being interested in southern development, decided to move into the South in the early 1970s, it did so in a calculated way. It set up medium-sized plants, not in urban areas with a politicised working class, but in rural areas with high unemployment. In decentralising its production and subcontracting many of its processes, it ensured not only that its ability to determine staffing and investment strategies could not readily be challenged by the unions, but also that production could not be so easily disrupted by industrial action. The advantages of these moves were later to prove of great importance in helping Fiat defeat the unions in the famous confrontation of 1980.

Barkan has argued in some detail that decentralisation was a response to workers' gaining more control over the work process.[16] The forms of decentralisation were many and varied. Much of the work formerly carried out in large factories was consigned to smaller units, and even to the home, creating what became known as the *fabbrica diffusa*. The process also made extensive use of illegal labour and contributed to the growth of Italy's underground economy. Large firms began to subcontract small assembly-line production work and noxious or dangerous tasks. Even highly skilled work, such as machine maintenance, was arranged on a

---

[15] See, for example, Regalia, Regini, Reyneri, 'Labour Conflicts and Industrial Relations in Italy', pp. 131ff. Some economists have claimed that decentralisation began in the 1960s.

[16] See particularly *Visions of Emancipation*, pp. 153-6.

freelance basis, since this proved cheaper than employing full-time technical experts. The *statuto dei lavoratori*, moreover, did not apply to companies with fewer than fifteen employees, where unions were, in any case, weak or absent. Industrial action was also less likely, and labour easier to replace, so that management enjoyed total control over the workforce.

Other types of production tended to focus on the underground economy and work in the home. The most common of these were to be found in such industries as textiles and clothing, shoe manufacturing and toy-making. Later such working methods were extended to the assembling of electronic, computer, and other appliances. Much of the work was done by women, unskilled southern workers, illegal immigrants and students on low pay, with no pension rights or benefits. Employers could thereby avoid having to comply with costly health and safety standards and save on social insurance contributions, which might otherwise have added as much as 38 per cent to labour costs.

When dealing with this form of activity statistics are unreliable, but we do know that the underground economy was more vigorous in the North, where the level of technology, even on a small scale, was generally more highly developed. Some economists believe that as much as 25 per cent was added to the country's GNP through the 'submerged' or underground economy, whose activity is not generally available to statistical computation. To some extent it offset the rather poor official rate of active labour participation in the country, which was as low as 35-6 per cent of the population during the seventies.[17] Some economists have argued that as much as 35 per cent of agricultural production in the seventies derived from the part-time labour of workers registered as employed outside the sector. This type of work was undertaken at weekends and after normal working hours.

Barkan has, in fact, argued that such a decentralised economy is not a sign of vitality and initiative. It is exploitative in nature, for the most part dependent on large industries, and it tends to create yet another duality in the Italian economy (i.e. a secure versus a precarious workforce). Much of this argument is true, yet it is not

---

[17] See Table 1, 'Appendice statistica', Fanfani, *Scelte politiche e fatti economici*, p. 247.

the whole picture. From the time of the oil crisis onwards, large industry, in both the private and public sectors, was in difficulty, and there was a genuine risk that the pressure on public spending would be worsened by a growing deficit in the balance of payments. Expanding imports were compensated for, however, by the increased energy, activity and productiveness, not of large industry, but of small and medium firms, in regions which were promoting new forms of economic growth. Employment in manufacturing industry between 1971 and 1981 thus grew exclusively in small-scale industry, particularly in Central and North-East Italy.[18] While large companies did indeed undertake decentralisation as an industrial relations strategy, it is nevertheless the case that 'there also existed the technological and organizational conditions to permit a transfer of production towards small firms, and indeed to work in the home, with no significant loss of efficiency'.[19]

In January 1973, in compliance with EC instructions, Italy introduced value added tax (Iva), which replaced the existing system of taxing each commodity transaction (Ige). This meant that subcontracting and other forms of decentralised production became cheaper. It should be noted, moreover, that the decentralisation of production was a global phenomenon then taking place also in western economies which enjoyed less turbulent union/employer relations. It has become evident that the greater shift towards small enterprises, which had in any case always played an important part in Italian industry, was not simply a matter of 'decentralisation'. It had its own inner dynamic in a process of industrial growth which was quite independent of large industry. In this sense, the idea that it was an unhealthy development, relying chiefly on large industry, was by no means entirely true.

Another sign of vitality within the small enterprise sector was the fact that it did not take place in the South, where financial incentives and even transfers of plants were being channelled. In

---

[18] See Salvati, *Economia e politica in Italia*, pp. 134-5. For a detailed breakdown of employment patterns for the period in relation to various industries, see Istat, *Annuario di contabilità nazionale. Serie 1960-1985*, vol. xv, table 3.3, pp. 128-9.

[19] Salvati, *Economia e politica in Italia*, p. 136.

the 1970s financial aid to the South more than tripled by comparison with the previous ten years,[20] yet the increased productiveness mentioned earlier took place in Central and North-East Italy, where there was no state intervention. Although employment in industry was subject to shifting patterns, overall it did not increase. Nevertheless, if we include other sectors, Italy was the only advanced economy in which total employment increased substantially during the 1970s. Employment in industry increased in the small enterprises of Central and North-East Italy and also in the less productive, large state-holding industries in the South. The major increase in total employment was in effect due to expansion in the services sector and to public employment in the South.[21]

The Italian economy in the 1970s thus presents a complex picture of a country in difficulty on a number of levels (e.g. inflation, public spending, currency devaluation), with a continuing North/South divide in which there was a significant degree of increasing vitality in the North, particularly in small enterprises. Economic development is always a crucial factor in determining the relative strengths of bargaining partners in industrial relations. The Italian *sindacato* had been able to establish itself in Italian society largely in the wake of a period of economic expansion unparalleled in the country's history. Clearly such a situation could not be prolonged indefinitely, especially following the profound economic changes taking place from the mid-seventies. The consequences of these developments, however, were not always very clear at the time to the *sindacato*, which continued to promote its social and political role while also having to deal with its changing relations with employers. But the increasingly difficult economic conditions provided the material framework within which it had to develop its aspirations.

---

[20] See statistics, Fanfani, *Scelte politiche e fatti economici*, p. 154.

[21] See ibid., p. 155 and Table 20, 'Appendice statistica', ibid., p. 265.

16

The Effects of the *Sindacato*'s New Centralised Role

A New Bargaining Hierarchy Established

In the period that runs from the 1960s to the mid-1970s, the three-yearly national contracts negotiated between the employers and the category federations became established as the focal point of industrial bargaining. During the cycle of intense protest between 1968 and 1972, plant bargaining was also placed on a secure footing. These two negotiating levels would remain central features of Italian bargaining practice. As the economy moved into recession between 1974 and 1976, interconfederate bargaining, that is, bargaining between the Confindustria and the Cgil-Cisl-Uil federation, returned to a position of prime importance. A major reason for this was that both employers and unions were anxious, at a time of crisis, to stabilise the situation as much as possible. Crucial in this was the 1975 agreement over the *scala mobile*, already discussed in chapter 15. The agreement subsequently reached in 1977 on the reduction of labour costs was another landmark in establishing the importance of this level of bargaining. By the mid-to-late 1970s, therefore, a centralised level of national bargaining between the employers' organizations and the union confederations was established, with significant effects on negotiations at lower levels.

There were numerous ways in which interconfederate bargaining affected lower-level negotiations. Guidelines were produced on holiday working, shift work and other matters, which the national negotiators for each category were then obliged to follow. Also fixed at this level, but this time with government involvement, was the proportion of wages covered by automatic increases in the *scala mobile*. Since the 1975 agreement set this cover at something like 80 per cent of wages, some room for bargaining at the lower levels remained. But the automatic increases took much of the urgency out of these negotiations. The government was sometimes present as mediator or as party to the agreements. The willingness of the employers to reach agreements on such matters as the *scala mobile*, increased social contributions, and investment depended on what the government was prepared to make available in the form of tax concessions, grants for capital investment, etc. Involvement in such tripartite negotiations was attractive to the confederations, for it promised to fulfil their ambitions to exert a broader social and political influence in society. But simultaneously it increased the pressure on the unitary federation Cgil-Cisl-Uil to demonstrate to the employers and to the government that it could control the demands of the federations and thus prove to be a dependable negotiating partner.

From the mid-1970s, therefore, there were three major bargaining levels, with the higher-order agreements imposing constraints on negotiators lower down. Interconfederate agreements established broad guidelines in a number of areas and fixed the terms of the *scala mobile*. The national contracts between the industrial federations and employers dealt with basic conditions of work for each category, for example job classification, minimum wage levels, training, hours of work, holidays, health and safety, disciplinary procedures, and union rights. From 1976 such contracts included provisions for information on plans for investment, restructuring and employment.[1] In the 1976 metalworkers' and chemical workers' contracts, this provision was the first article of the agreement.[2] These changes signalled the extension of bargaining into areas which were traditionally the preserve of managerial decisions. The working environment came increasingly within the remit of federal bargaining, and contracts usually stipulated, as we can see from a typical proviso, that 'the financial burden of meeting the requirements agreed by the employers and plant union

---

[1] For the importance of this development, see Treu and Negrelli, 'Workers' Participation and Personnel Management Policies in Italy', pp. 81ff.

[2] See *Contratto collettivo nazionale di lavoro industrie chimiche e affini 1976-9*, p. 7, and *Contratto nazionale di lavoro addetti all'industria metalmeccanica privata 1976*, p. 15.

representatives will be borne by the employers'.[3]

At plant level minimum wage rates fixed in national contracts could be further improved, although most pay negotiations at plant level were concerned with productivity bonuses, overtime, etc. Agreements on the working environment, union rights, job classification, and even restructuring and investments made at higher levels came into play in plant negotiations. In 1974 about fifty plant agreements were reached throughout central and northern Italy, in which employers undertook to invest in southern plants in exchange for wage restraint on the part of the workers. In the event, this was an unequal bargain, since the wage sacrifices were real and immediate enough, while the employers' side of the agreement concerned commitments for the future, which they were unable to honour because of the recession. Although not very fruitful, the agreements were nevertheless significant, for they demonstrated that it was possible for employers and unions to co-operate, at least in principle, on strategic objectives, from the interconfederate down to plant level,

Paradoxically, the economic crisis of the mid-1970s had in some ways helped the *sindacato* achieve one of its aims, namely that of placing the horizontal or confederate structures in a strategically commanding position. Cella and Treu observed:

> The presence of a strong horizontal component is no longer, as it was originally (and as it still is today in France), a sign of weakness or of excessive dependence on the world of politics. Rather it operates, despite uncertainties and contradictions, as a 'class-based' *sindacato*, with a strong desire to influence economic and social policies and to guide lower-level, 'autonomous' bargaining.[4]

By the mid-1970s the Italian *sindacato* had produced an organizational and bargaining structure which seemed, in principle, capable of carrying forward both its long-term strategic and its immediate workplace objectives.

---

[3] *Contratto nazionale di lavoro addetti all'industria metalmeccanica privata 1976*, article 27, p. 64.

[4] Cella e Treu (eds), *Relazioni industriali*, p. 356.

Some Effects of Change

Although from the time of the economic crisis in the mid-1970s the *sindacato* was pushed back on to the defensive, the atmosphere was no longer like that of the old days when employers ruled by diktat.

Union control over the membership was more secure in industry than in other sectors. In spite of the *scala mobile* agreement earlier in the year for example, the autumn of 1975 witnessed a succession of strikes in the public sector, among railway workers, postal workers, state employees, school workers and employees in the state-holding institutions. The first of these even began to support the increasingly vociferous autonomous unions, which were ready to break ranks with the major federations and promote the sectional demands of this group of workers. One of the effects of centralisation, therefore, was to provoke an increase of activity in the autonomous unions.

It was not easy, morever, for the *sindacato* to shape a cohesive strategy out of the diversity of demands being made from below. In the autumn of 1976 assemblies and strikes were organized throughout the country in protest against the government's economic policies and its unwillingness to promote development in the South. At one point, in retaliation, the government threatened to suspend the operation of the *scala mobile* for workers earning over eight million lire a year and to reduce its cover to 50 per cent of wages for those earning more than six million lire.[5] At the same time the *sindacato* was anxious to link the question of employment to investment, hoping thereby to engage both employers and government in a strategic response to the economic crisis which would avoid the shedding of labour. The unions' insistence that national contracts should contain provisions on the disclosure of information became more urgent than ever. The metalworkers' contract of 1976, which, as we have seen, contained such provisions, was not easily concluded. A national strike of metalworkers was required before they could be secured. In early July 1977 an agreement was reached with Fiat which created 5,000 new jobs in the Mezzogiorno. Such successes were isolated and

---

[5] See 'Cronologia 1974-7: vicende generali', *Quaderni di rassegna sindacale*, anno xx, gennaio-febbraio 1983, pp. 82-7.

modest, but through these efforts the *sindacato* managed to keep on the agenda issues which prevented the movement's activities from fragmenting in the pursuit of a myriad of sectional demands.

The congresses of the two major confederations held in June 1977 reflected these difficulties. The report of Lama, in particular, to the Cgil Congress in Rimini focused sharply on the difficulties faced by the movement. It was impossible to deny that the *sindacato* was now well established and that it held a position of considerable strength in Italian society. Italy was unique among western economies, in that, in the preceding three years, 'in spite of an annual rate of inflation of over 20 per cent, the purchasing power of wages had increased', and the reduction in productivity in 1975 'had not led to massive dismissals in large companies'.[6] Rights had been gained in the factories. These were inscribed in statutes and in comprehensive three-yearly contracts which covered controls on dismissals and rights of information on planning, restructuring and investment. But in spite of all this, Lama argued, little had been achieved in economic and industrial policy. The substance of the ensuing critique did not spare the government, the employers, or the unions themselves.

Lama took as his starting-point the argument that if the movement chose to claim recognition for its social and political role, it had to adjust its behaviour accordingly, for it was assuming new responsibilities. It could not continue to produce an endless list of demands while ignoring its own corresponding obligations. If it was right to be critical of both government and employers for their failures, it was also necessary to acknowledge the shortcomings of the *sindacato* itself and of its members' behaviour. This was essential because in becoming a *soggetto politico* the movement was shifting the centre of gravity of its operations from automatic adversarial postures to critically constructive ones.

It was becoming increasingly clear, Lama continued, that the restructuring which was required in industry demanded the creation of a more skilled workforce. In this regard, he argued, the congress had to face the problems associated with the *ugualitarismo* which held sway in the movement, since in failing to reward skills the *sindacato* was, in fact, alienating many workers with ability and

---

[6] *I congressi della Cgil*, vol. x, p. 41.

initiative.[7] Speaking a few days later at the Cisl Congress, however, the General Secretary, Macario, took a different view, arguing that 'a common commitment requires the development of our egalitarian line on the treatment of workers. This is also a necessary condition for a balanced development of structures of production and for expanding and protecting employment.'[8]

A further requirement of industry, Lama argued, was the flexibility and mobility of labour, and there was no doubt, furthermore, 'that the complete rejection of mobility seemed at times irrational and inimical to policies of company renewal and increased productivity.'[9] Italian industry would undoubtedly cope more effectively with the crisis if the workforce enhanced its flexibility. A serious obstacle to this, Lama pointed out, was the fact that many workers preferred to rely on the *cassa integrazione* rather than relocate or retrain. A number of workers who drew on the fund were also able to find unofficial work. Lama stressed the socially and morally negative effects of a sustained reliance on the *cassa integrazione* and drew attention to the disadvantages of those workers in regions and industries where it was impossible to find supplementary work. Economic restructuring, along with policies for creating employment, the report continued, required a more sustained regional orientation and input.

The toughest part of Lama's report concerned wage settlements. It was also the most controversial. The transformation of the country's economy could be achieved, he argued, only through a programme of 'austerity'. Unrestrained wage increases diminished the room for manoeuvre and damaged the possibility of diverting resources to the South. Combined with high levels of southern unemployment, such wage rises perpetuated already distorted patterns of economic behaviour and created mass discontent and resentment in the more deprived regions.[10] Lama's

---

[7] 'Professionalism', argued Lama, 'has to be reflected also in wage levels, otherwise we discourage the improvement of labour skills, which has a negative effect on productivity.' Ibid., p. 42.

[8] Cisl, *Atti del VIII Congresso confederale*, p. 82.

[9] *I congressi della Cgil*, vol. x, p. 45.

[10] See ibid., p. 47ff.

arguments were in line with the Pci's own 'austerity' programme and were intended to increase the Pci's prospect of entry into government by demonstrating that communist influence could be a force for controlled development. There was, of course, more than one way of interpreting the report. Some saw it as a return to the *cinghia di trasmissione*. But it could also be seen as an attempt to impress on the movement a style of operation which would enhance its own credibility as a responsible agent of social and economic development.

Many inside and outside the movement felt that Lama was creating a confusion of roles by abandoning the adversarial vocation of the *sindacato* and in the process doing the work of the government and employers. To large sectors of the student movement, for example, Lama was the symbol of a communist 'sell-out' to the establishment.[11] At a demonstration organized for 2 December 1977 by the metalworkers' federations, calling among other things for policies to create employment in the South, although support was still forthcoming for the *sindacato*, there were some significant changes in the composition of the demonstrators. In addition to 200,000 workers, young people from the associations of the unemployed, particularly strong in the area around Naples, were present, and there was considerable support from feminist groups. Student participation, however, was accompanied by criticism of the *sindacato*, and it was the last occasion for many years to witness students taking part in an organized manner in an event sponsored by the unions.

The associations of the unemployed mentioned above were often critical of the unions, and frequently relations were overshadowed by mutual suspicion. The collaborationist side of the movement's new role, and the image it sought to project of a 'responsible' agent of decision-making in the country, were difficult perspectives to sell to many of its supporters. As the *sindacato* was adopting a role which in some ways resembled the neo-corporatist tendencies of some other labour movements in Europe, it created a degree of disaffection among those sectors of society which had looked to it to challenge, rather than support, the system.

---

[11] At a rally at Rome University on 17 February 1977, organized groups of students disrupted Lama's speech and invaded the platform in protest at the Cgil leader's 'betrayal' of the working class.

Rank-and-File Representation

By the mid-1970s over 40 per cent of the employed population was unionised, thus reaching the levels of other advanced economies in Europe. In fact, union membership continued to grow throughout the 1970s, reaching over nine million by 1980. These figures, however, concealed some worrying developments. From the mid-1970s the unions were finding it difficult to represent new groups of non-industrial workers. The predominantly industrial orientation of the *sindacato* began to create problems in adapting to the needs and demands of the increasing number of service and white-collar workers. Even within industry itself the development of new skills among workers set the unions problems of representation, while autonomous unions started to make inroads into such areas as transport, clerical work and banking. But in addition to these difficulties, which arose from new patterns of employment, there were problems also within the very heart of the movement, where the *sindacato* felt it had achieved its greatest success, the *consigli di fabbrica.*

Factory councils were well established throughout the country as the base-structure for plant-level bargaining. But by the second half of the decade the *sindacato*, which was pressing at higher levels for greater investment and industrial development in the South and working for other long-term objectives, began to tie the hands of negotiators at lower bargaining levels. In plant negotiations, the presence of provincial and other union officials was increasingly felt as a restraining force anxious to contain rank-and-file demand in return for benefits promised at some higher level.[12] Such problems were further complicated by other difficulties which were emerging from within the councils themselves.

The first indications that things were going wrong in the *consigli di fabbrica* date back, in fact, to as early as 1972. In a speech at an Acli conference in the late summer of that year, Renzo Ferro Garel gave a critical report on the councils, including among his comments the observation that major decisions about the procedures and structures of the *consigli di fabbrica* were being

---

[12] See Regini, *I dilemmi del sindacato*, pp. 49ff.

taken at higher levels with no consultation.[13] He complained in particular about the methods of election. Council delegates were chosen by the workforce as a whole, and not by union members alone, in workshop or other homogeneous units. But in order to bring the *consigli* under greater union control, workshop units were abandoned in favour of larger factory constituencies. The argument in support of such a change was that choosing the best available candidates could not be reconciled with dividing elections along workshop lines. The net effect of the change was that the workers were invited to choose their representatives on the basis of their confederate affiliations. This produced greater hierarchical control, since the representatives were inevitably more disciplined union cadres. But it also reintroduced a competitive factor between the confederations, which was a constant reminder of the failure to unite.

Such developments towards greater control from the top were not simply the result of malevolent machinations. The simple fact was that once the initial period of intense protest had begun to die down after the 'Hot Autumn', it became increasingly difficult to find candidates who were not committed union militants. Such activists, understandably, sought to increase their influence among the workers and also to promote their own confederations. A Cgil working group produced a report in 1974 which reinforced many of the criticisms made by Ferro Garel. According to this report, the elections for council delegates were attempting to accommodate too many factors. In addition to selecting the best shop-floor candidates, the elections were endeavouring to 'preserve unity' by guaranteeing that at least some representatives would be chosen from each confederation and that all political persuasions would be represented on the lists.[14] The report highlighted how the choice of the best candidates was inhibited by the attempts to engineer parity of representation between the divided confederations. Such practices began to grow at all levels of the movement. The need to preserve unity among the confederations would often be translated into quotas on electoral lists, and proportional post allocations even at

---

[13] See *Atti del XIX convegno nazionale di studio alle Acli 1972*, pp. 812ff.

[14] For the Cgil report, see Aiello, Amoretti, Gordini, Pettine, Rosati and Treves, 'Evoluzione e problemi dei consigli di fabbrica e di zona', pp. 151-69.

the highest organizational levels. There was a justified feeling that internal democracy was being distorted in order to preserve parity among confederations which could not settle their differences.

Problems also arose in the functioning of factory councils. In the larger factories the *consigli* were able to form sub-committees and working parties, but even these frequently lacked the expertise to make informed judgements on technical matters, in areas ranging from health and safety to company investments. Consequently, union officials with greater experience or with access to technical advice were called in, thereby increasing once again the reliance on personnel and union organizations outside the factory. By the same token, when delegates from within the plant did begin to acquire expertise, there was a tendency for such workers to spend all their time on these technical matters and to distance themselves from the day-to-day problems on the production line. In the larger factories such delegates were often co-opted as full-time experts, who later became reluctant to return to the tedium and loss of status of shop-floor workers. 'In some factories', the Cgil report complained, 'this phenomenon has reached significant dimensions; there are even entire executives which are no longer in touch with production.'[15] At the National Conference of Council Delegates held in Rimini in May 1975, Lama severely criticised those delegates who themselves ceased to be workers.

The *consigli* were running the risk of losing touch with the membership in yet another way. 'In the factory councils', Ferro Garel argued, 'there are the very highly politicised groups who shift the discussion on to more general themes ... in order to analyse, in a highly ideological manner, the whole [political] system. Most delegates are not able to follow such debates and lose interest in arguments they fail to understand.'[16] Thus the factory assembly, instead of functioning as the centre from which policy originated, risked becoming a forum in which the more politically advanced conducted their internal battles, or in the worst cases a body which such elements attempted to manipulate.

For a variety of reasons, therefore, relations between the unions, and sometimes even the factory delegates, on the one hand,

---

[15] Ibid., p. 160.

[16] *Atti del XIX convegno nazionale di studio alle Acli 1972*, p. 810.

and the rank-and-file on the other were becoming increasingly bureaucratic. Yet despite all these problems, the *consigli di fabbrica* were in place, well-established, and on the whole carrying out necessary functions.

The case of the *consigli di zona* was different. As their name indicates, these committees were area councils which were meant to co-ordinate the activities of the *consigli di fabbrica* in given localities. They were similar to the factory councils in being unitary bodies, i.e. not divided along confederate lines, and were to give a strategic dimension to the activities of the factory councils. They did not, however, enjoy anything like the success of the plant-based units, and never really became a functional part of the movement. At the Acli conference mentioned earlier, Ferro Garel complained that in Turin in 1972 'the *consigli di zona* exist, essentially, on paper'.[17] The Cgil working group reported two years later that the area councils were not developing as intended. Where they did exist, instead of co-ordinating the industrial activities of the factory councils, they concerned themselves with the social or 'extra-contractual' dimensions of the factory, e.g. transport, nursery facilities, educational courses and the like.

The major problem of the *consigli di zona*, however, was their number. Official statistics recorded a total of 261 throughout the country in 1975, with an equal number planned for future development. Only 46 had premises. Of those in existence, 253 were in central and northern regions and only 8 in the South.[18] Most of those projected for the future were never created, and most of the others ceased to function within a few years.

We have seen something of the effect on the lower levels of the movement of the *sindacato*'s increasingly centralised role, as it attempted to assert itself as a *soggetto politico*. We now need to look a little more closely at some other political and ideological aspects of this development.

---

[17] *Atti del XIX convegno nazionale di studio alle Acli 1972*, p. 805.

[18] Cgil, *Organizzazione sindacale e rinnovamento unitario*, pp. 271-3.

Some Regional and Sectoral Developments

Numerous commentators have observed that the most potent symbol of the workers' movement during the 1960s and 1970s was the *operaio massa*, and even more typically the unskilled metalworker, such as at Fiat in Turin or at Breda in Milan. During the *sindacato*'s period of ascendancy, the industrial working class was able to aggregate the demands of all sectors of society in a remarkable way. Indeed, one of Italy's leading observers of the industrial relations scene has recently refined this point and argued forcefully that the most powerful ideological ingredient of the *sindacato*'s mobilising capacity was the egalitarianism of the Catholic and communist metalworkers' federations which underlay all the economic and social demands of the late 1960s and the 1970s.[1] Accornero contends that the centrality of this perspective, itself the result of a peculiarly Italian fusion of Catholic and communist ideological elements, was a major cause of the comparative decline which the movement later suffered in the 1980s.

While it is true that the *sindacato*'s egalitarianism eventually began to damage its capacity to mobilise, there were other reasons for its loss of momentum which should not be ignored. There was, for example, widespread support for the movement's ambitions as a social and political agent. But its subsequent inability to live up to expectations and promote reforms from the mid-1970s also contributed to a decline in its public credibility.

So long as ideological factors continued to weigh heavily on the *sindacato*'s development, the Catholic and communist union confederations were practically alone in shaping the destiny of the movement. But these confederations were not monoliths, and a brief discussion of how they differed in some regions and economic sectors, in addition to having an intrinsic value of its own, may also produce some insights into the broader question of the changing

---

[1] See A. Accornero, *La parabola del sindacato*, especially pp. 20ff.

role of ideology as a factor in the movement's development.

The Italian workers' movement constantly presents surprises to the outside observer. It would not be unreasonable, for example, to expect the bedrock of communist support to have been in the great industrial centres. But a comparison between the great industrial centre of Turin and the smaller and less heavily industrialised Modena, for instance, reveals that in 1981, of the unionised workers in industry in Turin 48 per cent belonged to Cgil federations and 24 per cent to those of the Cisl, while in Modena the figures were 86 per cent and 8 per cent respectively. Not only were the workers more unionised in the smaller town, with its local ties to agriculture still strong, but they were also more closely identified with the communists. Earlier, in 1971, the metalworkers' federations formed a single union, the FLM, while also retaining their separate identities as FIM-Cisl, FIOM-Cgil and UILM-Uil. Individual workers could join the unitary federation with or without confederate affiliation. Between 1975 and 1983, while workers not affiliating to a confederation varied between 50 and 60 per cent in Turin, in Modena only 5-7 per cent declined confederate allegiance.[2] The smaller, provincial capital of a mainly agricultural area, whose industrialisation was recent by comparison with Italy's industrial capital, was not only more highly unionised, but also more politicised.

Italy is a country with strong regional identities. Political and social commentators, when conducting national surveys or analyses, are faced with two main alternatives. They can use a purely geographical classification and divide the regions into North-West, North-East, Central and the South and Islands.[3] The North-East and Central regions can be varied slightly, to add a subcultural dimension to the classification. However, those analysts who wish

---

[2] See Golden, *Labor Divided*, pp. 176 and 190.

[3] The most commonly accepted classification for Italy's twenty administrative regions is as follows. North-West: Piemonte, Valle d'Aosta, Liguria, Lombardia; North-East: Veneto, Trentino-Alto Adige, Friuli Venezia-Giulia, Emilia Romagna; Central: Toscana, Marche, Umbria, Lazio; South and Islands: Abruzzi, Molise, Campania, Puglia, Basilicata, Calabria, Sicilia, Sardegna. This classification is sometimes varied. Emilia Romagna, for example, is occasionally put among the Central regions.

to focus on the country's major ideological divide between Catholics and communists tend to group the country's administrative regions, and in some cases provinces, as follows: the Industrial triangle of the North; the White, mainly Catholic, area; the Red, strongly communist, area; and the South and Islands.[4] But all such classifications have to be used with flexibility in a country which constantly surprises the analyst. There are provinces in the North where union membership favours the Cisl over the Cgil by more than 2:1. The strongest concentrations of communist Cgil support, moreover, are in traditionally agricultural areas in the Centre-North, where even industry is of small and medium dimensions, rather than in the large industrial cities where one might expect to find such support. One will find provinces in the South where the share of union membership is in the balance, and many which are so conservative as to regard even the Catholic Cisl with suspicion.

The Industrial Sector

Although the Cgil has always been stronger than the Cisl in the industrial sector, the degree of dominance has varied over time and according to region. Some of the variations can be clearly related to the developments described in earlier parts of this study. For example, the dramatic fall of Cgil unionisation between 1951 and 1961 was closely linked to the defeat of the Cgil in the 1955 Fiat elections for the internal commissions, as was its subsequent recovery in the 1960s and 1970s after the confederation's change of direction (see Appendix, Table 1). In most regions, the Cisl has

---

[4] A number of works, including the comparative study of the Cgil and the Cisl edited by Guido Romagnoli, *La sindacalizzazione tra ideologia e pratica* (see vol. i, p. 168), use the following grouping: <u>Industrial triangle</u>: Piemonte, Valle d'Aosta, Liguria, Lombardia (excluding the provinces of Bergamo, Brescia, Sondrio and Mantova), and the provinces of Piacenza and Lucca; the <u>White area</u>: Trentino Alto-Adige, Friuli Venezia-Giulia, Veneto (excluding the province of Rovigo), and the provinces of Bergamo, Brescia and Sondrio; the <u>Red area</u>: Emilia Romagna (excluding the province of Piacenza), Toscana (excluding the province of Lucca), Umbria, Marche (excluding the province of Ascoli Piceno), and the provinces of Mantova, Rovigo and Viterbo (the last of these from the region of Lazio); the <u>South and Islands</u>: all the remaining regions and provinces.

never been able to challenge seriously its communist counterpart in industry. In the White belt, however, it developed some of its industrial unions quite successfully to rival the Cgil. Along with the metalworkers' FIM, which eventually became the vanguard of the Cisl's industrial policy, the FILTA was often strong among textile workers, and the Federchimici achieved a reasonable level of membership among workers in chemical and related industries. The Cisl's industrial federations, moreover, had one important advantage over their Cgil counterparts, which undoubtedly won them some members. As the industrial federations began to build their organizations in the 1960s, their function was given great prominence through the Cisl's commitment to articulated bargaining, a practice which the Cgil took longer to endorse. On the other hand, as the decade witnessed an increasing willingness on the part of workers to support industrial action, the more experienced industrial leaders of the Cgil were able to generate new support for their own organizations.

But there were important local factors which affected union membership. Given the strong tradition of the territorially-based confederate organizations in the Italian *sindacato*, at local level the category unions often developed in the shadow of either the Cgil's *camera del lavoro*, or, in the case of the Cisl, the *unione sindacale*. Frequently, category unions were located in the headquarters of their respective confederate organizations. This could be a stimulus to development, but it could also lead to internal rivalries. Where the Cisl was weak in industry, for example, as in the communist stronghold of Emilia Romagna, its centre of local union activity was the provincial *unione sindacale*, which felt obliged to encourage the growth of the industrial unions, but which would often itself be funded by its agricultural federations. The Cisl hierarchy, far removed from the strains of local disputes and anxious to make inroads into the industrial monopoly of the Cgil, would, therefore, consider such shifting of resources productive, though this could generate enormous tensions at local level.

The ability of these provincial and sub-provincial structures to employ full-time officials was crucial. The time of union officials in these local headquarters, however, was not wholly spent in local and workplace negotiations. Much of it was given to assisting and advising their members on such matters as pensions, family allowances, health insurance payments, and a whole range of work-

and socially-related matters. The ability of the local *camera del lavoro* or *unione sindacale* to provide such assistance could be crucial in attracting members. This was even more so in the South, where before 1969 industrial federations had hardly existed. Even after 1969 in many parts of the South industrial unions were little more than formal creations. There were, however, as we shall see, exceptions to this.

After the 'Hot Autumn', the overall rate of unionisation in industry increased, and although the Cgil maintained its general position of dominance in this sector, patterns of development began to change. Workers were attracted to the unions more by the new issues which had been raised than by ideological traditions, though such traditions did not cease to count altogether. Particularly in the White areas, where the Cisl's industrial federations were stronger, they produced young and enthusiastic leaders, whose new ideas and conflictual orientation enabled the Catholic industrial unions to keep pace with the equally dramatic increase in membership in the rival communist-led federations.[5] But these Catholic federations were attracting new members for reasons which were not related to the Cisl's past. Numerous industrial unions established their own headquarters and became financially independent of local confederate structures, although such developments were rarer in the strongly communist areas of the Centre-North, where the Cisl found it difficult to keep pace with its rival. Some industrial federations, particularly on the Catholic side, tried to abandon the 'advisory' roles of local confederate structures, with their excessive attention to individual cases. *Assistenzialismo*, as it was called, conflicted with the increased professionalism and *contrattualismo* which the new brand of Cisl leaders within the industrial unions were trying to promote throughout the movement. But these critical ideas were much easier to sustain in the North, where category unions were able to develop more independently of collateral structures than in the South.

Common to members of Cgil and Cisl industrial unions during the 1970s, throughout the Centre and North of the country, was the enormous increase in support for greater unity. A growing number of workers wished to join unitary federations without confederate affiliations. This led to a certain relaxation of traditional

---

[5] See Romagnoli (ed.), *La sindacalizzazione*, vol. ii, pp. 32ff.

rivalries, and local officials on both sides began to pay less attention to the daily business of recruitment, which in the past had always been charged with a highly competitive edge.

The picture was a little different in the South. Although anti-communist polemics diminished in the 1970s, the unity which was given vigorous support in the northern part of the country received little more than formal acknowledgement in the South. Here not only did it remain standard practice for local headquarters to be shared by the Cisl and its federal structures, but offices would frequently be common to the Cisl, the Acli and even the Dc. The same was sometimes true for the Cgil and Pci.

Except for a few large factories in cities like Naples, the industrial federations in the South had to operate in a totally different environment from their northern counterparts. Even where the communist-led FIOM seemed to have a good base of support in local factories, such support would often owe more to the charisma of particular leaders than to policy or political conviction. Leaders occasionally transferred from one federation to another and would even take members with them. Surveys seem to have confirmed that this kind of relationship between cadres and rank-and-file was widespread in the South, as also were forms of *clientelismo*.[6] Frequently, industrial federations were the creation of a particular factory and sometimes of workers or cadres from the North. Such cadres, particularly in the case of the Catholic FIM, and especially if they were strong on unity, found themselves in difficulty with the local confederate structures. Occasionally, such unions would be regarded as not properly belonging to the Cisl. Such experiences were less likely to occur in the FIOM and Cgil. Overall up to the late 1970s at national level, policy and leadership within the industrial federations tended to be shaped predominantly in the northern part of the country.

Agriculture

Glancing at the figures in Table 1 of the Appendix, it may surprise the reader to find that even in the agricultural sector, except for a

---

[6] See ibid., pp. 99ff.

period in the White regions, the Cgil has had a higher membership than its Catholic rival. We must remember, however, that these figures are for unions which organize agricultural workers and they do not include peasants and other small-scale landowners, who constituted a solid base of support for the world of political Catholicism. The support for the Cgil is not so surprising if we recall the land occupations during the late 1940s and the role of communist leaders within these struggles. After the *Cgil unitaria* was split and cold war hostilities brought deep political divisions into the union camp, the Fisba-Cisl and the Cgil's Federbraccianti, which organized agricultural workers, were among the most ideologically and politically entrenched of the workers' organizations. This was the pattern up and down the country, certainly well into the 1970s.

Changes in the 1970s varied enormously between and even within regions. They also differed substantially from those in industry. The *assistenzialismo* towards which some of the industrial federations were becoming more and more hostile was, by contrast, increasingly important as a means of gaining membership for both the Fisba and Federbraccianti. In some northern regions, where the industrial unions were beginning to grow in organizational strength and membership, conflicts arose at local level between these and the agricultural unions over resources and even policy orientation, particularly on the question of 'unity', an issue on which the industrial federations were forcing the pace. Such internal tensions tended to be more frequent in Catholic organizations, although they were by no means absent from the Cgil.

The unevenness in patterns of development was particularly evident in the South, where unemployment was greater than in the North. Unionisation has always been of two types in agriculture. First, there were workers with fixed employment, whose requirements were largely contractual. The South, however, had a much higher proportion than the North of ill-protected *precari*, who made up the bulk of the agricultural unions' membership. Thus the southern local union official's time was often largely taken up with helping to obtain the various forms of assistance available. Competition between the rival organizations would often revolve around which was most effective in obtaining such assistance. The natural advantage which the Fisba enjoyed locally in being closer to the ruling party was a mixed blessing. On the one hand, good relations with the party in office were an advantage, particularly in the South, where clientelistic practices were ingrained. On the other hand, the Fisba was less able to develop autonomously from confederate structures and shape a distinctive identity for itself than its rival. By contrast, the Federbraccianti tended to gain some benefit from being the more 'natural' defender of the dispossessed.

The Tertiary Sector: Public Administration

Although global statistics for the 1960s and 1970s show the Cgil to have had a higher membership nationally than the Cisl in the tertiary sector as a whole, it must be remembered that this sector bands together workers ranging from the school porter to the airline pilot. Since some of these categories are discussed elsewhere in this study, we shall focus on an area of particular interest, one in which the Cisl has traditionally been dominant.

The category with which one traditionally associates Cisl domination in this sector is public administration. Even before the great increase in tertiarisation in the 1970s, in many parts of the country employees in public administration alone accounted for more than 20 per cent of the entire Cisl membership.[7] Membership of the Cisl was advantageous for public sector employees, even in traditionally Red areas, so it is not surprising that the Cisl/Cgil ratio of membership sometimes reached 3:1. Even in the Red regions, the Cgil found it difficult to compete with its Catholic rival. Indeed, Catholic resolve to remain ahead would often be stronger in the Red regions than in those areas where its dominance was not threatened. Prior to 1969, therefore, the main appeal of the Cisl to potential members lay either in its traditional ideological allegiance to the world of political Catholicism, or in the prospect of employment and promotion offered by the public administration's clientelistic structures, in which the Cisl was entangled. While in the North the motivation was mixed in roughly equal proportions, the clientelistic element was more important in the South.

Throughout the 1970s, however, Cisl domination in the world of public administration was reduced. And although the main

---

[7] See the vast range of regional statistics available in ibid., pp. 193-240. A very useful complementary volume, providing more detailed statistics in each category, is E. Biagioni et al., *Indagine sul sindacato*, pp. 14-164.

novelty overall seemed to be a shift in the proportion of membership in favour of the Cgil, a new factor emerged which in the 1980s would then spread to other sectors. In northern regions in particular, as a more unitarian approach developed in some of the confederate unions, 'autonomous' unions began to gain strength. But even here the pattern was varied. In some White areas, for instance, where co-operation between Cgil and Cisl was developing, particularly in the health sector, 'autonomous' unions emerged with closer ties to the Dc, which had lost control of the relevant collateral union (Fiso-Cisl). In some Red areas, however, the Cisl's public employees' union (Sinascel) was so conservative that even its membership of the Cisl seemed incongruous. Occasionally, in parts of the health sector where the left was in control, the Fiso-Cisl found itself in the unusual position of being able to accuse its rival of *clientelismo.*[8]

The Cisl remained uniformly dominant in the public administration unions in the South during the 1970s. Nevertheless, it did see its proportion of union membership drop, sometimes dramatically, in urban centres. From the early 1970s, however, there developed within the Cisl an internal opposition to the conservatism and clientelistic practices of the leaders within the public service unions. New leaders emerged who were less interested in anti-communist polemics, and who wished furthermore to see an end to the confederation's collateralism with the Dc. But the unitarians within the Cisl were never sufficiently numerous to create genuinely collaborative initiatives, and there were many areas in the South which remained almost untouched by change. Thus, given the peculiar arrangements which allowed unions a place within the managerial structures of the public administration, the Cisl was in a very strong position. In effect this was a source of *clientelismo* which brought little credit to the organization. The ties with the Dc within the Cisl's public sector unions remained strong. After the advances of the left in the 1975 local elections, for instance, many of the local administrators and civil servants who obstructed the initiatives of the new left-wing councils in their efforts to reform the notoriously inefficient and corrupt local services were Cisl members.

---

[8] See Romagnoli, *La sindacalizzazione*, vol. ii, pp. 64ff.

Conclusion

Over the twenty-year period upon which we have focused, there is little doubt that overall the federations obtained greater autonomy *vis-à-vis* horizontal/territorial structures, even though the degree to which this happened varied enormously from one locality to another. This was, of course, in line with the development of the federations at national level. This was accompanied by a tertiarisation of both labour and unions, a process which continued to expand, although our observations on the services' sector in this chapter have focused mainly on one group of employees.

Perhaps the most significant change from our point of view was taking place on the ideological level. There is little doubt that in many country areas, particularly in the South, a traditional conservatism still worked to the advantage of the Cisl. This was also true nationally for the middle-class membership of the public sector unions. But even in these situations, such a hold was less secure than previously, especially since many unions were moving towards closer collaboration. The unitary structure of the national federation Cgil-Cisl-Uil, although less uniformly replicated at lower levels, nevertheless had a powerful effect on the thinking of local officials up and down the country. In industry, as has already been indicated, traditional ideological allegiances were losing much of the overweening power they had exercised over workers' choice of union in the 1950s and 1960s.

The changing distribution of membership between the two major confederations, if examined by geographical region, overwhelmingly suggests that subcultural traditions were losing their hold on union members. In Table 2 (see Appendix), I have used a geographical distribution of regions into national areas which has the advantage of presenting a fairly homogeneous White North East, and a substantially Red Centre. It is clear from the figures in Table 2 that the most significant trend is the tendency for the proportions of membership to converge towards the centre, i.e. for the share of the combined membership in every case to move towards 50 per cent. In three of the areas, the larger of the organizations, the Cgil, loses ground to the Cisl. If we examine the figures for these three areas alone, it might seem reasonable to conclude that the Cisl is becoming more popular and that the convergence towards the centre is incidental. But what is of greater interest is what is happening in the fourth area, the predominantly White North East. If the trend of major significance were simply the fact that the Cisl was becoming more popular, why was this pattern reversed in its own stronghold?

One can make sense of this confusing pattern of shifts only by taking into account major changes in the 'ideological' factor. In other words, once we observe that there is a 'decline of ideology' the explanation becomes quite straightforward. Such a decline, however, takes place alongside a more general trend.

If we take the general trend first, we note that in simple numerical terms, union membership continued to increase for both confederations over the thirty-year period from 1960 to 1990. During this period, the Cisl was able to shake off its 'conservative', employer-oriented image of the 1950s and increasingly validate its credentials as a labour organization. The gradual growth in its share of the combined membership reflects this increasing acceptance of the Cisl as a 'proper' union confederation. In a very important sense, the 'unionisation' of the Cisl is by the same token a 'de-ideologisation' of its style of operation. The Cisl becomes more of a rival to the Cgil as a union, and less as the representative of an alternative subculture. The fact that this pattern of change is intensified in the Red regions and reversed in the White regions illustrates the greater adjustment required in those parts of the country where ideological and political allegiances are stronger. Thus the diminishing force of ideology has accelerated the trend towards the Cisl in the Red regions. But in the White areas, taken as a whole, the collapse of the 'White' factor cancelled out the 'natural' shift towards the Cisl, and in fact *reversed* it. In other words, the pattern of change was clearly damaging to the Cisl where it had been ideologically strong as a 'Catholic' union.

The weakening of the ideological factor in potential members' choice of union was accompanied by a greater ideological pluralism within the organizations themselves. But it is important to note the limitations of such change. Within the confederations, ideological change was not the same as political change. Traditional collateralist links between unions and parties were not based on ideology alone and were destined to survive for some time to come.

18

The Problems of a *Soggetto Politico*

From the Reform Strategy to EUR

There were two phases in the *sindacato*'s reform strategy in the 1970s. The reform strategy on which the *sindacato* embarked during its period of buoyancy at the beginning of the decade set out an ambitious programme, aimed at correcting the structural weaknesses of the national economy and impressing on it a new model of development. The confederations' proposals were wide-ranging. Those on public spending included the formation of a unified health system in place of the chaotic range of schemes previously available, as well as the reform of education and the creation of a housing programme with the necessary powers of land expropriation. The *sindacato* also proposed the reform of the grossly inequitable tax system, whose burden fell disproportionately on those taxed at source, and which at the same time allowed billions to be lost to the public purse. Initiatives were proposed for redirecting investment and for restructuring and modernising industry and agriculture. The proposals were clearly aimed at shifting the burden of development on to the internal market through a greater reliance on public consumption. The strategy was an attempt to create a set of objectives at the macroeconomic plane and thus provide a coherent framework within which to shape workers' claims right down to plant level.

The second phase of the *sindacato*'s strategy, however, entailed a major change of course, since the recession which followed the global oil crisis of 1973 made it impossible for the *sindacato* to pursue all its objectives simultaneously.[1] Employers and government began increasingly to see the solution to the

---

[1] For a comprehensive account of the *sindacato*'s change of strategy in response to the economic crises of the decade, see P. Lange and M. Vannicelli, 'Strategy under Stress: The Italian Union Movement and the Italian Crisis in Developmental Perspective', pp. 136ff.

country's economic problems in terms of lowering the costs of production, and the *sindacato* had to find ways of avoiding lay-offs and defending wages, without losing sight of its strategic aims. In practice, this meant that many of the *social* demands within the *sindacato*'s programme were suspended in favour of more urgent economic objectives. But even this modified agenda would prove difficult to implement. The reform strategy pursued up until the mid-1970s had not been successful, largely because mass mobilisation had not been sufficient to compensate for the lack of institutional and party support. Without such pressure the government, which had been the *sindacato*'s chief interlocutor in these early years, was unlikely to pay heed to the movement's demands. But despite these difficulties, there were changes in the political scene after 1975 which suggested that the situation might change.

In June 1975 local and regional elections saw a major increase in support for the Pci, producing six regional parliaments out of twenty with communist-led coalitions, and giving the communists a relative majority in eight out of the eleven largest Italian cities. The following year, in the national elections, the Pci gained an unprecedented 343 seats in both houses, and closed the gap considerably on the Dc with the latter's total of 398. Given the unwillingness of the Psi, under its new leader Bettino Craxi, to enter into another centre-left coalition, the Dc was forced into an arrangement whereby, from July 1976 onwards, the government could survive only with the 'abstention' of communist opposition votes. The Andreotti government was subsequently brought down in January 1978 by the Republican Party's insistence that the communists should be included in a government of national emergency. Although not given cabinet responsibility, the Pci was brought into what was called the *maggioranza programmatica* in March 1978. This meant that the government could now expect positive votes from the communists and not simply abstentions. Clearly, the new era of co-operation between 1976 and 1979 was a period which awakened new hopes and fears in the *sindacato*. After 1976 all discussions within the movement took place against the background of a possible entry of the Pci into government.

In January 1977 Enrico Berlinguer launched the Pci's 'austerity' programme, arguing that economic renewal could not be brought about painlessly. The social reforms for which the unions were pressing could not be achieved against a background of increasing labour costs. The Pci was adding its moderating influence to that of Lama within the Cgil. The agreements on containing labour costs which the unions reached with the employers in January 1977 and with the government two months later should be seen within the context of this additional pressure on the *sindacato* from the Pci, anxious as the latter was to demonstrate its ability to bridle union demands and so prove an effective force in government.

To numerous members of the Cisl and Uil, and to many socialists within the Cgil, it looked as if the Pci wished to impose sacrifices on the workers and control the unions so as to achieve its ambition of entering government, thus gaining full legitimacy in the political system. Yet it cannot be said that Berlinguer's 'austerity' line was in conflict with the direction being taken by the *sindacato* itself since the mid-1970s. There was widespread acceptance within the confederate leadership that an exclusively conflictual approach to industrial relations was out of tune with the *sindacato*'s ambitions to contribute to the formation of public policy.

But there was more to Berlinguer's proposals than an appeal for restraint from the workers. His remarks on wage moderation were made within the context of a shift to a form of economic development aimed at 'overcoming models of consumption and [economic] behaviour based on unrestrained individualism', and at remedying the major structural distortions within the Italian economy.[2] When we look at the matter more closely, therefore, we find a great deal in common between the framework of Berlinguer's 'austerity' proposals and the new priorities established by the *sindacato*. Luciano Lama, the leader of the Cgil, would shortly highlight such parallels even more plainly.

The new model of economic development projected by the confederations focused on a number of structural changes: industrialisation of the South, along with the modernisation of its agriculture; industrial reconversion and programmes of investment favouring productive activities and public consumption; more effective use of the state-holding sector in promoting these

---

[2] For Berlinguer's 'austerity' speech, see E. Berlinguer, 'Conclusioni al convegno degli intellettuali', pp. 293-308.

developments. These themes were restated at the congresses of the confederations, all held in 1977. The link with 'austerity' was most explicit in the Cgil, where Lama stressed that uncontrolled wage increases and irrational patterns of consumption militated against the objectives of long-term structural reform.[3]

The leader of the Uil, Giorgio Benvenuto, speaking at the Cgil Congress, shared the objectives of the Cgil but warned that 'austerity' needed concrete links with a coherent programme of development, otherwise the *sindacato*'s good will 'would be exploited in the direction of existing economic policy and end up consolidating dominant interests'.[4] In his report to the Cisl Congress a few days later, Luigi Macario decried the irrational effects of the unplanned and distorted economic development being pursued. The much-vaunted *centralità dell'impresa* (central role of enterprise) in Italian society being promoted by the employers could not remain an exclusively economic phenomenon, he argued, 'but had to confront the problems of employment and the need for development in the nation'.[5] The future leader of the Cisl, Pierre Carniti, in his speech, emphasised that 'it would be on the question of the South that the outcome of the crisis would be decided'.[6]

The General Secretary of the Cgil, Luciano Lama, declared in a press interview to *la Repubblica* on 24 January 1978 that just as the *sindacato* had refused to accept that profits were an 'independent variable' in the economy, so it was time to accept that wages and employment were not so either. In an open economy, he declared, there could be no 'independent variables', since all the major factors were mutually interdependent. His remarks were, in effect, a prelude to a Cgil-Cisl-Uil conference which produced what became known as the EUR strategy. On 13 and 14 February a conference of almost 1,500 delegates took place at the Palazzo dei Congressi in EUR, Rome. It had been organized by the Cgil-Cisl-Uil federation at a time when a possible Pci entry into the

---

[3] See *I congressi della Cgil*, vol. x, p. 47.

[4] Ibid., p. 168.

[5] Cisl, *Atti del VIII Congresso confederale*, p. 41.

[6] Ibid., p. 201.

maggioranza programmatica or 'governmental majority' was being widely discussed. There was, therefore, a reasonable expectation that increased Pci influence would improve the chances of a positive response from the government to any new union initiatives.

The conference in EUR gave the most formalised expression to date of the *sindacato*'s activity as a *soggetto politico*. In a radical break with past practice, it gave official recognition to the subordination of the usual bargaining objectives to longer-term advantages accruing to the workers as a whole. It accepted, in other words, wage restraint and the flexible use of labour both within and between places of work. But there were conditions attached to such sacrifices. Reforms were demanded in areas such as housing, agriculture, energy, transport, tax and state finance.[7]

But the immediate focus of the *sindacato*'s strategy was on the question of how the resources released on the union side of the bargain could be most effectively used for productive investment by both the government and the employers. The former was to re-examine the investment patterns of those productive sectors under its control, e.g. the *partecipazioni statali*, with the aim of redirecting economic activity more effectively. The regions were to be given greater power to allocate resources, along with adequate mechanisms and funds to make regional planning possible. The key to the *sindacato*'s approach towards the employers, however, both private and public, was control over investment. Provisions to discuss investments had been included more and more in national contracts ever since the first agreement between the metalworkers' unions and Fiat in 1970, in which the *sindacato* agreed to a phased introduction of the newly agreed 40-hour week in return for investment in the South. Investment planning, however, could be successful only if it combined both short- and medium-term objectives with plans prepared at the industrial-sector level on a regional basis. A massive vote in favour carried the EUR proposals.

The Confindustria was nevertheless sceptical, many employers regarding the proposals as a Trojan Horse intended to overwhelm the citadel of the entrepreneurs. But the success of the plan hinged also on the attitude of the government and its ability to

---

[7] For a more detailed discussion of the contents of the EUR proposals, see Lange and Vannicelli, 'Strategy under Stress', pp. 166-79.

respond to the terms of the proposals. Given the continued growth in inflation during the winter of 1977-8, the six parties of what was shortly to become the 'governmental majority' welcomed the proposals. Two weeks after the conclusion of the EUR conference on 14 February, the Secretary of the Dc, Aldo Moro, made a speech to his party's parliamentarians in which he was able to point to some concrete benefits of communist influence and win support for the entry of the communists into the 'governmental majority'. The linking of the Pci with the EUR strategy in this way, however, proved to be of dubious benefit to the *sindacato*.

In terms of its immediate aims, the strategy was a failure. There were various reasons for this. In spite of the substantial vote in favour of the EUR proposals at the conference itself, many union leaders, particularly those within the metalworkers' federations, were worried that acceptance of the 'austerity' aspects of the programme would depoliticise industrial conflict.[8] There was widespread concern over the marked shift from an adversarial to a collaborative stance. More immediately, however, the long-term operation of the *scala mobile* which had been agreed in 1975 was reducing differentials among workers and giving rise to considerable resentment among the more skilled operatives. Thus, the pressure on union negotiators in renewing contracts during the winter of 1978-9 'led practically all the category federations to find strategies for avoiding the co-ordinated restraint demanded by the secretariat of the Cgil-Cisl-Uil federation'.[9] Beneath the ritual acknowledgement of EUR, the industrial unions were seeking real wage increases for their members.

This ambiguity enabled the employers to claim that EUR was defunct. It was particularly the case with those employers in the Confindustria who were unwilling to accept long-term objectives imposed by political pressures. The government also used wage claims to justify its own failure to act, and with the Pci now within the 'governmental majority' and unable to oppose, it felt more than usually safe.

It was clear that the strategy had relied too much on the Pci's

---

[8] Miriam Golden has carried out a detailed study of internal dissent over the EUR proposals. See particularly her *Labor Divided*, pp. 89ff.

[9] Turone, *Il sindacato nell'Italia del benessere*, p. 65.

ability to obtain results from within the 'governmental majority'. By the end of 1978 many Cgil leaders were beginning to fear that they were losing touch with a base which was becoming increasingly impatient with the *sindacato*'s plea for sacrifices to no apparent purpose. In January 1979 the Pci, unable to make any headway, accused the government of deliberately undermining EUR. The Dc had skilfully exploited the communists' desire for respectability in order to moderate union demands. On 31 January the Pci withdrew its support from the government and returned to opposition. The failure of the EUR strategy marked the beginning of a period of prolonged crisis for the *sindacato*. Yet it is not at all clear that the experiment was an unqualified failure in every respect. However problematic it proved to be, it was in many ways a high point of programmatic cohesion. Its failure was in large part due to a government which presided over an increasingly degenerating political process which it could not control. It is doubtful whether it could have kept to the terms of EUR even if it had wished to do so, and it was certainly grateful for the excuse not to try. But the strategy had provided some important lessons for the *sindacato* as it continued to review its role in society.

Unions, Parties and Government

Following the 'Hot Autumn', the *sindacato*'s newly won strength in Italian society made it a direct bargaining partner with the government on reforms. From the mid-1970s, however, as pressing economic problems made the reforms more difficult, and as the opponents of reform gained increasing influence, the situation changed. Direct meetings between the unions and the government became less frequent, and the confederations were forced back into greater reliance on political parties to press their case. Thus some of the influence which the parties had been losing over the unions began to reassert itself. Within this context there was, in effect, a real link between the EUR strategy and the promotion of the Pci into the sphere of government.

There have been severe judgements on this aspect of EUR, and indeed on the *sindacato*'s apparent willingness to draw closer to the political parties. The fact remains, however, that there were not many alternatives. As far as the EUR strategy was concerned, without the Pci in the 'governmental majority' there were even fewer prospects of a positive response to the union proposals. But could renewed party influence ever amount to a return to the past?

From the time in the sixties when the confederations began to draw closer, a tendency had emerged to keep the *sindacato* equidistant from all political parties in the interests of unity. In his report to the June 1977 Cgil Congress, Lama rejected the assumptions underlying this tendency. It was absurd, he argued, not to recognise the Pci's greater claims to the *sindacato*'s support, and to turn a blind eye to the benefits which the party's inclusion in government could bring. This was different, he stressed, from giving the Pci unqualified support, and he repeated that the confederation would place the interests of workers, and of the country at large, before loyalty to any political party.[10]

At the Cisl Congress a few days later, various tendencies emerged. One group of Cisl leaders who seemed to be promoting a new *collateralismo* with the Dc, was in favour of the project to clean up the image of the party being promoted by the new party Secretary Benigno Zaccagnini, 'l'onesto Zac'. This group would support Dc-Pci collaboration if the party chose to follow this path, but it was clearly not pressing for it. A second tendency, which consisted largely of an alliance between the Catholic 'new left' and socialists who had begun to join the Cisl in the seventies, was suspicious of the 'historic compromise', since this threatened to weaken the adversarial role of the opposition in parliament, if not to obliterate it completely. Additionally, they feared that, by extension, union leaders, in support of their respective parties engaged in this *consociazione* (consociation), would be over-anxious to stabilise the political situation and restrain rank-and-file demands in order not to put the political alliance under strain. These reservations about a possible Dc-Pci collaboration had the effect of producing a consensus around the formula proposed by a third group, the *contrattualisti* or 'contractualists'. This compromise was well expressed by the General Secretary Macario, who held firm to the confederation's 'refusal to declare a preference for any particular government

---

[10] *I congressi della Cgil*, vol. x, especially pp. 48ff.

formula' since, he continued, the *sindacato* was unwilling to 'function as an extension of any party'.[11]

In the autumn of 1976 the socialist Giorgio Benvenuto had been elected General Secretary of the Uil, to replace the republican Raffaele Vanni. Ignoring communist claims that Berlinguer's 'historic compromise' did not exclude parties other than the Dc, Benvenuto attacked it as if it were intended as a proposal for power-sharing between the two major forces. In a press interview in early October 1976 he claimed that 'the country is positively sliding towards a bipolarised political situation, and this runs the risk of producing political stagnation, which in turn changes the whole strategy of the *sindacato*'.[12] At the Uil Congress the following year Benvenuto welcomed the fact that discrimination against the communists was at last breaking down but repeated his warnings against the illusion that a Dc-Pci political deal could solve the country's problems.

Despite the leading historic role of the Pci in the struggles of the working class, there was no single party which could, in government, command the automatic loyalty and co-operation of all sections of the *sindacato*. Indeed to some extent it was the fragmented nature of the *sindacato*'s party loyalties which had led it to seek an independent role as a *soggetto politico* and thus promote its centralising functions. There were, moreover, certain advantages for the government in encouraging the development of greater union centralisation and in engaging the *sindacato* in direct negotiations. It was clearly desirable to negotiate with a partner which could control internal dissent. This was all the more important since it was evident that developments in Italian society were making it impossible to manage the economy without union co-operation. The alternative, curtailment of union power through either legislation or a series of critical confrontations in which the *sindacato* would be defeated, a path which the UK, for example, would later choose to follow from 1980, was not a realistic possibility in Italy. In any case, the unions had displayed a willingness to co-operate from the mid-1970s, and the EUR strategy seemed to many to have consolidated the shift in the *sindacato*'s

---

[11] Cisl, *Atti del VIII Congresso confederale*, p. 64.

[12] S. Turone, *Storia dell'Unione Italiana del Lavoro*, p. 185.

orientation 'from systematic conflict to institutional bargaining'.[13]

To what extent such developments towards high-level bargaining were, as some commentators claimed at the time, neo-corporatist, will be discussed later. One can understand, however, how the *sindacato*'s political aspirations gave rise to such speculation, especially bearing in mind some of the comments of union leaders themselves. Writing in 1978, the leader of the Uil, Giorgio Benvenuto, claimed that the *sindacato*'s view of its political role 'leads to a completely original conception of institutional relations'.[14] At the macroeconomic level, he continued, 'the *sindacato* collaborates above all with the government (and prior to this with the political parties) in defining general objectives', subsequently 'employing its structures at sector, territorial and workplace level to achieve objectives which it has set itself in economic policy', although Benvenuto's comments, at least on this occasion, stressed the importance of continual reference back to the membership, precisely to *avoid* falling into neo-corporatism.[15]

It emerges clearly both from the debates within the movement and from official statements that most Italian *sindacalisti* considered moves in a neo-corporatist direction a threat to the *sindacato*'s autonomy. A variety of European experiences, not all of a neo-corporatist kind, were discussed. It was argued, for example, that the 'co-determination' (*Mitbestimmung*) of the German approach simply legitimised existing capitalist structures and that the *autogestion* (workers' self-management) being promoted in France lacked any capacity to transform economic structures.[16] There was no evidence in either experience that the unions had become a force for change. There was a difference between being involved in managing the economy and reaching agreements with the government about economic objectives. The

---

[13] M. Golden, 'Neo-corporativismo ed esclusione della forza-lavoro dalla rappresentanza politica', pp. 226-7.

[14] G. Benvenuto, *Il sindacato tra movimento e istituzioni*, p. 93.

[15] See ibid., pp. 100ff.

[16] See Lange and Vannicelli, 'Strategy under Stress', pp. 158ff, for a more comprehensive discussion of this.

latter option left each side free to take appropriate action if the other reneged on the bargain. The key to economic restructuring, and at the same time the most meaningful step in the direction of greater industrial democracy, was the contractual provision for influencing patterns of investment. The message was very clear. In order to participate in controlling social and economic development, 'it is not necessary to be inside the institutions ... . The movement cannot but reject any suggestion of co-determination or any form of absorption into public institutions.'[17] Each confederation stressed this point at its own 1977 congress. In 1978, the EUR agreement seemed to go even further, stressing 'the autonomy of the *sindacato* and the rejection of any concept of "social pact"'.[18] Despite such apparently forthright rejections of the neo-corporatist model, however, the question would resurface within the movement for a short but significant period before it could finally be laid to rest.

Paradoxically, the weakness in the *sindacato*'s quest for autonomy lay in the heterogeneous nature of its party affiliations. Although this need not, in theory, have been a weakness, it was indeed a problem in the Italian political situation, where the left was itself divided and unable to press a coherent direction on government. The problem for the *sindacato* was that the traditional loyalties of different sections of the movement were to parties which frequently pulled in different political directions. Nevertheless, there was no doubt that the *sindacato* had achieved some measure of autonomy which was irreversible, and it looked more critically at the policies of its historically collateral parties. The movement had also gained an unprecedented degree of legitimacy in the social and political system. Yet, as we have seen, towards the end of the decade it was forced back into a situation where it found itself at the mercy of inter-party relations without being able to influence them. The Cgil-Cisl-Uil federation had 'become part of the political system, but without being able to create effective mechanisms for political interplay with the other actors within it'.[19] This was the *sindacato*'s dilemma, and the

---

[17] Baglioni, *Il sindacato dell'autonomia*, p. 327.

[18] 'Per una svolta di politica economica: l'Assemblea dell'EUR', p. 150.

[19] Carrieri e Donolo, *Il mestiere politico del sindacato*, p. 98.

problem at the heart of the EUR strategy.

The Unions and Society

The failure of EUR provoked a series of reflections about the state of the *sindacato*, both internally and in its relations with other social forces. Internally, there was a rude awakening to the gap which had grown over the years between the leadership and the rank-and-file. Even union officials complained that more and more frequently their sources of information about internal discussions and decisions were the media and not the movement's own channels for debate and consultation.

But the collapse of the strategy also led to increased scepticism about the real intentions of leading politicians. Perhaps the legitimisation of the Pci had been used simply to serve the cynical intentions of the Dc. A number of laws were passed to facilitate industrial restructuring, youth employment, and planning by sector, but with few tangible results. Apart from the creation of a national health service with the passing of a bill in 1978, little or nothing seemed to change. A parliamentary committee had been established in 1976 with special responsibility for the problems of the Mezzogiorno, but once again proposals could not break down the usual obstacles to innovation. It had become clearer than ever that one of the major barriers to any form of social transformation was the simple fact that the public institutions through which changes had to be effected were themselves badly in need of reform. Given the entrenched interests at stake and the high level of corruption which accompanied any dealings concerned with reforms in the South, the prospects remained grim.

The failure of the Pci to have any effect on government during the period of 'national solidarity' emphasised the immobility of the political system. The inability of the country's leaders to make any headway on the proposed reforms highlighted the institutional paralysis which was creeping into all of Italian society. The idea that Italians were living in a 'blocked democracy' (*democrazia bloccata*) was increasingly evident after 1979.

Among the social forces which felt the full effects of this institutional and political impotence was the women's movement. By 1979 women represented almost 33 per cent of the country's total labour force. But whatever problems existed for their male counterparts, women were sure to be worse affected. In the period we are discussing for example, female earnings for comparable work in the blue-collar industrial sector were 74 per cent of male earnings. Whereas the unemployment rate for males was 4.8 per cent in 1980, it was 13.1 per cent for women.[20] This is not to deny that anti-discrimination initiatives had been taken during the 1970s. Law n.1204 of 30 October 1971 granted security of tenure to women in case of childbirth and protected them against heavy or hazardous forms of employment during pregnancy. Law n.903, was passed on 9 December 1977 on the equality of treatment between men and women. This law forbade discrimination against women in employment applications, wages, promotions, training and dismissals. It ensured equality in relation to pension schemes, family allowances and retirement, and it included a provision for paternity leave. But enforcement in many of these areas was quite another matter.

Bianca Beccalli has pointed out that law n.903 was passed almost entirely without the help of the unions. It was, she said, 'an initiative from the top, unaccompanied by any show of social conflict'.[21] It followed, belatedly, an EC directive, and was passed during a period when the Minister of Labour was a woman. This is not to say that the *sindacato* had ignored the problems of women, but rather that its commitment had been fitful and characterised by frequent ambiguities. Beccalli has indicated that since the War the unions have in fact fought for progressive legislation and defended women's interests. The Cgil in particular, in defending the weaker elements in the labour force, automatically fought for female workers. Contradictions arose, however, in the movement's tendency to accept the dominant values of Italian society, regarding the male as the breadwinner, which produced an equivocal attitude towards issues of equal rights and pay. The Italian *sindacato* found it difficult to focus attention on the problems of women as such, i.e. as distinct from those problems which women share with their male colleagues.

Within the unions themselves women have always been under-represented. In 1975, for example, women held under 1 per

---

[20] See Barkan, *Visions of Emancipation*, pp. 10ff and pp. 140ff.

[21] Beccalli, 'Le politiche del lavoro femminile in Italia', p. 260.

cent of the positions in the provincial secretariats.[22] The situation was improving, but slowly. In 1980, if we examine the case of the Fiat plants in Turin, 20 per cent of the workers, but only 7 per cent of the factory council delegates, were women. The local and provincial metalworkers' union offices employed 131 officials and staff. Of these, 98 were males. Of the 33 women, only 6 had a political role, the remainder being secretarial or related staff. Of the 98 males, on the other hand, 95 were union officials.[23]

The unfair employment practices in society at large were standard within the movement itself. This did not mean that women remained inactive on feminist issues within the unions. In 1974, at the University of Turin, they organized a course on the condition of women in Italian society for those workers who took advantage of the 150-hour study provision in the *statuto dei lavoratori*. These courses spread to other urban centres and attracted students, intellectuals and housewives. The topics began to vary and to include courses on the history of the family, female health care, women in culture, in politics, etc.[24] Women's groups were formed within unions in Turin, Genoa, Verona and Milan from 1975 onwards. Eventually these developed into cross-category networks of co-ordinating committees which received official Cgil-Cisl-Uil recognition in 1978. These groups challenged many traditional, value-laden assumptions inside the movement.

Inevitably, tensions and contradictions emerged from the discussions within these groups. Some of the ideas proved difficult to put into practice when tested against the daily realities of industrial relations. This was the case, for example, with critiques of the patriarchal structure of the *sindacato*. Although women proposed alternative, less combative ways of conducting internal affairs and discussions, in order to shape a less aggressive and male-dominated culture, this was seen by union negotiators, almost all male, as hopelessly utopian and impractical. It was one thing to speculate about such shifts in union culture, but it was quite another to face a tough and ruthless employer across the negotiating table.

---

[22] See A. Cammarota, *Donna, identità, lavoro*, pp. 74ff.

[23] Barkan, *Visions of Emancipation*, p. 143.

[24] See ibid., pp. 141ff.

Within this world, where legitimacy was felt to depend on results, women found themselves adopting patriarchal postures to achieve their own goals. Indeed, many women had been formed within a leftist culture in which class tensions held priority and, therefore, they tended to associate combativity less with patriarchy than with class domination and the need to liberate the working class from oppression. Some argued that it was impossible to resolve women's problems in the movement without first having achieved their own autonomy as women, while others saw union objectives and struggles as deserving priority.

Such differences frequently emerged in relation to concrete bargaining issues, for example on the question of whether or not to press for an increase in part-time employment. Some argued that such a development simply reinforced women in their domestic roles, when what was needed was an equitable division of domestic duties between men and women. These women felt that the *sindacato* should press only for full-time employment for both men and women, and that the problem of domestic responsibilities should be met by new and better services. Such ideas obtained limited support from male union activists. There were women, however, who argued for a more positive appraisal of part-time work. It could be seen, it was stressed, as an option for both men and women who were interested in seeking time for other kinds of activities and improving the quality, and not simply the material prosperity of their lives.

Many of the issues raised by women in the *sindacato*, already difficult problems in themselves, came up against the inertia of the Italian institutional and political system. There were other problems within the social fabric of the country, however, which institutional and political stagnation tended to fuel rather than simply leave unresolved.

The birth of terrorism in Italy came as a response to the 'Hot Autumn' of 1969, when explosives were placed in a bank in Piazza Fontana in Milan, and two others in Rome, all on 12 December of that year. Sixteen people were killed in Milan itself and a total of one hundred and six were wounded. This is now known to have been the work of right-wing terrorists, although terrorists of the left were soon to steal the limelight. The Red Brigades (*Brigate Rosse*, BR) came into existence around October 1970. These, and other left-wing terrorist organizations, drew their members from a variety of backgrounds. Many of them had been students and had progressed to these organizations from activity in student or revolutionary groups, such as *Lotta Continua* or *Potere Operaio*. Frequently terrorists were found to have a religious background.

The revolutionary groups which emerged in the late 1960s must, however, be distinguished from terrorism. They clung firmly to the objective of creating mass movements and conducting open protests in society. The terrorist groups, by contrast, opted for the clandestine destabilising tactics of violent action. Until 1974, the activity of the Red Brigades was mostly of a propagandist nature, although it included beating up employers or setting their cars on fire. But on 18 April 1974, the Red Brigades kidnapped the Genoese judge Mario Sossi, and declared that henceforth their attacks would be aimed at the heart of the state. Sossi was later released unharmed. As if in response to this, neo-fascist terrorists, using the name *Ordine Nero*, triggered a bomb at a demonstration in Brescia on 28 May, killing six people and wounding ninety. On 4 August, *Ordine Nero* managed to bomb the Florence-Bologna train in a tunnel, killing twelve people and wounding forty-eight. Whereas the Red Brigades seemed to target their victims - judges, politicians, employers, police and even union activists - in order to pass on clear political messages, the neo-fascists struck indiscriminately.

The darkest years of the Republic, the *anni di piombo* ('years of lead', or 'the bullet') between 1976 and 1979 coincided with the period when the Pci's collaboration with the Dc was at its maximum. The intensification of red terrorist activity was in part the result of the collapse of the political and electoral prospects of the ultra-left groups, and in part a reaction to what the extremists saw as the increasingly collaborationist postures of the Pci and the *sindacato*. The proletariat, and all prospects of its being persuaded to pursue a genuine revolutionary programme, had been abandoned by its traditional leaders. The sense of frustration was thus intensified in the minds of those prepared to achieve such objectives through violence.

A vigorous youth movement emerged around 1977, with protests caused by a combination of overcrowded universities, increasing unemployment with diminishing prospects for graduates, and the continued blocking of long-awaited reforms. Part of this movement expressed not only fury but a willingness to resort to armed insurrection. This was not terrorism, but it was a terrain from which terrorist groups hoped to recruit. The old ultra-left, which consisted of *Potere Operaio, Lotta Continua, Il Manifesto*, and the Pdup, was now operating within parliament under the umbrella grouping, *Democrazia Proletaria*. Already quite small and ineffectual, the ultra-left was eventually marginalised by these developments. The student movement, which went under the name of *Studenti dell'Autonomia*, openly attacked the Pci and the unions.

In February 1977, during the occupation of Rome University, the communist leader of the Cgil, Luciano Lama, was shouted down when trying to speak, and violent clashes broke out between the students, i.e. the *autonomi*, and the police. The period of demonstrations and clashes ended in September with an ill-tempered conference in Bologna, highly critical once more of the Pci, but avoiding repetition of earlier clashes with the police. Yet despite their frustration with the Pci and the *sindacato*, the majority of the *autonomi* were not in the end prepared to become armed revolutionaries, and their movement soon faded away. The BR had not succeeded in gaining the recruits they had hoped for. Nevertheless, they responded to the growing mood of Pci-government collaboration by opening up a new phase in terrorist activities. In this new 'strategy of annihilation', the Red Brigades announced that they would strike at 'servants of the state', with the intention of intimidating whole sectors of the establishment. Some groups even indicated that the Pci was the main obstacle to progress. The EUR strategy, with all its compromises and calls for restraint, together with the Pci's entry into government which this was meant to facilitate, were the ultimate betrayal by union and political leaders of the working class. Aldo Moro, President of the Dc, managed to persuade his party to accept the Pci into the 'governmental majority', albeit without direct cabinet responsibility. On 16 March 1978, on his way to parliament to vote on the new government, Moro was abducted by the Red Brigades and his five police guards killed. He was later 'executed' and his body dumped halfway between the headquarters of the Dc and the Pci, in an act of 'proletarian justice'. Numerous commentators have been puzzled by the seemingly slack security aspects of the entire affair. There have been suggestions of complicity between the Red Brigades, elements of the security forces and influential sectors of the ruling establishment, who were all equally horrified at Moro's achievements. Although nothing has yet been proved, evidence being uncovered looks increasingly likely to confirm this view.

The killings continued into 1979 and 1980. Left-wing terrorism, however, began to find itself in retreat with the appointment of the Carabiniere General Carlo Alberto Dalla Chiesa as head of the anti-terrorist forces. With the help of new laws granting reduced sentences to penitent ex-terrorists (the *pentiti*) willing to supply further information, the terrorist threat was defeated and, some argue, Italian democracy strengthened by its ability to resist and eventually conquer terrorist tyranny. One of the most stupefying instances of violence, however, consisted of a neo-fascist act of indiscriminate terrorism. On 2 August 1980 a bomb at Bologna station killed eighty-five people, wounding two hundred. Subsequent revelations, following declarations by the neo-fascist Vincenzo Vinciguerra at his trial in 1984, implicated the Italian secret services and the NATO-protected Gladio organization in this and other terrorist activities. Eventually, on 16 May 1994, three terrorists received life sentences and two officials of the SISMI, the military intelligence organization set up in 1977, were condemned to eight years' imprisonment for their part in the Bologna bombing.

Although there is little doubt that some young factory workers had mixed feelings about red terrorism, the Red Brigades never managed to attract significant numbers of these to their ranks, and regarded the *sindacato* as hopelessly institutionalised into the bourgeois state. In fact, throughout these difficult years, the organized working class played an important part in defeating the left-wing terrorists' aims of gaining support among its members. Unions publicly condemned and organized protests and demonstrations against terrorism. What residual ambiguities remained seemed to disappear after the protest marches against the Red Brigades' assassination in January 1979 of the young Genoese communist factory council delegate Guido Rossa, for reporting and testifying against a suspected terrorist at his place of work. The *sindacato*'s ability to combat the threat of terrorism within its ranks certainly won the movement public credibility. With this success to its credit it was able to proceed into the 1980s to face a new and difficult phase of its existence.

Part VI

THE *SINDACATO* SINCE 1980: YEARS OF CRISIS AND REAPPRAISAL

19

The Changing Shape of Industrial Relations

The fortunes of labour movements are inevitably bound up with the fluctuations of economic cycles. Unions may attempt to create for themselves a role in society which protects them from the negative effects of such changes, but this is no easy matter, as events in Italy since 1980 have shown. Economically, although the early years of the decade were somewhat troubled, matters slowly began to improve. Inflation having reached its highest point ever in 1980 at 21.1 per cent, was later brought down to 8.6 per cent, but not until 1985. By 1989 it stood at about 6.6 per cent.[1] A growth rate of over 2.5 per cent in GDP was sustained between 1983 and 1987. Throughout the decade labour costs fell and productivity increased. Italian industry continued to diversify, to restructure at home, and to prosper abroad.

The state-holding sector, under the leadership of such individuals as Romano Prodi at IRI and Franco Reviglio at ENI, became more efficient. This was accompanied by the emergence of entrepreneurs like Gardini, De Benedetti and Berlusconi, all intent on capturing foreign markets. The most dramatic effect of the 1980s seems to have been the demise of the collectivist values of the late sixties and the seventies and an enthusiastic embracing of the enterprise culture. Commentators in the late 1980s talked about a new 'economic miracle' and of Italy as one of Europe's success stories. In 1987 the claim was made that Italy had overtaken the UK as the fifth most powerful industrial nation in the West.

Yet a question mark remained over the enduring nature of this achievement. Flexibility and flair are the typically Italian qualities which contributed to the economic revival of the 1980s. But some would argue that such qualities are not enough to bring about a permanent transformation in the Italian economy, whose lasting health is by no means guaranteed. As the 1980s drew to a close the public sector deficit threatened to run out of control.

---

[1] Statistics from *Le regioni in cifre*, Rome: Istituto nazionale di statistica, edizione 1990, tavola 17.18.

There is still uncertainty about how well-prepared the large number of small and medium enterprises, not to mention the over-complex and ultra-traditional Italian banking system, have become to take advantage of the new European market. The economic divide between North and South is as wide as ever.

Finally, the economic revival of the eighties brought about a fragmentation of the industrial relations system, at least in appearance, with the *sindacato* attempting to revitalise itself with new ideas and objectives. As we shall see, this shock to the *sindacato* was not entirely negative in its effects.

Reshaping Bargaining Practices: the Employers

If the 1970s was the decade of conflict, the 1980s were characterised by the reassertion of employer ascendancy. During the 1970s the unions were too strong to be challenged in head-on confrontations. However, with the collapse of the EUR strategy, the return of the Pci into opposition in January 1979 and its subsequent disappointing performance in the June elections, the private sector employers took courage and began a counter-offensive. Labour costs had to be reduced, authority restored to management, and the centrality of market principles established.

Fiat took the lead in attempting to shape the new order. In October 1979 the company sacked sixty-one workers in Turin for alleged terrorist sympathies and threats of violence in the factory.[2] The union campaign in defence of the workers failed to prevent the management decision from being upheld in January 1980. The psychological effects of this first victory by an employer were profound. The old fears of Fiat management, which many thought had disappeared for ever, returned. The press speculated about Fiat's next step. The feeling that the period was to be a watershed in Italian industrial relations history proved to be right, even though the long-term effects of this are far from settled even today.

In the spring of 1980 Agnelli announced that a sharp fall in sales required a cut of 30 per cent in production and 20 per cent in

---

[2] Although a number of those sacked were undoubtedly innocent, there had been three deaths and a number wounded among management and senior workers. See Ginsborg, *A History of Contemporary Italy*, p. 403.

manpower. The blow came on 8 September when Fiat announced that 24,000 workers would have to go on to the *cassa integrazione* for 15 months, during which time they would receive about 90 per cent of their wages, and the company would re-employ only half of these workers when the period ended. On 14 September Fiat further announced that it was going to dismiss 14,000 workers immediately. The unions began a total strike, which lasted thirty-five days. On 27 September the company withdrew the dismissals but reduced the period of the *cassa integrazione* to three months. A feeling of relief among some workers caused divisions in the ranks, and solidarity began to weaken.

On 10 October an assembly of the co-ordinating committee of clerical workers and foremen was transformed into a protest march through the streets of Turin. The 30-40,000 protesters were complaining about the climate of intimidation against those employees who continued to work. It was clear that the strike, which was now being sustained with the help of pickets from outside the area, could no longer continue. An agreement was reached on 15 October. Funds from the *cassa integrazione,* guaranteeing 93 per cent of wages, would be granted to 23,000 workers until July 1983, when Fiat would consider taking back those still out of work.

The outcome was seen as a major defeat for the *sindacato.* There is little doubt that Fiat's primary objective was to restore employer authority. In simple financial terms the company could easily have negotiated on the union proposals to rotate the *cassa integrazione* and allow the normal attrition rate of 12,000 workers per year to take care of labour reductions. Instead, the firm chose the 23,000 workers who were to go on to the *cassa integrazione*, making sure that the militants of the 1970s were among them. In July 1983 Fiat did not re-employ those workers who were still unplaced. From the company's point of view the benefits of its new authoritarian line seemed considerable. Abstentions from work and lost hours generally, declined more than tenfold in a single year. Productivity increased immediately by 30 per cent and the company was restored to profitability by 1981. Membership of the unions declined, partly as a result of 12,000 workers taking voluntary severance by 1982. Management imposed a regime of labour mobility, closed several plants and made unilateral decisions on investments and modernisation.

The immediate effect of the Fiat victory was to increase employer confidence generally and to persuade some companies that the Turin firm's approach was necessary throughout industry. Many, but not all, employers took up Fiat's lead. The *sindacato*, however, as we shall see, was not slow to recognise its earlier mistakes and soon began to adapt to changing circumstances.

The Confindustria asked the government in January 1980 to lighten the burden of the *scala mobile*. This was an important psychological move because the *scala mobile* agreement dating from 1975 was regarded as one of the *sindacato*'s greatest achievements, expressed in the union slogan *la scala mobile non si tocca* ('the *scala mobile* must not be touched'). Later, in June 1982, the Confindustria announced that it had decided unilaterally to cease implementation of the terms of the 1975 agreement, which, in effect, would have taken the *scala mobile* back to the level of the 1957 settlement. The Cgil calculated that in 1981 indexation accounted for 64 per cent of wage increases, whereas previously it accounted for only 35 per cent. After nationwide consultation through plant assemblies, the Cgil-Cisl-Uil federation obtained approval for a nine-point document to act as a basis for negotiation with the Confindustria. Bargaining began late in 1982 and involved the government as mediator in the final stages, leading to a tripartite agreement in January 1983. The Confindustria's initiative led to a reduction of the *scala mobile* and was a further step in weakening union power. In numerous plant-level agreements in 1983, the employers won back total control in such areas as shift-work and labour mobility in the factories, and regained greater authority over working conditions generally.

After these developments, a further attempt to weaken the unions came from the hawkish Federmeccanica. In December 1984, it issued a 'manifesto' aimed at recasting the entire system of industrial relations by proposing that bargaining should proceed according to two quite different patterns of negotiation. Traditional collective bargaining could persist in industries protected against foreign competition by the government. The most radical part of the plan, however, was concerned with the greater part of Italian industry, which had to operate on the open market. What was suggested was not so much a restructuring of collective bargaining as a huge curtailment of its scope and application. According to the plan, bargaining was to be limited largely to the sphere of unskilled labour, and individual contracts were to be introduced for an increasingly diversified and technologically competent workforce. Furthermore, union influence was to be kept out of important areas where planning, innovation and reorganization were required. In short, the document sought to re-establish managerial prerogatives, bypassing the unions in the process.

Although the Federmeccanica's view won a certain measure of support within the Confindustria, many private employers rejected its extremist anti-union flavour, preferring a more constructive collaboration with the somewhat humbled and more 'realistic' *sindacato* which seemed to be emerging from its recent defeats. Despite these defeats the movement remained a powerful influence on both the industrial and political scenes, a fact which the Federmeccanica underestimated. It was better to co-operate with such a force than risk the unpredictable effects of attempting to humiliate it. Thus the early 1980s gave rise to a dichotomy in employers' approaches to industrial relations in Italy.[3]

The collaborative approach was best illustrated by the employers in the state-holding sector, where it was formalised in important agreements. This, of course, was the sector most subject to Dc and Cisl influence. It had often been seen as the instrument for implementing Catholic 'solidaristic' perspectives in employment and industrial development policy, and had a history of better relations with the unions. On 18 December 1984, IRI, the most powerful and the largest of the state-holding corporations, signed an agreement, known as the 'Protocollo IRI', with the Cgil, Cisl and Uil confederations. Coming in the same month as the unveiling of the Federmeccanica's 'manifesto', it appeared as a clear alternative to the model of industrial relations proposed by the latter and originally initiated by Fiat in 1980. The 'Protocollo IRI' was seen by both sides to the agreement as a constructive development in industrial relations. It proposed the setting up of joint consultative committees at company and area levels. The *sindacato* was to be involved in industrial and economic policy, employment, labour mobility, professional training and all major aspects of the group's activities. Forms of self-management, so far eschewed by the Italian

---

[3] See Treu and Negrelli, 'Workers' Participation and Personnel Management Policies in Italy', pp. 85ff for case studies and examples of the two trends in the 1980s.

sindacato, were to be encouraged, particularly in the South. By signing this agreement, the *sindacato* was, in effect, entering into a direct co-decisional arrangement with the managements of the IRI group, a position it had always resisted in the past. Thus, while its hegemony was being undermined in some quarters, the *sindacato* was, in fact, entering a new collaborative phase in others. As one analyst has said of the agreement, 'no matter how much it conflicted with tradition, for the *sindacato* it meant the recognition of its indispensable role in managing industrial relations and was thus the seal on its credibility: a seal which the hawks of the Confindustria - with Fiat at the head - had withdrawn from it, with no intention of giving it back'.[4] An updated version of the agreement was renewed on 16 July 1986. A few days later, on 22 July, an agreement was signed between the confederations and employers in the private sector of the chemical industry on rights of information and joint consultation on major aspects of employment and industrial development.[5] The hawks among the employers were not able to impose their will even within the private sector.

During the first half of the decade, negotiations at Fiat were almost at a standstill. The company's attempt, along with that of the more hawkish employers in the Confindustria, to bring about a large-scale blockage of contract renewals, created difficulties for the *sindacato*, yet nationally this effort was not a great success.[6] It is, in any case, uncertain whether unity around a strategy aimed at union marginalisation could be sustained. Many employers value the capacity of the unions to maintain discipline among the workforce, so that the employers' front is likely to remain divided. In June 1989, for instance, while the Confindustria was engaged in

---

[4] U. Romagnoli, 'L'anno zero della democrazia industriale', p. 325.

[5] The texts of both agreements can be found in Giugni, *Diritto sindacale*, Appendice II, pp. 281-7 and 288-300.

[6] Later in the decade, in July 1988, Fiat signed separate agreements with the FIM-Cisl and the UILM-Uil, the FIOM-Cgil refusing to go along with agreements which fell too far short of demands without first consulting the membership. Commentators' speculations about a return to the practice of the separate agreements of the 1950s, however, so deeply-rooted in the movement's memory, did not materialise.

wide-ranging negotiations with the *sindacato* on revising rules for plant bargaining and re-examining major features of the industrial relations system, the hawks of the association let it be known through the press that they intended once again, unilaterally if necessary, to repudiate the *scala mobile*. This renewed attack on the *scala mobile* was aimed at undermining the collaborative stance of the Confindustria's President, Sergio Pininfarina, and sabotaging the negotiations, which looked like consolidating the position of the unions as negotiating partners.

The ensuing difficulties over the *scala mobile* were subsequently resolved in a tripartite agreement between the government, the Confindustria and the *sindacato* on 6 July 1990. In essence, the employers agreed to continue to implement the *scala mobile* in its existing form until January 1992, and reopen negotiations for the national agreements which they had been refusing to renew since late 1989. The government, in turn, agreed to a downward readjustment of employers' contributions. The Federmeccanica, however, would not be bound by the Confindustria's decision to sign the agreement. The result was that the employers in the metalworking sector refused to negotiate national contracts with the unions, a difficulty which took until January 1991 to be resolved.

Most experts were agreed that by 1990 metalworkers' pay had declined by Western European standards and that union demands were reasonable. The Federmeccanica's behaviour made sense only in the light of the organization's original objectives, which have remained unchanged since its creation in 1972: namely, to be in the front line of opposition to the *sindacato*'s 'power to affect the material conditions of work, and to proceed from this point to influence industrial policy'.[7] The Federmeccanica, in other words, with Fiat at its head, was behaving like the champion of the employers' right to govern alone in the factories.

Economic factors reveal that the 1980s did, in a very real sense, restore employer ascendancy. To take a simple indicator, labour costs were reduced, while productivity increased. Manpower in large-scale industry was cut by about 33 per cent. In the

---

[7] F. Chiaromonte, 'Sindacato così sbagli', *Rinascita*, Nuova serie, Anno 1, N. 36, 21 ottobre 1990, p. 13.

metalworking industry it was reduced by 22.7 per cent, whereas productivity increased by 50 per cent. Indexation of wages was greatly reduced during the 1980s, and workers had to rely increasingly on overtime to maintain their earnings.[8]

In spite of these changes to the disadvantage of the labour force, the overall development of industrial relations in the 1980s was not entirely negative for the *sindacato*. In reality, the process of change was characterised by a certain amount of creative adaptation on both sides. One of the dominant features of the 1980s was a tendency towards greater decentralisation of collective bargaining. This was noticeable, for example, in the innovations at company-level negotiations. Whereas clauses covering rights of information on employers' plans had been a feature of national contracts since 1976, the 1980s saw these extended to local bargaining, along with a tendency to create joint committees to examine specific issues such as the organization of work and professional training. The greater emphasis on company-level negotiations was not a fragmentary or chaotic process, moreover, but it tended to operate within the limits set at higher levels. There was, accordingly, a redefinition of areas appropriate to the different negotiating levels,[9] and the devolution of bargaining was largely controlled because employers, on the whole, still considered national, industry-level bargaining a necessity.

A feature of the greater shift towards company-level bargaining was that negotiations became more concerned with how the *sindacato*, and indeed the workforce in general, were to be involved in innovation. Thus more attention was given to the methods and stages of union/management co-operation than at any time in Italy's industrial history. This is a necessity for an employer who wishes to utilise all the advantages of a workforce and its representatives in an increasingly competitive world economy. Ironically, the return to authoritarian methods at Fiat in the 1980s has been an object-lesson in support of this idea. Work rhythms

---

[8] For further discussion and statistics, see S. Negrelli and E. Santi, 'Industrial Relations in Italy', pp. 174ff, and E. Carra e R. Mancini, 'Salario e salasso', pp. 20-2.

[9] See Negrelli and Santi, 'Industrial Relations in Italy', pp. 182ff for a more detailed treatment of these tendencies.

were increased without consultation, nervous strain quickly became more perceptible among the workforce, and experienced workers of a more combative stamp were removed, so that a general atmosphere of anxiety about union activity pervaded the plants.[10] Simultaneously, however, Fiat lost ground slowly but steadily both in the domestic and foreign markets. In comparative terms, by 1990, new models at Fiat were taking longer to be produced and had more than twice as many faults as those manufactured by the company's Japanese rivals. They also broke down earlier than those of the company's major European competitors. Cesare Romiti's launch of a campaign, with worker participation, for *qualità totale*, was viewed by most analysts with considerable scepticism. In the first place, Romiti was himself the architect of the *sindacato*'s earlier defeat, and he has since remained in the forefront of opposition to the reinstatement of the unions in Italian industrial relations. His view of 'participation', which seems to consist largely of the idea that workers follow management's instructions, but with good grace, has even been repudiated by Umberto Agnelli, who has always insisted that competitiveness will be restored in Italy only through a more productive working relationship with the unions.[11] Many are convinced that in its anxiety to rid the firm of those workers who were prepared to take the lead in tough negotiations, Fiat's management deprived itself of those valuable human assets which, productively utilised, could have been of immense benefit in improving the company's performance.

There are thus strong indications that most employers will continue to look for a productive relationship with the *sindacato*, if only for the sake of survival. There are signs that both management and unions see mutual advantages in moving towards new forms of co-operation. The *sindacato* has certainly learned that innovation and change are not the enemies of progress, but it is still concerned that too eager a move into participation could weaken its independence and ability to retain a conflictual stance, if this becomes necessary, to defend its members' interests.

---

[10] See 'L'inchiesta: viaggio nella Fiat', pp. 26-34.

[11] For a lengthier discussion see *La qualità totale alla Fiat*, Rome: Ediesse, 1990.

The Role of the Government

Although the *sindacato*'s relationship with the government throughout the 1980s was not as subject to traumatic episodes as were its dealings with the employers, it was by no means without its turbulent moments. After the elections of 1979 and the abandonment of the 'historic compromise', the Dc and Bettino Craxi's Psi began to draw closer, with the aim of creating a stable governing coalition. The socialists wished to foster greater co-operation with labour, both in order to legitimise the new centre-left coalition which replaced the government of 'national solidarity', and also to demonstrate their superiority over the communists in obtaining union co-operation to solve the country's economic problems. Given the Dc's links with the Cisl, many of the Catholic party's leaders were not opposed to such a development. Thus an important element of the new stabilising strategy was the involvement of the *sindacato* within what an astute observer of the period has called a *logica di maggioranza*.[12]

The government was particularly active in mediating between the unions and the employers over the Confindustria's threat to abandon the *scala mobile* from January 1983. Many national contracts had not been renewed, and there was talk of some employers attempting to bargain directly with workers, factory by factory, and bypassing the *sindacato*. After much background work the government, alongside the employers and unions, signed a tripartite agreement on 22 January 1983. The agreement enabled the blocked contracts to be renewed, averted the employers' abandonment of the *scala mobile*, and seemed to provide a new framework for future developments in industrial relations.

The *scala mobile*'s protection against inflation was reduced by between 10 and 15 per cent. Limits were set on the use of the *cassa integrazione*, and the employers were given greater freedom of choice in filling job vacancies. Some wage groups' taxes were lowered, and the government promised to increase family allowances and hold down the prices of public services. Ceilings on wages were to be established at interconfederate level, and plant or company pay bargaining could not be undertaken within eighteen

---

[12] Chiaromonte, *Quattro anni difficili*, p. xxxiv.

months of such agreements. The government also agreed to lower the burden of employers' contributions to pensions. It was further stipulated that a 'solidarity fund', an idea which had divided the Pci and the Cgil communists, would be set up, whereby workers would contribute 0.5 per cent of wages for the purpose of investment and job-creation, particularly in the South. Finally, the agreement contained provisions for legislation which would give part-time and other forms of flexible labour greater security and enable them to become part of future collective agreements.[13]

The objectives of the agreement were to promote economic stability through a form of wage control, achieve a greater degree of labour flexibility, and reorganize the system of industrial relations in such a way that interconfederate bargaining would act as the chief regulator of lower-level negotiations. This would have considerably reduced the role of national/category agreements. But in reality, both unions and employers have been reluctant to weaken national bargaining at industry level, and even company-level bargaining has increased.

After a poor performance by the Dc in the 1983 elections, Bettino Craxi became the first socialist to head an Italian government, albeit within a Dc-led coalition. He was determined to show that a socialist Prime Minister was capable of breaking the traditional paralysis of Italian government. Determined to reduce inflation by wage control, he presented a plan whereby levels of wage indexation would not only be reduced, but fixed *in advance* of inflation targets each year. The Pci was opposed to the plan. The Cisl and the Uil wished to support Craxi, as did the socialists within the Cgil. The communists within the Cgil, however, opposed Craxi's plan. Craxi was determined to isolate his leftist competitors both in the Pci and in the Cgil and show that decisions could be made without having to compromise with the communists. Seeing the opportunity to exploit the split within the *sindacato*, in an act of governmental *decisionismo*, Craxi issued an emergency decree on 14 February 1984, cutting the *scala mobile* through a legislative device which bypassed the need for union approval. The communist decision to call for a national demonstration in Rome against this

---

[13] The full text of this agreement is contained in Giugni, *Diritto sindacale*, pp. 301-7.

act of authoritarian contempt for consultation was not supported by the non-communist union leaders. The latter did not distinguish between their support for Craxi's policies and his method of implementing them. The demonstration, nevertheless, went ahead on 24 March, and received massive support. The emergency legislation was withdrawn and a new set of proposals prepared, less draconian but still reducing the cover of the *scala mobile*. These were voted on in a referendum in June 1985, which the government won, with a majority of 54 per cent in favour to 46 per cent against. The Cisl, the Uil and the Cgil socialists had campaigned for the new Craxi proposals, and the Cgil communists against. The *patto federativo* which had held the confederations together since 1972 was shattered.

Although the referendum result was a defeat for the communists, government supporters were disappointed by the narrowness of the victory. It was clear that many traditional supporters of other parties and members of the non-communist unions had voted with the communists. Craxi had not crushed the communists as he had hoped, and the whole episode demonstrated that within the Italian political system long-term agreements on economic matters still had to be negotiated with the opposition. What Craxi's aggressive handling of the *scala mobile* episode achieved in a singular manner was the most serious split in the *sindacato* since the bitter experiences of the 1950s, far surpassing the achievements of any Dc leader. It should be said, however, that relations between the confederations had been deteriorating ever since the beginning of the decade. There soon followed attempts on all sides to rediscover common ground. The three confederations constructed a common position on the *scala mobile* shortly after the referendum and reached the agreements discussed earlier.

A new feature of the 1980s was the increasing role played by the public sector in the world of industrial relations in Italy. This brought the government more into the picture, whereas the Confindustria was keen to reduce the amount of government mediation in the *sindacato*'s relations with industry, because it recognised that the unions were stronger in the political field than in the market. Italian industrial relations thus remain closely bound up with the political and institutional system. At the same time collective bargaining has remained strong, has become increasingly diversified, and shows signs of continuing to adapt.

20

Some Repercussions within the Movement

Political and Internal Tensions

During the 1980s the degree of convergence between the Uil's positions and those of the Psi remained strong, as the socialists continued with some success to promote their function in government. The Cisl, at its organizational conference in January 1980, vigorously restated its neutralist assertion that the *sindacato* could be truly autonomous only if it were prepared to be equally troublesome to all political parties in the interests of its members. Yet many commentators spoke of a 'demochristianisation' of the Cisl as the decade progressed. At the Cisl Congress of July 1989, the leader of the metalworkers' federation, Raffaele Morese, forcefully defended the Cisl's autonomy, insisting that: 'never, I repeat, never will we be reduced to discussing the leadership of the Cisl at the headquarters of a political party'.[1] One of the confederation's deputy leaders, Mario Colombo, rejecting the thesis of those who continued to speak of the *due anime* ('two souls') of the Catholic organization, insisted that 'the Cisl can possess only a single soul, inspired by the spirit of autonomy'.[2] The General Secretary, Franco Marini, repeated that the Cisl had over the years demonstrated its 'independence from all outside centres of political, economic and ideological power'.[3] Less than two years later, in May 1991, the Dc Minister of Labour heading the negotiations with the three confederations on the *scala mobile* and the costs of labour was none other than Franco Marini. Nor is this all. At the time of his vigorous defence of the 'spirit of autonomy' at the 1989 Cisl Congress, Mario Colombo had already been appointed by the government as director of INPS, the state body which handles

---

[1] F. Chiaromonte, 'La scommessa dell'autonomia', p. 9.

[2] Ibid.

[3] Ibid.

national health contributions, pensions and other state benefits. Such appointments could hardly but reinforce scepticism about the Cisl's repeated claims of non-alignment.

The Cgil, on the other hand, historically alien to the 'neutral' *sindacato* thesis, had greater difficulty with the idea of a free-floating *soggetto politico*. Luciano Lama, in a newspaper interview, summarised the confederation's position thus: 'We are a *soggetto politico* wanting change. We cannot bring this about alone. We do not pass laws, we do not govern banks, nor do we administer local government. We can, however, promote change ... and we must work for a change in the political leadership of the country.'[4] But although the majority within the Cgil were favourable to a change of government with a strong communist input, the 1980s, nevertheless, witnessed the increasingly common practice of public disagreement between communist *sindacalisti* and Communist Party leaders. Such differences became more apparent after the collapse of the 'national solidarity' experiment in 1979. In fact, the period between 1979 and 1983 put a definitive end to any suggestion of even a partial revival of the *cinghia di trasmissione*.

1979 was a crucial year because of the twin failures of EUR and the government of 'national solidarity'. To most Pci leaders the two initiatives were closely linked, each requiring the other for its own success. In an article in November 1979 on the Fiat sacking of the sixty-one suspected terrorist sympathisers, the communist politician Giorgio Amendola attacked the *sindacato*, particularly the metalworkers' federations, not only for being slow to speak out unambiguously against terrorism, but also for undermining EUR and therefore the government of 'national solidarity', a clear assault on the left of the *sindacato*, which had ignored the agreement when making its wage claims. Furthermore, he argued, the confederations 'spoke an ambiguous, coded, diplomatic and circuitous language in order to preserve the balance of a precarious unity, without openly facing their real differences. They resorted increasingly to demagogic tactics, which resulted in their being outmanoeuvred by the left.'[5]

---

[4] Interview with G. Pansa, 'Niente patto sociale e la scala mobile guai a chi la tocca', *la Repubblica*, 26 giugno 1981, p. 5.

[5] G. Amendola, 'Interrogativi sul "caso" Fiat', p. 14.

In truth the notion of the *sindacato* acting as a *soggetto politico* caused the Pci some discomfort. There were certainly problems of a conceptual nature concerning the function of a political actor with no parliamentary mandate and no clear institutional role in legislation or national and local government. Consequently, there developed a tendency among some party intellectuals to argue in favour of shifting the locus of decision-making back to parliament.

In July 1980 the government announced its intention to issue a decree, including among its provisions the establishment of a 'solidarity fund', secured by the deduction of 0.5 per cent of wages from all employed workers, aimed at the creation of investment and jobs in the South. This measure, initially proposed by the Cisl and supported by the communists within the Cgil, was strongly opposed by the Pci. There were sharp exchanges between Lama, the Cgil General Secretary and Berlinguer, the party Secretary. The Pci was, in short, firmly opposed to the notion, extremely widespread within the Cisl and seemingly infecting the Cgil, that the unions could 'secure for themselves a slice of the proceeds of capital accumulation and manage it efficiently'.[6]

These developments within Italian communism were highlighted at a Pci Conference in January 1985, where the party was debating its influence on the working population. It was abundantly clear that the existence of the Cgil in the workplace was no longer considered a guarantee of party influence. As one of the Pci's leading intellectuals, Aldo Tortorella, stated:

> In fact, communists want a party presence in the factory and workplace precisely because they have abandoned the 'transmission-belt' theory. They want to promote their own policies without entrusting such work to any union - and conversely - *without allowing any union to use the Communist Party as a 'transmission belt' for its own policies.*[7]

Tortorella's apparent fear that the historical tables between the Pci and the Cgil had been turned may seem exaggerated but it did, in fact, have some basis in reality. As the *sindacato* had been

---

[6] Chiaromonte, *Quattro anni difficili. Il Pci e i sindacati*, p. 68.

[7] *I comunisti: dove si lavora e si studia*, p. 72. My italics.

consolidating its position in the factories during the 1970s, the nature and degree of Pci influence among workers had been changing.[8] The Cgil, in its quest for unity, and also in promoting the *sindacato*'s role as a *soggetto politico*, found itself operating alongside sectors of the movement which were tied to parties in competition with the Pci. Being in government, moreover, such parties were able to offer the *sindacato* deals which promoted the *sindacato*'s role as a political actor. Thus the Pci was exposed to the prospect of political isolation without the support of its traditional labour wing. Conflict among communists was thus inevitable. When, for example, in 1983 the Cgil's communist leader Luciano Lama welcomed the fact that the country had at last acquired a socialist Prime Minister, the first in its history, the Pci replied that the Cgil had been hasty in its comments. Subsequent developments seemed to justify this judgement. Craxi's attempt in 1984 to reduce the *scala mobile* produced the deepest split in the *sindacato* since the 1950s. His determination to marginalise the Pci put additional strains on the *sindacato* as the movement was attempting to forge a new unity.

Given all these factors, it was clear that greater unity between the components of the *sindacato* required more explicit ruptures between these components and their collateral political parties than they had so far been prepared to permit.

Relations between the Confederations

When the November 1981 Cgil Congress took place, the confederations were already in open disagreement over possible adjustments to the *scala mobile*. Perceiving a threat to the unity of the movement, Lama warned that if the *sindacato* failed to agree on such a crucial issue, unity at a political level would be impossible, and a tendency for each component to lapse back into a new collateralism would result.[9]

---

[8] In 1983, for instance, at Fiat Mirafiori, out of the total workforce of almost 52,000, only 1,400 were Pci members. See Golden, *Labor Divided*, pp. 237ff.

[9] See L. Lama, 'Relazione al X Congresso della Cgil', p. 31.

The Confindustria first asked the government to suspend the *scala mobile* in January 1980. Although the Cgil and the Uil initially announced their total opposition, the Cisl was stating publicly by April 1981 that it was prepared to consider modifying the mechanism as part of a comprehensive economic package. At a meeting with the government that same month, the confederations were divided. Fiat threatened to abandon the *scala mobile* unilaterally, and this lead was followed by similar threats from numerous employers' organizations: Federmeccanica, Confapi, Confcommercio and Confagricoltura.

The Cisl's claim was that accepting downward adjustment of the indexation mechanism gave the *sindacato* a stronger moral argument for its claim to influence economic policy overall. A number of *cislini* were pushing this line in order to promote the *scambio politico* ('political exchange') as a central function of the *sindacato*. On 28 June 1981, Giovanni Spadolini, a republican, became Prime Minister, the first non-Dc Premier since 1945. Anxious to take advantage of the Cisl's attitude and also to prove himself in the economic arena, he promised the unions that he would stand by future agreements. The confederations responded by agreeing, in December, a position which pinned the *scala mobile* to 16 per cent, i.e. below the existing inflation rate, although inflation was itself going down. The Cgil's insistence on putting the agreement to the rank-and-file for approval, however, caused further divisions, since the other components of the *sindacato* wanted a quick settlement to support their own parties, thus seeming to confirm Lama's prophecy of a new collateralism. By 1982, as the polemics continued, Carniti and Benvenuto, leaders respectively of the Cisl and the Uil, were arguing strongly for centralised negotiations with the employers and the government to restructure the *scala mobile*, and accusing the Cgil communists of promoting a 'democrazia movimentista e assemblearista' in order to undermine these negotiations. The conversion of the Uil to the Cisl camp was clearly connected to socialist support for the government and, some argued, to Craxi's known ambition to become the first ever socialist Prime Minister of Italy.

When Craxi fulfilled this ambition in August 1983, relations between the confederations were still deteriorating. Numerous national category contracts were eighteen months behind their renewal dates, owing partly to the divisions between the confederations over the *scala mobile*, which remained as deep as ever. We have noted Craxi's attempt to reduce the *scala mobile* by emergency decree in February 1984, and how this move dealt a death-blow to the Cgil-Cisl-Uil federation. But it was largely the *sindacato*'s attachment to its party-political alliances which transformed Craxi's decision into such a powerfully destructive act. His initiative on 14 February was born of impatience with the unions. A week before, on 7 February, deliberations between the confederations had broken down, since each component, including the socialists within the Cgil, was firmly supporting the position of its own party. The desire of the Cisl, the Uil, and the Cgil socialists to see the Craxi-headed coalition succeed in bringing inflation under control where others had failed, and the determination of the communists to preserve the *scala mobile* intact at all costs, were stronger than their resolve to find a compromise. Each side thus raised its initial position to the status of a battle-cry, thus radicalising internal conflict, which led to the referendum of the following year.

But party loyalties during the referendum campaign had suffocated subtler points of convergence After the results of the referendum, there were indeed many in the Cisl and the Uil who were glad to have taught the Cgil a lesson, as they saw it. But even within the Cgil there were communists who were aware of the burden imposed by the *scala mobile* and who secretly accepted the need for its modification. On the other hand, there were those within the Cisl who were horrified at Carniti's overreaction to communist opposition, manifest in his call for the creation of a single *sindacato* which excluded the communists.[10] Indeed some Catholic metalworkers' leaders felt that at least the communists had acted as 'genuine' union leaders, and not simply as party pawns. It was clear that crossing the divides there were mutual sympathies which had been temporarily submerged.

Thus the will to compromise and rediscover a path towards unity was rekindled soon after the bitter debates had ended. And it was not limited to the *sindacalisti*. Beneath the surface there was unease within the Dc, the Pri, the Psi and even within the Confindustria about the fact that a kind of Craxi-Carniti-Agnelli

---

[10] Turone, *Il sindacato nell'Italia del benessere*, p. 100.

axis seemed to be developing, with the aim of striking a blow at the communists. While each of these major figures might have had his own reasons for wishing to weaken communist opposition, their separate motivations did not combine to form a cohesive rationale. Indeed they created considerable alarm in some quarters. The leader of the Milanese Cisl, for instance, was extremely critical of his own leader: 'I am opposed to the theory of the *scambio politico*; politics does not consist only of dealing and trading. Carniti has taken a perverse course, which at present is creating tensions within the *sindacato*'.[11] Even within the Confindustria there were employers who wished to distance the organization from the anti-communist line which was developing. One member of the Confindustria's Executive Council argued that it was ill-judged to take a course 'which inevitably frustrated the communist element within the Cgil, for this element remained one of the most judicious and sensible components in the *sindacato*'.[12]

After the referendum in June 1985, steps to heal the rift which had occurred were taken almost immediately. On 23 July the confederations met, and the following day they worked out a programme which included an agreement that the *scala mobile* should be fixed at 100 per cent indexation for the first 600,000 lire of monthly wages and at 30 per cent for the remainder. The period of automatic revision was to be six-monthly. This was the first unitary platform agreed since 1982.

The *sindacato*'s historical divisions along party lines have not only given rise to the existence of different confederations, but also to the creation of a variety of cumbersome administrative and electoral arrangements, in order to preserve collaboration between the confederations. These practices have a long tradition in the postwar history of the *sindacato*. In both the *Cgil unitaria* between 1944 and 1948 and the Cgil-Cisl-Uil federation between 1972 and 1984, the principle of *pariteticità* (parity of numbers and representation) has operated, alongside the creation of tripartite structures at various levels, to preserve unity. This arrangement has, however, had two unintended consequences. First, although it undoubtedly enabled unity to be preserved at a formal level, it did

---

[11] G. Caldarola, 'Due voti di fiducia non fanno una maggioranza', p. 4.

[12] Ibid., p. 5.

so by giving lasting structural expression to the different political traditions of the confederations. Secondly, *pariteticità*, by limiting the choice of candidates through operating lists, inhibited democracy within the movement. Restricting choice in order to protect the party-political loyalties of candidates did not enhance the credibility of the movement either as a *sindacato* or as an independent *soggetto politico*.

The problem of adjusting candidatures in order to preserve unity also proved to be an intractable one within the Cgil itself. From the beginning, communists and socialists in the confederation had organized and discussed policy within their separate *correnti*, or 'currents'. Traditionally, full-time posts were distributed and candidatures at elections organized in such a way as to preserve an approximate 2:1 communist/socialist ratio within the confederation's ranks. For over twenty-five years, however, many within the organization had been arguing for the abandonment of the *correnti*. In the summer of 1990, thirty-nine Cgil communist men and women wrote a document calling for the abolition of the *correnti* and the basing of internal union democracy on 'one person, one vote', with no special arrangements to protect party affiliations. On 20 September the Cgil General Secretary, Bruno Trentin, himself a communist, announced that the communist component (known as *unità sindacale*) would be disbanded.[13] At a conference of the *unità sindacale* current, held on 18 and 19 October 1990, Trentin's initiative was endorsed. Speaking at the conference, Trentin's deputy and leader of the socialist component, Ottaviano Del Turco, announced that his *corrente* would not follow suit until new rules governing internal relations within the confederation had been worked out. Some socialists suspected that since Trentin's move came at a critical moment of internal debate within the Pci,[14] it was

---

[13] V. Sivo, 'Trentin fa la rivoluzione nella Cgil', *la Repubblica*, 20 settembre 1990, p. 13.

[14] In July 1989 a debate arose within the Pci following the decision of the General Secretary, Achille Occhetto, to set in motion the creation of a new and transformed political force out of the existing membership of the party and others who were prepared to collaborate in setting up the new organization. This occurred in January 1991 when the Pds (Partito democratico della sinistra) was founded, replacing the Pci.

intended to prevent the development of organized parallel communist factions within the Cgil and the Pci of supporters and opponents of Occhetto's initiative. The habit of reading party-political implications into union initiatives of the kind taken by Trentin is all too easy to understand in an Italian context. By the time of the Cgil's October 1991 Congress, however, the socialist request for a review of internal procedures had been met, and Del Turco announced that 'party components no longer have any justification' within the confederation.[15]

Were such changes steps in the direction of organic unity? The year before Trentin's move to break up the communist group within the Cgil in September 1990, Franco Marini, in his speech to the Cisl's July 1989 Congress, insisted that 'unity does not mean a single *sindacato* [i.e. confederation], a kind of enforced institutionalisation ... but a free-flowing change towards a large and pluralistic organization, open and flexible, accommodating differences, but without factions'.[16] Organic unity was not possible, he continued, because both the Cgil and the Uil were still tied to political parties. As we have already had occasion to note, by 1991 Marini was himself Dc Minister of Labour in the Andreotti Government. Observers might be forgiven for noting a certain incongruity in his remarks.

The Cgil Congress in October 1991 witnessed what could turn out to be major turning-points in the confederation's complex relations with the country's political forces and its own attempts to find a path to unity. The Pds leader, Achille Occhetto, speaking as a guest at the congress, expressed his party's desire to see 'a *sindacato* which was not only autonomous, but independent of all political connections, even of possible alternative governments and realignments of the forces of the left'.[17] In publicly declaring his party's break with any concept of an automatic 'special relationship' with the *sindacato*, Occhetto was finally removing all obstacles to unity not only for the socialists within the movement, but also for the Catholics of the Cisl. In this momentous statement,

---

[15] Report on the Cgil Congress, R. D'Agostini, 'L'unità più vicina', p. 9.

[16] F. Marini, 'Relazione al XI Congresso, luglio 1989', p. 7.

[17] D'Agostini, 'L'unità più vicina', p. 11.

the leader of the Pds was finally demonstrating that his new party had abandoned the traditional concept of a 'labour movement', that is, a force composed of a bloc or alliance between union and party. The *sindacato*, henceforth, would be viewed as 'free-floating', as it were. As if in response to Occhetto's speech, and also to the Cgil's disbandment of its *correnti*, the new leader of the Cisl, Sergio D'Antoni, also a guest at the congress, surprised the delegates with an attack on the government, and with the declaration which followed: 'We must work for our convictions and interests in establishing new norms for alternating governments, thus enriching the fabric of democracy in our country. There can be no "companion governments" for the *sindacato*, nor any privileged relations with political parties. In this sense, the Cgil decision to disband its internal components is a positive step.' Finally, D'Antoni declared, 'we feel closer [to the Cgil] than we did yesterday.'[18]

In July 1992 the Cgil, Cisl and Uil signed an agreement with the employers abolishing the *scala mobile*. On this occasion, pressure was brought upon the socialists by the newly elected socialist Prime Minister, Giuliano Amato, and the Cisl once again chose to support the majority Dc government. Trentin, notwithstanding his own party's opposition to the move, and fearing a split within the movement if he did not do so, signed on behalf of the Cgil, and offered his resignation immediately. Although this was not accepted, the episode highlighted once more how party pressures continued to exercise a definite hold on at least the Cisl, the Uil, and the socialist members of the Cgil. Paradoxically, it seemed to be the ex-communists who had become most disposed to break the old collateralist links in the interests of unity.

What we have discussed in this chapter lends further support to what has been argued earlier about the weakening of ideological links and the more durable nature of other connections. It was even clearer, by 1992, that the enduring force of collateralism lay less in subcultural traditions, although these were far from spent, than in the sphere of *realpolitik*.

---

[18] Ibid., p. 12.

21

The Crisis of Representation

Changing Patterns of Membership

During the 1980s the Italian *sindacato* lost much of the negotiating power and capacity to mobilise that it enjoyed in the 1970s. We have already seen how the *scala mobile*, the jewel in the crown of the movement's achievements in the 1970s, was dramatically cut in the mid-1980s. In July 1992 the Cgil, Cisl and Uil signed an agreement with the employers abolishing the mechanism altogether.[1] Italian commentators sometimes paint a picture of terminal decline for the *sindacato*. Yet this decline, real enough in the Italian context, must be seen in perspective. The *scala mobile*, uniquely in the capitalist world, provided automatic three-monthly wage rises, in line with increases in the cost of living for most wage- and salary-earners, and for many years provided equal pay rises for all. The *cassa integrazione*, another benefit which was unique in the advanced economies, is still in operation. The *sindacato*'s negotiations and policy statements are reported daily in all the newspapers, and its leaders are still national figures and important interlocutors of the government and employers. When judged, therefore, from the standpoint of its own achievements in the 1970s, the Italian *sindacato* has indeed suffered a decline, but if seen alongside the position, let us say, of British trade unions, its position seems remarkably strong and resilient.

Early in the 1980s, experienced activists all over the country began to complain of the *sindacato*'s diminishing capacity to achieve results through traditional forms of industrial action. It became difficult to muster support. Even where mobilisation enlisted large numbers, the employers were able to ignore the protests. Underlying this difficulty was the fact that the industrial

---

[1] It is ironic that the second, in this case fatal blow to the mechanism should occur with the support of the second socialist Prime Minister, this time Giuliano Amato.

working class, traditionally the main protagonist in social and economic struggles, no longer held a position in society which enabled it to exercise this role of leadership. The 'universalism' which, in the 1970s, the Italian *sindacato* had been able to build around its egalitarian demands was breaking down. At the 1981 Congress of the Cgil, the confederation historically most tied to the industrial working class, delegates called on the movement to place itself at the head of new and diverse groups, such as technicians, clerical workers, researchers, part-time workers, women and even the unemployed, and to create a new 'social bloc'. Otherwise it would lose its power to shape the future. As the decade progressed the very concept of the centrality of the working class was questioned. In an interview in November 1986, Bruno Trentin of the Cgil argued that the '*centralità operaia*' was an *ideological* rather than a *social* reality. The worker on the assembly-line, for instance, the symbolic figure of class mobilisation, had never represented more than 25-30 per cent of those who worked in industry. But whereas the working class, in the traditional sense of the term, was in numerical decline, dependent labour as a whole was in continual expansion.[2] The world of wage-earning and salaried workers could no longer be assumed to revolve around the traditional Marxist image of the industrial worker as its strategic centre of gravity. The organized expression of such a class-based movement, the '*sindacato dei consigli*', was having difficulty in drawing together and consolidating its leadership over a labour force which was being reorganized and restructured out of all recognition.

The movement in the 1980s was thus confronted with the problem of how to remain a propulsive force in a world of labour which was being changed at unparalleled speed and to an unprecedented degree. If we take a global view of the changes which, according to Paolo Sylos Labini, had already taken place between 1951 and 1988, we find that the proportion of the country's workforce in agriculture had diminished from 40 per cent to 7 per cent in the North and from 56 per cent to 16 per cent in

---

[2] 'Quel mondo in crescita del lavoro subordinato', interview with Bruno Trentin by Marcello Villari, p. 9.

the South.[3] The services sector had expanded from about 20 per cent to around 60 per cent, and although workers in industry still counted for 32.5 per cent of the working population in 1985,[4] the most significant fact in this connection was that the balance had shifted from large to small industry, i.e. to areas where the *sindacato* was weaker. To these simple statistics, however, we must add the increase in the complexity of the industrial workforce itself, now much less homogeneous, and ranging from casual, unqualified labour to the highest levels of skilled operators in the new technologies. These skilled workers, moreover, were rejecting the egalitarianism which, years earlier, had been imposed upon the movement by the metalworkers.[5]

The difficulties of the *sindacato* in the 1980s and early 1990s came, therefore, from a variety of sources. In part they were due to changes in the nature of employment. At the same time the movement did not find it easy to develop policies capable of mobilising workers in areas like the tertiary sector, where it needed to do so. Unionisation has been too low among the young, among women in general, among professional workers and technicians and other atypical groups of membership which have, on the other hand, become of increasing importance in the labour force as a whole. Finally, fewer individuals are being drawn to the *sindacato* for ideological or political reasons than in the past.

Is the picture, therefore, totally negative? Some commentators have pointed out, for instance, that union membership in Italy started to grow once again in 1986, and that in 1990 the three confederations together enlisted more than ten million members for the first time in their history. If we consider what has been happening to union membership elsewhere, this looks impressive at

---

[3] P. Sylos Labini, 'Il lavoro e la produzione', pp. 35-6.

[4] Tavola n.4, Istat, *Annuario di contabilità nazionale. Serie 1960-85*, volume xv, p. 64.

[5] The egalitarian ideal was proving remarkably difficult to shift among masses of unskilled workers. In an investigation carried out in 1980 at Fiat, the very place where the march of the 40,000 dealt the *sindacato*'s egalitarianism its first major defeat, only 2 per cent of workers thought that better educational qualifications should be rewarded by higher pay. See Accornero, *La parabola del sindacato*, p. 35.

first sight (see Appendix, Table 3). But if we look at the statistics for union membership among the *active* workforce (see Appendix, Table 4), the situation seems to change quite significantly. Whereas in the decade from 1981 to 1990 the total membership of the confederations increased by 14.46 per cent, the total membership of *active* workers declined by a similar figure of 14.95 per cent. What accounts for this apparent anomaly is the enormous increase in the number of pensioners joining all three confederations over the decade. Pensioners currently account for more than 38 per cent of the total confederate membership (see Appendix, Table 5). Is this an altogether unhealthy development? Certainly, the decline in membership of the *active* workforce is a serious cause for concern.[6] But pensioners are important in social policy; they are profoundly affected not only by problems relating to pensions, but also by decisions in the areas of housing, transport, health and benefits in general. The tendency of pensioners to turn to the *sindacato* reflects the position of relative importance which it continues to have, in Italian society, as a social and political actor.

The spread of membership between the confederations has not altered significantly since the early 1970s (see Appendix, Table 6). The Cgil share of the membership still exceeds 50 per cent overall, i.e. slightly more than the Cisl and the Uil combined. While ideological motivations have continued to lose a great deal of their power, the two major confederations remain substantially stronger in their traditional White and Red regions. Having said this, the geographical distribution of membership is showing a tendency for regional affiliations to be spread more evenly within each confederation, with a trend for each of them to experience an increased proportion of southern membership.[7]

If we examine changes in membership sector by sector (see Appendix, Table 4), we note that the Cgil retains its highest concentration of membership in industry. This distinguishes it from

---

[6] According to the relevant Cesos report, *Le relazioni sindacali in Italia. Rapporto 1990-91*, p. 83, the trend towards a falling rate of membership among the *active* workforce was reversed in 1990. Whether this a lasting change of direction remains to be seen.

[7] For a more detailed breakdown of regional membership figures for each confederation, see *Laser*, n.1, p. 12, Table 5.

the other two confederations. Nevertheless, the Cgil too is undergoing the same gradual process of tertiarisation of its membership as its rivals. There are other changes worthy of note. Between 1981 and 1990, the Cgil was the only confederation which suffered an absolute decline in membership in all sectors. In the tertiary sector as a whole, the Cisl increased its membership by 2.25 per cent, while proportionately the Uil performed best of all with an overall rise of 10.27 per cent. Also in the tertiary sector, the confederations increased their combined membership among the *active* workforce by 1.18 per cent.

In many ways a more important indicator of the confederations' fortunes is the degree of unionisation they manage to sustain among the workforce. The picture here is on the whole more worrying (see Appendix, Table 7). Even where membership increased in absolute terms, as in the services sector, the process of unionisation did not keep pace with the rise in employment. Though not dramatic in all instances, the decline in unionisation between 1981 and 1990 took place in all sectors.

The biggest decline was in agriculture. But here, we must bear in mind that by 1981 the confederations had unionised a staggering 99.88 per cent of agricultural workers. There has been no comparable experience in labour history, and even with its reduced figure of 84.30 per cent, unionisation in this sector remains remarkably high.

The percentage of decline in unionisation was almost identical in industry and the services, most of it taking place during the first half of the decade. In industry the decline can be partially explained by the diversification of the workforce, and also by the decentralisation of production, which created problems for recruitment. Unionisation in the tertiary sector reached a peak of about 40 per cent in the late 1970s, since when it has been falling. What was worrying to the *sindacato* was the fact that it was losing members in industry, a sector in decline, but without gaining them in an advancing sector where it needed to do so.

Once again there is more than one way of interpreting these developments. Non-membership of the confederations does not necessarily signify hostility towards the unions. It may reflect the difficulties the confederations are facing in learning how to appeal to new types of workers, in a world where even the traditional subcultures which sustained the major confederations are in decline.

More importantly, non-membership does not even necessarily indicate an unwillingness to take industrial action. Many workers, particularly in the services sector, do take action, but not in the confederations. To understand this point we must examine the development of the new autonomous unions.

The New 'Autonomous' Unions

The increased unionisation of workers in the services sector and among white-collar public employees which has been under way since the 1970s has given special cause for concern because of the tendency in these sectors towards a high level of fragmentation. In 1974, for instance, no less than thirty category unions representing state employees and civil servants were affiliated to the Cgil alone.[8] Given the heavy penetration of the public administration by the Dc, the dominant influence in the sector had been that of the Cisl. Historically, moreover, this mixture of Catholic groupings produced a situation in which the *sindacato* was actually represented on bodies concerned with the management of personnel.

It is commonly agreed that the *sindacato*'s involvement in these sectors has compromised its independence, and has been used to maintain, rather than challenge, a status quo which remains substantially tainted by *clientelismo*. At the official level, the confederations called repeatedly for a revision of the bargaining system, and there was mounting pressure to bring industrial relations in the public sector under the same procedures as those in the private sector. It is generally recognised that one of Italy's major problems is the great divide between policy and realisation and that reform of the antiquated and clientelistic system of public administration is an urgent necessity if this is to be remedied. The *sindacato*, and the Cisl in particular, needed to extricate themselves from the tangled web of self-protecting connections within the public administration in order to exert pressure for its reform. The restructuring of workplace representation, finalised in December 1993, along with the *sindacato*'s withdrawal from the administrative councils, which will be discussed later, finally resolved this

---

[8] Cella e Treu, *Relazioni industriali*, p. 124.

problem.[9]

One of the most fundamental differences between white-collar public sector workers and industrial workers, at least traditionally, is that whereas the latter have found the workplace a source of unity, the former create their identities around their differences. It is no surprise, therefore, to find the creation of a large number of autonomous unions in the non-industrial world of labour. These have emerged independently of the confederations, indeed usually in competition with them.

The autonomous unions began to make an impact with the 'tertiarisation' of industrial conflict in the 1970s.[10] The taboo on strike action among non-industrial workers was broken by the white-collar workers in industry during the 'Hot Autumn', and the practice spread in the early 1970s to public employees, teachers, transport staff and others. In these sectors, particularly where the influence of the confederations was weak, the demands which emerged tended to conflict with the strategic objectives of the confederate *sindacato*. Between 1974 and 1983 the services sector's share of time lost through industrial action was slightly less than 30 per cent. By 1985 it had increased to about 43 per cent.[11]

Figures on membership of autonomous unions are unreliable. For the mid-1970s, the most feasible estimates put the combined national membership at somewhere between 320,000 and 500,000.[12] Among bank employees and teachers, there was a respectable level of membership (see Appendix, Table 8), seemingly reaching almost a quarter of that of the confederations. Membership of the autonomous unions in the more troubled transport sector, however, was still small. Among railworkers, even if we accept their own

---

[9] See the text of the original proposal of March 1991, 'L'Intesa sulle rappresentanze sindacali unitarie', particularly Section V, paragraph 1, p. 37, which stipulated that the terms of this agreement are binding on all forms of union representation, including the white-collar public sector.

[10] The most comprehensive study of the development of the autonomous unions in the seventies is to be found in R. Stefanelli (ed.), *I sindacati autonomi*.

[11] Cesos, *Le relazioni sindacali in Italia. Rapporto 1985-86*, tavola 6, p. 56.

[12] See Biagioni, Palmieri, and Pipan, *Indagine sul sindacato*, pp. 53-6.

figures, the membership was less than a tenth of that of the Cgil alone.

But even in the late seventies there were visible signs of the growing strength of autonomous unions. In the 1979 elections for union representatives to the National Schools Council, for example, while the confederate candidates together obtained 56.2 per cent of the votes, the share of the autonomous unions was 43.8 per cent.[13] The problem for autonomous unions at this stage was that they had little or no official negotiating role, which meant that they could be ignored by the major parties to negotiations.

In the public administration, unions were important since they were represented on the *consigli di amministrazione* (Administrative Councils). In elections to these bodies in the various government ministries, in November to December 1979, the autonomous unions obtained 18.1 per cent of the votes,[14] whereas by 1984 in similar elections the figure had increased to 28.1 per cent.[15] Although it was clear that the autonomous unions were getting increased support at the expense of the confederations, the latter continued to dominate negotiations on the union side. This led the confederations to ignore the danger signals.

One of the factors which took the confederations by surprise was the disruptive power of the new forms of industrial action which the autonomous unions could promote in the tertiary sector. The public was hit in 1984 when flight controllers challenged the military regulations limiting their power to strike. This action was followed by strikes by pilots and airport workers for more pay. These events set the scene for the emergence in 1986 of the *Cobas* (*comitati di base*, or rank-and-file committees), which, through their promotion of disruptive industrial action among railworkers, teachers, and others, created the impression among large sections of the public that the autonomous unions were out of control and that the confederations were losing their capacity to hold the workers' movement together. During 1988 and 1989 there were

---

[13] See ibid., p. 55.

[14] See details in ibid.

[15] My own calculations, based on detailed results in Cesos, *Le relazioni sindacali in Italia. Rapporto 1984-85*, p. 246.

strikes which almost led to civil disorder in overcrowded airport lounges, train and ferry stations and in the Metro in Milan. In Naples there was even a demonstration against bank staff who were on strike. Such events generated a great deal of highly-charged debate, much of it ill-informed or excessively dramatic.

An argument arose in 1987 when eleven autonomous unions claimed the right to negotiate alongside the confederations for contract renewals which affected about 600,000 health workers and 85,000 doctors. After withdrawing from the negotiations, the autonomous unions relented and signed the agreement which the confederations had reached with the employers in March of that year. According to the most reliable statistics, by 1990 the Cgil and the Cisl represented respectively only 6 and 7 per cent of medical staff nationally, while the number rose dramatically among non-medical staff, where the confederate share was 84 per cent.[16]

The autonomous unions began to make inroads into the confederations' territory, partly owing to the latter's 'solidarity' culture which tends always to play down the differences between groups of employees. Thus the autonomous airline pilots' union Anpac gained much support in 1986 when it put forward proposals on insurance provision, health schemes and a number of other matters relating to the pilots' special conditions of work. The same feeling that the confederations were not sufficiently attentive to their particular needs led other airport workers and staff to reject the agreement between Intersind and the confederations in the autumn of 1987. This was the prelude to the industrial action and disruption which followed at regular intervals over the next two or three years, causing much public alarm.

Perhaps the *autonomi* who would make the greatest impact were the *Cobas*, groups with a loose organizational structure, which first grew out of the teachers' rejection of the official *sindacato*'s bargaining platform in May 1986. Before this, the traditional autonomous teachers' union (Snals) had unionised about 15 per cent of teachers, the confederations 35.2 per cent, and about 49.8 per cent remained unaffiliated.[17] In February 1987, the confederations

---

[16] See Cesos, *Le relazioni sindacali in Italia. Rapporto 1990-91*, pp. 199-200.

[17] Cesos, *Le relazioni sindacali in Italia. Rapporto 1985-86*, pp. 211-2.

and the Snals signed the new contract with the government. The *Cobas* spearheaded a series of strikes and demonstrations which culminated in 40-50,000 teachers demonstrating in Rome to reject the contract which had been signed by the confederations and the Snals. The *Cobas* thus emerged as a challenge also to the traditional autonomous union in the sector. Strongest in the cities, and reaching 50 per cent of unionised teachers in Naples, the *Cobas* tackled deeply-felt professional grievances, which many teachers felt the traditional unions had ignored, and brought criticism of the whole structure of the teaching profession into public prominence. They also demanded a monthly increase of L40,000 for all teachers. The pressure exerted by the *Cobas* was such that the Snals dissociated itself from the agreement it had signed earlier, and by the spring of 1988 even the confederations had made the *Cobas'* salary claim their own, a demand which would have been unthinkable a year earlier. According to Antonio Ceccotti, undisputed leader of the schools' *Cobas* in 1989, the movement grew among teachers 'because the *sindacati* were never a true expression of the sector, but simply an extension of the political parties'.[18]

Later, the *Cobas*, the Snals and the *Gilda* (an offshoot of the *Cobas* appearing in 1988), joined forces and, in a strange alliance of left and right extremes, called the most successful demonstration in the history of the teaching sector. On 25 June 1991, up to 100,000 teachers descended on Rome from all parts of the country to reject the new contract which was being proposed on salaries, the harmonisation of regulations governing public sector employees with those of the private sector, and the agreement over a minimum services guarantee in the case of industrial action.

The autonomous unions, of which there were more than twenty among railworkers, had been growing in the railroad sector as a whole since 1976. By 1986, with 19,900 members, they represented about 12.6 per cent of unionised workers. They were thus almost a quarter of the size of the Cgil (80,000 members) and actually larger than the Uil (18,000 members). These were still, however, the traditional autonomous unions, of which Fisafs, with

---

[18] R. Greco e L. Macchiavelli, 'I guerrieri del pubblico impiego - Inchiesta sui Cobas', p. 14.

a membership of about 13,600, was the largest. In 1986, Fisafs called a strike and inflicted losses which amounted to the equivalent of almost £7 million in five days. The disruptive power of these unions in public services was considerable, a fact which contributed to their high profile.

The following year the railroad sector saw the formation of the *Cobas* among the engine drivers. Between May and June 1987, these workers rejected confederate and Fisafs agreements, made claims of their own and organized several strikes, which paralysed rail traffic. But the most notable feature of this new development was the fact that the majority of the *Cobas* leaders in the sector were members of the Cgil and the Pci. Indeed, one of these leaders stated 'most of us have no intention of tearing up our membership cards. We simply want to be taken into account.'[19] The railway *Cobas* complained that the confederations had become bureaucratic, distant and conservative, and that many local leaders did not even know the official union representatives who met the employers on their behalf. They demanded *Cobas* representation at negotiations. These developments were particularly worrying for the Cgil. The *macchinisti* (engine drivers), for example, who supported the *Cobas*, were about 70 per cent habitual Pci voters.

In March 1989 yet another group of employees, telephone workers for the Sip, dissatisfied with the official unions, established *Cobas* groups in their sector. But the most disturbing feature of all these new developments from the *sindacato*'s point of view was the absence of medium- or long-term perspectives in the *Cobas* and their seeming indifference to the need to co-ordinate the objectives of different groups of workers. To a *sindacato* which prided itself on the support it had been able to build up in the country at large around the need for a united *soggetto politico* operating in the broader interests of working people, the spontaneist activism of the *Cobas* constituted a rejection of the strategic sense which the movement had constructed through many years of patient effort.

Yet in many ways it was precisely the particular configuration of this 'culture of solidarity' which created a large part of the problem. Clear signs of a serious problem existed among ordinary members many years before the emergence of the *Cobas*.

---

[19] Ibid., p. 13.

The demonstration by the Fiat clerical workers, foremen and skilled operatives in 1980 which forced the *sindacato* to abandon the strike was accompanied by slogans which accused the unions of neglecting the technically qualified and of undervaluing the tertiary sector. This attack on the *sindacato*'s egalitarian line was the first open sign of worker discontent with the official unions. The subsequent emergence of militant autonomous activity among such groups as doctors, teachers, pilots, engine drivers and many others, gave expression to a desire for greater recognition of their skills and training against a *cultura di coordinamento* which was seen as a levelling down of widely different professional activities. What the *sindacato* first saw as the 'craft' orientation of the *Cobas* and other autonomous unions was simply articulating the desire of those who supported these unions to have their professional status given proper recognition.

A further problem was that of negotiating rights. Although autonomous unions had existed for many years prior to 1986, in practice the confederations monopolised bargaining on the union side. For many years problems relating to negotiating rights were shelved in the interests of parity between the three major confederations. Owing to pressure within the public administration sector, however, it was agreed in 1988 that a minimum of 5 per cent of votes in elected bodies such as the administrative councils would be required for a union to be admitted to negotiations.

Subsequent events intensified the call for clarification in the area of negotiating rights. The *Cobas* refused to sign an agreement which was acceptable both to the railway employers and the confederations in March 1992. Strikes were called in April, and estimates concerning support for the strikes varied from between 29 and 41 per cent of workers concerned. In the event, most services were kept going, to the satisfaction of the confederations, which claimed that support for the autonomous unions was at last on the decline. The previous year, owing to union splits, the railway employers had negotiated separately, on different occasions, with the confederations and the autonomous unions. Frustrated by the events of April 1992, the minister concerned, Lorenzo Necci, declared that the benefits of the March agreement would not be paid to those who took industrial action against it. A debate ensued about the legality of such an initiative. What emerged with force was the necessity for legislation on negotiating rights.

Another factor which contributed to increased autonomous activity was the absence, until June 1990, of any legislation regulating industrial conflict. Some have argued that support for autonomous unions, particularly the *Cobas*, fed on their readiness to promote conflict, even in essential services. The autonomous unions were resentful of the way in which the confederations had for years created codes of self-regulation without consulting them. Although the Cisl showed signs as early as 1981 of being prepared to consider legislation, on the whole the confederations remained hostile to the idea until the level of conflict generated by the *Cobas* from 1986 onwards began seriously to damage their public image. In 1988, the confederations accepted the idea of legislation on strikes in essential services. The law (*legge* n.146) was passed in parliament on 12 June 1990. In services such as energy, schools, health service, transport, refuse collection, the judicial system and telecommunications, it imposed an obligation to give 10 days' advance notice of industrial action. The level of services to be maintained during industrial action was to be established by collective bargaining between employers and unions and submitted to a special committee of experts appointed by parliament to assess the adequacy of such agreements.

What, therefore, is the extent of the challenge to the confederations represented by the autonomous unions? Reliable statistics are not available, but it seems reasonable to suppose that such unions may command a combined membership of up to two million. But this number represents three different types of autonomous unions: (1) the traditional autonomous unions which have existed for many years among teachers, civil servants and bank employees; (2) unions which have emerged to promote the professional status of employees such as doctors and airline pilots; (3) militant unions of recent origin such as the *Cobas* recruiting among teachers and engine drivers. But increase in support for unions in group (3), for instance, did not affect the membership of the confederations very profoundly. Among teachers, many *Cobas* supporters were previously unaffiliated, and among groups such as the engine drivers many retained their confederate membership. Even in the heady period of 1986-7 there was no collapse of confederate membership in the sectors affected by the new *autonomi*. Indeed, in these years the confederations successfully signed agreements covering ten million workers in the private and public sectors. Even in the sector with the highest proportion of autonomous union membership, the public administration, elections to the administrative councils continued to see 70 per cent of confederate candidates chosen.

When we look at levels of industrial action, we find that the image of a *sindacato* which had lost control of the situation is hard to sustain. Statistically, the total number of hours lost in strike action in 1986 and 1987 was less than in any year since 1959. Why, therefore, was the impact on the public so powerful? There are a number of reasons for this. If we look carefully at the statistics, we find that while conflictual levels from 1986 were not high in global terms, they did, in fact, increase in the tertiary sector, where the autonomous unions were most active.[20] In 1986, the services sector was able to transform its 37.93 per cent share of strikers into 59.42 per cent of total hours lost through industrial action. Thus the impact of strikes in the services sector was greater in terms of hours lost than in industry. When we consider the potential for disruption in the public administration, on buses, trains and airlines, in banks, hospitals and schools, we can see that the effect on the public is more immediate than are most forms of industrial action in industry. Thus, despite the fact that the total number of hours lost in strikes, if we leave aside the the years 1984 and 1985, reached an all-time low in 1986, the public gained the impression that it was more difficult to live with industrial action. There are some additional points to make in this connection.

Whereas many traditional forms of industrial action inconvenienced the greater part of the population indirectly, strikes undertaken by the autonomous unions in the late eighties and early nineties tended to be aimed more directly at the public. Partly for this reason, newspapers often carried advance warning of strikes, often with the co-operation of the unions. Whatever the intentions, however, the effect of this publicity was not altogether beneficial to the unions, autonomous or confederate. The popular perception of the 'good strike', the egalitarian and 'social' strike, which had enabled the *sindacato* to muster widespread support in the late sixties and throughout the seventies, no longer existed. The other

---

[20] See statistical tables in Bordogna, '"Arcipelago Cobas": frammentazione della rappresentanza e conflitti di lavoro', pp. 277-82.

factor which influenced public thinking was the high profile of the divisions between the confederations and the autonomous unions. Taken together, all these factors produced in the public mind an image of a movement in crisis.

There are signs that the law passed in June 1990 (*legge n.146*), has affected the level of activity of the new unions, some of which tried either to ignore the law or else to find loopholes in its provisions.[21] But the committee overseeing the application of the legislation soon prevented both the *Cobas* and *Gilda*, for example, from organizing strikes in infant schools and also rejected their codes of self-regulation as inadequate in guaranteeing essential services. The support for these organizations seems also to have suffered. In the elections to provincial schools' councils in 1991, the *Gilda* went down from a 3.4 per cent share of the vote in 1989 to 2.0 per cent, and the *Cobas* from a high point of 6.7 per cent in 1989 to 0.4 per cent. In the same period the confederations jointly increased their share of the votes from 45.6 per cent to 60.6 per cent. Even the traditional and less militant Snals went up slightly from 25.2 per cent to 26.5 per cent.[22]

The restraining effect of the law on strikes in essential services was also felt by the autonomous unions in the railway sector and among air traffic control staff, both of which had to abandon industrial action in 1991 in order to keep within the law. Thus it seems that the new autonomous unions will find it difficult to regain the level of support attained in the late 1980s. The confederations may be able to draw some comfort from the fact that the prospect of a long-term threat to their future from the newly emerged *autonomi* seems less likely now than it did around 1987-8. But they will no longer be able to ignore the autonomous sector of the *sindacato* in many areas of negotiation.

Problems within the Confederations

The crisis of representation was felt not only in the confederate

---

[21] See the report by D. Carrieri, 'I sindacati non confederali', in Cesos, *Le relazioni sindacali in Italia. Rapporto 1990-91*, pp. 197-202.

[22] Ibid., Table 3, p. 201.

sindacato's relations with the *autonomi*, but also within its own internal structures. At the Cgil Congress in 1981 the General Secretary, Luciano Lama, warned that 'the factory councils had to express the demands of white-collar workers, technicians, administrators and researchers', otherwise they would lose credibility.[23] Mechanisms for the swift consultation of the rank-and-file *before* making decisions had to be found so that workers would not habitually find themselves asked to ratify decisions already taken.[24]

Increasingly, slogans began to appear at demonstrations, protesting against these developments. A major factor in provoking such complaints was the tendency, particularly strong within the Cisl and the Uil, to compensate for the movement's loss of power *vis-à-vis* the employers by tying it more closely to the government and seeking forms of political bargaining (*scambio politico*). This had two effects: it encouraged union leaders, particularly those tied to the parties in government, to make decisions without consultation, and it also put the unity of the Cgil-Cisl-Uil federation under considerable strain. At a rally in March 1982, 30,000 demonstrating metalworkers shouted down the Uil leader Benvenuto for blocking a confederate proposal demanding a general strike. Benvenuto, it was alleged, was in collusion with the Psi leader Craxi and more interested in promoting the party's fortunes in government than the workers' demands. The slogans on the banners at the demonstrations against Craxi's emergency decree to slash the *scala mobile* in 1984 showed a clear awareness of the connections between a broad array of political problems: 'real union unity is in the workers themselves', 'the workers do not want to be divided', 'neither with Jaruzelski nor with Craxi', 'ban emergency decrees', etc. At the root of the movement's problems was the simple fact that there were no formal mechanisms for rank-and-file consultation before decisions were taken at confederate level. As a contemporary source asserted, 'such decisions are questioned only when there is disagreement between the confederations'.[25]

---

[23] Lama, 'Relazione al X Congresso della Cgil', p. 29.

[24] See ibid., pp. 29-30.

[25] Cella e Treu, *Relazioni industriali*, p. 177.

After the break-up of the Cgil-Cisl-Uil federation in 1984 it became evident that moves towards rediscovering unity would need to include a revitalisation of the links between the membership and the higher echelons of the *sindacato*. The metalworkers' federations immediately began to argue strongly for the restoration of the central role of the local factory council, 'the skeletal structure of the unitary *sindacato*', which had suffered serious decline as the powerhouse for the generation of new ideas.[26]

At the Cgil Congress in February 1986, speakers complained that the strategy which aimed at making the *sindacato* a *soggetto politico* had resulted in greater centralisation of its activity at the expense of the membership's involvement.[27] In 1986, 20.8 per cent of metalworkers voted against the *sindacato*'s national agreement; by 1990 the figure had risen to 26.2 per cent.[28] There was clearly a need to create more effective mechanisms for consultation. In July 1986, the three confederations of Milan reached an agreement on how to renew the base structures of the *sindacato*. The agreement emphasised the importance of continuity with the 'factory council' experience, but stressed the need for the existence of workplace organizations for employees such as 'doctors, technicians, researchers, junior executives and managers in the public sector'.[29] After a great deal of preparatory groundwork, an agreement was signed on 1 March 1991 by the leaders of the three confederations, Trentin for the Cgil, Marini for the Cisl, and Benvenuto for the Uil,

---

[26] P. Galli, 'E allora rendiamoli più rappresentativi', pp. 7-8.

[27] See particularly the contributions of A. Amoretti, G. Cazzola and R. Bianchi, in 'I lavori dell'XI Congresso Cgil', pp. 23-6. At its own congress the year before, the Cisl's final resolutions stressed the importance of increasing internal democracy within the unions, but expressed none of the Cgil's anxiety about the distancing effects, *vis-à-vis* the rank-and-file, of the *scambio politico* (political bargaining) or *concertazione sociale* (social concertation). See resolution 56 (*La democrazia interna*), in Cisl, 'Le mozioni del X Congresso Nazionale, 1985', pp. 94-7. As we shall see in the final chapter, this attitude, at least in the confederation's official statements, would change rather abruptly soon after the Cisl's Congress.

[28] Accornero, *La parabola del sindacato*, p. 16.

[29] 'Le intese unitarie raggiunte da Cgil, Cisl e Uil di Milano sulle strutture di base e sull'azione sindacale (2 luglio 1986)', p. 273.

outlining the replacement of factory councils and their equivalent in the tertiary sector by the Rsu (*Rappresentanze sindacali unitarie*) in all workplaces.

The proposals expressed a clear desire to minimise the confederate divisions which might be reflected in workplace structures. By now, the confederations were beginning to respond to the problem of the *autonomi*, and they drafted detailed regulations governing the relations between representatives with different confederate affiliations, and between these and the autonomous unions.[30]

Representatives would still be elected by a secret ballot of all workers and not simply union members. However, there would now be a clear advantage in joining the *sindacato*, since the Cgil, Cisl and Uil candidates would themselves be elected in 'primaries' strictly confined to the membership. This was an improvement over their simple nomination by union officials outside the factory. Autonomous unions would also be able to put forward candidates. Where possible the Cgil, the Cisl and the Uil would present unitary lists, and in all eventualities 67 per cent of all places would be distributed strictly according to votes for the candidates, irrespective of their affiliations. For the remaining 33 per cent, as a stimulus to unity between the confederations, the places going to confederate candidates would be divided equally among the confederations. Non-confederate candidates would obtain places in the normal way according to the votes cast in their favour.

With the agreement over the Rsu, the *sindacato* took an important step in attempting to adapt to a radically transformed labour environment. Although it is too early to pass judgement on the success of these new bodies, the process of replacement has started. Rsu elections took place in May 1992 at the naval construction port in La Spezia. More significantly perhaps, owing to the development of the *autonomi* in the railway sector in recent years, the first Rsu elections in this sector took place at the end of March 1992 at two large depots in Bologna (Centrale and Arcoveggio). Candidatures were open to all, including the *Cobas*, and the elections were conducted broadly according to the guidelines described earlier. In the ballot, 77 per cent of personnel

---

[30] See footnote 9.

voted, and 80 per cent of the votes went to confederate candidates, more than half, in fact, to the FILT-Cgil. This was seen as a success for the confederations.[31]

The Cgil Congress in October 1991 addressed itself to what remains in some ways the most serious distortion in its representational function, namely in respect of its female members. The urgency of the matter derives from the fact that this is not an issue which affects only certain categories of workers. If left unresolved, it threatens to impair whatever improvements are made in all sections of the movement. Even within the Cgil, which is arguably the most historically and ideologically sympathetic of the confederations to the demands of women, at the time of writing only one of its national category federations, namely the FISAC (bank employees) is led by a woman. Despite the fact that women provide about two fifths of the national membership, there is only one female Assistant General Secretary (i.e. in the Abruzzo) in all of the confederation's regional organizations, and out of 174 *Camere del lavoro* throughout the country, only five are led by women, those of Reggio Calabria, Gela, L'Aquila, Varese and Pomezia. Although details of implementation need to be worked out, the new statutes of the Cgil stipulate that both in the vertical and horizontal structures of the organization, positions of leadership must be held by at least 40 per cent of both sexes. The most encouraging aspect of this change was its level of support at the congress. In a congress enjoying an impressive degree of pre-congressional participation at all levels,[32] the voting figures for the new statutes containing these changes were 900 in favour, 35 against and 15 abstentions.[33] There will almost certainly be pressure on the Cisl and the Uil to follow the Cgil's lead in an initiative which will undoubtedly enrich and consolidate the *sindacato*'s representational function.

---

[31] See M. Guerzoni, 'A Bologna si parte', p 16.

[32] For a breakdown of figures on delegates attending preparatory congresses and assemblies, see D'Agostini, 'L'unità più vicina', p. 10.

[33] G. Iocca, 'Nuovi attori e nuove regole', p.16.

22

Which Way Forward?

Arguments about Neo-Corporatism

In its bare essentials neo-corporatism defines a formalised system for arriving at trilateral agreements between the state, the employers and the unions. Sympathetic commentators have pointed to the stability of countries such as Austria, Denmark, Norway, Sweden, Switzerland and the former West Germany, which have developed neo-corporatist industrial relations procedures. They have argued that these societies have evolved a wide range of institutional innovations and that neo-corporatism has an enhanced capacity to pursue the interests of union members in a disciplined manner.[1]

Against those who question the democratic character of neo-corporatist decisions in matters of economic and social policy, the supporters of neo-corporatism have argued that it has given coherence and power to the chosen representatives of vast sectors of the working population. It offers access to high-level negotiations for shaping economic and social policy through a system which attempts to rationalise modes of representation which otherwise would remain scattered, fragmented, and prey to the powerful. Neo-corporatism has thus been described by analysts such as Walter Korpi as a more advanced and better organized form of democracy in which the capacity for collective action is more evenly distributed and controlled and the relations with authority are rendered more open and stable.[2]

Opponents of neo-corporatism from the left of the *sindacato* have produced a variety of counter-arguments. It is seen by them as a manoeuvre to favour the interests of the establishment. The

---

[1] See P. C. Schmitter, 'Teoria della democrazia e pratica neo-corporatista', pp. 118ff.

[2] This is the argument presented in W. Korpi, *The Democratic Class Struggle*.

purpose of neo-corporatism is always, in their view, to institutionalise and absorb the *sindacato* in such a way as to deprive it of any ability to act independently. By drawing the *sindacato* into binding agreements, all capacity for rank-and-file participation in policy-making is destroyed, and the *sindacato* thereby loses its character as a 'movement' or social force, retaining only its 'institutional' or bureaucratic function.

In practice, intellectuals associated with the Italian *sindacato* have not expressed these arguments in such polarised forms. They have, however, employed a variety of arguments, with those decisively in favour of neo-corporatist developments in the minority. Although Catholic and communist intellectuals did not form totally homogeneous blocs, it would be true to say that arguments sympathetic to neo-corporatism were more common within the Cisl and the Uil, whereas the Cgil on the whole retained a more critical posture.

By the early 1980s there were a number of reasons why neo-corporatist arrangements should have begun to interest some of the movement's intellectuals. The *sindacato* had attempted to develop its role as a *soggetto politico* without placing its macroeconomic collaboration with employers and the state within a highly formalised framework. But this strategy had largely failed to bring about the reforms for which the movement had pressed since the early 1970s. One of the main reasons for this was that, whereas the *sindacato* had considerable bargaining strength through its ability to disrupt the economy, this was true only when the economy was stable. But economic crises from the mid-1970s had led to collaborative strategies, epitomised in the EUR experience, and generated increasing dissatisfaction with the movement's reliance on a purely 'conflictual' model of bargaining which was by its very nature unpredictable in its results.

In July 1978 the socialist Sandro Pertini was elected President of the Republic. In June 1981 Pertini invited Giovanni Spadolini to form the first non-Dc-led government in the Republic's history. These changes, together with Spadolini's apparent determination to provide the government with fresh solutions to the country's problems, led some to see in the new situation 'a trend towards a major change in the [industrial relations] system ... because in the meantime theories about a "democratic neo-corporatism" had gained some credibility on the margins of the *sindacato*'s cultural environment'.[3] The idea of a stable arrangement in which economic policy could be determined through the co-option of the unions and employers into government agencies had some appeal. Agreements could be made which the government and the employers could not simply ignore when it suited them. But the confederations would have to pay a price. They would have to adopt a tripartite agenda and be willing to reduce labour conflict. Some commentators argued that such an arrangement would even require legislation limiting the right to strike.

At the 1981 Cgil Congress, the left of the confederation, headed by Sergio Garavini, attacked the high-level exchange of political favours, and compromises between the *sindacato*, the government and the employers, all of which seemed to be leading in a neo-corporatist direction. Such developments, it was argued, reduced the unions to a subordinate role and did nothing to challenge the capitalist system. But concern was not limited to the left of the confederation. Even the majority of communists, who had long since ceased to adopt 'anti-system' political positions, were worried. The leader, Luciano Lama, was critical of the growing tendency to circumscribe the role of the movement within the confines of a neo-corporatist perspective. The employers wanted centralised bargaining (at least on the price of labour), he argued, 'in order to inhibit articulated bargaining, i.e. at the level of the area, the sector and the plant'.[4] There were two further dangers: that of losing contact with rank-and-file demands and the associated threat to internal democracy within the *sindacato*.

Opposition to neo-corporatist developments did not, however, imply an unwillingness to engage in tripartite negotiations as such, nor did it weaken support for the notion of the *sindacato* as a *soggetto politico*. In fact some argued, particularly within the Cgil, that a neo-corporatist vocation was incompatible with such a role. In order to act effectively as a political actor within the system, the *sindacato* had to retain its capacity to promote social struggles and independent action, whereas neo-corporatist arrangements would turn it into an organ of the state. Autonomy of action was essential if the movement were to retain those elements of pluralism and creative conflict necessary to effect change and avoid the total

---

[3] Mariucci, 'I rapporti tra sindacato e stato', p. 34.

[4] L. Lama, 'Relazione al X Congresso della Cgil', p. 19.

institutionalisation of the unions. More recently, at the Cgil Congress in October 1991, the leader of the confederation, Bruno Trentin, argued that a pluralist democracy which defends the freedom of union activity must uphold 'the legitimacy of social conflict as a fundamental element in a free order'.[5]

But this is not the whole story. There were also commentators who argued that what was emerging could best be described as a form of neo-corporatist pluralism where the best elements of democratic practice, creative conflict, and institutionalised co-operation could co-exist. The problem was that a comprehensive theory of neo-corporatism in relation to democratic institutions had not been developed. This was partly due to the fact that where such neo-corporatist arrangements did exist, they had evolved pragmatically, in a piecemeal fashion, and not according to any obvious theoretical design. Developments in Italian industrial relations, moroever, conformed less than most to traditional patterns, and there was even uncertainty over whether such developments could be described in any strict sense as neo-corporatist.

The impression that Italy might be moving in a neo-corporatist direction arose initially because of the *sindacato*'s practice from the early seventies of negotiating with both government and employers. The Italian *sindacato* differed from unions which were shaped according to the 'trade union' model, where negotiating with government on such matters as pensions, health policy and family allowances, or with employers on investments and company strategy, were excluded from the normal conduct of labour relations. Roughly speaking, only two broad models of industrial relations seemed possible within the conceptual horizons of industrial relations theory, the neo-corporatist and the 'trade union' models. The EUR strategy, moreover, although hardly a success, appeared nevertheless indicative of the *sindacato*'s willingness to enter into the kind of tripartite relationship which was typical of neo-corporatist practice.

What to many seemed to confirm the trend towards neo-corporatism in Italy was the agreement reached between the unions, the employers and the government on 22 January 1983. This agreement was not conducted through a series of parallel

---

[5] D'Agostini, 'L'unità più vicina', p. 10.

discussions with the government acting as mediator, as was the common practice, but rather the outcome was a genuine tripartite agreement. There were two additional features of this agreement which reinforced the views of those who perceived a general movement towards neo-corporatism. First, central to the settlement were those parts of the agreement, such as wage ceilings and the adjustment of the *scala mobile*, which were aimed at the global objective of achieving economic stability. Secondly, there appeared to be an intention to reorganize the system of industrial relations in such a way that centralised bargaining would act as the chief regulator of lower-level negotiations.

The 'Protocollo IRI' of December 1984 proposed the setting up of joint consultative committees at company and area levels which would involve the *sindacato* in decision-making in industrial and economic policy, employment and labour mobility. Although this agreement was confined to the state-holding sector, IRI had in the past set the pace on the employers' side for the development of industrial relations practice in Italy. An updated version of the agreement was signed on 16 July 1986. This was followed on 22 July by an agreement between the confederations and employers in the private sector of the chemical industry which included provision for joint consultation on major aspects of employment and industrial development. There seemed, at least to some observers, to be mounting evidence that industrial relations in Italy were moving in a neo-corporatist direction.

But even on the basis of such evidence, the counter-arguments turned out to be stronger. The *scambio politico* and *concertazione sociale* which commentators used to describe bargaining practices in Italy fell far short of neo-corporatism. While these terms do indeed describe some of the characteristics which are to be found in neo-corporatist systems generally, they do not imply the highly centralised set of permanent and formalised relations sanctioned by legislation, which are the essential components of neo-corporatist systems. This difference is borne out by closer scrutiny of the agreements in question. The 1983 tripartite agreement fell considerably short of a neo-corporatist type of settlement. There was no co-ordination between any of its components and any legislative mechanisms, nor did it contain any provision for introducing more formal procedures at a centralised level. Nor did the 1984 and 1986 agreements mentioned above go any further towards establishing a tighter regulatory framework. For this reason it remains true to assert that the 'Italian industrial relations system is still based primarily on collective bargaining'.[6] There continues to be, moreover, too much devolved bargaining in Italy to conceive of a shift towards a strongly institutionalised system in the near future.

Far from being the outcome of a planned move towards neo-corporatism, the increase in centralised bargaining seems, on the contrary, to have been the result of competing strategies. The first crucial high-level agreement, that of 1975 over the *scala mobile*, although a stabilising event in the light of the preceding years of conflict, was also an important defensive stratagem for both the *sindacato* and the employers. But the repercussions of this agreement caused the government to reflect on its own inability to conduct effective political bargaining with the different social actors, for it seemed to be 'surrendering an important part of its role in shaping economic policy'.[7] The government, therefore, in the face of social forces which were highly organized and able to mobilise interests and negotiate them at a highly centralised level, could not afford to be excluded from such bargaining and risk allowing macroeconomic developments to escape its influence.

Government involvement in subsequent tripartite negotiations was thus not inspired by a coherent view of how the major social forces in Italian society should regulate their interactions. The tendency of the government in such encounters was to use them either to resolve its own internal conflicts or simply to stabilise the economic situation by controlling the cost of labour and the level of public spending. One of the most important effects for the government of the January 1983 tripartite agreement was momentarily to interrupt the growing social and political conflict and re-establish its authority. The agreement contributed little to the long-term solutions of the country's problems, provided no guidelines for future negotiations of a similar kind, and was unceremoniously abandoned by the peremptory government decision under Craxi in 1984 to cut the *scala mobile*. It became abundantly clear that far from being part of any neo-corporatist blueprint, the *sindacato* found itself being treated as simply 'a

---

[6] Negrelli and Santi, 'Industrial Relations in Italy', p. 179.

[7] M. Regini, 'Relazioni industriali e sistema politico: l'evoluzione recente e le prospettive degli anni ottanta', p. 141.

cinghia di trasmissione for stability and governability as defined by the government'.[8] Given the perennial internal conflict both within the major party itself and between its coalition partners, it is not surprising that the *sindacato* should have found itself being pulled in different directions by its components' collateral partners in government. The simple fact is that there were too many hidden agendas within the Italian political system to allow any government seriously to consider promoting a neo-corporatist system which would tie its hands and inhibit its capacity to use policy as a regulator of its ever-shifting alliances.

If we turn next to the employers, an analysis of events since the 1975 agreement on the *scala mobile* makes it as difficult to perceive in their behaviour any serious intention of building neo-corporatist structures. One of the puzzling questions on this front was why the Confindustria pressed for centralised bargaining from about 1975, and later acquiesced in government involvement, when the trend elsewhere in Europe was to weaken the unions as bargaining partners. The neo-corporatist thesis, attractive perhaps at first glance, tends to vanish if we look more closely at the *content* of negotiations and not simply at their ostensible institutional forms.

The contents of all the major centralised agreements we have discussed tended to focus on wage containment and the reduction of labour costs, which were indeed effective, and investments and social spending which, by contrast, were not. Such agreements had clearly worked in the employers' interests. Ever since the 'Hot Autumn' of 1969, the two major developments which had worried them were the increase in decentralised bargaining, and the *sindacato*'s greater control over industrial strategy for which national category contracts provided. Far from wanting neo-corporatist developments, which might have reinforced such provisions, the major objective of the employers in pursuing interconfederate bargaining was to weaken national category contracts and plant bargaining, and as a consequence wrest back control of industry. The disparity of objectives between employers and unions was sufficient to demonstrate that there never was any serious prospect of a neo-corporatist industrial relations settlement being reached in Italy.

It is evident that the trend which had been emerging since the

---

[8] Carrieri e Donolo, *Il mestiere politico del sindacato*, p. 110.

mid-1970s towards new forms of tripartite bargaining was not the result of a genuinely consensual operation. The three major parties to the process entertained different, and often conflicting agendas. Some did indeed wish to bring innovations to the industrial relations system. Others wanted to use bargaining to promote little more than a kind of stasis between periods of tension, and even to weaken the capacity of the *sindacato* to influence economic policy. Yet others saw in the increase of high-level negotiations an opportunity to change the political balance of power between political parties, often within the government coalition itself. There were many reasons within the Italian social and political order that impelled the *sindacato* to negotiate on a broader basis than is found in 'trade union' systems. But they did not amount to a desire to move closer to a highly regulated and codified neo-corporatist system. For a variety of reasons, each party to such high-level agreements as existed was anxious to retain as much room for manoeuvre as possible.

Are the Two Major Labour Cultures Closer?

We have seen in the course of this study that both Catholics and communists have changed and adapted, partly in response to external pressures and partly as a result of mutual interaction. Increasingly, too, the third component of the movement, the Uil, has played an important part in these developments. How far have the major labour cultures converged? It is sometimes difficult to judge how cohesive Cisl thinking is around particular ideological or theoretical positions. We do know, however, that those intellectuals who were sympathetic to the practices of *scambio politico* and *concertazione sociale*, which, rightly or wrongly, were associated with neo-corporatism, were part of the intellectually vigorous left-wing current, led by Pierre Carniti, which had gained the leadership of the confederation in the 1970s and shaped much of its official policy. Very briefly, Carniti's view of the *sindacato*'s political role hinged around a number of key ideas. First among these was the notion that no political party automatically enjoyed a privileged position *vis-à-vis* the *sindacato*, which, as a *soggetto politico*, engaged in political bargaining in its own right. Carniti's view of the function of political parties differed fundamentally, as we shall see, from that of the orthodox left. Contained in his position was, of course, a trenchant critique of the *partitocrazia* endemic in Italian society. A conceptual severance of the legitimate domain of party-political activity from the dynamics of social development found expression in the Cisl's notion of the *autonomia del sociale*. The division of Italian society into 'political' and 'social' spheres created a separate 'social' space, free from the contamination of the *partitocrazia*, within which the *sindacato* could negotiate, even on political matters, with the state. The parties should perform their major functions in parliament and contain their activities within the political institutional framework. The unions, however, operated from a 'social' base. The *sindacato* could thus practise a *scambio politico* with the state, without engaging in deals with political parties, in the open and according to rules which would protect the *sindacato*'s autonomy.

The Cgil's position differed from that expressed by Carniti. In his report to congress in 1981, Luciano Lama rejected the Cisl's concept of the *autonomia del sociale*, which, he stated, was considered essential by the Cisl 'for renovating democracy and the state, and capable of providing a basis for negotiating a *scambio politico* with the state without the involvement of political parties'. Such a view, he argued, artificially removed from the scene 'all the specific characteristics of the individual political formations', leaving them unrepresented in 'civil society'.[9] The *sindacato*, committed to autonomy from all political parties, could not provide such representation. Underlying Lama's critique there was, of course, a profoundly different evaluation of the nature of political parties. But as debate continued on this question, further discussion was later rendered futile by an abrupt change of course within the Catholic confederation.

At the Cisl Congress of 1985 the leadership of the confederation passed into the hands of the strongly pro-Dc Franco Marini, without any organized opposition from the Carniti camp, or any serious debate on the divisive issues which one could have expected to have played an important part in a change of command.[10] At the level of policy, the congress itself reflected the

---

[9] 'Relazione al X Congresso della Cgil', p. 11.

[10] For a discussion of this change in the confederation's leadership and its aftermath, see P. Kemeny, 'Le politiche di concertazione: storia di una rinuncia', pp. 95-132.

positions of the outgoing leadership, with no hint of what was afoot. The *concertazione triangolare*, which the incoming leadership secretly intended to drop, since Dc supporters argued that in recent years it had served simply to strengthen Craxi and the Psi, actually received congress approval.[11] Resolution 52 stressed that the policy of bilateral and trilateral encounters 'so far put into practice demonstrates that it is possibile to manage and direct change through a relationship of collaboration between the state and society'. The motion did recognise, however, that the practice of *concertazione sociale* raised doubts in the minds of some observers about the democratic legitimacy of a practice which might curb the free play of the various social and political forces in society. To this end, it was claimed, every effort was to be made to define procedures which, 'when applied within the clear framework of each institution's role, would strengthen the democratic process by incorporating within it the method of *concertazione*'.[12]

It was precisely on this point, however, that the new leader, Marini, once installed, would unilaterally change the policy of the confederation. Pietro Kemeny has described how debate within the Cisl about the political role of the *sindacato* declined after Marini's leadership victory in 1985. The relationship between the confederation and the intellectuals who had generated new ideas from the early 1970s began to weaken. There were complaints that no attempts to improve internal democracy within the Catholic confederation were being made.[13] By the July 1989 Congress of the Cisl, however, the victory of the right was complete, and this time, once again without argument, the delegates accepted the line of their new leader. In his opening report, Marini, in a clear reference to resolutions 28 and 52 of the 1985 Congress, which touched on the necessity of co-ordinating bilateral and trilateral negotiations, stated that bilateral agreements were sufficient. He proposed the key concepts of 'economic democracy' and 'participation' as the means

---

[11] See resolution 28, where congress discussed the restructuring of the bargaining system, and stressed that the confederations 'need to operate on both the interrelated trilateral and bilateral levels'. Cisl, 'Le mozioni del X Congresso Nazionale, 1985', p. 56.

[12] Ibid., pp. 90-1.

[13] See particularly Kemeny, 'Le politiche di concertazione', pp. 123-9.

by which 'the pitfalls of neo-corporatism [with which Marini equated his predecessor's *scambio politico*] could be avoided'. In Marini's perspective these key concepts had their point of application in the workplace and did not imply any involvement in the higher reaches of decision-making in matters of economic policy. All Marini's efforts seemed bent on weakening the *sindacato*'s political ambitions: 'We do not pursue, as some people think, neo-corporatist forms of democracy, nor do we support a democracy based purely on a *scambio politico* ... we must look with suspicion upon all attempts to steer our democracy in the direction of *neodecisionismo*, just as we have rejected the theory and practice of *consociazione*.'[14]

It would be a mistake to give these comments of the highly pragmatic Marini too much theoretical weight. His aversion to union involvement in political decisions was in part due to his desire to relaunch the role of his party, which, in the eyes of many Dc sympathisers, had lost ground to the socialists, who seemed able to gain political capital out of trilateral agreements. Marini's fears were perhaps unduly alarmist. What his leadership reminded commentators of, however, was the fact that there were numerous Cisls, with their centres of gravity in either the industrial or the agricultural sectors, in public employment, in the South or in the Dc itself and that, on some issues at least, we have probably not seen the end of abrupt, and perhaps baffling, changes of direction.

Marini's defeat of Carniti seemed to take the Catholic confederation into a phase of marked pragmatism, but a pragmatism, according to one of the Catholic movement's own intellectuals, without vision and direction, in which 'nothing emerges which looks beyond the specificity of the sector, the category or the particular geographical location'.[15] This may not remain a permanent state of affairs. Marini has been replaced, but we must wait to see whether the Cisl led by his successor will reverse this strongly pragmatic orientation. So far, the confederation, which launched itself into the 1990s as the *sindacato della solidarietà* has, under the new leadership of Sergio D'Antoni shown signs of wanting a somewhat strengthened 'political contractualism' in which the *sindacato* emerges once again as a

---

[14] Marini, 'Relazione all' XI Congresso, luglio 1989', pp. 5-6.

[15] Kemeny, 'Le politiche di concertazione', p. 80.

strong interlocutor of both government and employers. Nevertheless, we shall have to await further developments.

Within the Cgil there has been a process of pluralisation which, together with the reconstitution of the Pci into a new political party (the Pds) and its final break with the Comintern's historical tradition, now renders the very use of the term 'communist' redundant. With the greater acceptance of pluralist values on all sides, there is no doubt that compact and cohesive 'ideological' positions no longer retain their former power of appeal. Although alongside the so-called 'christian democratization' of the Cisl there was in the 1980s an increase in susceptibility to Psi party pressure within the Uil, this was likewise due less to 'ideological' factors than to the desire to promote the party's electoral prospects.

The ideological roots of the two major confederations still remain discernible. And although this will continue to produce tensions for some time, there are also complementary strengths within the two traditions which retain the potential for increasing the effectiveness of the movement as a whole. Despite the enormous changes in the composition of the labour market, for instance, the Cgil still retains much of the class instincts which enabled it to take a global view of workers' requirements. This remains true even where it is attempting to adapt to change, as illustrated in the *piano d'impresa* (enterprise plan) which the confederation launched at its 1981 Congress. The plan originated at a meeting of the Cgil Directorate in October 1979, after the Pci had abandoned the government of national solidarity and by which time it was clear that the EUR strategy had failed. It was argued at the meeting that national contracts which required employers to disclose information on investment and planning had had little effect in shifting patterns of investment. The *piano d'impresa* was intended to remedy this failure.

The *piano* was not intended as an exercise in centralised planning. On the contrary, its purpose was to decentralise decisions on industrial and economic policy agreed at national level and to bring into play new spheres of decision-making at sector and area levels. The proposal that public agencies should be involved in co-ordinating these developments was part of a general rethinking of the role of the state whereby it would activate its smaller, decentralised regional units. Finally, such a global strategy was also aimed at relieving unemployment and renewing the economy of the

Mezzogiorno.[16] While the plan was never adopted as policy by the movement as a whole, much of the thinking which lay behind it has become common currency within the *sindacato*.

On the question of the movement's political role, large sectors of the Cgil remained unimpressed by the experiments in tripartite bargaining which had been going on since the late 1970s. A debate conducted in the pages of *Rinascita* in a series of articles in February and March 1988 showed Cgil intellectuals to be more worried than their Cisl colleagues about the negative effects of 'social pacts' between employers, government and *sindacato*. It was too easy, it was argued, for the parties to such agreements to ignore their representative institutions lower down. The Cgil General Secretary, Antonio Pizzinato, suggested, for instance, the setting up of annual consultations between the unions and parliamentary committees on matters of social and employment policy. It was, after all, parliament which legislated and not the government. Such consultations, moreover, could be set up at regional, provincial and even municipal levels. The *sindacato*, he added, should change the existing practice of bargaining exclusively with the executive and broaden its negotiating activity 'within the wider framework of interaction with elected assemblies'.[17]

Thus while the Cgil remains in a sense the guardian of rank-and-file involvement within the *sindacato*'s activity, the Cisl, by contrast, is by tradition more sensitive to the tensions this can create in institutional arrangements. The Cgil's ingrained habit of mobilising popular support carries attendant risks. Once aroused, rank-and-file feeling is not easily controlled and, in the thinking of the Cisl, is rarely attuned to the subtleties and compromises which are necessary in high-level agreements. The Cisl's approach, often supported by the Uil, has led these two confederations to accuse the Cgil of retaining an excessive reliance on 'conflict'. Replying to the communist Chiaromonte in a round table discussion, for example, the Uil leader, Benvenuto, argued that 'union initiatives cannot continue along traditional lines alone, i.e. on the basis of struggle. In order to achieve the democratic planning described by Chiaromonte, it is necessary to create institutional space for the

---

[16] See particularly, Lama, 'Relazione al X Congresso della Cgil', pp. 20ff.

[17] A. Pizzinato, 'Non è più il tempo della concertazione', p. 7.

sindacato'.[18]

But the characteristic which in the late 1970s and early 1980s emerged as the one which perhaps most markedly distinguished the Cisl from both the other confederations was its *contrattualismo*, i.e. its tendency to see the contract between union and employer as the mainspring of the *sindacato*'s activity and the nerve-centre of the industrial relations system. At its organizational conference in January 1980 the Cisl proposed the exclusive use of union-employer contracts to bring about the objectives aimed at in the Cgil's *piano d'impresa*. In other words, the political dimension of the *piano*, which emphasised the importance of 'participation' at the decentralised levels of both industry and the state, tended to be replaced in the *contrattualismo* of the Cisl by well-formulated agreements at a higher level. Rank-and-file mobilisation are conceptually marginal in the 'contractualist' perspective, which does not see workplace relations as essentially antagonistic. Problems which the Cgil continued to see as rooted in relations of class were perceived instead by the 'contractualists' as 'technical' and capable of being resolved through skilfully drafted agreements.

The *contrattualismo* of the Cisl was further emphasised during the debates in late 1981 and early 1982 over the unions' possible administration of the 'solidarity fund' discussed earlier. In his growing impatience with the Cgil's repeated calls for popular consultation, the Cisl leader, Pierre Carniti, remarked that 'democracy within the *sindacato* cannot be reduced to a confused relationship full of mistrust between the workers and the union leadership'.[19] The Cisl began to intensify its critique of the *movimentismo* and *assemblearismo* to which the Cgil was, allegedly, prone. Intent as it was on promoting high-level agreements as part of its new, invigorated 'contractualism', the Cisl found it could no longer accept union behaviour which depended on the need to be continually ratifying decisions in assemblies. The permanent risk that decisions would be overturned was disruptive. In negotiations, it was argued, the *sindacato* could not operate with its hands tied. It needed to act with greater flexibility, make rapid decisions, and most of all be dependable in the eyes of its negotiating partners once agreements had been reached. The Cisl

---

[18] 'I "mestieri" del sindacato italiano', p. 6.

[19] Bianchi, *Storia dei sindacati in Italia*, p. 254.

thus began to call for new structures in the *sindacato*, which would be both adaptable and allow for rank-and-file participation, yet at the same time not require consultation at every step. Well grounded as parts of this argument were, it was difficult to sustain it without seeming to wish to curtail democracy within the movement.

The Cisl's critique of *movimentismo* has remained constant. It was very much in evidence at the Cisl Congress in July 1989. In his congress report, Franco Marini asked: 'What sense is there in electing union representatives if their decisions can be subjected daily to referenda, and be questioned and disclaimed?'[20] The precariousness of the class perspective within the Cisl was witnessed by a resurgence of the confederation's *associazionismo*, another of its time-hallowed tendencies. Marini gave explicit support at the July 1989 Congress to the renewed emphasis on the *sindacato degli iscritti* (members-only union), when he condemned the 'opportunism of those who use the *sindacato* only when it is to their advantage' and asked the congress to give serious consideration to a proposal from the transport workers' federation, 'to withdraw the benefits which result from negotiations from those workers who go on strike against the agreements'.[21]

Thus while the major confederations have over the years considerably modified many of their positions and have even learned a great deal from each other, they continue to manifest the strengths and weaknesses of their own traditions and origins. The Cgil remains more attentive to the moods of the rank-and-file. It will probably continue to experience greater difficulty than the Cisl and the Uil in re-adapting its bargaining position in mid-course or in improvising during negotiations. Its habit of looking over its shoulder at rank-and-file reaction and its tendency to take agreements back to the membership before modifying its position will inevitably be regarded by the other confederations as either rigidity or stonewalling. The Cisl and the Uil, however, run the opposite risk, namely that of attempting to legitimise the *sindacato*'s decisions from above rather than below. The Cisl's faith in the skill of the negotiator, moreover, tends to substitute contractual obligations for rank-and-file support.

---

[20] 'Relazione all'XI Congresso, luglio 1989', p. 7.

[21] Ibid.

Which Way Forward?

The characteristics which have been discussed describe a *sindacato* whose components, while still manifesting the influence of their origins, nevertheless now find ideological differences less of an obstacle to united action than in the past. This means that the links between unions and parties are now sustained more than ever before by pragmatic considerations. In the long term, this may prove to be favourable to the prospect of unity.

Commenting on the *sindacato* within the broad framework of Italian society, Luigi Mariucci states: 'It is clear that the "political" dimension of union activity, in its relation to public policy, belongs to the physiology and not the pathology of our institutional system.'[22] Paradoxically, the very plurality of party affiliations was instrumental in leading the confederations to establish their 'autonomy' from their respective parties for the sake of internal unity and in fashioning for the *sindacato* a position as a *soggetto politico*. Although by the early 1980s this political role of the *sindacato* was no longer questioned within the movement itself, there remained some resistance within the Pci to this historically unique development among western labour movements.[23] Nevertheless, by the time of the 17th Congress of the Pci in September 1986, the concept of the *sindacato* as a *soggetto politico* had found its way into the official theses approved by congress:

> To seek to overcome the tendencies towards centralisation and neo-corporatism does not entail minimising the importance of the relationship between the *sindacato*, national planning and institutions. The increase in the political and contractual weight of the *sindacato* which has been witnessed in these past decades in economic policy decisions is a highly positive development. The full recognition of the unions as promoters of economic policy is a cultural and civil achievement, and guarantees the consolidation and enduring nature of our democratic system. All narrow conceptions of the *sindacato*'s role

---

[22] Mariucci, 'I rapporti tra sindacato e stato', p. 39.

[23] See 'I "mestieri" del sindacato italiano', pp. 6ff., where Lama publicly opposes his party colleague Giorgio Amendola on this issue.

deny its function as an active participant within the planning process.[24]

The leader of the newly-formed Pds, Achille Occhetto, a guest speaker at the Cgil's Congress in October 1991, stressed his party's view of the *sindacato* as 'an important social and political actor'.[25]

In many ways, the *sindacato*'s widespread acceptance in Italian society as a *soggetto politico* can be seen as one of its greatest achievements. But by the time the Pci, for example, had given its official support to this function, it was clear that the *sindacato* was finding it difficult to sustain itself at the head of a vast social movement. Many of the developments discussed in earlier pages, such as the growth of the tertiary sector, the development of autonomous unions, and the increasingly complex needs of more technologically skilled workers, had brought about both an enlargement and at the same time a fragmentation of the *sindacato*'s traditional constituency. The movement thus found itself surrounded by a plurality of demands which could no longer be reduced simply to those of the working class, but rather required new instruments and methods for their enhancement. The movement reached the position by the early 1990s in which, although it had not lost its 'political citizenship', it needed to renew its methods and perspectives in order to retain its central position in the world of work.

Such a task of renewal is difficult for a movement which has traditionally seen itself as the champion of the continuity and uniformity of guarantees for workers. From the time of its early struggles against the *gabbie salariali* to its successes with the *scala mobile*, the concept of a substantial continuity underlying the needs and conditions of all working people has sustained its thinking and its strategies. The commonality of the demands of the working class was to a large degree rooted in a corresponding homogeneity in the world of production. The productive order, however, has changed almost out of all recognition, so that the highly differentiated aspirations and demands of working people which the *sindacato* now has to address have their basis in very different conditions of production. .

---

[24] *Tesi, programma, statuto. I documenti approvati dal XVII Congresso del Pci,* pp. 60-1.

[25] D'Agostini, 'L'unità più vicina', p. 11.

New groups of workers including non-European immigrants, both men and women, come to Italy for different reasons and from a variety of countries and backgrounds. They range from young Catholic women, from the Philippines and elsewhere, who find in the Church a meeting-place and source of mutual support, to black African youths in search of any kind of labour, from seasonal tomato-picking in the South to factory work in the North. The problems presented by these developments are new to the *sindacato* but are none the less real and urgent for that.

The *sindacato* is, accordingly, undergoing a major cultural transformation in which the promotion of flexibility is as important as the creation of stability. It is a mistake to think that employers need flexibility and workers stability. Both require the capacity to adapt within coherent frameworks. Greater flexibility in industrial relations does not mean chaotic and disordered deregulation. Apart from a minority among Italian employers, neither side seems to feel that it would benefit from the banishment of collective bargaining to the margins of economic life. Indeed, in March 1992, an important agreement was signed between the FULC (Unitary Federation of Chemical Workers) and the state-holding sector employers Enichem and Asap (both part of ENI), establishing a committee of equal numbers (six from either side) to discuss the planning and development of industrial and employment policy in the chemical industry. Regional and other territorial bodies will follow this initial development. This is an important step, which takes co-operation between employers and unions a stage beyond the exchange of information. What is required is nothing less than a new historic interaction between stability and flexibility which will provide a framework for development.

A further area in which the confederations require greater flexibility is in their relations with the autonomous unions. In some professional groups, such as teachers, airline pilots, and workers in new technology, autonomous unions may even grow and become an enduring part of the industrial relations scene. The traditional unions will thus have to collaborate with bodies representing a world of labour in which the culture of collective guarantees, backed by universal appeals to the principles of class, have either never existed or have been abandoned.

This will have important repercussions on the role of the confederations. High-level and even tripartite national negotiating structures could have an increased role in co-ordinating a growing network of *ad hoc* agreements at both workplace and area levels. Such agreements, in the words of one of the Cgil's own intellectuals, would have to emerge from 'a more streamlined system of bargaining: free from the ritual need to harmonise different agreements, and from fixed and inflexible time scales, in brief a system which is more responsive to changes in the economy and in production, and at the same time to social and political change ... . We can no longer think in terms of agreements which cover all matters, for all workers in the whole country.' Accornero thus describes a new model of union activity requiring 'a transition from a mechanical and standardising defence of workers, grounded in principles of equality and collective identity, to a more organic and diversified defence of their interests based more on principles of reciprocity and co-operation'.[26]

One of the most interesting concepts to emerge from the image of a more decentralised and dispersed organization of bargaining practices is that of the increased importance of the geographical unit. Health and many other services are under regional control. Some, such as the banking system, often have deeply-rooted provincial or regional structures. But linked to the emphasis on regional and local factors is a growing tendency within the *sindacato* to turn its attention to the problems workers face as citizens. The Cgil, for instance, is, in the early 1990s, moving in the direction of a *sindacato dei diritti* (union for rights), but without abandoning its identity as a union. At its October 1991 Congress, the Cgil took a major step in defining its new role, while at the same time offering a corrective to the tendency which had recently emerged within the Uil to transform the *sindacato* into a *sindacato dei cittadini* (citizens' union).[27] While the congress resolutions affirmed the confederation's intention to shift the centre of gravity

---

[26] A. Accornero, 'Il sindacato nella società flessibile', p. 335-6.

[27] See the draft resolutions for the Uil's 1989 Congress, particularly the section 'Politica sociale e sindacato dei cittadini', pp. 42-68. It should be noted, however, that the Uil, in the person of its leader, Benvenuto, was also widely criticised for seeming to suggest at the congress that the *sindacato* needed to integrate itself more fully into some of those institutional arrangements which, to his critics, were the very cause of civic malaise in the nation. See, for example, Orazio M. Petracca, 'Il sindacato dei cittadini? È possibile ma rinunciando ad essere Uil', *Corriere Della Sera*, 30 ottobre 1989, p. 2.

of the *sindacato*'s activity to cover the *general* interests of workers, the General Secretary, Bruno Trentin, was careful to insist: 'I wish to stress that the Cgil intends to remain an organization of workers and not transform itself into a citizens' union.'[28]

Developing the European Dimension

In May 1991 the three confederations produced an agreed document setting out their proposals for the reform of collective bargaining. The document stressed the importance of moving in two strategic directions. One was the development of more decentralised bargaining along the lines discussed earlier, together with a declaration of the confederations' willingness to adopt four-yearly contracts.[29] But the greater priority, the document asserted, was the creation of negotiating structures at the European level.

The Italian *sindacato* possesses a sense of urgency over the need to develop effective union representation at the European level. This is not just a response to increased European integration in other spheres, which it has supported for many years. Although the support of both the Cisl and the Uil for Europe predates that of the Cgil, even the communist-dominated confederation began to rethink its position as early as the 1960s and has in recent years developed detailed proposals, which converge in essentials with those of the other two confederations, for the development of union strategies at the European level.[30] The unanimous view of the Italian confederations is that union strategies which are confined within national perspectives will become increasingly ineffectual and defensive, given the globalisation of economic processes and the implementation of the Single European Market.

Born of the common conviction of the confederations that 'future development and employment creation can no longer be solved only by national strategies', the Cgil proposed in its 1988 European Programme the formation of a European strategic identity.

---

[28] M. Carrieri (ed.), 'Il senso di una svolta', p. v.

[29] See 'Documento unitario sul confronto per la riforma della contrattazione', p. 77.

[30] See 'The Cgil's European Programme'.

The proposal entailed three radical initiatives: the *sindacato* should become a European bargaining agent; an employer counterpart should be created at the European level; and there should be a political mediator at the European level with transnational powers.[31] The Cgil restated these views in its October 1991 Congress in Rimini. Italian calls for such levels of bargaining nevertheless create difficulties for some ETUC member confederations. Only national confederations, and not national trade, or industry-based, unions are affiliated to the ETUC. But many national confederations of labour, such as the German DGB and the British TUC, do not have negotiating powers. Hence the Italians proposed that a way be found of enabling national trade or industry unions to participate in ETUC activities.

The ETUC, at its May 1991 Congress in Luxembourg, elected an Italian from the Cisl, Emilio Gabaglio, as its new General Secretary. At the same time the three Italian confederations took their proposals for bargaining at the European level a stage further. The creation of European negotiating structures should, they suggested, be pursued on three fronts. First, national confederations should enter the debate in progress concerning a 'social Europe' and evolve a common strategy aimed at influencing its development. Secondly, trade or category unions should attempt at the European industrial or sector levels to reach agreements with employers in traditional bargaining areas such as hours of work, shift work, labour mobility and training. Finally, procedures should be worked out for reaching agreements between unions, employers and institutions at the European level, together with a system for shaping a comprehensive scheme whereby the various negotiating levels, from the European level down to the local level, can be co-ordinated.

European labour relations are, however, very much in their infancy, and it is difficult to see the Italian proposals appearing on any immediate agenda. The redefinition of European structures which will be necessary in the light of the collapse of communist regimes makes future developments more difficult than usual to predict. The Italian *sindacato* is unlikely, however, to drop its proposals, and this may well help generate the motivation which has so far been lacking in the ETUC for the creation of European

---

[31] See ibid., pp. 3-4 for further elaboration of these proposals.

negotiating structures, which are long overdue.

The Italian *sindacato* has a great deal to contribute at a European level. Italian labour legislation is the most advanced in the EU countries with respect to individual and collective rights of working people, despite some negative judgements by the European Court on the question of Italian employer compliance with European rules.[32] As we have seen, the impact of divisive ideological traditions has diminished considerably within the movement. It has, nevertheless, retained its strong theoretical and strategic proclivities and is unlikely to lapse into the untheorised pragmatism which has characterised some labour movements. In fact, a case can be made for arguing that the interplay between the Catholic and communist subcultures has been a strength rather than a weakness. The creative conflict and competition, which have been a constant feature of the Italian *sindacato*, have led it to experiment more widely with new ideas than most labour movements. Its various components have, at different times in the *sindacato*'s postwar history, entertained, scrutinised or at least debated a wide range of industrial relations options from both the 'trade unionist' and the neo-corporatist camps, while the movement has introduced some highly distinctive and innovative practices of its own into the world of labour relations. It is thus familiar with the problems and perspectives of a variety of labour traditions in Europe. Throughout its history, however, it has retained an important characteristic common to both the Catholic and the communist traditions, namely a strong sense of the interconnectedness of the various aspects of working people's lives. This has led the movement to demand a broader than usual social and political role in society. Its ambition to function as a *soggetto politico* has, as we have seen, taken its components of Catholic and communist origins to a point of ideological convergence on the important question of the *sindacato*'s autonomy from all political parties, an itinerary which is unique in labour history. The Italian *sindacato*'s present difficulty lies in translating this convergence into practice, for although ideological collateralism with political parties has now disappeared, each of the confederations still carries with it a subcultural heritage too distinctive to ignore or submerge. But at least these issues are

---

[32] See G. Atanasio, 'Community Objectives and National Goals in the Field of Social Policy', pp. 227-34.

being discussed. The movement's potential contribution to the future development of European industrial relations is, therefore, a patrimony of rich and varied experiences, wedded to a well-tested capacity to create a sense of strategic direction. It remains to be seen whether the Italian *sindacato* will succeed in realising its potential in Europe.

Postscript: Developments Since 1992

With the kind permission of the publishers, I have taken advantage of a slight delay in production to update the manuscript following the dramatic developments which have taken place in Italy since 1992.

The *sindacato* has escaped the effects of involvement in the illegal and corrupt practices which have so damaged most of the political parties in Italy since early 1992. It has thus been able to consolidate some of its initiatives both internally and in the broader framework of the industrial relations system.

The most important internal development was the setting up of the new plant structures, the *Rappresentanze sindacali unitarie* (Rsu), agreed by the unions in March 1991. These were accepted by the Confindustria and Intersind in an agreement with the confederations on 20 December 1993. Elections to these new bodies, which will replace the *consigli di fabbrica*, are ongoing all over the country in 1994.

Relations with the employers continue to exhibit the differences and polarities discussed earlier. February 1994, for example, was dominated by strikes and difficult negotiations brought about by the unilateral dismissal of workers at Fiat. At the same time, Olivetti adopted a more consensual approach in its negotiations with the unions, in an attempt to secure its financial viability. An agreement was reached which included talks with the Ciampi government, aimed at bringing forward budget resources which the government had decided to make available and transforming the *cassa integrazione* from a simple 'welfare' mechanism into an instrument for retraining and redeployment. This consensual approach has, in fact, typified the development of *contratti di solidarietà*, which have been agreed by unions and employers all over the country. Such settlements have helped safeguard employment, in return for greater flexibility and mobility on the part of the workforce, thus facilitating restructuring in various sectors.

In the area of public administration the unions have, between 1992 and 1994, extricated themselves from the *consigli d'amministrazione* (administrative councils), in which they had been involved in areas of management. They have thus disengaged from an ambiguous and compromising relationship with government agencies and established clear negotiating procedures in line with other employment sectors.

The practice of tripartite negotiations between government, employers and unions continued with an agreement in July 1992 over labour costs, the standardization of private and public sector bargaining, price controls and the use of the *cassa integrazione*. This agreement failed, largely because the containment of inflation and incomes did not result in the protection of the purchasing power of pay and pensions, nor did it produce growth and improvement in employment. The appointment of Ciampi, a former President of the Bank of Italy who had never belonged to a political party, as Prime Minister in 1993 restored a measure of stability and public confidence in the beleaguered political system. A more comprehensive and flexible agreement was subsequently reached in July 1993, known as the 'Protocollo Ciampi'. This agreement covered four major areas of labour and production.

The first part of the agreement attempted to improve on the previous 'Protocollo' by stipulating that the government would meet employers and unions twice yearly to review its objectives. The second area of agreement, over the reform of negotiating structures, took place against the background of employers' efforts to reduce the role of plant bargaining. The employers dropped these attempts in return for more flexible arrangements with the unions in a number of areas. Henceforth national category negotiations will be on a four-yearly basis, although pay structures will be renewed every two years. Two major levels of negotiation have been agreed, with the employers accepting, as we have seen, in December 1993, the new plant negotiating structures, the Rsu. On the labour market, there was agreement on government initiatives to promote retraining and employment programmes and greater use of the European social fund for this purpose. The final section of the agreement was aimed at improving production nationally, and it covered research and technological innovation, professional training, and further progress in the areas of regional investment policies, and public services and infrastructures. The agreement was voted on nationally by the unions and was supported by a large majority.

The future of the developments described so far, and much else besides, may depend, more than at any other point in the history of the postwar Republic, on the shape of the government following the elections of 27 and 28 March 1994. After two years of unrelenting inquiries in the courts, revelations of corruption among politicians, businessmen and industrialists threw the major political parties into turmoil and resulted in a victory for the right-wing alliance between Forza Italia, the Lega Nord and Alleanza Nazionale at the polls. Republicans, social democrats and liberals have disappeared as political parties. The much-reduced Dc party, in an attempt to revamp its damaged image, reconstituted itself as the Ppi in January 1994, and the Psi, which suffered massive defections, also attempted to clean up its image by electing new party Secretaries, significantly from its *sindacato* components. After a short spell as Secretary of the Psi, Giorgio Benvenuto, former leader of the Uil, resigned and was succeeded by Ottaviano Del Turco, who had led the socialist component of the Cgil. The only traditional party to have escaped relatively unscathed was the Pds, which had begun its process of renewal back in 1989. Judicial inquiries have so far revealed no direct involvement of the party (then the Pci) in the illegal activities so widespread in other parties. Despite losing at the 1994 national elections, the Pds emerged as the strongest opposition party, and even improved on its 1992 performance. Indeed, it won the second highest number of seats in the Chamber of Deputies, and more seats than any other party in the Senate. Despite being part of the defeated *polo progressista*, it obtained the highest total number of parliamentarians in the two Houses combined.

During the election campaign in early 1994, the political right gave indications that it intended to reduce the influence of the unions in the workplace and in society at large. There was alarming talk of the possible return of the *gabbie salariali* and the dismantling of the welfare state. Threats were made about abandoning the *cassa integrazione* and even the *statuto dei lavoratori*. Whether or not such impulses will be transformed into concrete plans remains to be seen. A large infusion of candidates for the right produced an unusually high number of newcomers to politics, and in platforms which were remarkably short of specifics even by normal standards, inexperience frequently resulted in a variety of extravagant claims. The success of Berlusconi, in particular, who used his extensive media empire to great effect, concealed a past which in reality was profoundly indebted to the system he was proposing to clean up. Given the deep divisions within the right, moreover, it is difficult to foresee the pursuit of coherent programmes of government. However, within days of being asked to form a government, aware of the *sindacato*'s apprehensions, Berlusconi announced, on 3 May 1994, that he viewed the tripartite agreement reached between the government, the employers and the unions in July 1993, the 'Protocollo Ciampi', as positive and constructive, and that he had no intention of weakening that agreement. The confederations gave this announcement a guarded welcome.[33] Two weeks later, however, Berlusconi presented a programme to parliament which hinted at possible deregulatory initiatives in the labour market. The confederations expressed alarm, with the leader of the Cisl demanding the retention of a 'politica di concertazione'. Even the Cisnal leader, Mauro Nobilia, strongly asserted the need to retain state involvement in the economy.

The debate about the *sindacato*'s role as a *soggetto politico* raised a new issue in 1993. A line of argument emerged within the Cisl that since the *partitocrazia* which had paralysed the political system had collapsed, the need for the *sindacato* to continue its role as a *soggetto politico* would diminish. In this sense, the unions may be able to take on a more 'associational' and 'partisan' role, one which is in keeping with a deeply-rooted tendency within the Cisl. Both the Cgil and the Uil, however, remain suspicious of the Cisl's *associazionismo*. Speakers at the Uil's May 1993 Congress expressed the view that in a less consensual political system there is likely to be an even greater need for the *sindacato* to be able to make a political impact.

Although some commentators have speculated that the collapse of centrist government in Italy may well speed up the drive towards unity, this change in the political scene is unlikely in itself to lead to the 'organic unity' which was once the objective of the *sindacato*. Developments in the nineties have indeed been towards greater unity, and there have been calls for a constituent assembly in 1994 to bring such unity about. But the Uil and Cisl Congresses

---

[33] 'La Pax Sociale di Berlusconi', *la Repubblica*, 3 maggio 1994, p. 1.

in 1993 stressed that a *sindacato unitario* should not be conceived of as a *sindacato unico*. The Cgil, morever, accepted that the idea of a *sindacato unico* as planned in the early seventies was no longer on the immediate agenda, although Trentin argued that the confederations will have to find a way of dispensing with three separate confederate structures at all levels. The Cisl has also indicated that it is not opposed to abandoning separate designations. There is now common acceptance that the ideological and historical traditions of the components can enrich the pluralistic fabric of the *sindacato* and that they should be seen as a positive patrimony which can enhance the flexibility of the movement rather than as an obstacle to greater unity. It will be interesting to observe how such delicately balanced objectives can be transformed into new institutional arrangements.

Although provisional figures suggest that the confederations continue to unionise almost 40 per cent of the workforce, a new factor has emerged with the creation of Lega Nord unions which are recruiting aggressively in the North of the country. The Cisnal, formerly tied to the neo-fascist Msi, enjoyed a remarkable expansion in the months leading up to the March 1994 elections and claimed, not altogether credibly, to have overtaken the Cisl in terms of national membership by the first quarter of 1994. Ten groupings of non-confederate unions, including those mentioned above, formed the Isa (*Intesa dei sindacati autonomi*) a few weeks before the elections of March 1994. The Isa maintains that it has a membership of six million although the confederations claim that it is unlikely to be more than one million in total. The Isa met the Prime Minister designate, Berlusconi, in early May and was given the encouraging assurance that its representatives would be included in the tripartite meetings which were scheduled to review the 'Protocollo Ciampi' of July 1993. Although Isa's representatives see themselves as the 'social wing of the new government',[34] this may not be an unmixed blessing to the delicate right-wing alliance of deregulatory and statist political forces which hope to govern the country. Isa representatives have already stated that the Ciampi agreement needs to be strengthened. The Cisnal, moreover, proposed a call for the restoration of the *scala mobile*, which the

---

[34] R. Petrini, 'L'"altro" sindacato invitato a Palazzo', *la Repubblica*, 4 maggio 1994, p. 3.

new organization subsequently sanctioned. However, the ability of these new forces to make a lasting impact on the world of labour will have to face the test of time. If such developments were to prove significant, however, the political parties of the right would weaken their ability to manage their electoral base. For this reason, they are unlikely to be given anything more than a 'spoiling' role, intended to weaken the confederations, by any government espousing deregulatory ambitions, and they would be wise to treat favours with caution. Such a government would be unlikely to pass on to the new unions any power it managed to wrest from the confederations. The Isa's claim to be the 'social wing' or collateral force of the heterogeneous mix of right-wing elements of which the Berlusconi government is composed has the appearance of a somewhat hastily contrived conception. This does not enhance its chances of survival.

The future shape and direction of Italy is perhaps more uncertain in mid-1994 than it has ever been since the creation of the postwar Republic. In its first few months of life, however, it cannot be said that the new right-wing government has shown strong evidence of its professed spirit of reform. Nevertheless, the country is undoubtedly at a critical point of its history, one at which the major traditional components of the Italian *sindacato* will once again be called upon to deploy the energies and resources of their considerable historical imagination.

APPENDIX

Table 1   Percentages of workers unionised by the two major confederations by economic sector in different regions

	Industrial triangle	White area	Red area	South and Islands
Agriculture				
1961 Cgil	52.1	15.3	76.9	14.6
Cisl	9.9	12.3	7.9	10
1971 Cgil	49.3	23	69.1	20.1
Cisl	17	24.3	11.3	14.7
1977 Cgil	49.5	38.3	80.3	48.4
Cisl	28.6	33.3	20	40.9
Industry				
1961 Cgil	12.3	8.7	25.3	6.3
Cisl	6.5	8.6	4.3	3.1
1971 Cgil	22.8	18.1	33.8	11.4
Cisl	13	18.5	7.9	6.5
1977 Cgil	25.9	21.9	40.7	19.1
Cisl	14.4	21.9	9.9	11.8
Services				
1961 Cgil	13.5	7.1	18.3	8.6
Cisl	11.2	14	11.7	13.6
1971 Cgil	15.3	9.1	21.5	10.3
Cisl	13.9	17.8	13.4	14.6
1977 Cgil	22.9	16	29.9	15
Cisl	17.3	21.9	16.4	17.7
Overall				
1951 Cgil	40	19.7	89.3	19.8
Cisl	10.1	13.2	9.6	10.9

Appendix

Table 1 (continued)

	Industrial triangle	White area	Red area	South and Islands
1961 Cgil	14.5	8.9	42.4	9.7
Cisl	8.2	11.3	9.4	9.3
1971 Cgil	20.7	15.1	36.5	12.9
Cisl	13.4	18.8	11.4	11.8
1977 Cgil	25.2	20.2	41.1	22.2
Cisl	15.6	22.6	14.2	20

These figures are extrapolated from those contained in Romagnoli (ed.), *La sindacalizzazione tra ideologia e pratica*, vol. ii, pp. 100-2.

Table 2 Changing distribution of Cgil and Cisl membership by geographical area. The proportion of their combined membership held by each of the confederations is given in parenthesis in percentages.

Confeds	North West	North East	Centre	South and Islands
1960 Cgil	697,831 (64.1)	170,743 (47.0)	1,080,208 (82.5)	634,388 (55.4)
Cisl	391,235 (35.9)	192,899 (53.0)	229,054 (17.5)	511,210 (44.6)
1975 Cgil	1,219,493 (60.6)	349,606 (48.2)	1,324,570 (77.3)	1,187,730 (53.4)
Cisl	791,498 (39.4)	376,037 (51.8)	388,825 (22.7)	1,037,185 (46.6)
1990 Cgil	1,309,270 (59.9)	509,859 (50.5)	1,864,765 (69.5)	1,466,482 (53.0)
Cisl	890,665 (40.5)	499,792 (49.5)	817,027 (30.5)	1,300,923 (47.0)

This table has been compiled using statistics from various sources, which vary slightly in their classification of regions into the geographical areas. In reorganizing the statistics and recalculating the proportions of membership, I have used the following classification of the regions:

North-West: Piemonte, Valle d'Aosta, Liguria, Lombardia.
North-East: Veneto, Trentino-Alto Adige, Friuli Venezia-Giulia.
Centre: Emilia Romagna, Toscana, Marche, Umbria, Lazio.
South & Islands: Abruzzi, Molise, Campania, Puglia, Basilicata, Calabria, Sicilia, Sardegna.

The advantage of placing Emilia Romagna in the central area for this particular group of comparative statistics, is that the North-East and Centre become, broadly speaking, White and Red areas respectively.

Table 3 Total membership of the confederations since the 1980s

		1981	1985	1990
Cgil	total membership	4,598,569	4,592,014	5,150,376
	as a % of 1981	100	99.86	112
Cisl	total membership	2,988,813	2,953,095	3,508,407
	as a % of 1981	100	98.8	117.38
Uil	total membership	1,275,944	1,249,408	1,485,758
	as a % of 1981	100	97.92	116.44
Total	all confederations	8,863,326	8,794,517	10,144,541
	as a % of 1981	100	99.22	114.46

Source: a collection of data and statistics on union membership, contained in *Nuova rassegna sindacale*, n. 22, 8 giugno 1992, *Laser*, n. 1, Laboratorio sulla sindacalizzazione e la rappresentanza, p. 7.

Table 4   Active-worker membership of the confederations since the 1980s, along with trends in membership

	1981	1985	1990	1981-5	1981-90
Cgil					
Agriculture	521,217	410,661	336,057	-21.21	-35.52
Industry	1,775,145	1,463,581	1,341,893	-17.55	-24.41
Services: marketed	567,248	523,621	531,130	-7.69	-6.37
Services: non marketed	526,988	541,507	515,722	+2.76	-2.14
Total	3,390,598	2,939,370	2,724,802	-13.31	-19.64
Cisl					
Agriculture	378,975	300,933	251,664	-20.59	-33.59
Industry	959,138	729,757	715,510	-23.92	-25.40
Services: marketed	450,341	443,875	461,099	-1.44	+2.39
Services: non marketed	583,017	581,098	595,545	-0.33	+2.15
Total	2,371,471	2,055,663	2,023,818	-13.32	-14.66

Table 4 (continued)

	1981	1985	1990	1981-5	1981-90
Uil					
Agriculture	120,649	114,256	121,154	-5.30	+0.42
Industry	481,947	405,737	407,078	-15.81	-15.53
Services: marketed	262,547	261,366	270,807	-0.45	+3.15
Services: non marketed	277,613	282,751	324,848	+1.85	+17.01
Total	1,142,756	1,064,110	1,123,887	-6.88	-1.65
Total all confederations					
Agriculture	1,020,841	825,850	708,875	-19.10	-30.56
Industry	3,216,230	2,599,075	2,464,481	-19.19	-23.37
Services: marketed	1,280,136	1,228,862	1,263,036	-4.01	-1.34
Services: non marketed	1,387,618	1,405,356	1,436,115	+1.28	+3.49
Total	6,904,825	6,059,143	5,872,507	-12.25	-14.95

Source: *Laser*, n. 1, p. 8.

Table 5   Pensioners as a percentage of membership of the confederations 1980-90

Cgil		Cisl		Uil		Total	
1980	1990	1980	1990	1980	1990	1980	1990
24.0	45.7	14.6	36.2	5.8	18.0	18.1	38.4

Source: Cesos, *Le relazioni sindacali in Italia. Rapporto 1990-91*, p. 86

Table 6   Each confederation's share of membership since 1970

	1970	1975	1980	1985	1990
Cgil	53.2	53	51	52.2	50.8
Cisl	32.7	33.6	34	33.6	34.6
Uil	14.1	13.4	15	14.2	14.6
	100	100	100	100	100
Degree of unionisation	38.5	48.5	48.7	42.1	39.3

Author's calculations based on membership figures from a variety of sources.

Table 7   Degree of unionisation of active workforce, by sector, in each
confederation, in percentages, 1981-90

	1981	1985	1990
Cgil			
Agriculture	50.99	45.85	40.13
Industry	26.60	24.61	22.73
Services:marketed	13.86	11.04	10.13
Services:non marketed	19.35	18.99	17.26
Services:Total	16.05	14.03	12.72
Cisl			
Agriculture	37.08	33.60	29.82
Industry	14.37	12.27	12.14
Services:marketed	11.00	9.36	8.79
Services:non marketed	21.41	20.38	19.93
Services:Total	15.16	13.50	12.84
Uil			
Agriculture	11.80	12.76	14.35
Industry	7.22	6.82	6.91
Services:marketed	6.42	5.51	5.16
Services:non marketed	10.19	9.92	10.87
Services:Total	7.93	7.17	7.24
National Total			
Agriculture	99.88	92.21	84.30
Industry	48.19	43.70	41.78
Services:marketed	31.28	25.91	24.09
Services:non marketed	50.95	49.30	48.06
Services:Total	39.14	34.69	32.79

Source: *Laser*, n. 1, p.9.

Table 8   Membership of autonomous unions among various categories of workers in 1976

Industry		Public services	
Metalworkers	18,713	Postal	2,500
Other	2,500	Telecommunications	700
		Banking	38,000
Total	21,213	Electricity	500
Public sector		Total	41,700
Civil service	13,000		
Health service	35,000	Various	
State holding bodies	18,000	Insurance	8,500
Schools	150-180,000	Commercial salesmen	15,000
		Pensioners	150,000
Total	216-246,000		
		Total	173,500
Transport			
Railways	10,800	Entertainment	2,000
Public transport	3,500		
Air transport	2,300		
Seamen	800		
Total	17,400	Overall Total	471-501,313

Source: Biagioni, Palmieri and Pipan, *Indagine sul sindacato*, p. 54.

Table 9   Membership of the confederations since 1950, along with degree of unionisation

Year	Cgil	Cisl	Uil	Total	% Unionisation
1950	4,640,528	1,189,882			50.8
1951	4,490,776	1,337,848			50.9
1952	4,342,206	1,322,038			48.8
1953	4,074,648	1,305,361			45.6
1954	4,134,417	1,326,542			44.6
1955	4,194,235	1,342,204			43.9
1956	3,665,989	1,706,818			42.0
1957	3,137,800	1,261,839			34.2
1958	2,595,490	1,654,242			32.7
1959	2,600,656	1,283,892			29.7
1960	2,583,170	1,324,398			28.5
1961	2,531,254	1,398,864			28.2
1962	2,610,843	1,435,626			28.2
1963	2,625,580	1,503,555			28.6
1964	2,711,842	1,515,154			29.7
1965	2,542,933	1,467,990			28.5
1966	2,457,945	1,490,807			28.0
1967	2,423,480	1,522,864			27.7
1968	2,460,961	1,626,786			28.7
1969	2,626,388	1,641,289			29.4
1970	2,942,517	1,807,586	780,000	5,530,103	38.5
1971	3,138,396	1,973,333	825,000	5,936,729	41.1

Table 9 (continued)

Year	Cgil	Cisl	Uil	Total	% Unionisastion
1972	3,214,965	2,184,279	842,912	6,242,156	43.2
1973	3,435,576	2,214,099	901,916	6,551,591	44.6
1974	3,826,622	2,472,701	965,051	7,264,374	47.2
1975	4,081,399	2,593,545	1,032,605	7,707,549	48.5
1976	4,313,131	2,823,780	1,104,888	8,241,799	48.7
1977	4,475,436	2,809,802	1,160,089	8,445,327	49.0
1978	4,527,962	2,868,837	1,284,716	8,681,515	48.9
1979	4,583,474	2,906,230	1,326,817	8,816,521	48.4
1980	4,599,050	3,059,845	1,346,900	9,005,795	48.7
1981	4,598,569	2,988,813	1,275,944	8,863,326	47.9
1982	4,570,252	2,976,880	1,358,004	8,905,136	46.5
1983	4,556,052	2,953,411	1,351,514	8,860,977	45.0
1984	4,546,335	3,097,231	1,344,460	8,988,026	43.5
1985	4,592,014	2,953,095	1,249,408	8,794,517	42.1
1986	4,647,038	2,975,482	1,305,682	8,928,202	40.1
1987	4,743,036	3,080,019	1,343,716	9,166,771	39.9
1988	4,867,406	3,288,279	1,398,071	9,553,756	40.0
1989	5,026,851	3,379,028	1,439,216	9,845,095	39.4
1990	5,150,376	3,508,407	1,485,758	10,144,541	39.3

These statistics are taken mainly from Cella and Treu, *Relazioni industriali*, p. 92, and Cesos, *Le relazioni sindacali in Italia. Rapporto 1990-91*, p. 84. Some recalculations were needed, making use of other sources. Reliable figures are not available for Uil membership before 1970, so that the degree of unionisation is based on Cgil and Cisl figures alone.

Figure 1   Organizational structure of the confederate unions

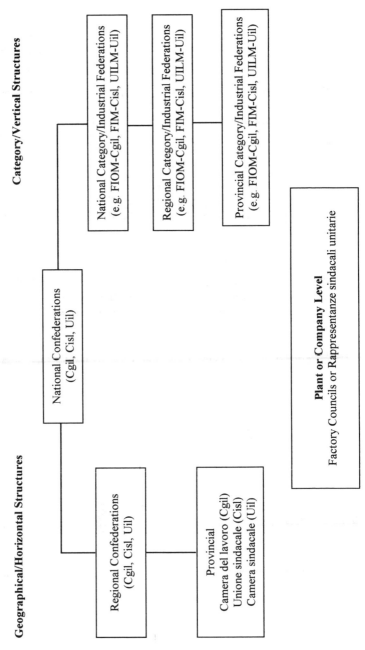

Geographical/Horizontal Structures

Category/Vertical Structures

National Confederations
(Cgil, Cisl, Uil)

National Category/Industrial Federations
(e.g. FIOM-Cgil, FIM-Cisl, UILM-Uil)

Regional Category/Industrial Federations
(e.g. FIOM-Cgil, FIM-Cisl, UILM-Uil)

Provincial Category/Industrial Federations
(e.g. FIOM-Cgil, FIM-Cisl, UILM-Uil)

Regional Confederations
(Cgil, Cisl, Uil)

Provincial
Camera del lavoro (Cgil)
Unione sindacale (Cisl)
Camera sindacale (Uil)

Plant or Company Level
Factory Councils or Rappresentanze sindacali unitarie

Glossary of Terms and Abbreviations

Acli (Associazioni cristiane dei lavoratori italiani) Catholic Associations of Italian Workers. A non-union organization for promoting the study, development and application of Catholic social teaching in the world of labour.

AFL American Federation of Labor. Joined with the Congress of Industrial Organizations (CIO) in 1955 to form AFL-CIO.

Alleanza Nazionale. National Alliance. From 1994, new name of the former neo-fascist Msi. Under the leadership of Gianfranco Fini, part of the victorious right-wing alliance at the national elections of March 1994.

Asap (Associazione sindacale per le aziende petrolchimiche) Employers' association for petrochemical companies within the Eni branch of the state-holding sector.

assemblearismo Term used to denote the tendency in some sections of the *sindacato* to rely too heavily on rank-and-file or assembly forms of decision-making to the detriment of executive functions. See also *movimentismo*.

associazionismo The tendency to give priority, in negotiations with employers, to the interests of members of the union rather than to the workforce as a whole. The more implacable proponents of this view argue that only members of unions should enjoy the benefits of such negotiations. This tendency has been in constant tension with the predominantly 'class' orientation of some unions.

aziendalismo The tendency to focus exclusively on the short-term objectives of, or gains from, plant-level bargaining.

bargaining levels For the major bargaining levels, see under *interconfederate bargaining*; *national industry bargaining*; *plant-level bargaining*; *provincial bargaining*.

bracciante Agricultural worker on a wage; day labourer.

Camera del lavoro Chamber of labour. The Cgil's confederate structure at territorial (horizontal) level, incorporating the industrial or category federations at this level. The *Camera del lavoro* remained with the communist/socialist Cgil after the secessions which began in 1948. The Cisl and the Uil formed their own territorial structures thereafter (see under *Unione sindacale* and *Camera sindacale*).

Camera sindacale Chamber of labour. The Uil's confederate

structure at territorial (horizontal) level, incorporating the industrial or category federations at this level. See also *Camera del lavoro* and *Unione sindacale*.

cassa integrazione guadagni   Short-term wage guarantee scheme. A scheme whereby workers in industry, agriculture and commerce are guaranteed an agreed proportion of their pay in the case of redundancy or work reduction. The greater part of the remuneration is paid by the government, and employers' contributions are subject to regular renegotiation. The scheme has been in operation for the whole of the postwar period, and its provisions were widened into their modern form in 1968. It has been utilised with some success in periods of difficulty for employers and for purposes of industrial restructuring.

category   For industrial relations purposes, this describes an industrial grouping consisting of a number of productive sectors. Thus each national category federation represents workers in a number of sectors. For instance, the metalworkers' federations FIOM, FIM and UILM represent workers in the following sectors: auto vehicle, electronics, electromechanical, mechanical, metallurgical, and shipbuilding. Similarly the category of chemical workers is subdivided into the following sectors: chemicals, pharmaceuticals, rubber and plastics, artificial fibres, petrochemicals, glass and ceramics.

Cei   (Conferenza episcopale italiana) Conference of Italian Bishops.

Cgil   (Confederazione generale italiana del lavoro) General Confederation of Italian Labour. The original united confederation, and the communist/socialist confederation after 1948.

Cgl   (Confederazione generale del lavoro) The pre-fascist General Confederation of Labour founded in 1906.

Cil   (Confederazione italiana dei lavoratori) The pre-fascist Catholic Italian Workers' Confederation; small and not very influential.

cinghia di trasmissione   'Transmission belt'. Used to describe the theory, often associated with communist movements, whereby the strategic objectives of labour organizations are directed by and encompassed within the guiding role of the party. The theory has its origins in a resolution of the 1907 Stuttgart

Congress of the Second International, which attempted to outline the spheres of party and union responsibility.

Cisl (Confederazione italiana sindacati lavoratori) The Italian Confederation of Workers' Unions. Founded in 1950, after the 1948 secession from the Cgil, as the mainly Catholic labour confederation.

Cisnal (Confederazione italiana sindacati nazionali lavoratori) The Italian Confederation of National Workers' Unions. Small and not very influential confederation close to the neo-fascist Msi, now the Alleanza Nazionale. Founded in 1950.

Cln (Comitato di liberazione nazionale) National Committee of Liberation.

Clnai (Comitato di liberazione nazionale alta Italia) National Committee for the Liberation of Northern Italy.

Cnel (Consiglio nazionale dell'economia e del lavoro) National Council for the Economy and Labour. An advisory body on economic and labour affairs for the government and for the Houses of Parliament. The Cnel is an organ of the state, provided for by article 99 of the Constitution, with the power to present legislation to parliament. It includes representatives from the unions, the employers, institutions of credit, the state-holding sector, and a number of independent experts.

Coldiretti   (Confederazione nazionale dei coltivatori diretti) National confederation, of Catholic inspiration, established in 1944 to protect the interests of peasant proprietors.

collateralismo   A term used to describe the organic relationship existing between Catholic organizations operating within different spheres of society. Frequently refers to the relationship between the Dc and Cisl. The term is often extended to other parties and confederations.

concertazione sociale   Social concertation. Frequently used to describe the tendency towards global collaboration on social and economic matters, involving government, unions and employers. To be distinguished from 'neo-corporatism'. See also *scambio politico*.

Confagricoltura (Confederazione generale dell'agricoltura italiana) Organization for employers in agriculture.

Confapi (Confederazione italiana della piccola e media industria) Employers' organization in small and medium-sized industry.

Confcommercio   (Confederazione generale del commercio e del turismo) Employers' organization in commerce and tourism.

Confindustria   (Confederazione generale dell'industria italiana) General Confederation of Italian Industry (private sector).

conglobamento   Name given to the agreement of June 1954 between the Confindustria and the Cisl and Uil (i.e. excluding the Cgil) which sought to rectify wage anomalies and consolidate a range of supplementary payments into a more rationalised pay structure.

Consigli di fabbrica   Factory councils, also known as *consigli dei delegati* (delegates' councils). These bodies emerged out of the 'Hot Autumn' as the unitary plant-level negotiating organizations for the unions.

consociativismo   see *consociazione*.

consociazione   Consociation. A situation in which the forces of political opposition and those of the government majority, instead of playing out their adversarial roles in parliament and in national politics, co-operate with each other. Also known as *consociativismo*.

contadino   This term is used in different ways. In popular usage it often refers simply to the agricultural worker. Although sometimes loosely used to cover all categories of non-waged agricultural workers (i.e. the share-cropper, the tenant farmer, the small landowner, and so on), it refers strictly speaking to the peasant owner as distinct from the simple agricultural labourer (*bracciante*).

contrattualisti   The name given to those within the Cisl who argue that the *sindacato*'s objectives can be attained exclusively through its contractual and negotiating activity. They tend to minimise the importance of mobilisation as an industrial relations instrument, and some are sceptical of the value of the movement's social and political objectives.

Cub   (Comitato unitario di base) Unitary rank-and-file committee. These emerged in the factories independently of union affiliation in the protest period of the late sixties. They were the immediate forerunners of the *consigli di fabbrica*.

Dc   (Democrazia cristiana) Christian Democratic Party. Since 18 January 1994 known as the Partito popolare italiano.

DGB   (Deutscher Gewerkschaftsbund) German national trade union confederation.

ENI   (Ente nazionale idrocarburi) National Hydrocarbon Corporation. A public body within the state-holding sector (see *Partecipazioni statali*), established in 1953 to promote research and development in the fields of fuel and energy. It subsequently developed, through a number of subsidiaries, into related areas, such as chemicals, textiles, etc.

ETUC   (European Trade Union Confederation)

Federazioni di categoria   Category federations or unions which represent their members according to industry and not trade. Thus all workers employed by a food manufacturer, for instance, whether on the shop floor, in electrical maintenance, carpentry, or transport, would belong to the foodworkers federation.

Federazione Unitaria Cgil-Cisl-Uil   The federation of the three confederations created in July 1972, with a tripartite organizational structure giving parity of membership in the secretariat and executive committee. The tripartite model was extended to all levels of the *sindacato* except the unitary factory councils. Ceased to function in 1984.

Federmeccanica   (Federazione delle aziende meccaniche) Organization of employers in the metalworking industry, founded in 1972.

FIM-Cisl   (Federazione italiana metalmeccanici) Italian Federation of Metalworkers, affiliated to the Cisl.

FIOM-Cgil   (Federazione impiegati e operai metallurgici) Federation of Office and Industrial Workers in the Metalworking Industry, affiliated to the Cgil.

Forza Italia   Political organization set up by Berlusconi which, as part of the right-wing alliance, won at the national elections in March 1994.

FULC (Federazione unitaria lavoratori chimici) Unitary Federation of Chemical Workers.

gabbie salariali   So-called 'wage traps' first introduced in the interconfederate agreements of 1945, in which wage structures operated within geographical and sexual confines.

general strike   Called by the confederations, this is a strike involving all categories of workers. A general strike can be on a national, local or regional level. See also *national strike*.

ICFTU   International Confederation of Free Trade Unions. See also *WFTU*.

Ige   (Imposta generale sull'entrata) General goods tax, levied on each commodity transaction, replaced in 1973 by *Iva*.

incompatibilità   The term used to describe the inappropriateness of holding simultaneous positions of leadership in more than one organization. Positions of union leadership are normally incompatible with equivalent responsibilites within a political party, with candidatures in parliamentary elections and with holding office in local or regional governments.

inquadramento unico impiegati-operai   Single scheme of white- and blue-collar workers' job-classification, this was the system of job-classification first agreed in 1970, consisting in most cases of 7-8 gradings. The *inquadramento unico* replaced previously separate systems of gradings for blue- and white-collar workers, which totalled up to 50 gradings in some industries.

integralismo   The tendency to see a particular set of religious or political teachings as the basis for organizing the whole fabric of society and its institutions. Usually applied to Catholic tendencies in politics, morality, etc.

interclassismo   The idea, deeply-rooted in the Catholic social tradition, that a party can represent the interests of a number of social classes, and mediate between the aspirations of social groups that are held by some to be inherently antagonistic.

interconfederate bargaining   Negotiations at national level between confederations both of employers and of labour. This bargaining does not have fixed procedures, and until the early 1950s was the major form of negotiation used. Now it covers wide-ranging economic matters concerning whole sectors of the economy. The negotiations are not industry-specific and deal with such areas as the *scala mobile*, labour costs, labour relations, etc. The government is frequently involved at this level, giving rise to the use of the term *concertazione sociale* to describe this practice.

Internal commissions   Plant-level committees of workers, not official union bodies, elected by the whole workforce, irrespective of union membership or not. They had no negotiating powers after 1947, but consulted with employers. Until the early 1970s, when they ceased to exist, the internal commissions were led mostly by union members, working in close collaboration with their respective and often competing federations.

Intersind   (Sindacato delle aziende a partecipazione statale) Employers' association for state-controlled companies within the IRI group.

IRI   (Istituto per la ricostruzione industriale) Institute for Industrial Reconstruction. A state body originally set up in 1933 to salvage the banking and industrial systems in Italy, it is now the largest of the public bodies among the *partecipazioni statali* or state-holding organizations. It has subsidiaries operating in such industries as ironworks (Finsider), metalworking (Finmeccanica), shipbuilding (Fincantieri), telecommunications (STET), food manufacturing (SME) and civil construction (Italstat).

Istat   (Istituto centrale di statistica) Central Institute for Statistical Information. Provides government information on various aspects of economic and social life, e.g. on population, agriculture, industry and commerce.

Iva   (Imposta sul valore aggiunto) Value Added Tax (VAT) which replaced Ige in 1973.

Lega Nord   Northern League. Federalist northern party led to victory by Umberto Bossi in the national elections of March 1994, as part of the right-wing alliance.

missini   Members of the Msi. The use of the term is frequently extended to include the party's supporters.

movimentismo   Term used to denote a tendency within some sections of the *sindacato* to rely on rank-and-file mobilisation at the expense of contractual or other institutional procedures. See also *assemblearismo*.

Msi   (Movimento sociale italiano) Italian Social Movement. Neo-fascist party. From 1994 known as Alleanza Nazionale.

national industry bargaining   Bargaining at national level between the industrial or category federations both of employers and of workers. This form of negotiation, now central to the Italian industrial relations system, became important after 1954, when the national category federations took over responsibility for bargaining from the confederations. Industry-wide and plant-level agreements are the major features of the Italian dual system of bargaining.

national strike   A nation-wide strike, usually, but not exclusively, by a single category or sector of workers, called by the relevant federation. See also *general strike*.

pansindacalismo   This term was created with the emergence of the *sindacato*'s claim, from the late sixties onwards, for recognition as a *soggetto politico*. It denotes a resurgence of the ideas of revolutionary syndicalism, which was strong in

Italy during the first two decades of this century. The term is normally used in a critical vein, to denote the tendency within the unions to claim a broad social and political role for the movement which encroaches on the territory of existing political forces or parties.

Partecipazioni statali   (State participations) State-holding organizations or bodies, such as IRI and ENI, set up by the government to obtain a controlling interest in otherwise private companies through the acquisition of shares. Such an arrangement is meant to combine the advantages of public control and accountability with those of private management.

Partito d'azione   Action Party. Strongly anti-fascist, founded in 1942 by radical, republican and socio-liberal elements close to the socialists. At its dissolution in 1947 most of its members joined the Psi.

partitocrazia   Term used in Italy to describe a system dominated by the excessive power of political parties, or of the central organs and officials of parties. Its characteristics range from the tendency of political parties to usurp parliamentary powers, to the spread of party influence and control into important areas of 'civil society'.

Pci   (Partito comunista italiano) Italian Communist Party. See also *Pds*.

Pds   (Partito democratico della sinistra) Democratic Party of the Left. In January 1991 the Pci voted to reconstitute itself and change its name to Pds. The change, following internal debate and discussion from July 1989, represented the final break with the party's historical links with the Comintern tradition.

plant-level bargaining   Plant- or company-level bargaining is the normal form of decentralised negotiation in industry and in the services sector. Multi-plant bargaining is also to be found in some areas. In some sectors, however, a territorial, usually provincial, form of bargaining is more common. See also under *sector*.

Pli   (Partito liberale italiano) Italian Liberal Party.

Ppi   (Partito popolare italiano) Italian Popular Party. Pre-fascist Catholic party founded in 1919. Now the name of the reconstituted Dc since 18 January 1994.

Pri   (Partito repubblicano italiano) Italian Republican Party.

provincial bargaining   In agriculture, the construction industry and some areas of commerce, provincial or area agreements are more common than plant-level bargaining. These agreements, which tend to take account of the labour market features of the different territories where they are made, either improve on items referred down from national agreements, or they give more detailed specification within some areas agreed nationally.

Psdi (Partito socialdemocratico italiano) Italian Social Democratic Party.

Psi (Partito socialista italiano) Italian Socialist Party.

Psiup (Partito socialista di unità proletaria) Italian Party of Proletarian Unity. Created in January 1964 by socialists opposed to the Psi's entry into the centre-left. It was also the original name of the immediate postwar Socialist Party, although this is commonly referred to as the Psi by commentators.

Rsu (Rappresentanze sindacali unitarie) The new elective works- or plant-level bodies which replaced the factory councils from 1994. These bodies include provision for representatives from the autonomous unions. The regulations governing election procedures were first agreed by the confederations in March 1991.

scala mobile Index-linked wage scale. A mechanism whereby an agreed proportion of salaries and wages is automatically increased at regular levels in line with the retail-price index. The level of cover is agreed by the unions, the government and the employers.

scambio politico Political exchange or barter. Used to describe the tendency in Italian industrial relations to accept political trade-offs with parties or government in the process of bargaining.

sector For industrial relations purposes, a productive sector within a larger category. See under *category*.

sindacato The Italian word for 'union'. The Italian *sindacato* is used in a number of ways. It can refer to individual unions, e.g. *sindacato dei metalmeccanici*. It can also be used to denote any component of the workers' movement, e.g. *sindacato cattolico*. Finally, it is the word most commonly used to describe the sum total of unions in Italy looked at in their organizational capacity or as a 'movement' or 'force'. There is no exact equivalent in English which serves all these purposes. In this study both *sindacato* and 'workers' movement' are used according to considerations of style and context.

soggetto politico   The term used by the Italian *sindacato* to describe itself as an 'actor' on the country's broader social and political scene.

TUC   Trade Union Congress.

ugualitarismo   Egalitarianism. Used to denote the tendency, which became strong in the *sindacato*, following the protest movements of the late sixties, to frame demands in an egalitarian manner, e.g. equal wage increases for all categories of employees.

Uil   (Unione italiana dei lavoratori) The Italian Workers' Union. Mainly republican, social democratic and socialist confederation after 1948, becoming increasingly dominated by socialists from the early seventies.

UILM-Uil   (Unione italiana lavoratori metalmeccanici) The Italian Union of Metalworkers, affiliated to the Uil.

Unione sindacale   Union of labour. The Cisl's confederate structure at territorial (horizontal) level, incorporating the industrial or category federations at this level. The Cgil and the Uil have their own territorial organizations, i.e. the *Camera del lavoro* and *Camera sindacale* respectively.

verticismo   The tendency to take decisions at the highest level, at the expense of rank-and-file consultation or participation.

WFTU   World Federation of Trade Unions. Founded in October 1945. Many western trade unions and confederations subsequently left to form the ICFTU, leaving the WFTU as a mainly communist organization.

Bibliography

Accornero, A., *Fiat Confino*, Rome: Edizioni Avanti, 1959.

----- *Dalla rissa al dialogo*, Rome: Editrice Sindacale Italiana, 1967.

----- 'Autonomia operaia e organizzazione sindacale', *I 30 anni della Cgil*, 1975, pp. 199-210.

----- 'Per una nuova fase di studi sul movimento sindacale', Accornero, Pizzorno, Trentin, Tronti, *Movimento sindacale e società italiana*, 1977, pp. 5-154.

----- 'Il sindacato nella società flessibile', Ferrante (ed.), *Il futuro del sindacato*, 1986, pp. 327-40.

----- *La parabola del sindacato*, Bologna: il Mulino, 1992.

Accornero, A., Pizzorno, A., Trentin, B., Tronti, M., *Movimento sindacale e società italiana*, Milan: Feltrinelli, 1977.

Acli, *L'unità sindacale un anno dopo*, Rome: Industria grafica moderna, 1967.

----- *Idee e documenti per l'unità sindacale*, Rome: Industria grafica moderna, 1969.

Aglieta, R., Bianchi, G., Merli-Brandini, P., *I delegati operai*, Rome: Coines, 1970.

Aiello, A. M., Amoretti, A., Gordini, U., Pettine, B., Rosati, L., Treves, C., 'Evoluzione e problemi dei consigli di fabbrica e di zona', *Quaderni di rassegna sindacale*, anno xii, n. 49, luglio-agosto 1974, pp. 151-69.

Albanese, L., Liuzzi, F., Perella, A., *I consigli di fabbrica*, Rome: Editori Riuniti, 1973.

Amendola, G., 'Interrogativi sul "caso" Fiat', *Rinascita*, n. 43, anno 36, 9 novembre 1979, pp. 13-15.

Annali dell'economia italiana, 14 volumes, Milan: Ipsoa, 1981-1985.

Atanasio, G., 'Community Objectives and National Goals in the Field of Social Policy', Francioni (ed.), *Italy and EC Membership Evaluated*, 1992, pp. 219-34.

Atti della Assemblea Costituente, vol. viii, Rome: Tipografia della Camera dei Deputati, 1947.

Atti della Ia conferenza nazionale consultiva della Cgil. Ariccia, 5-6-7 ottobre 1967, Rome: Editrice Sindacale Italiana, 1968.

Bibliography

Atti della riunione unitaria dei consigli generali Cgil-Cisl-Uil. Firenze, 22-24 novembre 1971, Rome: Edizioni Seusi, 1972.

Atti del XIX convegno nazionale di studio alle Acli. Roccaraso 31 agosto-2 settembre 1972, Quaderni di azione sociale, anno xxiii, nn. 7-12, luglio-dicembre 1972, pp. 581-1000.

Baglioni, G., (ed.), *Analisi della Cisl*, 2 volumes, Rome: Edizioni Lavoro, 1980.

----- *Il sindacato dell'autonomia: l'evoluzione della Cisl nella pratica e nella cultura*, Bari: De Donato, 1977.

----- *La politica sindacale nel capitalismo che cambia*, Rome-Bari: Laterza, 1986.

Baglioni, G. and Crouch, C. (eds), *European Industrial Relations*, London: Sage Publications, 1990.

Barkan, J., *Visions of Emancipation: The Italian Workers' Movement since 1945*, New York: Praeger, 1984.

Bartocci, E., *Alle origini della contrattazione articolata (1960-64)*, Rome: Editrice Sindacale Italiana, 1979.

Basso, L., 'Il partito nell'ordinamento democratico moderno', Pestalozza, *La costituzione e lo stato*, pp. 307-14.

----- 'L'utilizzazione della legalità nella fase di transizione al socialismo', *Problemi del socialismo*, nn. 5-6, terza serie, anno xiii, settembre-dicembre 1971, pp. 818-62.

Beccalli, B., 'Le politiche del lavoro femminile in Italia: donne, sindacato e stato tra il 1974 e il 1984', Ferrante (ed.), *Il futuro del sindacato*, 1986, pp. 241-67.

Bedani, G. L. C., 'Giuseppe Di Vittorio e il movimento dei lavoratori. Un profilo ideologico', *Lettera*, n. 3, febbraio 1983, 24-43.

Bellardi, L., Groppi, A., Liso, F., Pisani, E. (eds), *Sindacati e contrattazione collettiva in Italia nel 1972-74*, Milan: Franco Angeli, 1978.

Bellotti, L., *Achille Grandi e il movimento sindacale cristiano*, Rome: Cinque Lune, 1977.

Benvenuto, G., *Il sindacato tra movimento e istituzioni*, Padua: Marsilio Editori, 1978.

Bergamaschi, M., *Statuti dei consigli di fabbrica. Il settore metalmeccanico milanese 1970-80*, Milan: Franco Angeli, 1986.

Berlinguer, E., 'Conclusioni al convegno degli intellettuali', *Teoria e politica della via italiana al socialismo*, pp. 293-308.

Biagioni, E., Palmieri, S., Pipan, T., *Indagine sul sindacato. Profilo organizzativo della Cgil*, Rome: Editrice Sindacale Italiana, 1980.

Bianchi, G. A., *Storia dei sindacati in Italia*, Rome: Editori Riuniti, 1984.

Bianchi, G., Frigo, F., Merli-Brandini, P., Merolla, A., *I Cub: comitati unitari di base*, Rome: Coines, 1971.

Blackmer, D. L. M., 'Continuity and Change in Postwar Italian Communism', Blackmer and Tarrow (eds), *Communism in Italy and France*, 1975, pp. 21-68.

Blackmer, D. L. M. and Tarrow, S., (eds), *Communism in Italy and France*, Princeton: Princeton University Press, 1975.

Bobbio, L., *Lotta Continua: Storia di una organizzazione rivoluzionaria*, Milan: Savelli, 1979.

Bordini, M., 'I sindacati e il dibattito sulla programmazione (1960-67)', *Quaderni di rassegna sindacale*, n. 77, 1979, pp. 3-16

Bordogna, L., '"Arcipelago Cobas": frammentazione della rappresentanza e conflitti di lavoro', Corbetta e Leonardi, *Politica in Italia*, 1988, pp. 257-92.

Boschini, A., *Chiesa e Acli*, Naples: Edizioni Dehoniane, 1975.

Brezzi, C., Camerini, I., Lombardo, T., *La Cisl 1950/1980. Cronologia*, Rome: Edizioni Lavoro, 1980.

Brunetta, R., *Economia del lavoro*, Padua: Marsilio Editori, 1981.

Caldarola, G., 'Due voti di fiducia non fanno una maggioranza', *Rinascita*, n. 16, anno 41, 20 aprile 1984, pp. 4-5.

Cammarota, A., *Donna, identità, lavoro*, Milan: Giuffrè, 1984.

Carocci, G., *Inchiesta alla Fiat*, Milan: Parenti, 1960.

Carrieri, D.,'I sindacati non confederali', in Cesos, *Le relazioni sindacali in Italia. Rapporto 1990-91*, pp. 197-202.

Carrieri, M., (ed.). Round table discussion, 'Il senso di una svolta', *Nuova rassegna sindacale*, n. 38-39, 28 ottobre - 4 novembre 1991, pp. iv-xxiv.

Carrieri, M. e Donolo, C., *Il mestiere politico del sindacato*, Rome: Editori Riuniti, 1986.

Carra, E. e Mancini R., 'Salario e salasso', *Rinascita*, nuova serie, anno i, 15 aprile 1990, pp. 20-2.

'Carteggio 1949-51 "degli intrighi e delle manovre" USA - Italia. Gli americani, la scissione sindacale italiana, le polemiche fra Cisl e Uil', Appendix in Turone, *Storia del sindacato in*

Italia, 1981, pp. 519-46.

Castellina, L., 'Il movimento dei delegati', *Il Manifesto*, n. 1, gennaio 1970, pp. 26-7.

Castelvetri, L., 'Le relazioni industriali bipolari', Peschiera (ed.), *Sindacato industria e stato negli anni del centrismo*, 1976-83, vol. ii, pp. 256-339.

Cecchi, A. (ed.), *Storia del Pci attraverso i congressi*, Rome: Newton Compton Editori, 1977.

Cella, G. P., Manghi, B., Piva, P., *Un sindacato italiano negli anni sessanta: la FIM-Cisl dall'associazione alla classe*, Bari: De Donato, 1972.

Cella, G. P. e Treu, T. (eds), *Relazioni industriali. Manuale per l'analisi della esperienza italiana*, Bologna: il Mulino, 1982.

Cesos, *Le relazioni sindacali in Italia. Rapporto 1984-85*, Rome: Edizioni Lavoro, 1986.

Cesos, *Le relazioni sindacali in Italia. Rapporto 1985-86*, Rome: Edizioni Lavoro, 1987.

Cesos, *Le relazioni sindacali in Italia. Rapporto 1990-91*, Rome: Edizioni Lavoro, 1992.

Cgil, *Organizzazione sindacale e rinnovamento unitario. Atti della riunione nazionale sui problemi della politica organizzativa. Roma, 15-16-17 settembre 1975*, Rome: Editrice Sindacale Italiana, 1975.

----- *Una nuova organizzazione per la nuova politica. Atti del convegno nazionale Cgil di organizzazione. Ariccia, 26-7 ottobre 1977*, Rome: Editrice Sindacale Italiana, 1978.

----- *Prospettive della contrattazione collettiva*, Rome: ediesse, 1985.

----- *Documenti, materiali, attività dal X all'XI Congresso*, 2 vols, Rome: ediesse, 1986.

Cgil e programmazione economica, 2 volumes, Rome: Editrice Sindacale Italiana, 1966.

Chiaberge, R., 'Le strutture di base negli anni sessanta', *Quaderni di rassegna sindacale*, anno xii, n. 49, luglio-agosto 1974, pp. 122-36.

Chiaromonte, F., 'La scommessa dell'autonomia', *Rinascita*, n. 29, anno 46, 29 luglio 1989, pp. 8-9.

----- 'Sindacato così sbagli', *Rinascita*, nuova serie, anno i, n. 36, 21 ottobre 1990, pp. 12-15.

Chiaromonte, G., *Quattro anni difficili: il Pci e i sindacati*

1979-1983, Rome: Editori Riuniti, 1984.

Cicchitto, F., *Pensiero cattolico ed economia italiana*, Rome: Editrice Sindacale Italiana, 1970.

Cisl, *Una economia forte per un sindacato forte*, Rome: Uesisa, 1953.

----- *Terzo Congresso nazionale, Roma 19-22 marzo 1959*, Rome: Soc. Abete, 1960.

----- *Il risparmio contrattuale*, Rome: Ufficio Studi, 1965.

----- *Le politiche e l'attività della confederazione nel triennio 1962-65. Relazione della Segreteria confederale al V Congresso nazionale*, Rome: Arti grafiche Wanzer, 1965.

----- *Atti del V Congresso nazionale. Roma 22-25 aprile 1965*, Rome: Arti grafiche Wanzer, 1969.

----- *Atti del VI Congresso confederale, Roma 17-20 luglio 1969*, Rome: Arti grafiche Wanzer, 1970.

----- *Atti del VII Congresso confederale, Roma 18-21 giugno 1973*, Rome: Arti grafiche Wanzer, 1974.

----- *Atti del VIII Congresso confederale. Roma 14-18 giugno 1977*, Rome: Edizioni Lavoro, 1978.

----- *La Cisl dal IX al X Congresso*, 2 volumes, Rome: Edizioni Lavoro, 1985.

----- *La Cisl dal X all'XI Congresso*, 2 volumes., Rome: Edizioni Lavoro, 1989.

----- 'Le mozioni del X Congresso Nazionale, 1985', Cisl, *La Cisl dal X all'XI Congresso*, vol. i, Documenti, pp. 9-124.

Colarossi, B. Corridori, T., Macchiusi, M. (eds), *I giornali sindacali. Catalogo dei periodici Cgil 1944-76*, Rome: Editrice Sindacale Italiana, 1977.

Contratto collettivo nazionale di lavoro industrie chimiche e affini 1976-1979, Rome: Nuova Grafica Operaia, 1976.

Contratto nazionale di lavoro addetti all'industria metalmeccanica privata 1976, Rome: Stabilimento Grafico Fratelli Spada, 1976.

'Convegno delle organizzazioni sindacali dell'Italia liberata alla presenza della delegazione sindacale anglo-americana e del segretario della Federazione Sindacale Mondiale. Roma 15-16 settembre 1944', *La Cgil dal Patto di Roma al Congresso di Genova. Atti e documenti*, vol. i, pp. 15-59.

Coppo, D., 'La Cisl e i partiti politici', Baglioni (ed.), *Analisi della Cisl*, 1980, vol. i, pp. 97-119.

Corbetta, P. e Leonardi, R. (eds), *Politica in Italia. I fatti dell'anno e le interpretazioni. Edizione 1988*, Bologna: il Mulino, 1988.

Costantini, S., 'La formazione del gruppo dirigente della Cisl', Baglioni (ed.), *Analisi della Cisl*, 1980, vol. i, pp. 121-57.

Costituzione Italiana, Turin: Einaudi, 1975.

Couffignal, G., *I sindacati in Italia*, Rome: Editori Riuniti, 1979.

Craveri, P., *Sindacato e istituzioni nel dopoguerra*, Bologna: il Mulino, 1977.

'Cronache e documenti della scissione della corrente sindacale cristiana', Tatò (ed.), *Di Vittorio, l'uomo, il dirigente, 1968-70*, vol. iii, pp. 321-43.

'Cronologia 1974-77: vicende generali', *Quaderni di rassegna sindacale*, anno xx, gennaio-febbraio 1983, pp. 82-7.

Crouch, C. and Pizzorno, A. (eds), *The Resurgence of Class Conflict in Western Europe since 1968*, 2 volumes, London: Macmillan, 1978.

Cuminetti, M., *Il dissenso cattolico in Italia*, Milan: Rizzoli, 1983.

D'Agostini, R., 'L'unità più vicina', *Nuova rassegna sindacale*, n. 40, 11 novembre 1991, pp. 9-12.

D'Aloia, G., 'Conquiste contrattuali e controllo degli investimenti', *Proposte*, nuova serie, anno iv, n. 45-46, febbraio-marzo 1977.

Danco, C., *Agricoltura e sviluppo capitalistico in Italia*, Turin: Einaudi, 1972.

De Gasperi, M. R. (ed.), *De Gasperi scrive. Corrispondenza con capi di stato, cardinali, uomini politici, giornalisti, diplomatici*, 2 volumes, Brescia: Morcellania, 1974.

De Rosa, G., 'Sindacato unico per il 1973', *Civiltà cattolica*, anno 122, n. 2916, 18 dicembre 1971, pp. 589-99.

Decimo congresso del partito comunista italiano. Atti e risoluzioni, Rome: Editori Riuniti, 1963.

Delegati e consigli di fabbrica in Italia, various authors, Milan: Franco Angeli, 1974.

Della Rocca, G., 'L'evoluzione delle strutture di categoria', *Quaderni di rassegna sindacale*, anno xii, n. 49, luglio-agosto 1974, pp. 59-83.

Di Gioia, A., *La Cgil nei suoi statuti 1944-1974*, Rome: Editrice Sindacale Italiana, 1975.

'Dieci anni di processo unitario. Conversazione con Luciano Lama', *Quaderni di rassegna sindacale*, anno ix, n. 29, marzo-aprile

1971, pp. 3-28.

'Documento della sezione sindacale del Psi', Acli, *L'unità sindacale un anno dopo*, 1967, pp. 8-16.

'Documento unitario sul confronto per la riforma della contrattazione', *Nuova rassegna sindacale*, n. 18, 20 maggio 1991, pp. 76-8.

Dogmatic Constitution on the Church of the Second Vatican Council, (De Ecclesia 1965), London: Catholic Truth Society, 1965.

Esperienze, problemi e sviluppo della prospettiva sindacale unitaria, Rome: Edizioni Stasind, 1971.

Eurostat, *Basic Statistics of the Community*, Luxembourg: Office for official publications of the European Communities, 1981.

Faenza, R. e Fini, M., *Gli Americani in Italia*, Milan: Feltrinelli, 1976.

Falconi, C., *La contestazione nella chiesa*, Milan: Feltrinelli, 1969.

Fanfani, T., *Scelte politiche e fatti economici in Italia*, Turin: Giappichelli Editore, 1987.

Ferrante, G. (ed.), *Il futuro del sindacato*, Rome: ediesse, 1986.

Flamini, G., *Operai nell'Italia industriale*, Naples: Edizioni Dehoniane, 1969.

Foa, V., *Sindacati e lotte operaie 1943-1973*, Documenti della Storia 10, Turin: Loescher Editore, 1977.

----- *La cultura della Cgil: scritti e interventi. 1950-70*, Turin: Einaudi, 1984.

----- 'Sindacato e corporazione', Ferrante (ed.), *Il futuro del sindacato*, 1986, pp. 3-18.

Fontana, S., *I cattolici e l'unità sindacale (1943-1947)*, Bologna: il Mulino, 1978.

----- 'La concezione sindacale della Cisl e la cultura sociale cattolica', Baglioni (ed.), *Analisi della Cisl*, 1980, vol. i., pp. 25-46.

Forbice, A., *La federazione Cgil-Cisl-Uil fra storia e cronaca*, Verona: Bertani, 1973.

Forbice, A. e Favero, P., *I socialisti e il sindacato*, Milan: Palazzi, 1968.

Francioni, F., (ed.), *Italy and EC Membership Evaluated*, London: Pinter Publishers, 1992.

Frigerio, P. e Zanetti, G., *Efficienza e accumulazione nell'industria italiana: gli anni dello sviluppo e della crisi*, Milan: Franco

Angeli, 1983.

Galantini, E., (ed.), 'Delegati e consigli nei documenti sindacali', *Quaderni di rassegna sindacale*, 86-87, settembre-dicembre 1980, pp. 105-47.

Galli, P., 'E allora rendiamoli più rappresentativi', *Rinascita*, n. 16, anno 41, 20 aprile 1984, pp. 7-8.

Gherardi, G., *Amici e compagni. Le Acli, la gerarchia e il socialismo*, Rome: Coines, 1976.

Giannotti, R., *Lotte e organizzazione di classe alla Fiat (1948-1970)*, Bari: De Donato, 1970.

Ginsborg, P., *A History of Contemporary Italy. Society and Politics 1943-1988*, London: Penguin Books, 1990.

Giugni, G., 'Concertazione sociale e sistema politico in Italia', Ferrante (ed.), *Il futuro del sindacato*, 1986, pp. 271-83.

----- *Diritto sindacale*, Bari: Cacucci Editore, 1988.

Giuntella, M. C., '*Testimonianze* e l'ambiente cattolico fiorentino', Ristuccia (ed.), *Intellettuali cattolici tra riformismo e dissenso*, 1975, pp. 289-93.

Golden, M., 'Neo-corporativismo ed esclusione della forza-lavoro dalla rappresentanza politica', Pasquino (ed.), *Il sistema politico italiano*, 1985, pp. 208-31.

----- *Labor Divided. Austerity and Working-Class Politics in Contemporary Italy*, Ithaca and London: Cornell University Press, 1988.

Gorresio, V., *I bracci secolari*, Rome: Guanda, 1951.

Gradilone, A., *Storia del sindacalismo*, 3 volumes, Milan: Giuffrè, 1959.

Grandi, M., *L'attività sindacale nell'impresa*, Milan: Franco Angeli, 1976.

Greco, R. e Macchiavelli, L., 'I guerrieri del pubblico impiego - Inchiesta sui Cobas', *Rinascita*, n. 12, anno 46, 1 aprile 1989, pp. 12-14.

Guerzoni, M., 'A Bologna si parte', *Nuova rassegna sindacale*, n. 16, 27 aprile 1992, p. 16.

Guidi, E., 'Analisi e valutazione degli accordi sui delegati', *Quaderni di rassegna sindacale*, n. 24, dicembre 1969, pp. 54-72.

Horowitz, D. L., *The Italian Labour Movement*, Cambridge, Massachusetts: Harvard University Press, 1963.

I communisti: dove si lavora e si studia, various authors, Bari:

Edizioni Dedalo, 1985.

I congressi della Cgil, 10 volumes, Rome: Editrice Sindacale Italiana, 1949-78.

I congressi nazionali della Democrazia cristiana, Rome: Tipografia A.G.I., 1959.

'I lavori dell'XI Congresso Cgil, Roma 28 febbraio-4 marzo 1986', *Nuova rassegna sindacale*, n. 7-8, 7-14 marzo 1986, pp. 4-191.

'I "mestieri" del sindacato italiano', a cura di F. Rampini, *Rinascita*, n. 17, anno 37, 25 aprile 1980, pp. 5-9.

'I tre interrogativi', *Il Giorno*, 27 dicembre, 1967, p. 13.

I 30 anni della Cgil, Rome: Editrice Sindacale Italiana, 1975.

Il piano del lavoro della Cgil, 1949-1950. Atti del Convegno organizzato dalla Facoltà di economia e commercio della Università di Modena, 9-10 maggio 1975, Milan: Feltrinelli, 1978.

Il sindacalismo libero, Modena: Usp-Cisl, 1954.

Inchiesta sull'unità sindacale. Mille risposte alla rivista Rinascita, Rome: Editori Riuniti, 1967.

Iocca, G., 'Nuovi attori e nuove regole', *Nuova rassegna sindacale*, n. 40, 11 novembre 1991, pp. 16-18.

Istat, *Sommario di statistiche storiche dell'Italia 1861-1975*, Rome: Tipografia F. Failli, 1976.

----- *Compendio statistico italiano*, Naples: Tipografia Sagraf, 1978.

----- *Annuario di contabilità nazionale. Serie 1960-85*, vol. xv, Rome: Arte grafica S.p.A., 1987.

Istituto Gramsci, *Tendenze del capitalismo italiano. Atti del convegno di Roma*, 2 volumes, Rome: Editori Riuniti, 1962.

Kemeny, P., 'Le politiche di concertazione: storia di una rinuncia', *Prospettiva sindacale*, 77, anno xxi, settembre 1990, pp. 95-132.

Kemeny, P. e Ranci Ortigosa, E., 'La Cisl dei primi anni e l'ideologia del mondo cattolico', in Baglioni (ed.), *Analisi della Cisl*, 1980, vol. i, pp. 47-76.

Korpi, W., *The Democratic Class Struggle*, London: Routledge and Kegan Paul, 1983.

La Cgil dal Patto di Roma al Congresso di Genova. Atti e documenti, 6 volumes, Rome: Poligrafia dello Stato, 1949-52.

La Palombara, J., *The Italian Labor Movement*, Ithaca, New York: Cornell University Press, 1957.

La qualità totale alla Fiat, various authors, Rome: ediesse, 1990.

'La risoluzione del Direttivo approvata all'unanimità il 31 maggio 1972', *Rassegna sindacale*, anno xviii, n. 238, 18 giugno-2 luglio 1972, pp. 12-13.

Lama, L., 'L'impegno della Cgil per lo sviluppo e l'unità del sindacato in Italia', *I 30 anni della Cgil*, 1975, pp. 349-69.

----- *Intervista sul sindacato*, a cura di M. Riva, Rome-Bari: Laterza, 1976.

----- *La Cgil di Di Vittorio 1944-1957*, Bari: De Donato, 1977.

----- 'Relazione al X Congresso della Cgil, Roma, 16-21 novembre 1981', *Rassegna sindacale*, anno xxvii, n. 43, 26 novembre 1981, pp. 7-31.

Lange, P., Ross, G. and Vannicelli, M., *Unions, Change and Crisis: French and Italian Union Strategy and the Political Economy 1945-80*, London: George Allen and Unwin, 1982.

Lange, P. and Vannicelli, M., 'Strategy under Stress: The Italian Union Movement and the Italian Crisis in Developmental Perspective', Lange, Ross, Vannicelli, *Unions, Change and Crisis*, 1982, pp. 95-206.

Laser, n. 1. Laboratorio sulla sindacalizzazione e la rappresentanza. Supplement in *Nuova rassegna sindacale*, anno xxxviii, n. 22, 8 giugno 1992.

'Le intese unitarie raggiunte da Cgil, Cisl e Uil di Milano sulle strutture di base e sull'azione sindacale (2 luglio 1986)', Giugni, *Diritto sindacale*, 1988, pp. 272-4.

Le regioni in cifre, Rome: Istituto nazionale di statistica, edizione 1990.

Lettieri, A., 'L'inquadramento unico all'Italsider', *Quaderni di rassegna sindacale*, n. 100, xx, gennaio-febbraio 1983, pp. 48-50.

'L'inchiesta: viaggio nella Fiat', *Rinascita*, nuova serie, anno 1, 29 aprile 1990, n. 12, pp. 26-34.

'L'intesa sulle rappresentanze sindacali unitarie', supplement in *Nuova rassegna sindacale*, n. 10, 18 marzo 1991, pp. 35-8.

L'Isolotto. Documenti. La crisi della chiesa locale di Firenze, Bologna: Il Regno, 1969.

Lorini, M., '30 anni di lotte e di conquiste delle lavoratrici italiane', *I 30 anni della Cgil*, pp. 223-30.

Bibliography

Low Beer, J. R., *Protest and Participation: The New Working Class in Italy*, Cambridge: Cambridge University Press, 1978.

Magister, S., *La politica vaticana e l'Italia 1943-1978*, Rome: Editori Riuniti, 1979.

Manghi, B., *Passaggio senza riti*, Rome: Edizioni Lavoro, 1987.

'Mansioni, qualifiche, professionalità e salario nell'analisi della FIOM di Torino', *Quaderni di rassegna sindacale*, anno xx, gennaio-febbraio 1983, pp. 46-8.

Marini, F., 'Relazione all'XI Congresso, luglio 1989', testo integrale, *Conquiste del lavoro*, n. 166, 15 luglio 1989.

Mariucci, L., 'Negoziato politico e nuovi rapporti di lavoro', Cgil, *Prospettive della contrattazione collettiva*, 1985, pp. 37-71.

----- 'I rapporti tra sindacato e stato. Percorsi di lettura', Ferrante, (ed.), *Il futuro del sindacato,* 1986, pp. 19-40.

Merli, G., *De Gasperi ed il sindacato*, Rome: Cinque Lune, 1977.

Ministero del Bilancio, *Osservazioni presentate dai membri della Cnpe al rapporto del vice-presidente*, Rome: Stab. Failli, 1964.

'Modifiche proposte allo statuto confederale', *La Cgil dal Patto di Roma al Congresso di Genova. Atti e documenti*, vol. iii, pp. 363-4.

Morelli, U., *I Consigli di Gestione dalla Liberazione ai primi anni cinquanta*, Turin: Fondazione G. Agnelli, 1977.

'Mozione della corrente sindacale cristiana', *La Cgil dal Patto di Roma al Congresso di Genova. Atti e documenti*, vol. iii, pp. 19-26.

Nacamulli, R. C. D. (ed.), *Sindacati e organizzazione d'impresa in Italia*, Milan: Franco Angeli, 1982.

Negrelli, S. and Santi, E., 'Industrial Relations in Italy', Baglioni and Crouch (eds), *European Industrial Relations*, 1990, pp. 154-98.

New Light on Social Problems, encyclical letter of Pope John XXIII, *Mater et Magistra (1961)*, London: Catholic Truth Society, 1963.

Ottavo congresso del partito comunista italiano. Atti e risoluzioni, Rome: Editori Riuniti, 1957.

Pandolfo, A., 'La Cisl e il pubblico impiego', Baglioni (ed.), *Analisi della Cisl*, 1980, vol. ii, pp. 709-29.

Papuzzi, A., *Il provocatore. Il caso Cavallo e la Fiat,* Turin: Einaudi, 1976.

Pasini, G., *Le Acli delle origini*, Rome: Coines, 1974.

Pasquino, G. (ed.), *Il sistema politico italiano*, Rome-Bari: Laterza, 1985.

Peace on Earth, encyclical letter of Pope John XXIII, *Pacem in Terris (1963)*, London: Catholic Truth Society, 1963.

Pepe, A., *Classe operaia e sindacato. Storia e problemi 1890-1948*, Rome: Bulzoni Editore, 1982.

'Per una svolta di politica economica: l'Assemblea dell'EUR', *Quaderni di rassegna sindacale*, anno xx, gennaio-febbraio 1983, pp. 148-50.

Peschiera, F. (ed.), *Sindacato industria e stato negli anni del centrismo. Storia delle relazioni industriali dal 1948 al 1958*, Firenze: Felice Le Monnier, 3 volumes in 4 parts, 1976-83.

Pestalozza, L., *La costituzione e lo stato*, Rome: Editori Riuniti, 1975.

Piccioni, A., *La Cgil nei suoi congressi*, Rome: ediesse, 1986.

Pillon, C., *I comunisti e il sindacato*, Milan: Palazzi Editore, 1972.

Pirzio Ammassari, G., *Teorie del sindacalismo e delle relazioni industriali*, Naples: Liguori editore, 1979.

Pistillo, M., *Giuseppe Di Vittorio 1907-1924*, Rome: Editori Riuniti, 1977.

----- *Giuseppe Di Vittorio 1924-1944*, Rome: Editori Riuniti, 1977.

Pizzinato, A., 'Non è più il tempo della concertazione', *Rinascita*, n. 8, anno 45, 5 marzo 1988, p. 7.

Pizzorno, A., 'Political Exchange and Collective Identity in Industrial Conflict', Crouch and Pizzorno (eds), *The Resurgence of Class Conflict*, 1978, vol. ii, pp. 277-98.

Prandi, A., *Chiesa e politica. La gerarchia e l'impegno politico dei cattolici*, Bologna: il Mulino, 1968.

'Preambolo dello Statuto della Cisl - 30 aprile 1950', Appendix to Di Gioia, *La Cgil nei suoi statuti 1944-1974*, pp. 99-100.

'Quel mondo in crescita del lavoro subordinato', interview with Bruno Trentin by Marcello Villari, *Rinascita*, n. 45, anno 43, 22 novembre 1986, p. 9.

Regalia, I., *Eletti e abbandonati. Modelli e stili di rappresentanza in fabbrica*, Bologna: il Mulino, 1984.

Regalia, I. e Regini, M., 'Sindacato, istituzioni, sistema politico', Cella e Treu (eds), *Relazioni industriali*, 1982, pp. 311-41.

Regalia, I., Regini, M., Reyneri, E., 'Labour Conflicts and Industrial Relations in Italy', Crouch and Pizzorno (eds), *The Resurgence of Class Conflict*, 1978, vol. i, pp. 101-58.

Regini, M., *I dilemmi del sindacato*, Bologna: il Mulino, 1981.

----- 'Relazioni industriali e sistema politico: l'evoluzione recente e le prospettive degli anni ottanta', Ferrante (ed.), *Il futuro del sindacato*, 1986, pp. 139-63.

Relazione della segreteria confederale al terzo congresso nazionale, Rome: Cisl, 1959.

Relazione della segreteria confederale al quarto congresso nazionale, Rome: Cisl, 1962.

Reyneri, E., 'Il ruolo della Cisl nel ciclo di lotte 1968-1972', Baglioni (ed.), *Analisi della Cisl*, 1980, vol. ii, pp. 731-59.

Ricciardi, M., 'La Cgil e lo statuto dei lavoratori', *I 30 anni della Cgil*, 1975, pp. 157-70.

Riosa, A., *Lezioni di storia del movimento operaio*, Bari: De Donato, 1974.

----- 'Le concezioni sociali e politiche della Cgil', *I 30 anni della Cgil*, 1975, pp. 89-154.

'Risoluzione della 1a Commissione del Consiglio Generale Cgil (Roma, 7 dicembre 1977)', Cgil, *Una nuova organizzazione per la nuova politica,* 1978, pp. 299-305.

Ristuccia, S. (ed.), *Intellettuali cattolici tra riformismo e dissenso*, Milan: Comunità, 1975.

Romagnoli, G., *Consigli di fabbrica e democrazia sindacale*, Milan: Mazzotta, 1976.

----- 'La Cisl e il sindacato in fabbrica', in Baglioni (ed.), *Analisi della Cisl*, 1980, vol. ii, pp. 635-58.

----- (ed.), *La sindacalizzazione tra ideologia e pratica: il caso italiano 1950-1977*, 2 volumes, Rome: Edizioni Lavoro, 1980.

Romagnoli, U, 'L'anno zero della democrazia industriale', Ferrante (ed.), *Il futuro del sindacato*, 1986, pp. 319-25.

----- e Treu, T., *I sindacati in Italia: storia di una strategia (1945-1976)*, Bologna: il Mulino, 1977.

Rosati, D., *La questione politica delle Acli*, Naples: Edizioni Dehoniane, 1975.

Rossi, M., *I giorni dell'onnipotenza*, Rome: Coines, 1975

Rusconi, G. E. e Saraceno, C., *Ideologia religiosa e conflitto sociale*, Bari: De Donato, 1970.

Salerni, D., *Il sistema di relazioni industriali in Italia*, Bologna: il Mulino, 1981.

Salvati, M., *Economia e politica in Italia dal dopoguerra a oggi*, Milan: Garzanti, 1984.

Santi, F., 'Il movimento sindacale di fronte alla nuova situazione politica', *Rassegna sindacale*, anno viii, n. 51, marzo 1962, pp. 2589-91.

Schmitter, P. C., 'Teoria della democrazia e pratica neo-corporatista', Ferrante (ed.), *Il futuro del sindacato*, 1986, pp. 89-121.

Sciarra, S., 'L'influenza del sindacalismo "americano" sulla Cisl', Baglioni (ed.), *Analisi della Cisl*, 1980, vol. i, pp. 283-307.

Scoppola, P., *La proposta politica di De Gasperi*, Bologna: il Mulino, 1978.

Secchia, P., *Organizzare il popolo per conquistare la pace. Intervento al VII congresso nazionale del Pci, Roma, 4 aprile 1951*, Rome: La Stampa Moderna, 1951.

Simoncini, F., *Dall'interno della Uil 1950-1985*, Milan: Franco Angeli, 1986.

Sivo, V., 'Trentin fa la rivoluzione nella Cgil', *la Repubblica*, 20 settembre 1990, p. 13.

Spesso, R., *L'economia italiana dal dopoguerra a oggi*, Rome: Editori Riuniti, 1980.

Spriano, P., *Storia del partito comunista italiano*, 5 volumes, Turin: Giulio Einaudi editore, 1967-75.

'Statuto approvato all'unanimità dal Congresso di Napoli 1945', *La Cgil dal Patto di Roma al Congresso di Genova. Atti e documenti*, vol. i, pp. 255-74.

Stefanelli, R., *Lotte agrarie e modello di sviluppo 1947-67*, Bari: De Donato, 1975.

----- (ed.), *I sindacati autonomi. Particolarismo e strategie confederali negli anni Settanta*, Bari: De Donato, 1981.

Sylos Labini, P., 'Il lavoro e la produzione', *Lettera dall'Italia*, anno v, n. 17, gennaio-marzo 1990, pp. 35-6.

Tarrow, S., *Democracy and Disorder. Protest and Politics in Italy 1965-75*, Oxford: Clarendon Press, 1989.

Tatò, A. (ed.), *Di Vittorio, l'uomo, il dirigente*, 3 volumes, Rome: Editrice Sindacale Italiana, 1968-70.

Teoria e politica della via italiana al socialismo. I testi principali della elaborazione del Pci dalla dichiarazione programmatica del 1956 al discorso sull'austerità, Rome: Editori Riuniti, 1979.

Tesi per il X Congresso Nazionale Uil. Venezia 23-28 ottobre 1989, Stampa Grafica Ariete S.p.A., 1989.

Tesi, programma, statuto. I documenti approvati dal XVII Congresso del Pci, Rome: Editrice 'L'Unità' S.p.A., 1987.

'The Cgil's European Programme', Supplement to *Nuova rassegna sindacale*, n. 43, 12 dicembre 1988.

Tobagi, W., *Il sindacato riformista*, Milan: SugarCo Edizioni, 1979.

Togliatti, P., *Rinnovare l'Italia. Rapporto al V congresso nazionale del Pci, Roma, 29 dicembre 1945 - 4 gennaio 1946*, Roma: Società Editrice 'L'Unità', 1946.

----- *Opere*, 6 volumes, Rome: Editori Riuniti, 1974-84.

Tredicesimo congresso del partito comunista italiano. Atti e risoluzioni, Rome: Editori Riuniti, 1972.

Trentin, B., *Da sfruttati a produttori. Lotte operaie e sviluppo capitalistico dal miracolo economico alla crisi*, Bari: De Donato, 1977.

----- *Il sindacato dei consigli*, intervista di Bruno Ugolini, Rome: Editori Riuniti, 1980.

Treu, T., *Sindacato e rappresentanze aziendali*, Bologna: il Mulino, 1971.

Treu, T., and Negrelli, S., 'Workers' Participation and Personnel Management Policies in Italy', *International Labour Review*, vol. 126, No. 1, Jan-Feb 1987, pp. 81-94.

Turone, S., *Storia del sindacato in Italia 1943-1980*, Rome-Bari: Laterza, 1981.

----- *Il sindacato nell'Italia del benessere*, Rome-Bari: Laterza, 1989.

----- *Storia dell'Unione Italiana del Lavoro*, Milan: Franco Angeli, 1990.

Uil, *Statuto approvato dal primo congresso nazionale tenuto in Roma il 6-7-8 dicembre 1953*, Roma: ITER, 1953.

----- *Relazione presentata al primo congresso nazionale della Unione Italiana del Lavoro, Roma 6-7-8 dicembre 1953*, Roma: ITER, 1954.

----- 'Politica sociale e sindacato dei cittadini', *Tesi per il X Congresso Nazionale Uil*, 1989, pp. 42-68.

----- *Tesi per il X Congresso Nazionale Uil. Venezia 23-28 ottobre 1989*, Stampa Grafica Ariete, S.p.A., 1989.

Bibliography

United Nations, *1981 Statistical Yearbook*, New York, 1983.

Valentino, N., *Il presidente. Elezione e poteri del capo dello stato*, Turin: ERI, 1973.

Zangheri, R., *Agricoltura e contadini nella storia d'Italia*, Turin: Einaudi, 1977.

INDEX

Index